x2 Times

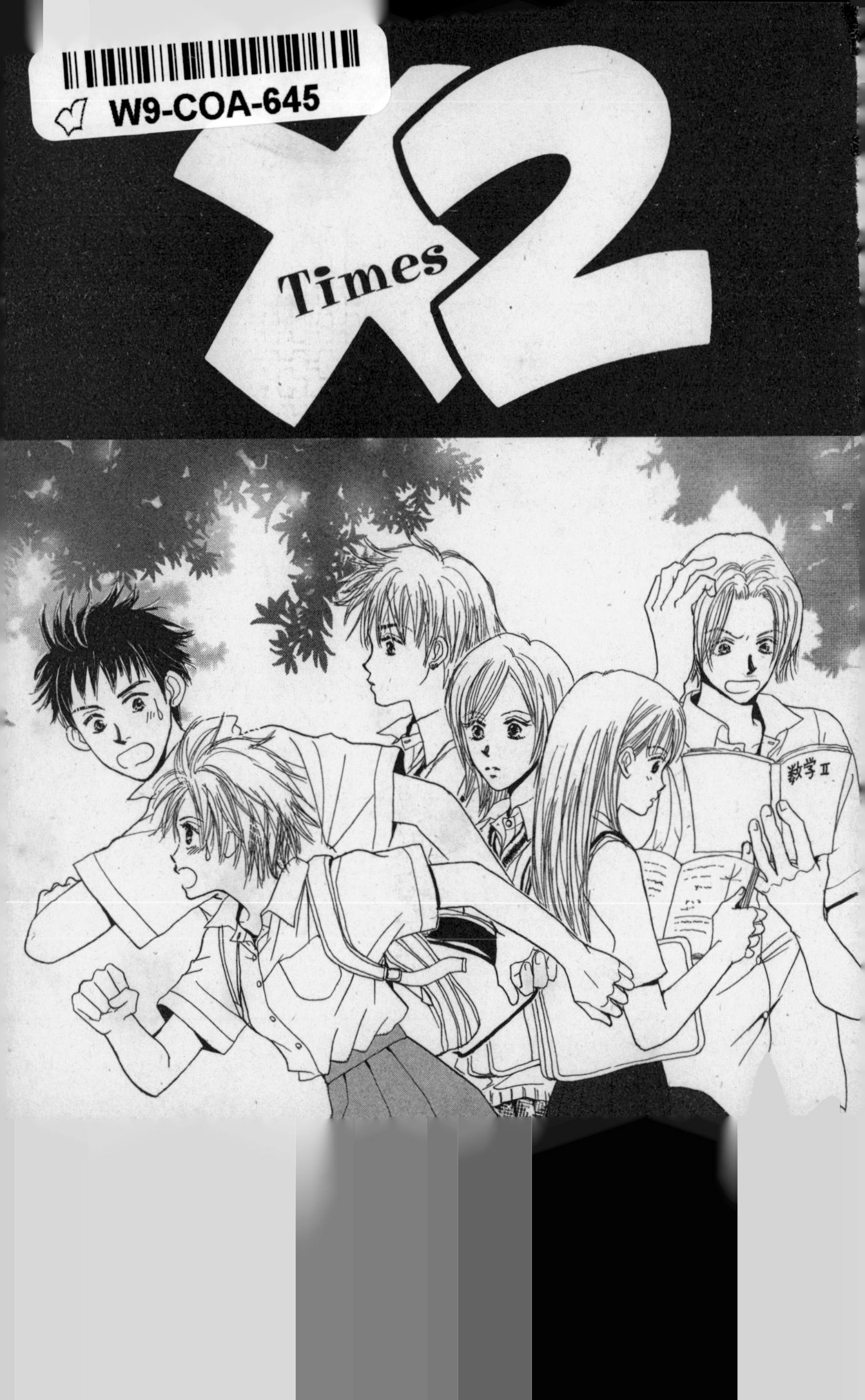
数学Ⅱ

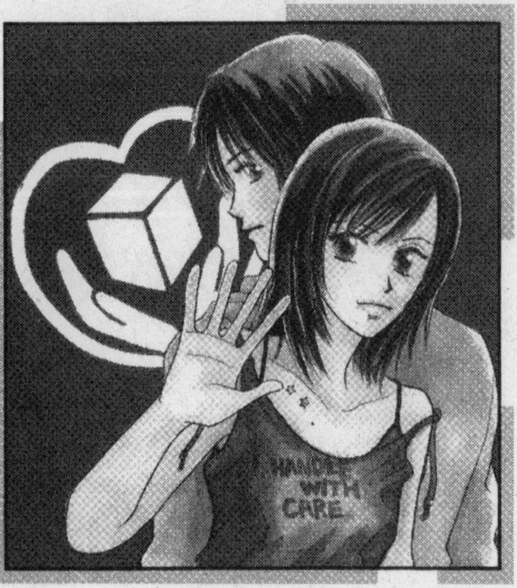
HANDLE
WITH
CARE

X2 • Times Two

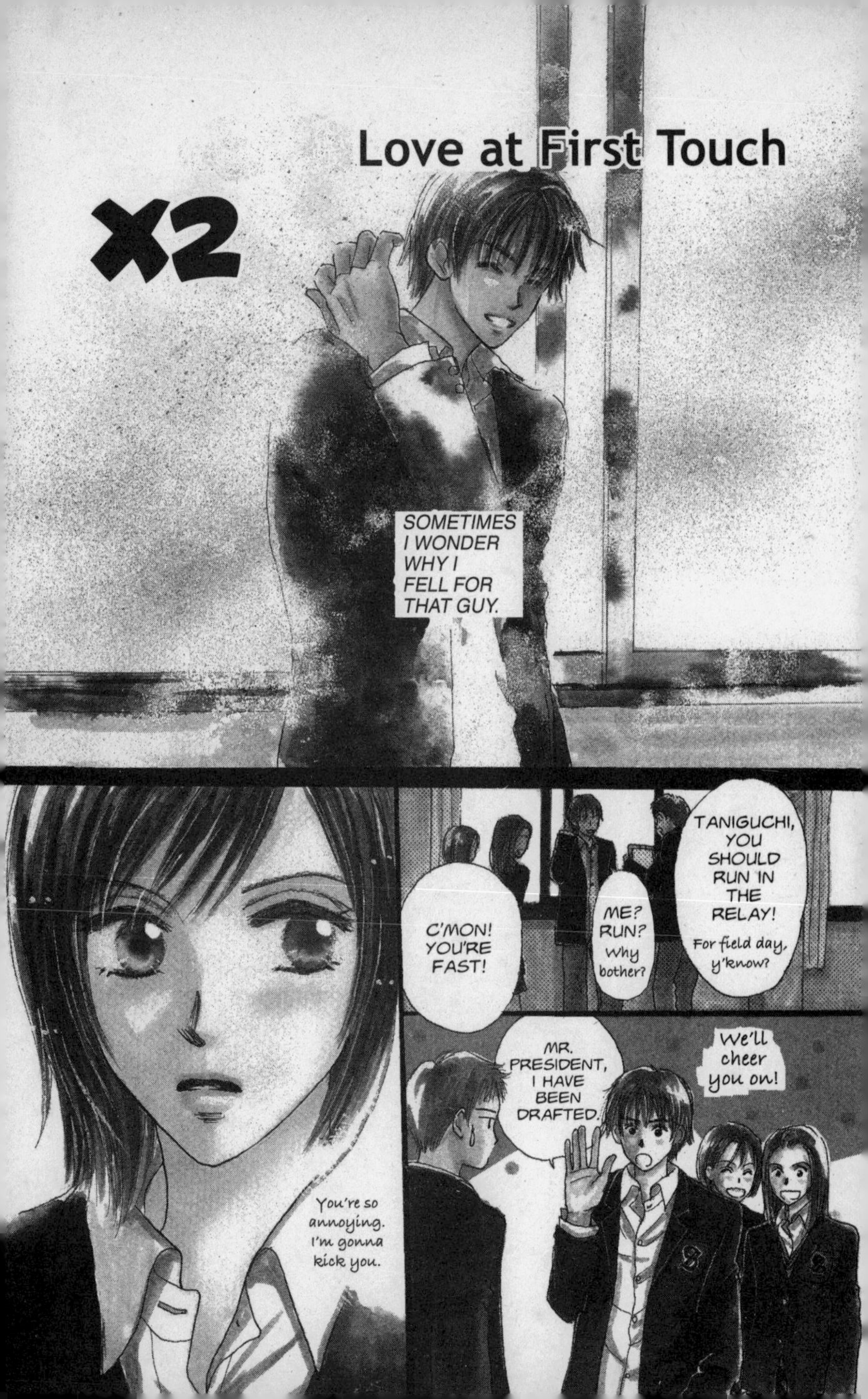
Love at First Touch
X2
SOMETIMES I WONDER WHY I FELL FOR THAT GUY.
TANIGUCHI, YOU SHOULD RUN IN THE RELAY!
For field day, y'know?
ME? RUN?
Why bother?
C'MON! YOU'RE FAST!
We'll cheer you on!
MR. PRESIDENT, I HAVE BEEN DRAFTED.
You're so annoying. I'm gonna kick you.

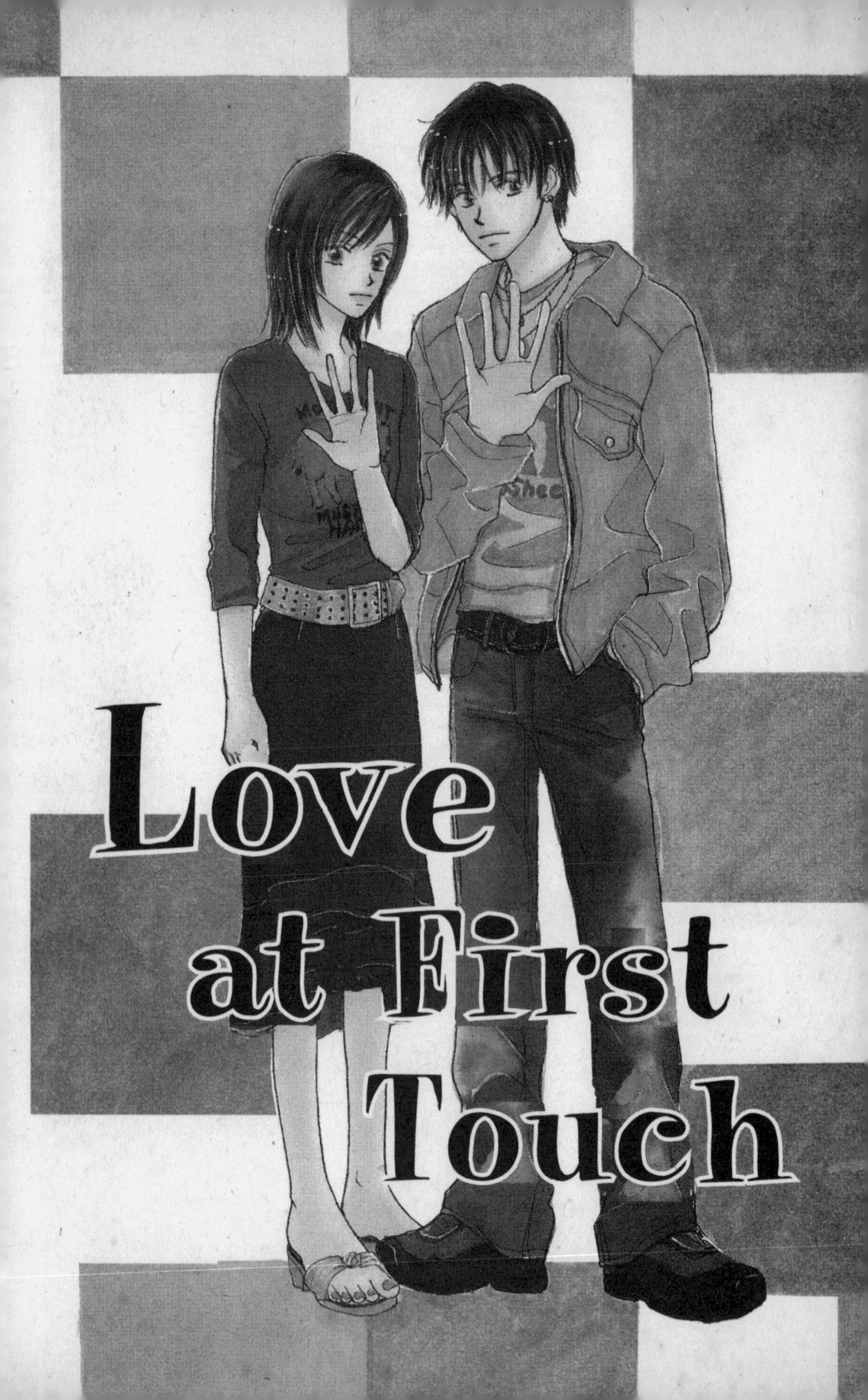
Love
at First
Touch

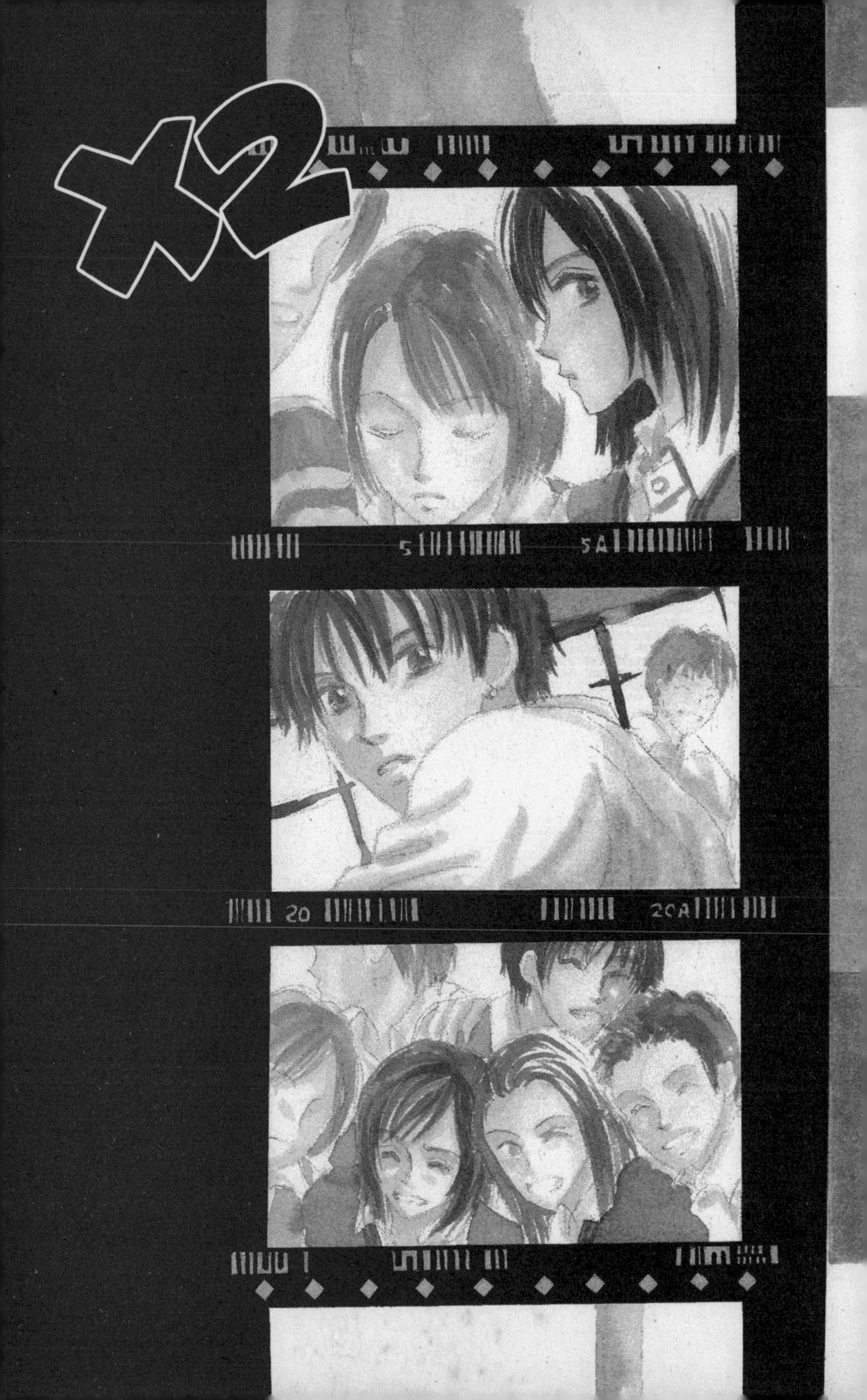
x2

Love
at First
Touch

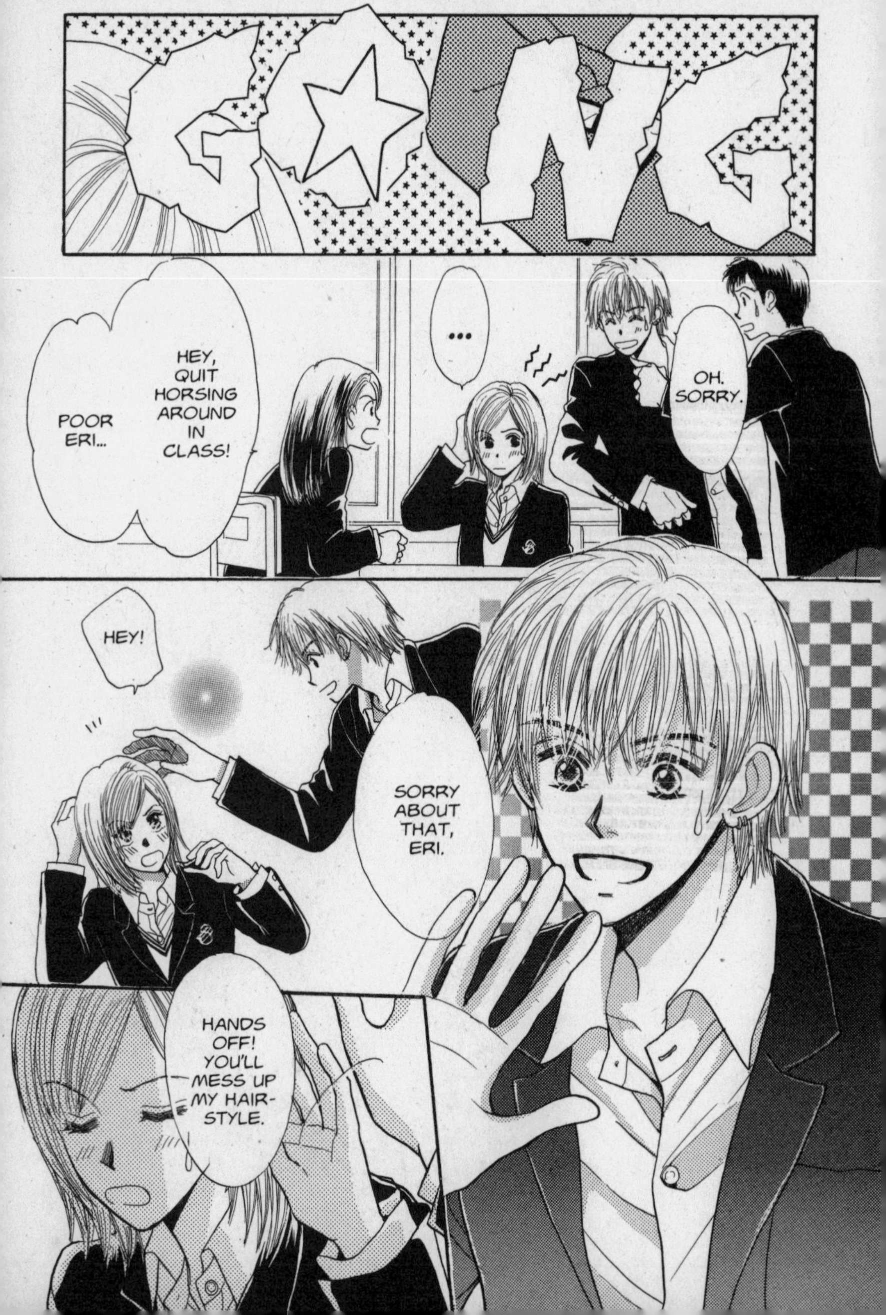
GONG
OH. SORRY.
...
HEY, QUIT HORSING AROUND IN CLASS!
POOR ERI...
SORRY ABOUT THAT, ERI.
HEY!
HANDS OFF! YOU'LL MESS UP MY HAIR-STYLE.

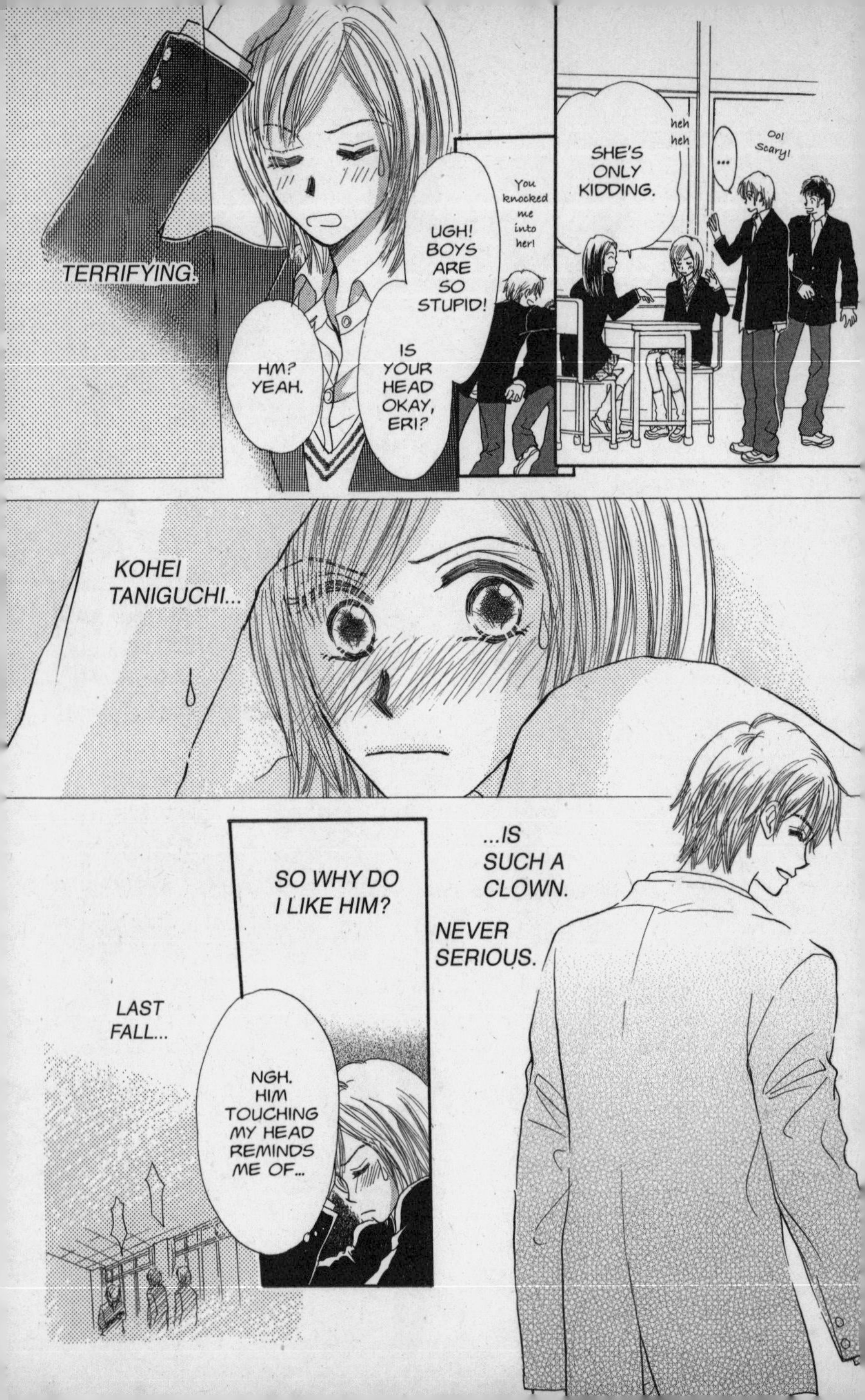
Oo! Scary!
...
heh heh
SHE'S ONLY KIDDING.
You knocked me into her!
UGH! BOYS ARE SO STUPID!
IS YOUR HEAD OKAY, ERI?
HM? YEAH.
TERRIFYING.
KOHEI TANIGUCHI...
...IS SUCH A CLOWN.
NEVER SERIOUS.
SO WHY DO I LIKE HIM?
NGH. HIM TOUCHING MY HEAD REMINDS ME OF...
LAST FALL...

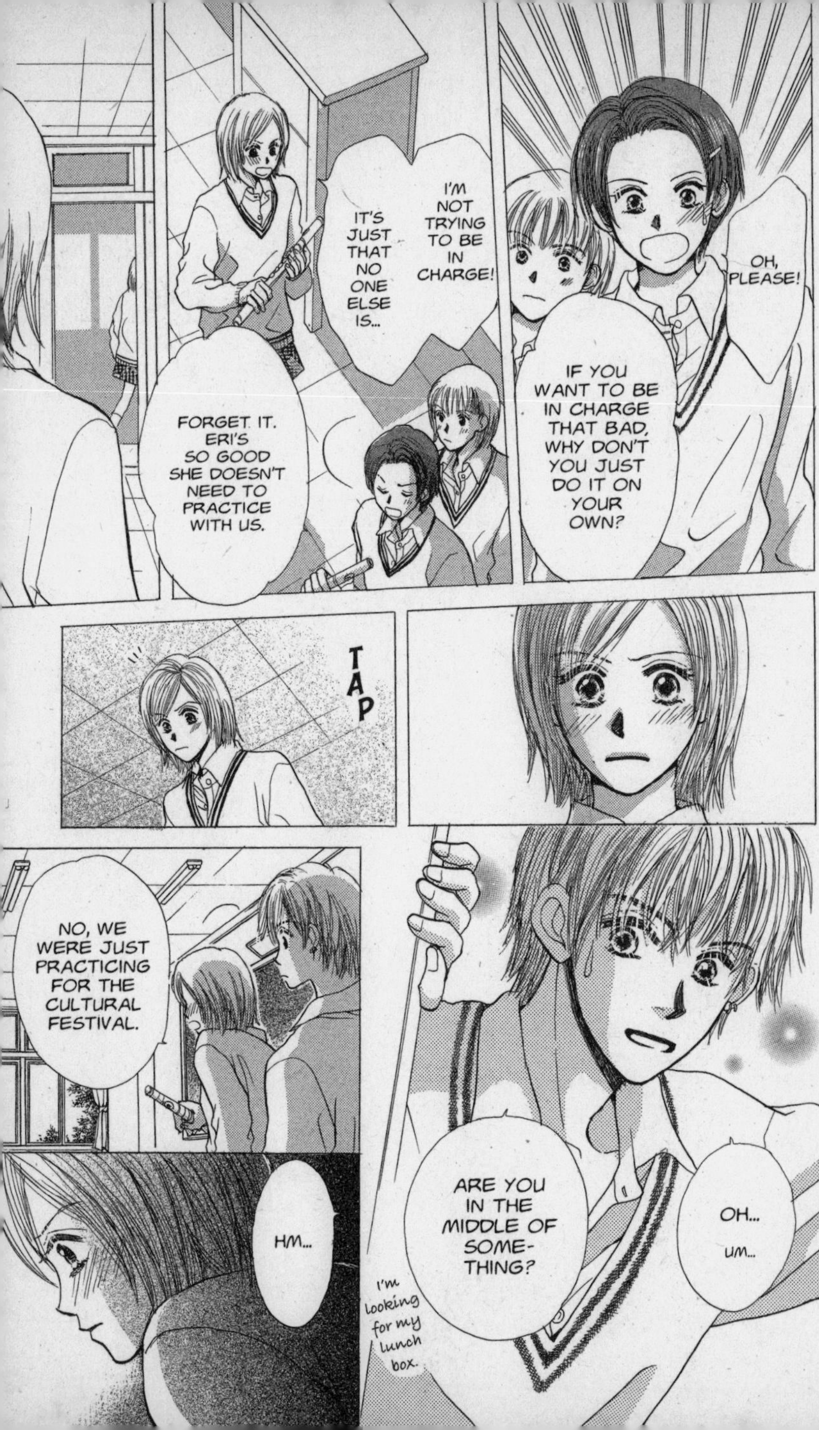
OH, PLEASE!
IF YOU WANT TO BE IN CHARGE THAT BAD, WHY DON'T YOU JUST DO IT ON YOUR OWN?
I'M NOT TRYING TO BE IN CHARGE!
IT'S JUST THAT NO ONE ELSE IS...
FORGET IT. ERI'S SO GOOD SHE DOESN'T NEED TO PRACTICE WITH US.
TAP
ARE YOU IN THE MIDDLE OF SOME-THING?
OH... um...
I'm looking for my lunch box.
NO, WE WERE JUST PRACTICING FOR THE CULTURAL FESTIVAL.
HM...

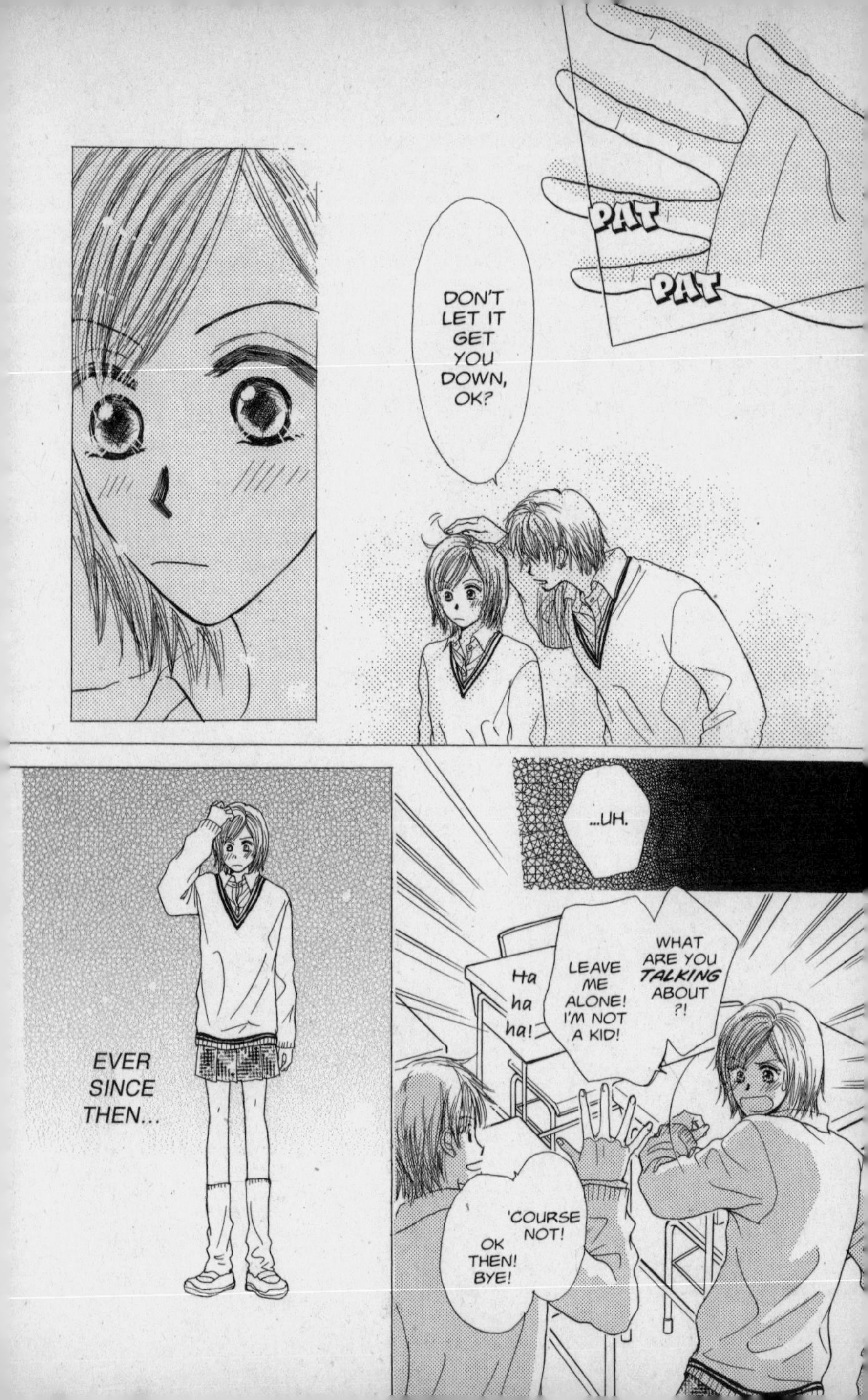
PAT
PAT
DON'T LET IT GET YOU DOWN, OK?
...UH.
WHAT ARE YOU *TALKING* ABOUT ?!
LEAVE ME ALONE! I'M NOT A KID!
Ha ha ha!
'COURSE NOT!
OK THEN! BYE!
EVER SINCE THEN...

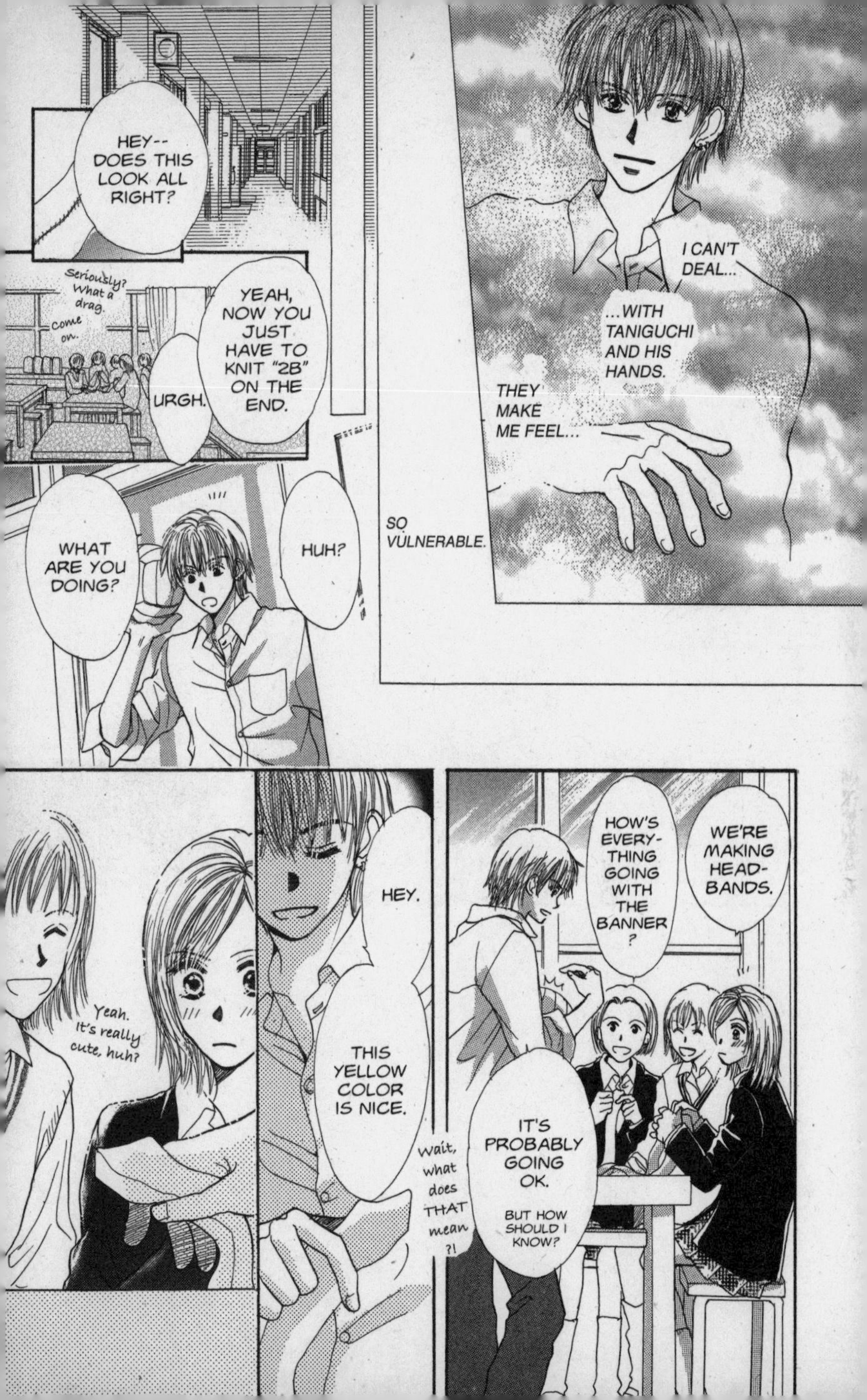
I CAN'T DEAL...
...WITH TANIGUCHI AND HIS HANDS.
THEY MAKE ME FEEL...
SO VULNERABLE.
HEY-- DOES THIS LOOK ALL RIGHT?
YEAH, NOW YOU JUST HAVE TO KNIT "2B" ON THE END.
URGH.
Seriously? What a drag.
Come on.
HUH?
WHAT ARE YOU DOING?
WE'RE MAKING HEAD-BANDS.
HOW'S EVERY-THING GOING WITH THE BANNER?
IT'S PROBABLY GOING OK.
BUT HOW SHOULD I KNOW?
HEY.
THIS YELLOW COLOR IS NICE.
Wait, what does THAT mean?!
Yeah. It's really cute, huh?

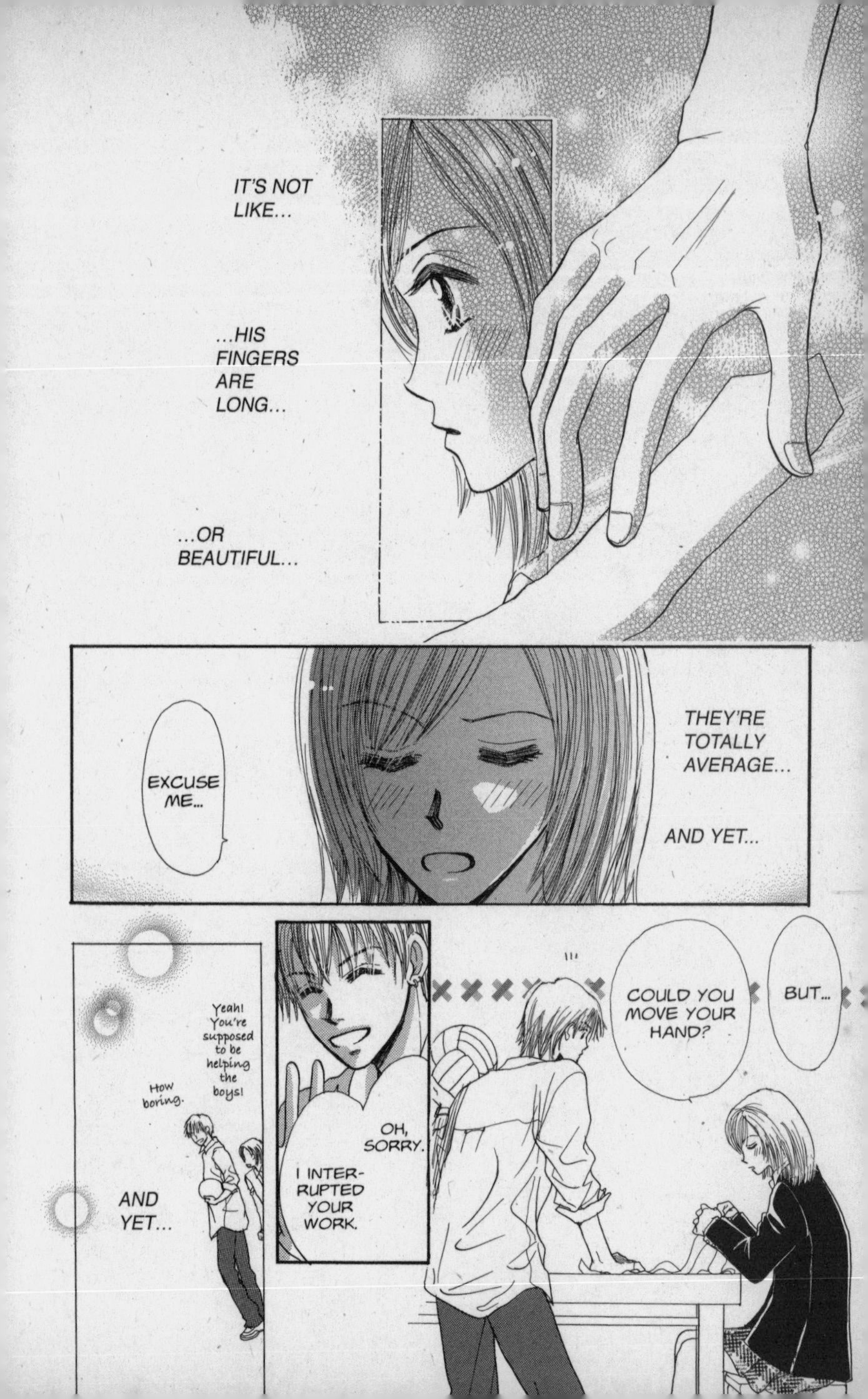
IT'S NOT LIKE...
...HIS FINGERS ARE LONG...
...OR BEAUTIFUL...
THEY'RE TOTALLY AVERAGE...
AND YET...
EXCUSE ME...
BUT...
COULD YOU MOVE YOUR HAND?
OH, SORRY.
I INTER-RUPTED YOUR WORK.
Yeah! You're supposed to be helping the boys!
How boring.
AND YET...

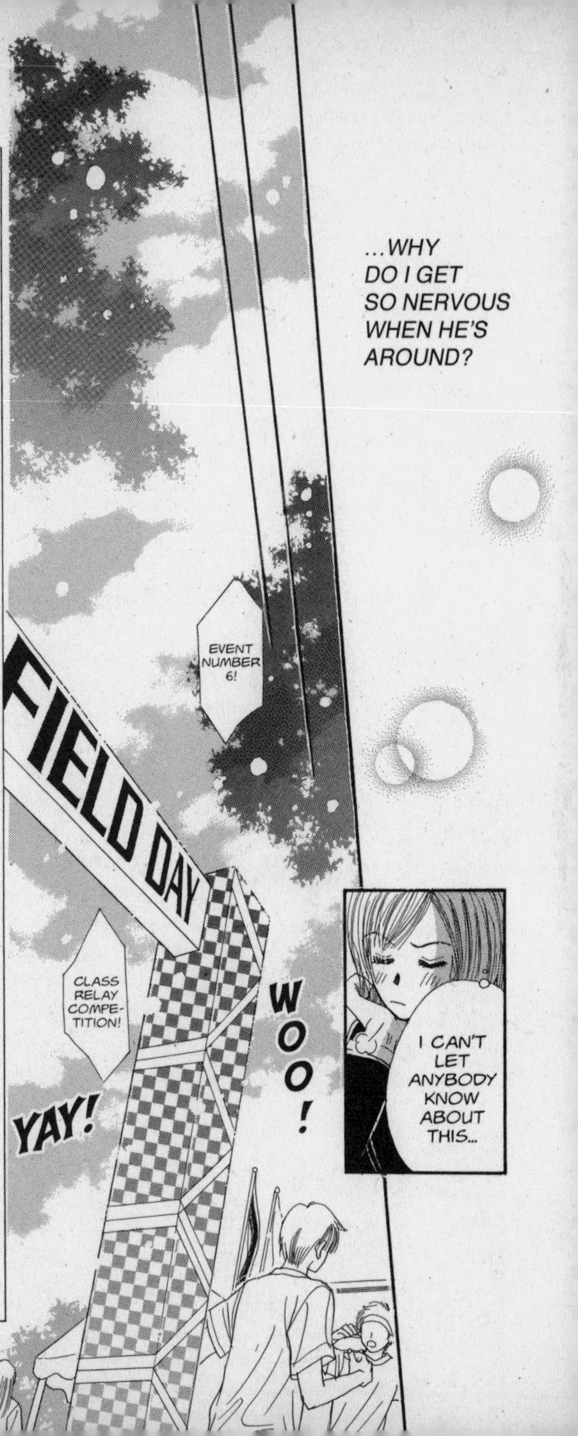
...WHY DO I GET SO NERVOUS WHEN HE'S AROUND?
EVENT NUMBER 6!
FIELD DAY
WOO!
CLASS RELAY COMPETITION!
YAY!
I CAN'T LET ANYBODY KNOW ABOUT THIS...

Greetings! Hi, this is Shouko Akira. This book ended up being a collection of short stories. I hope you like it!

About *Times Two:* These stories deal with school and yearning for love (actually that's what all my manga are about...). It wasn't easy to wrap each one up within 35 pages, though, I've gotta say.

"Love at First Touch": I remember field day when I was in school... there'd be so much commotion it would make me cry. So do you think these two could be a couple without fighting all the time?

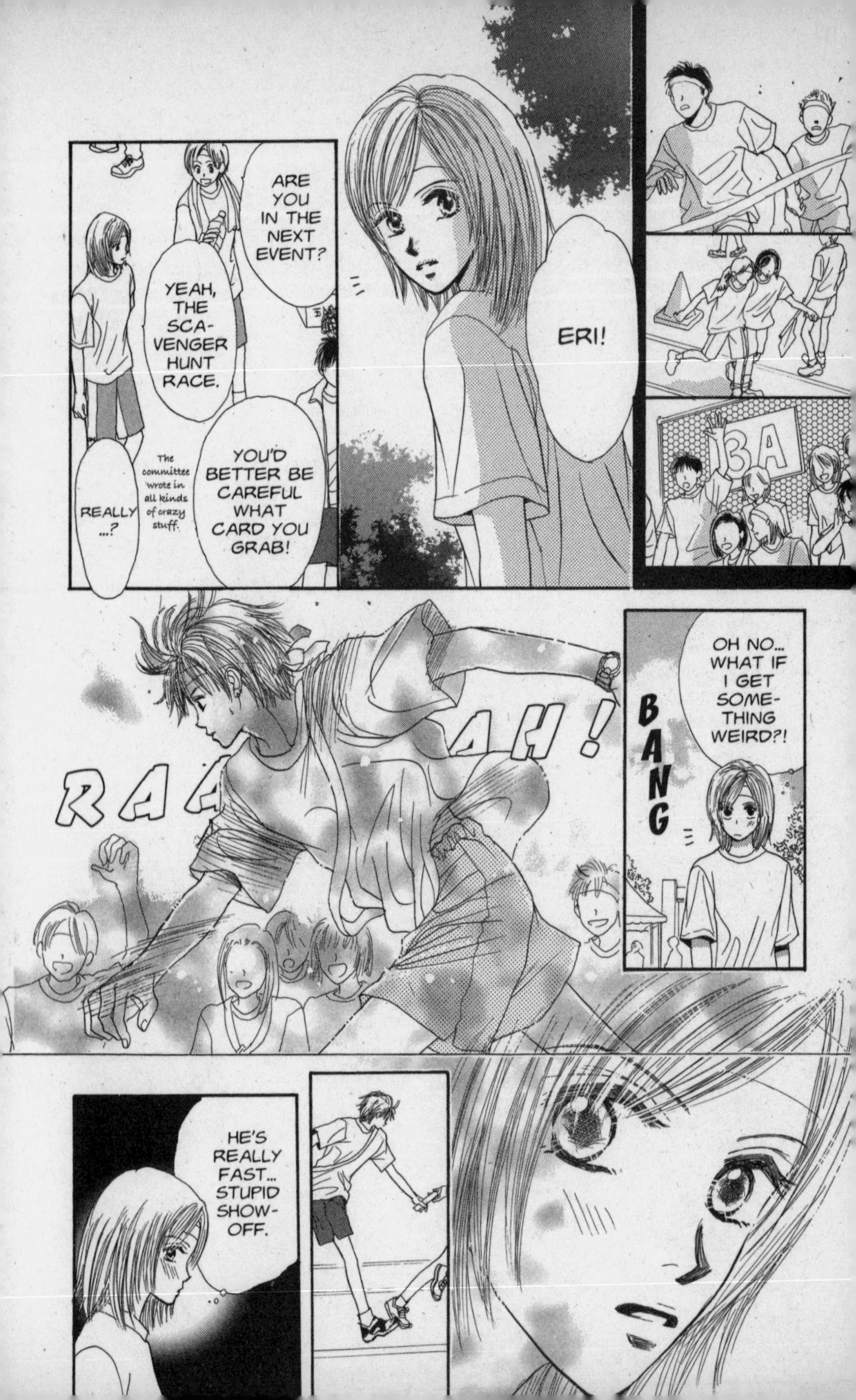
ERI!
ARE YOU IN THE NEXT EVENT?
YEAH, THE SCAVENGER HUNT RACE.
YOU'D BETTER BE CAREFUL WHAT CARD YOU GRAB!
The committee wrote in all kinds of crazy stuff.
REALLY ...?
OH NO... WHAT IF I GET SOMETHING WEIRD?!
BANG
RAA
AH!
HE'S REALLY FAST... STUPID SHOW-OFF.

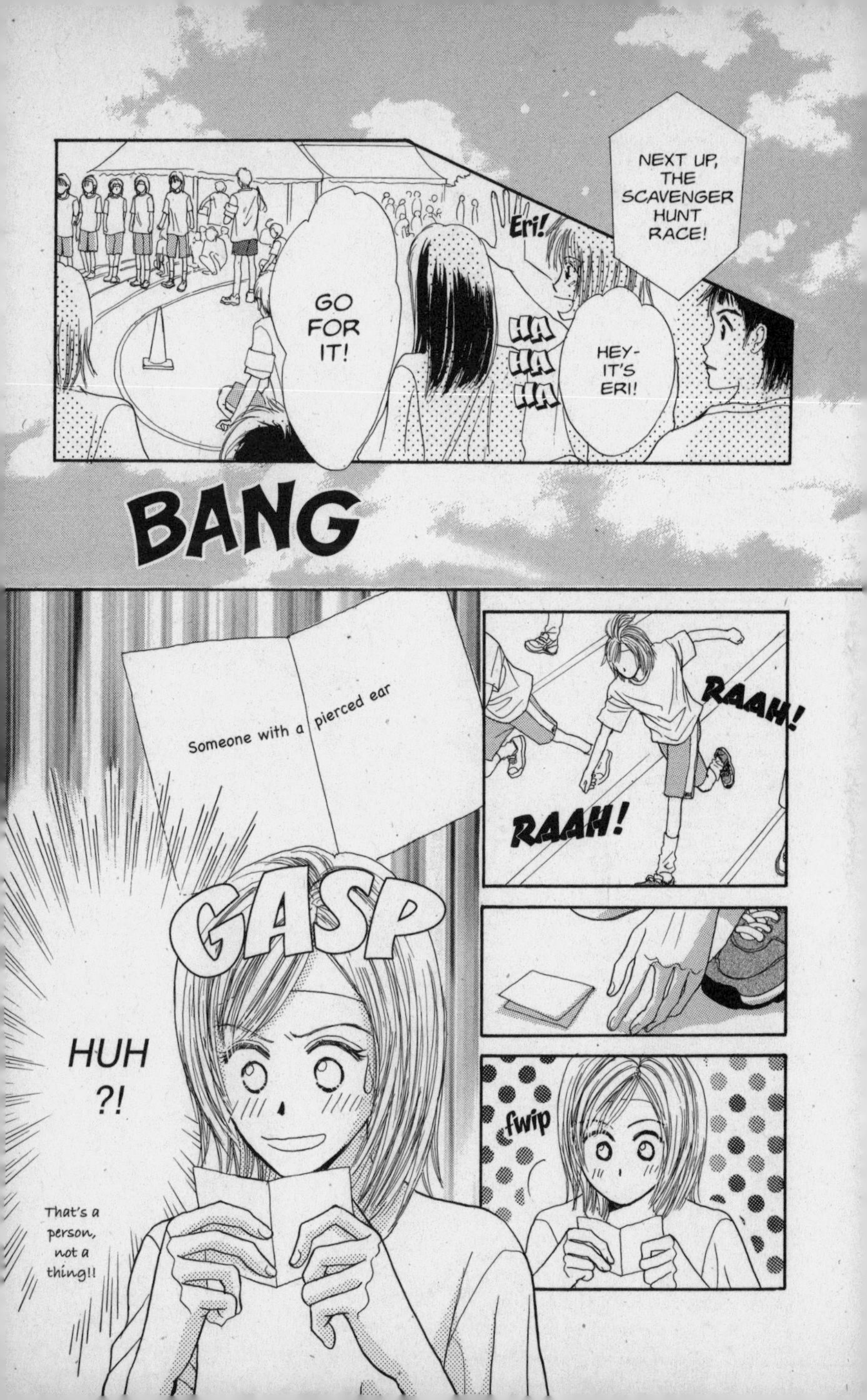
NEXT UP, THE SCAVENGER HUNT RACE!
Eri!
HEY- IT'S ERI!
HA HA HA
GO FOR IT!
BANG
RAAH!
RAAH!
fwip
Someone with a pierced ear
GASP
HUH ?!
That's a person, not a thing!!

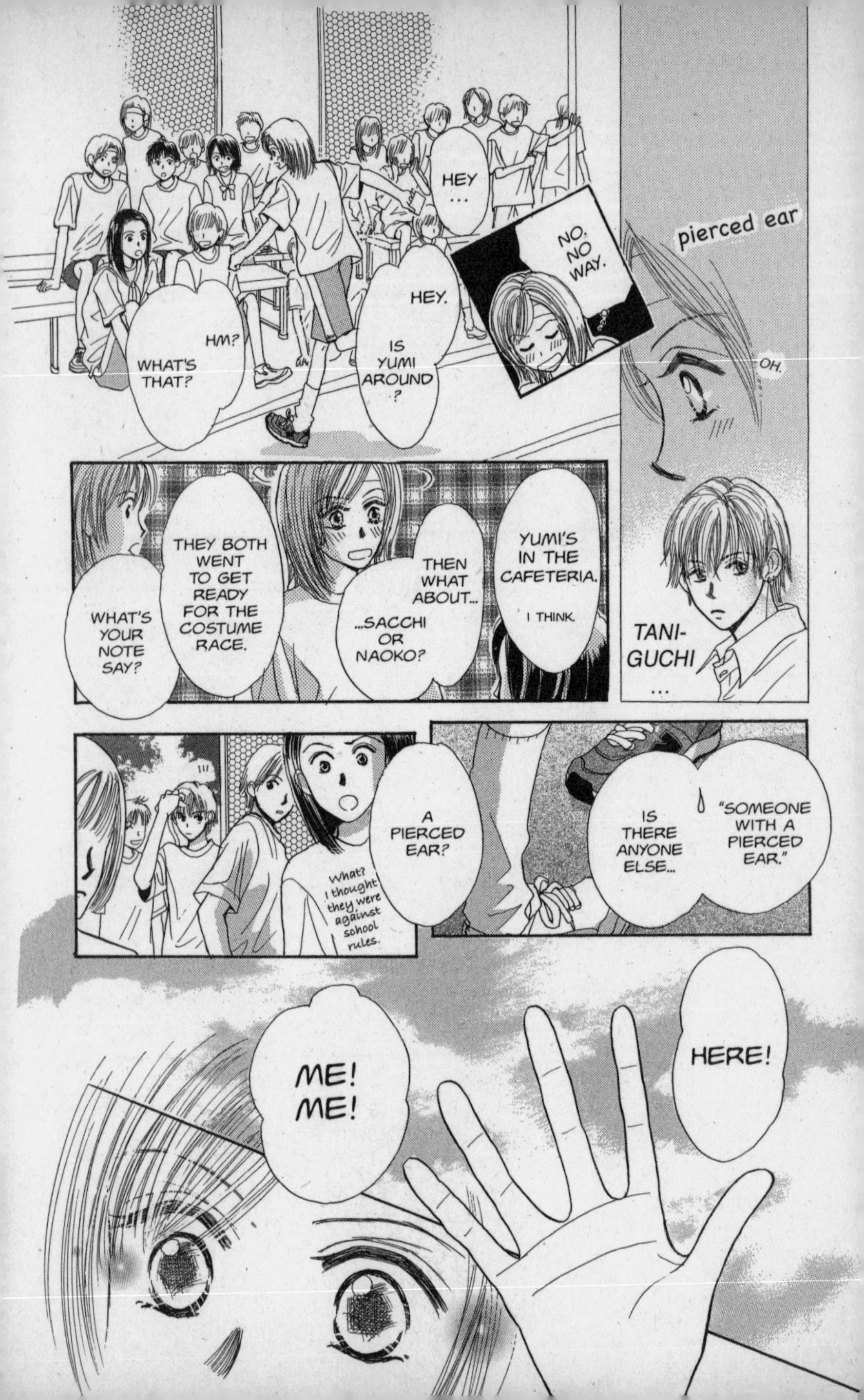
pierced ear
OH.
TANI-GUCHI ...
HEY ...
NO. NO WAY.
HEY.
IS YUMI AROUND?
HM?
WHAT'S THAT?
YUMI'S IN THE CAFETERIA.
I THINK.
THEN WHAT ABOUT...
...SACCHI OR NAOKO?
THEY BOTH WENT TO GET READY FOR THE COSTUME RACE.
WHAT'S YOUR NOTE SAY?
"SOMEONE WITH A PIERCED EAR."
IS THERE ANYONE ELSE...
A PIERCED EAR?
What? I thought they were against school rules.
HERE!
ME! ME!

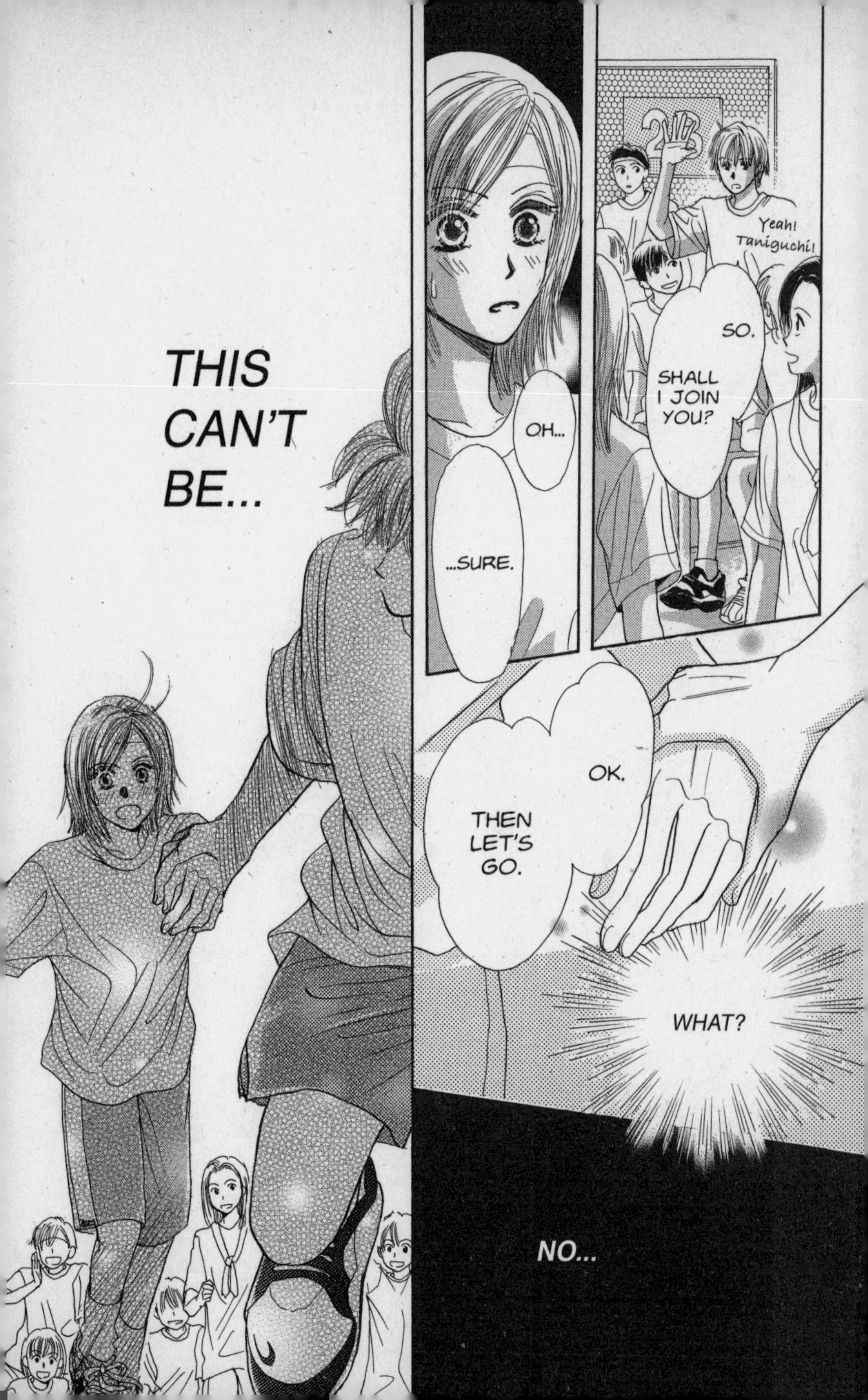

Yeah! Taniguchi!
SO.
SHALL I JOIN YOU?
OH...
...SURE.
OK.
THEN LET'S GO.
WHAT?
NO...
THIS CAN'T BE...

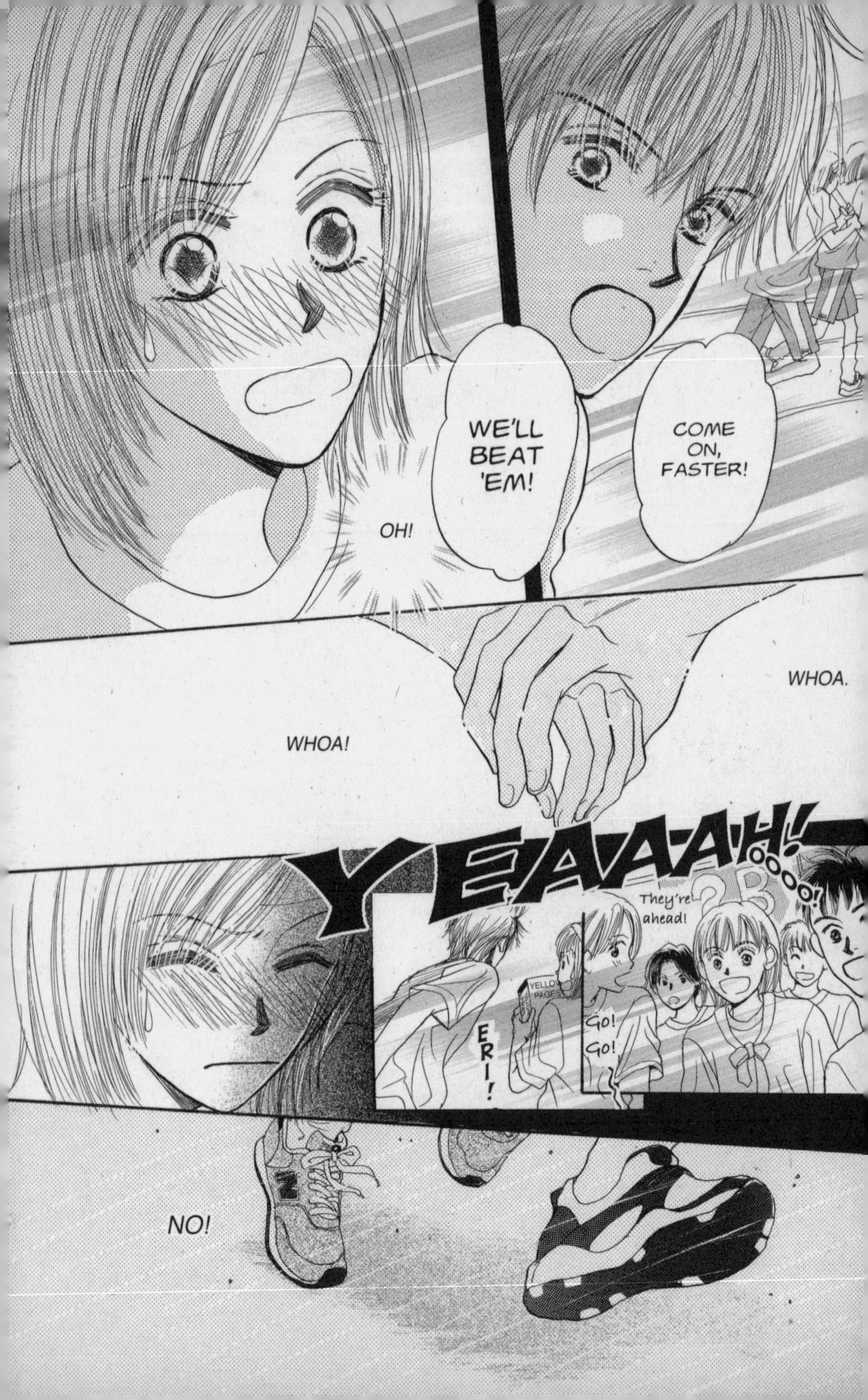
COME ON, FASTER!
WE'LL BEAT 'EM!
OH!
WHOA.
WHOA!
YEAAAH!
OOOO!
They're ahead!
Go! Go!
ERI!
NO!

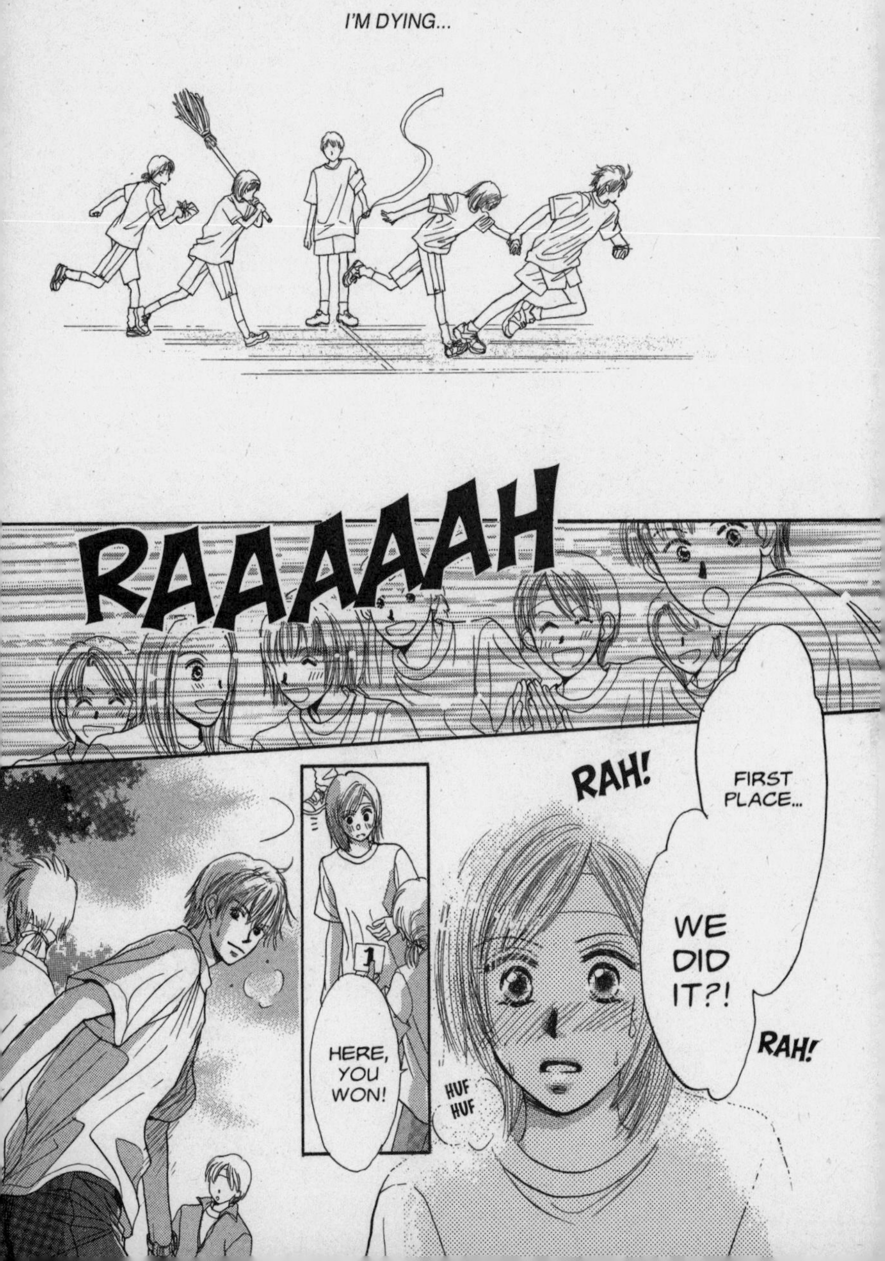
I'M DYING...
RAAAAAH
RAH!
FIRST PLACE...
WE DID IT?!
RAH!
HUF HUF
HERE, YOU WON!

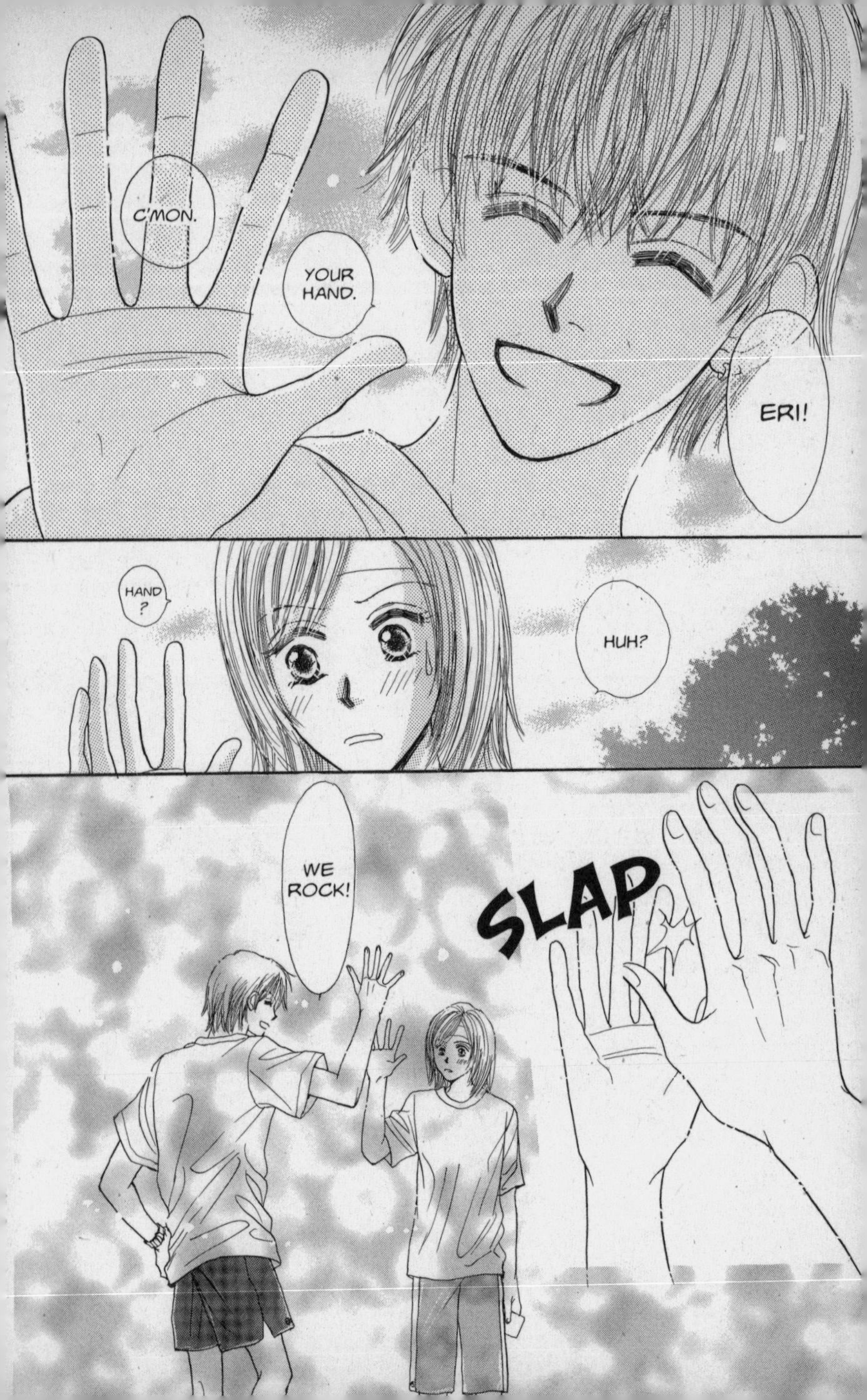
ERI!
YOUR HAND.
C'MON.
HUH?
HAND?
WE ROCK!
SLAP

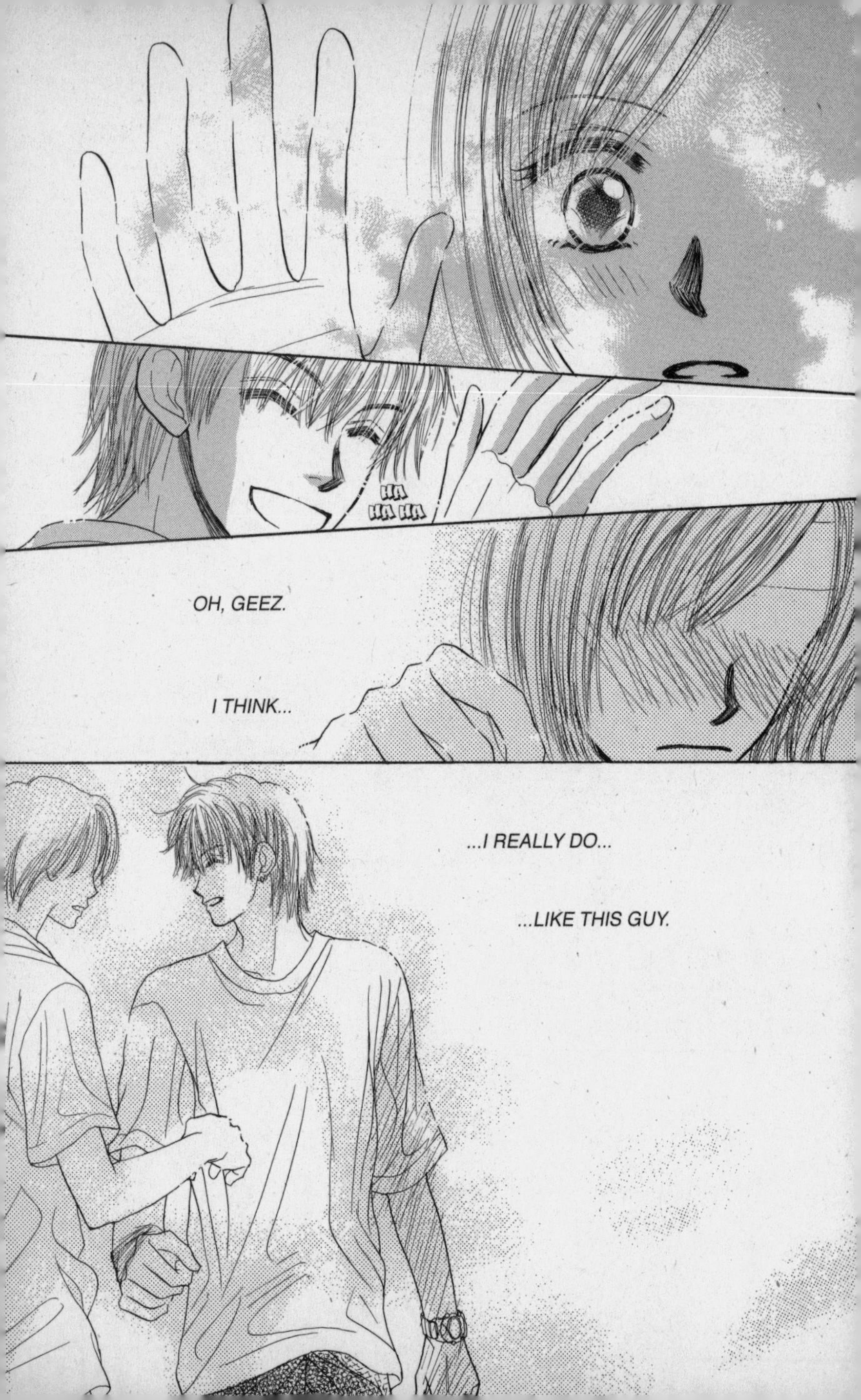
HA HA HA HA
OH, GEEZ.
I THINK...
...I REALLY DO...
...LIKE THIS GUY.

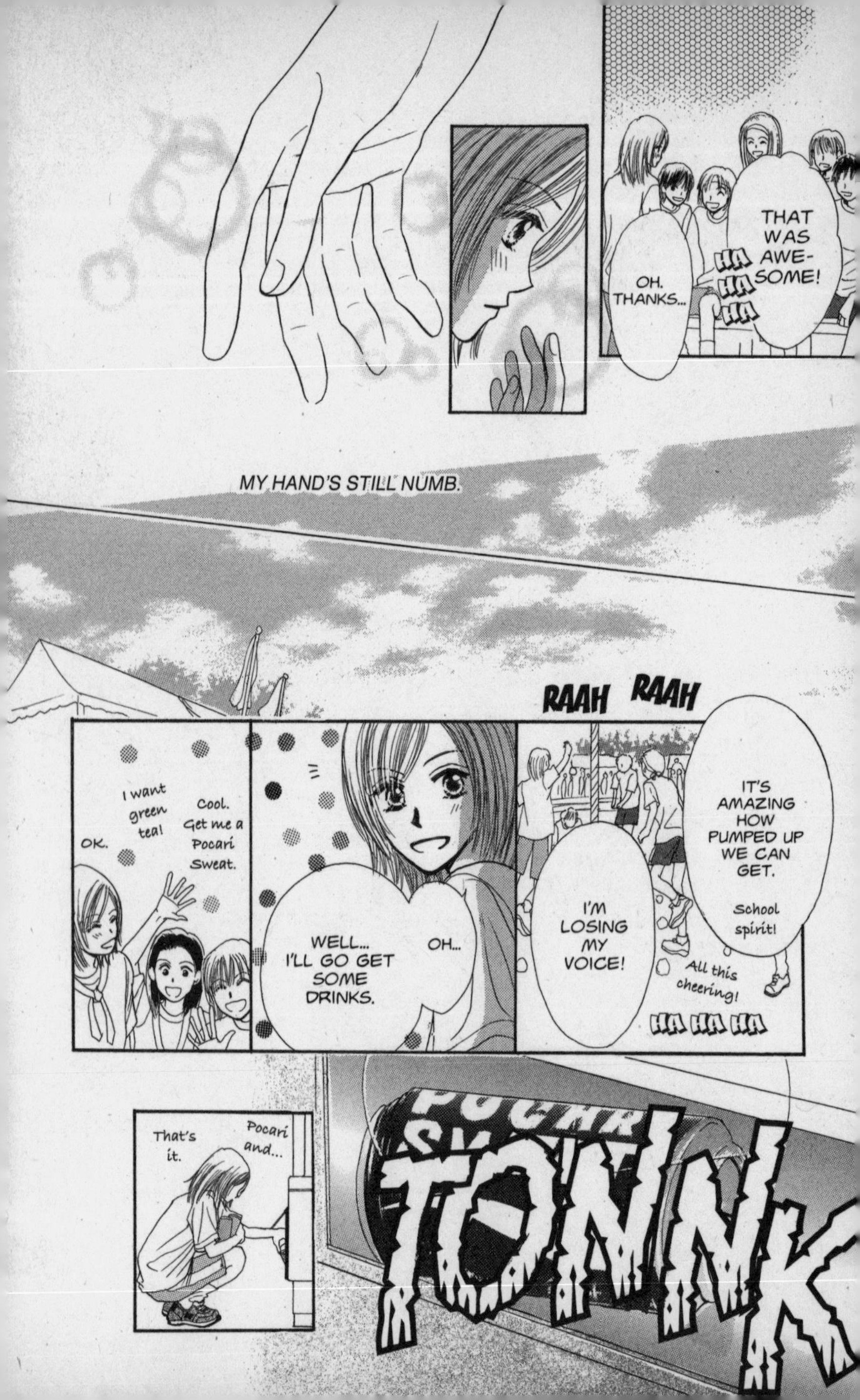
THAT WAS AWESOME!
HA HA HA
OH. THANKS...
MY HAND'S STILL NUMB.
RAAH RAAH
IT'S AMAZING HOW PUMPED UP WE CAN GET.
School spirit!
I'M LOSING MY VOICE!
All this cheering!
HA HA HA
OH...
WELL... I'LL GO GET SOME DRINKS.
Cool. Get me a Pocari Sweat.
I want green tea!
OK.
TONNK
Pocari and...
That's it.

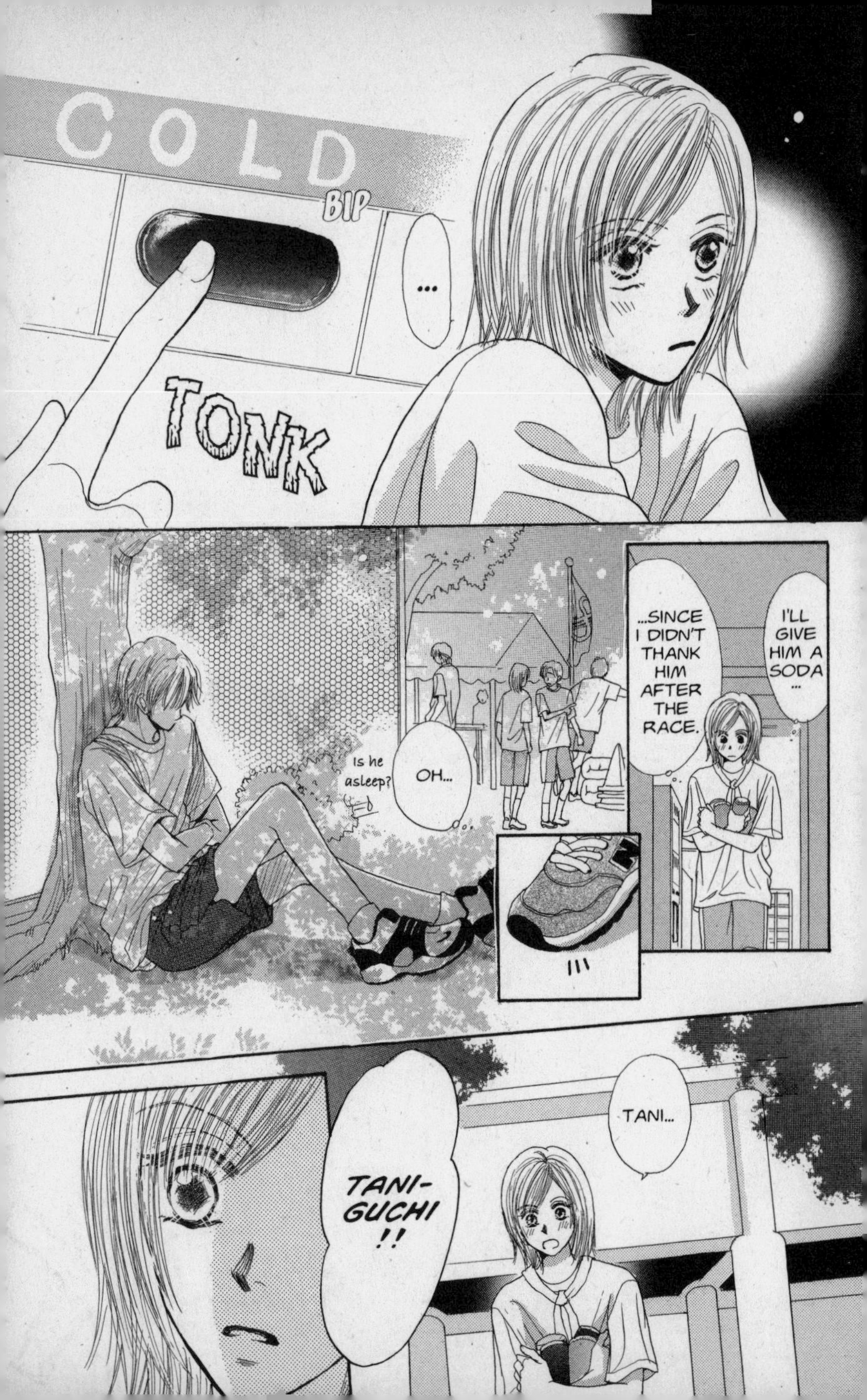
COLD
BIP
...
TONK
I'LL GIVE HIM A SODA...
...SINCE I DIDN'T THANK HIM AFTER THE RACE.
OH...
Is he asleep?
TANI...
TANI-GUCHI!!

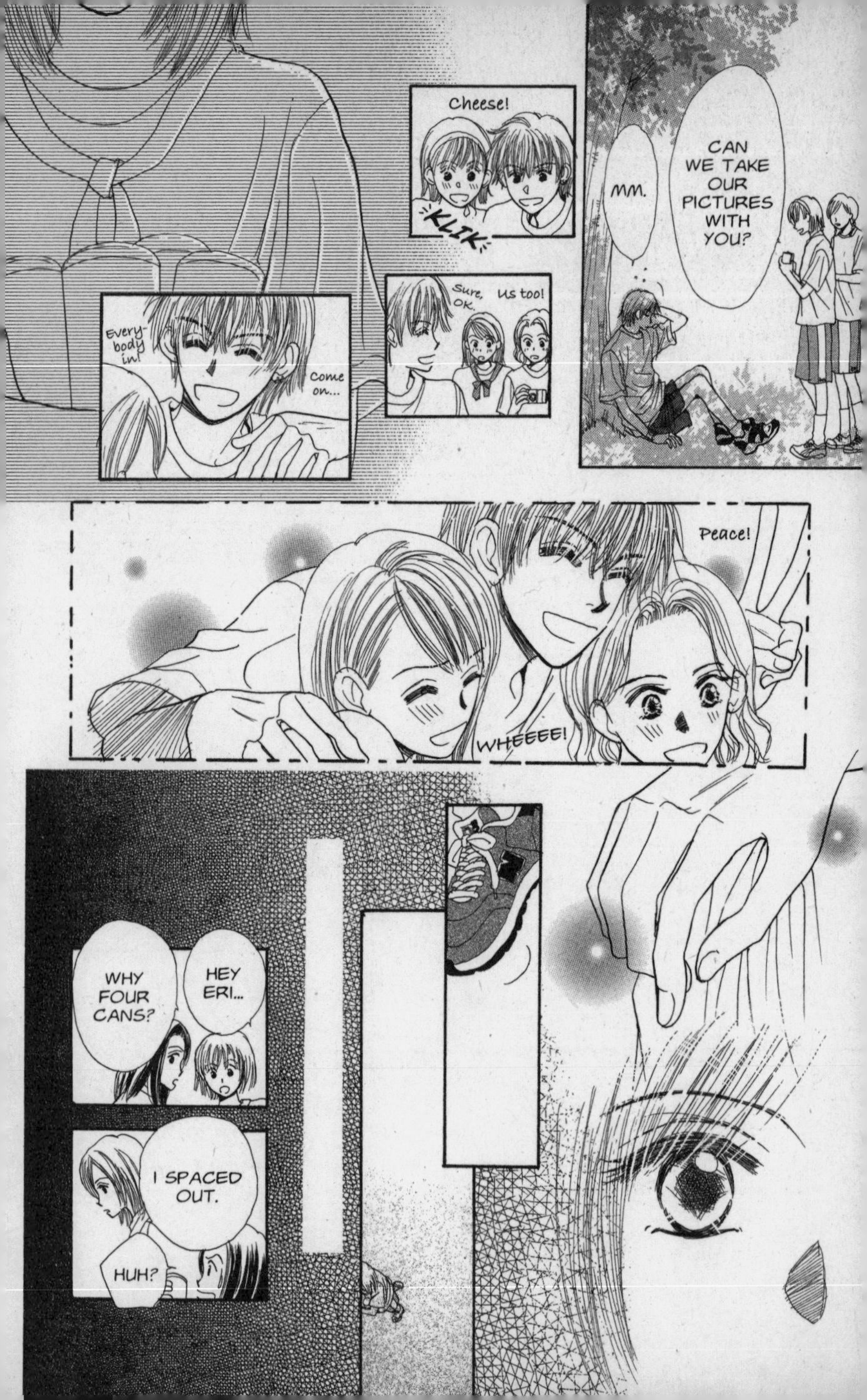
CAN WE TAKE OUR PICTURES WITH YOU?
MM.
Cheese!
KLIK
Us too!
Sure, OK.
Every-body in!
Come on...
Peace!
WHEEEE!
HEY ERI...
WHY FOUR CANS?
I SPACED OUT.
HUH?

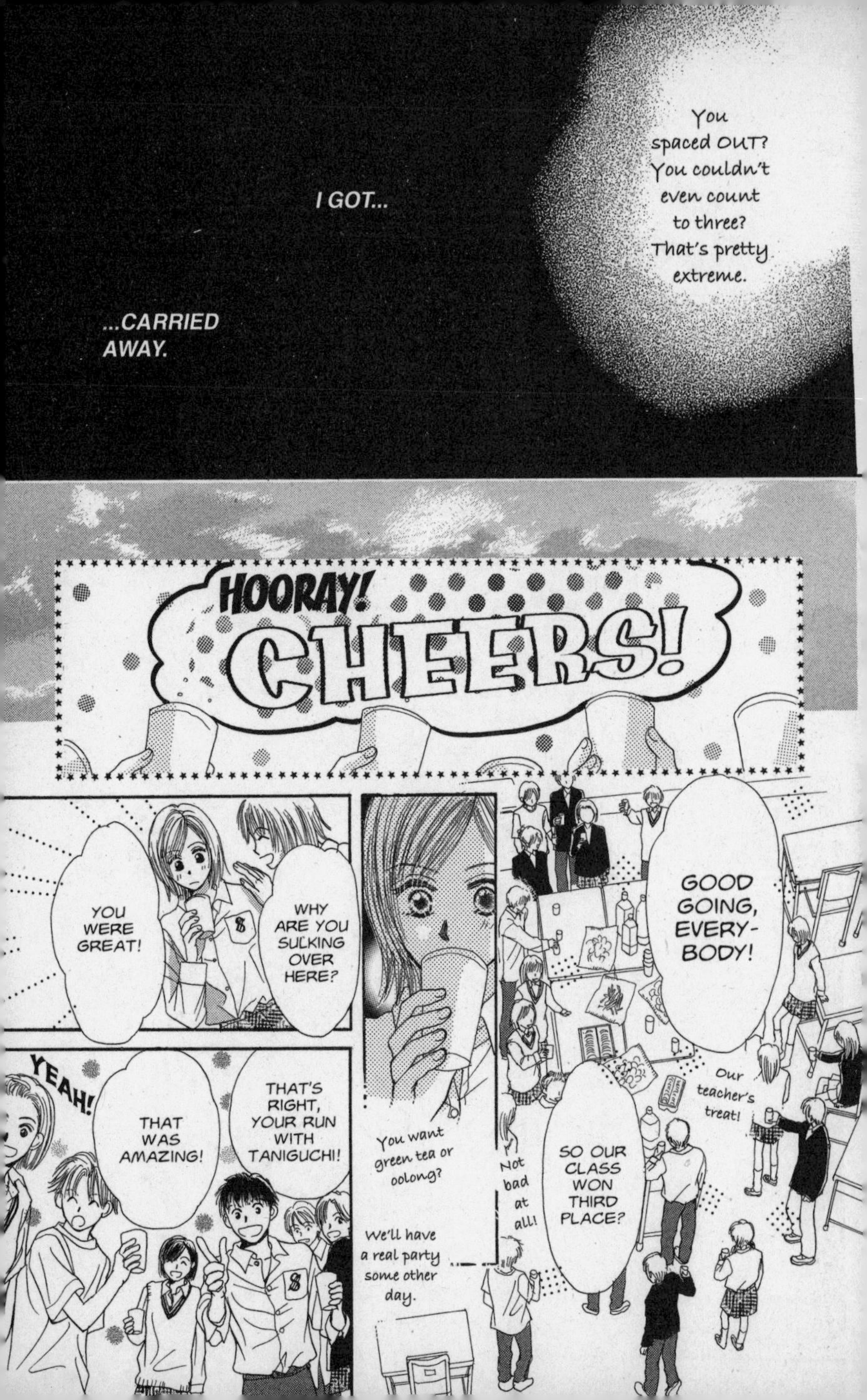
You spaced OUT? You couldn't even count to three? That's pretty extreme.
I GOT...
...CARRIED AWAY.
HOORAY!
CHEERS!
GOOD GOING, EVERY-BODY!
Our teacher's treat!
SO OUR CLASS WON THIRD PLACE?
Not bad at all!
You want green tea or oolong?
We'll have a real party some other day.
WHY ARE YOU SULKING OVER HERE?
YOU WERE GREAT!
THAT'S RIGHT, YOUR RUN WITH TANIGUCHI!
THAT WAS AMAZING!
YEAH!

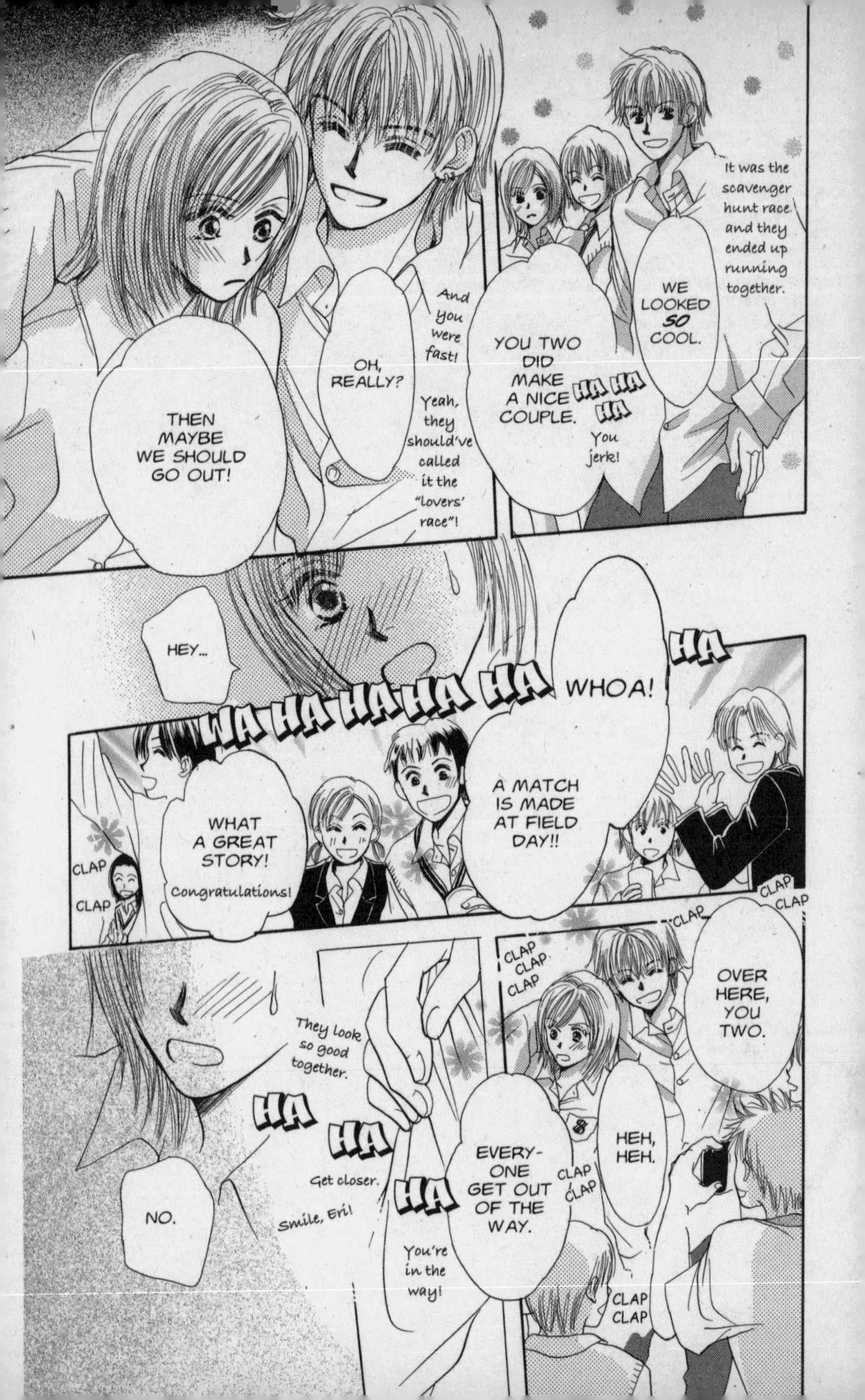
It was the scavenger hunt race and they ended up running together.
WE LOOKED SO COOL.
YOU TWO DID MAKE A NICE COUPLE.
HA HA HA
You jerk!
And you were fast!
OH, REALLY?
Yeah, they should've called it the "lovers' race"!
THEN MAYBE WE SHOULD GO OUT!
HA
WHOA!
HEY...
WA HA HA HA HA HA
A MATCH IS MADE AT FIELD DAY!!
WHAT A GREAT STORY!
Congratulations!
CLAP
CLAP
CLAP
CLAP
CLAP
OVER HERE, YOU TWO.
CLAP
CLAP
CLAP
HEH, HEH.
EVERY-ONE GET OUT OF THE WAY.
CLAP
CLAP
CLAP
CLAP
You're in the way!
They look so good together.
HA
HA
HA
Get closer.
Smile, Eri!
NO.

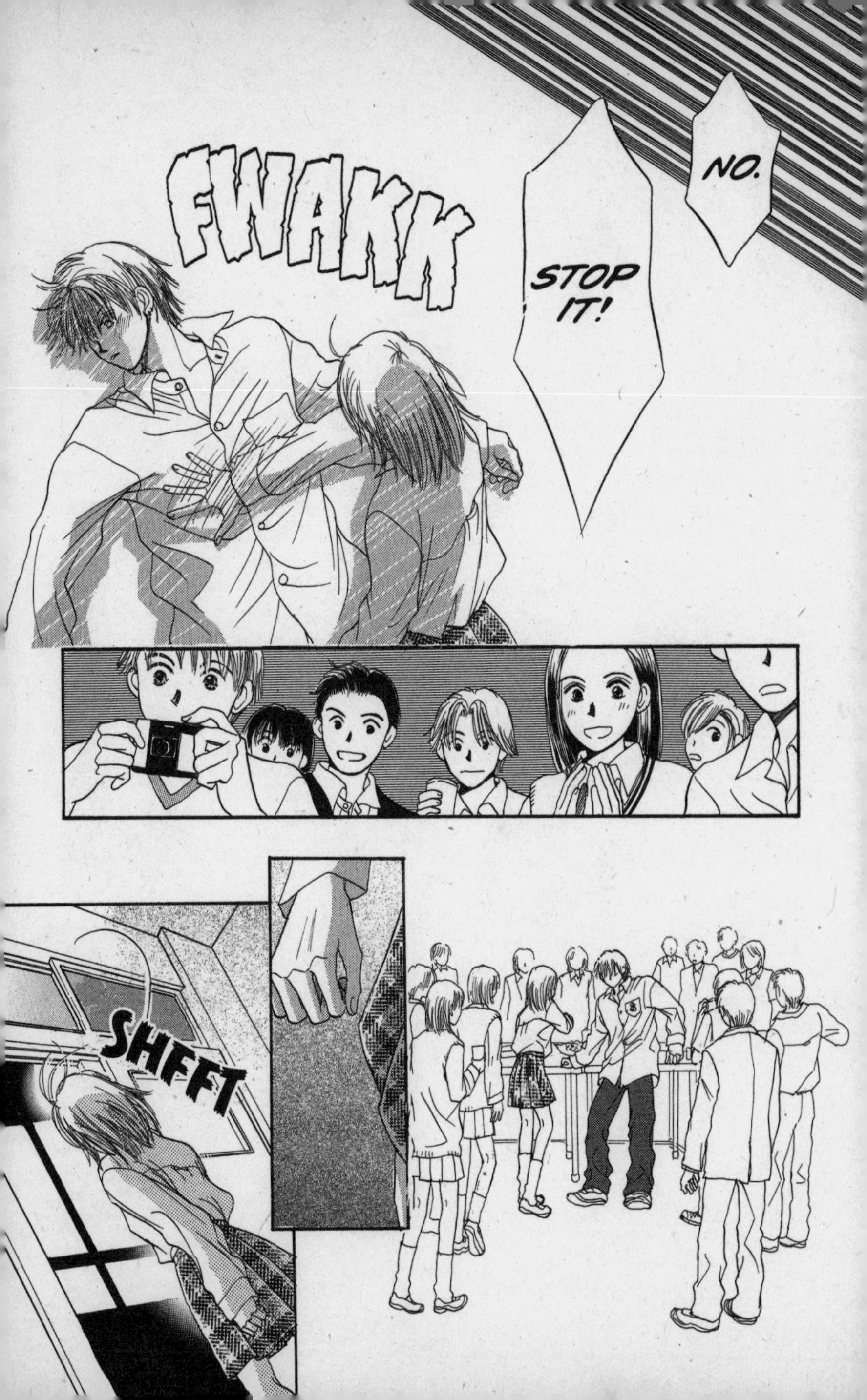
NO.
STOP IT!
FWAKK
SHFFT

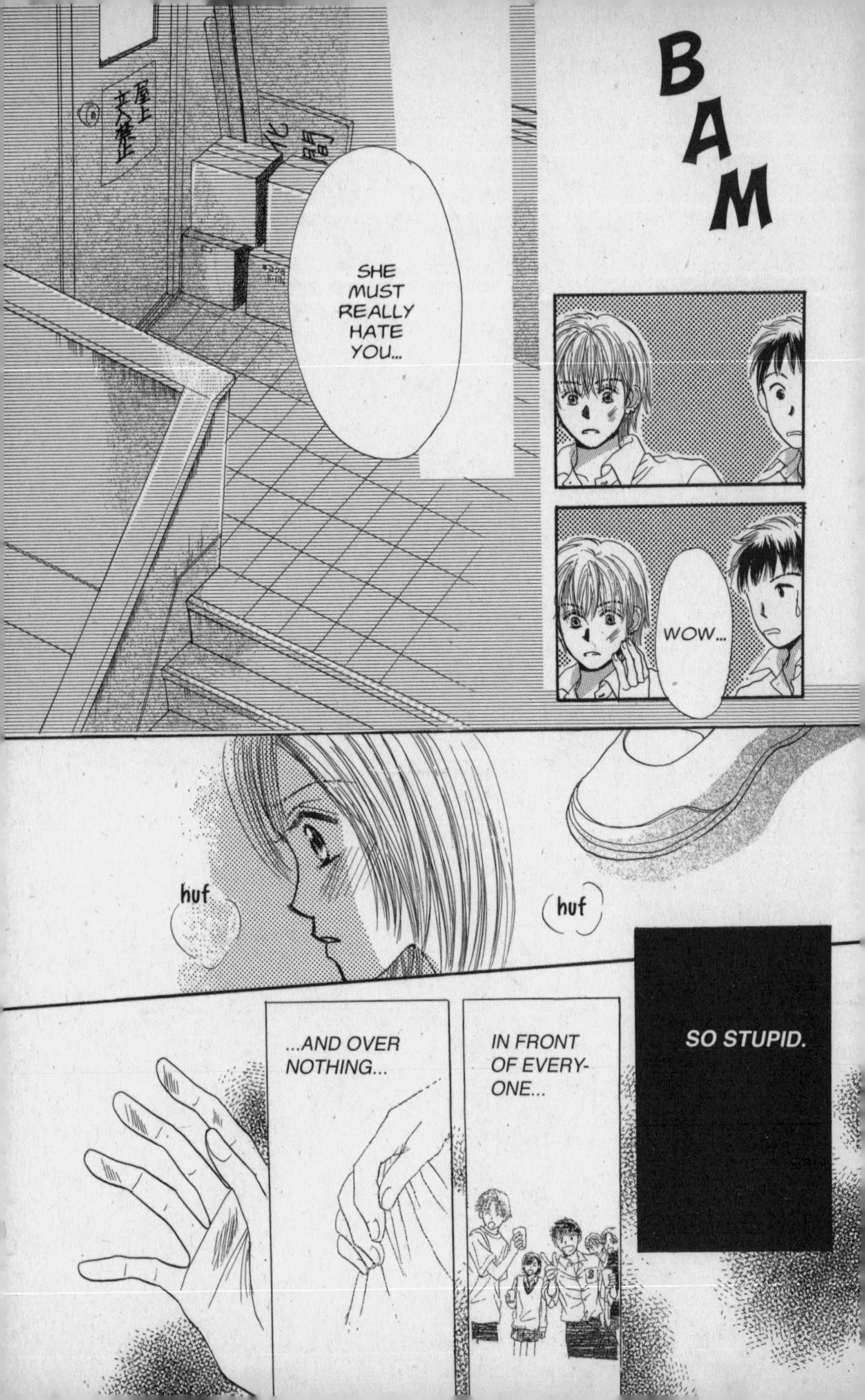
BAM
WOW...
SHE MUST REALLY HATE YOU...
屋上立入禁止
huf
huf
SO STUPID.
IN FRONT OF EVERY-ONE...
...AND OVER NOTHING...

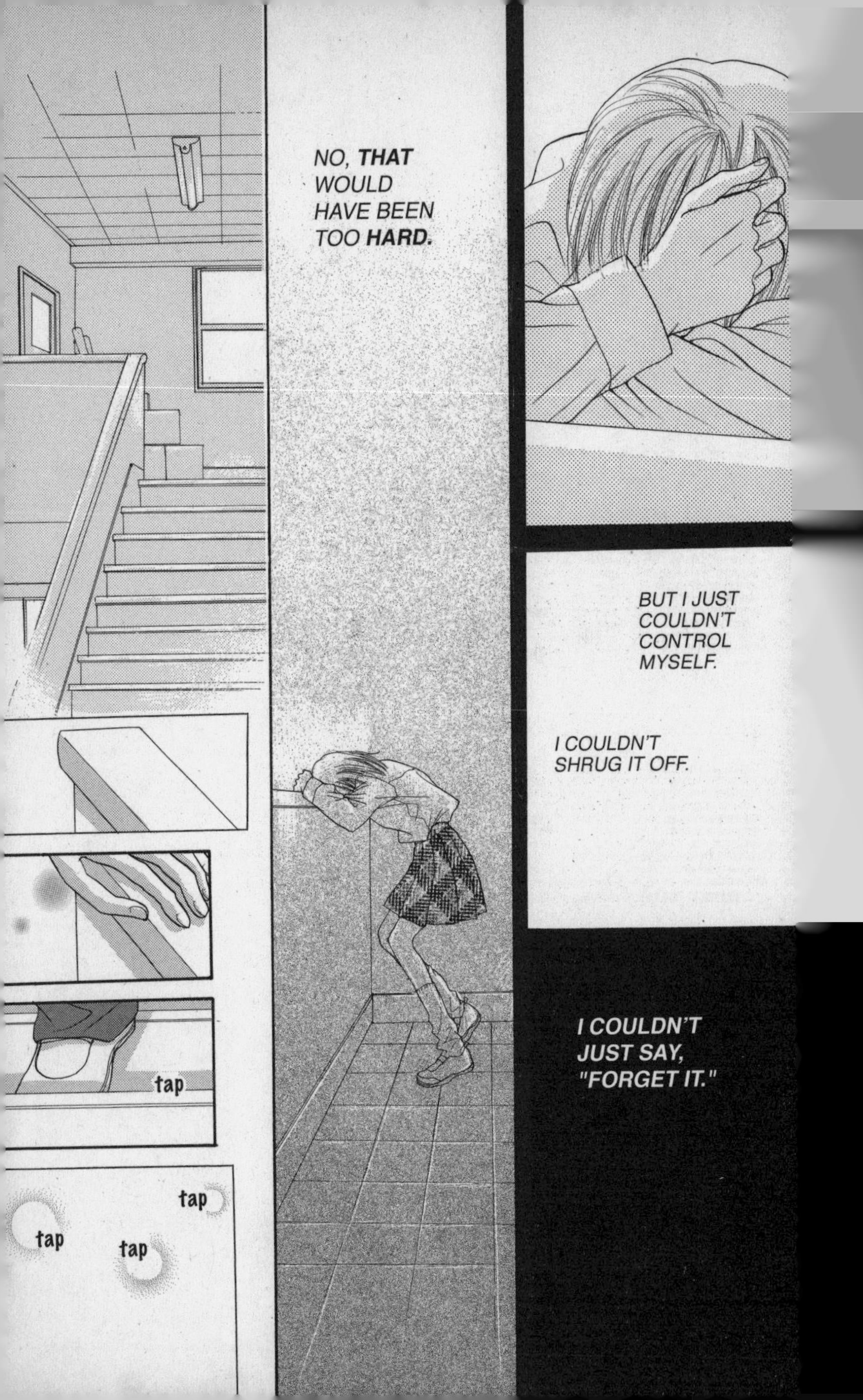
BUT I JUST COULDN'T CONTROL MYSELF.
I COULDN'T SHRUG IT OFF.
I COULDN'T JUST SAY, "FORGET IT."
NO, THAT WOULD HAVE BEEN TOO HARD.
tap
tap
tap
tap

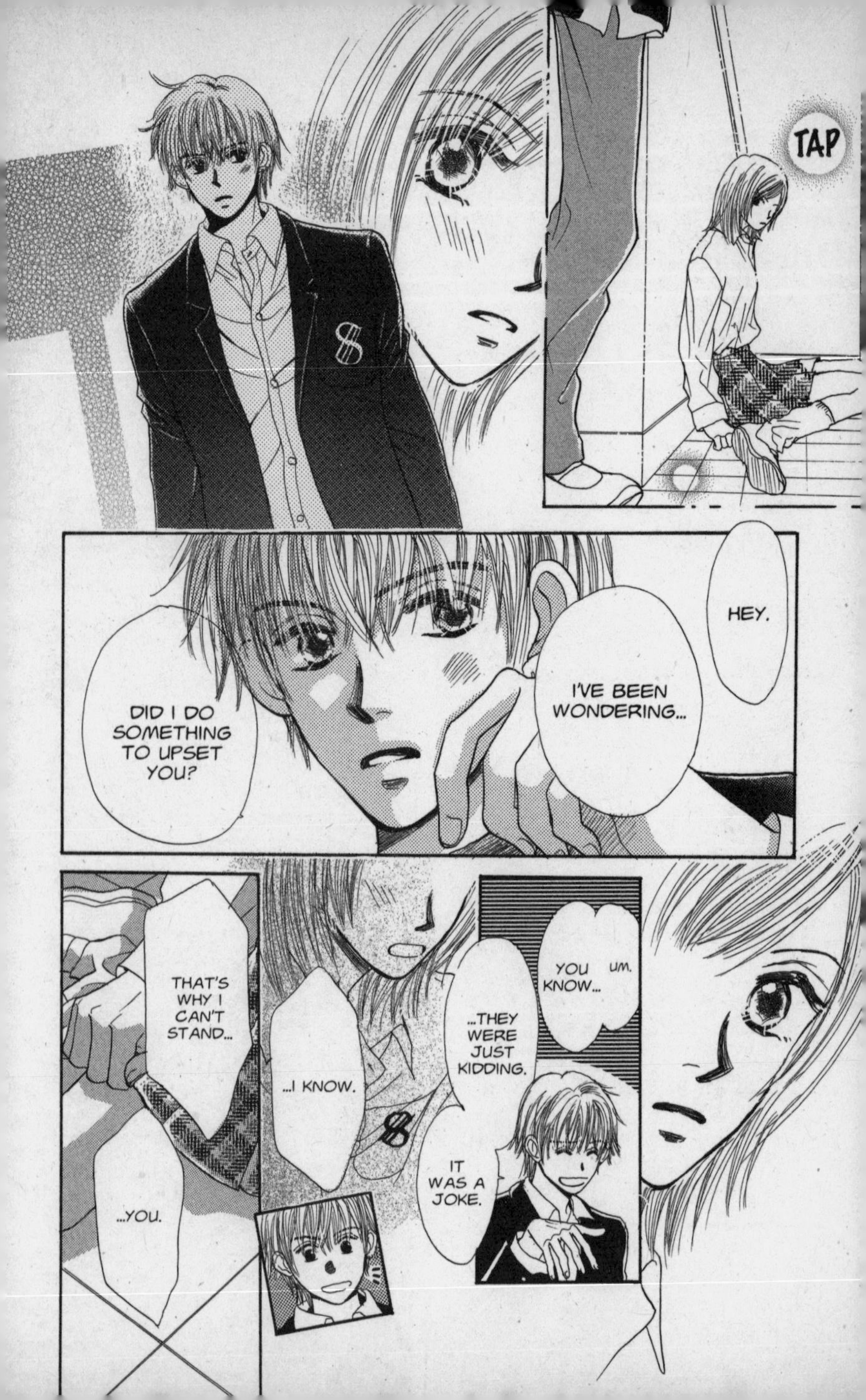
TAP
HEY.
I'VE BEEN WONDERING...
DID I DO SOMETHING TO UPSET YOU?
UM.
YOU KNOW...
...THEY WERE JUST KIDDING.
IT WAS A JOKE.
...I KNOW.
THAT'S WHY I CAN'T STAND...
...YOU.

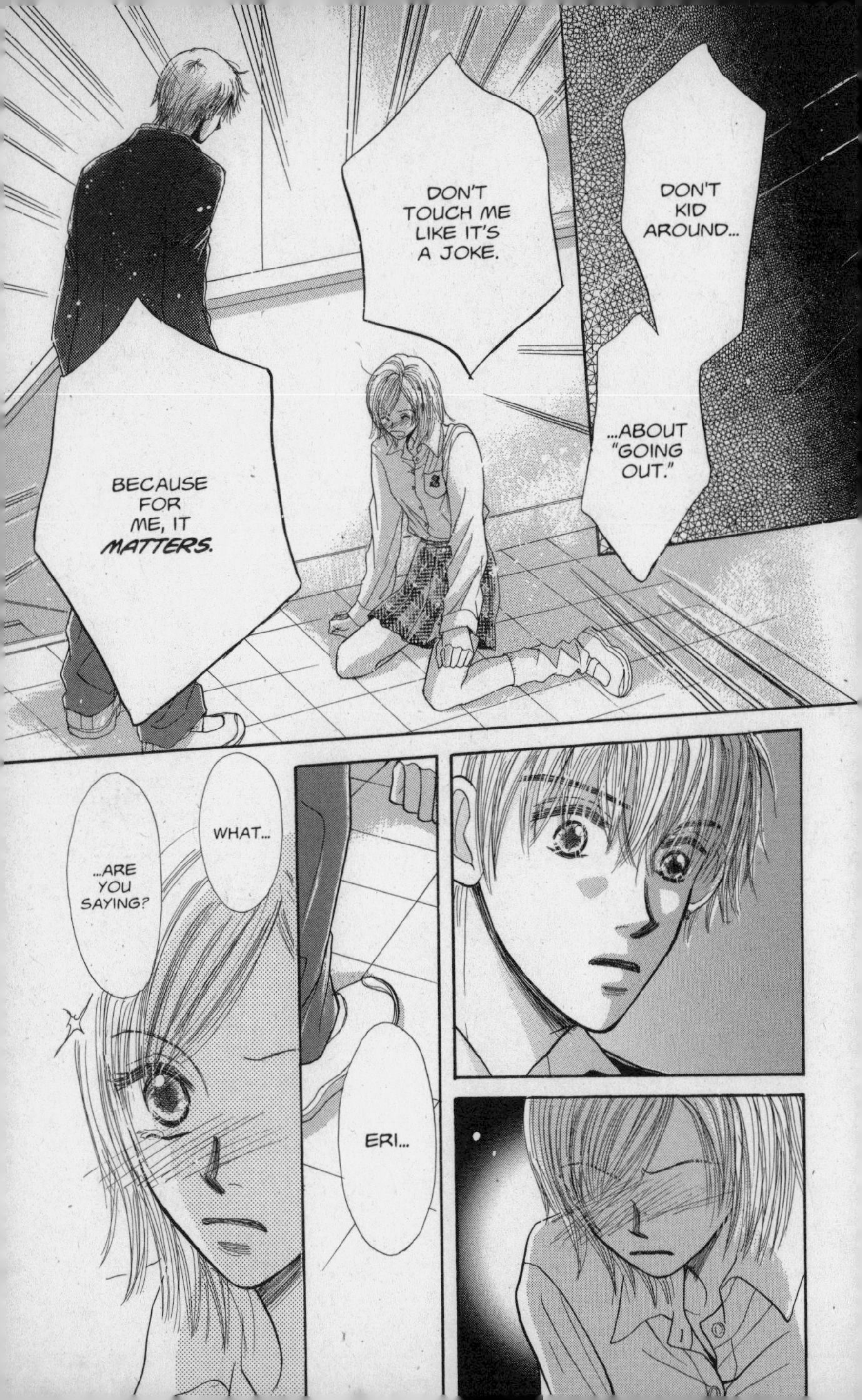

DON'T KID AROUND...
...ABOUT "GOING OUT."
DON'T TOUCH ME LIKE IT'S A JOKE.
BECAUSE FOR ME, IT *MATTERS.*
ERI...
WHAT...
...ARE YOU SAYING?

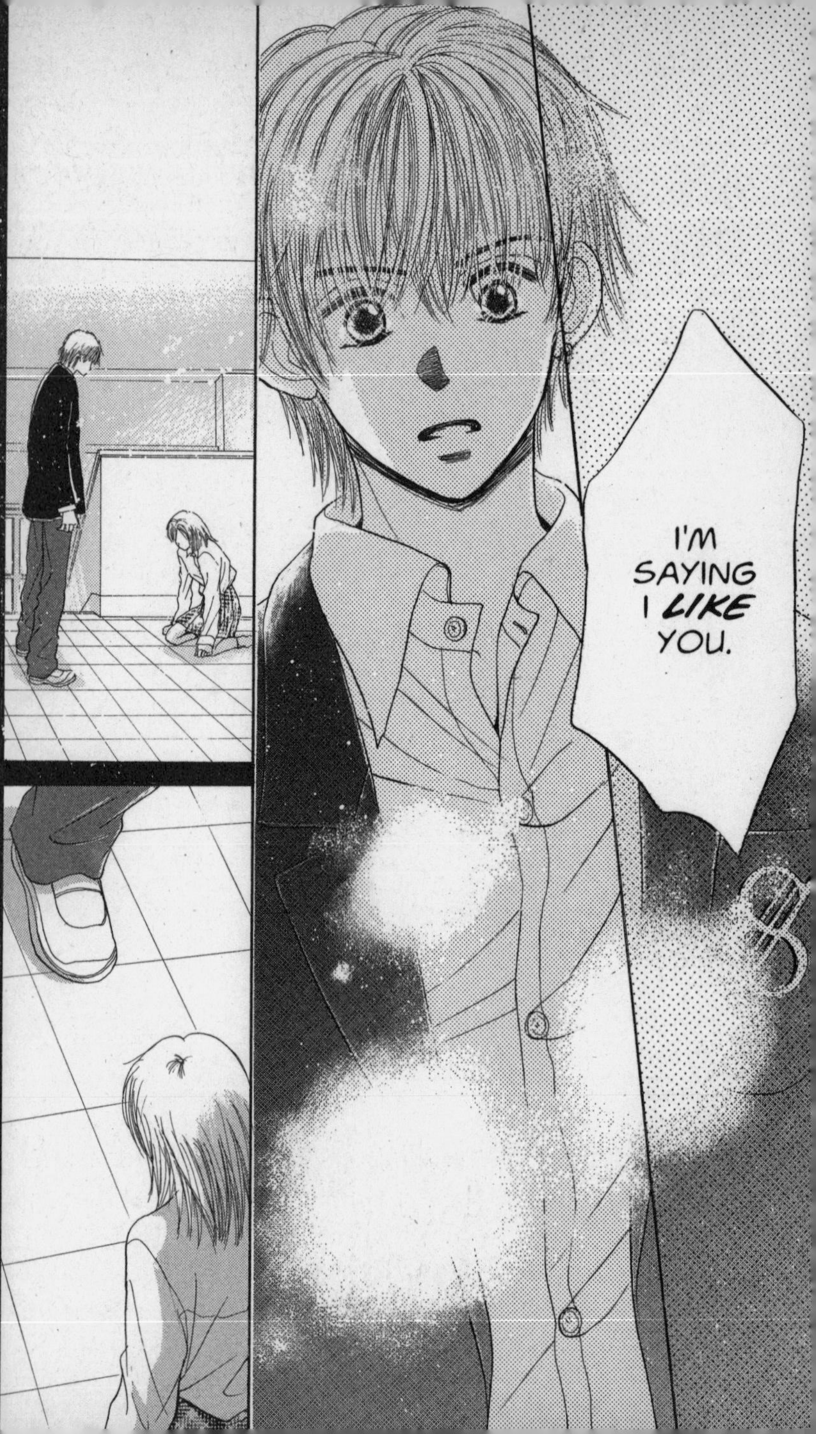
I'M SAYING I LIKE YOU.

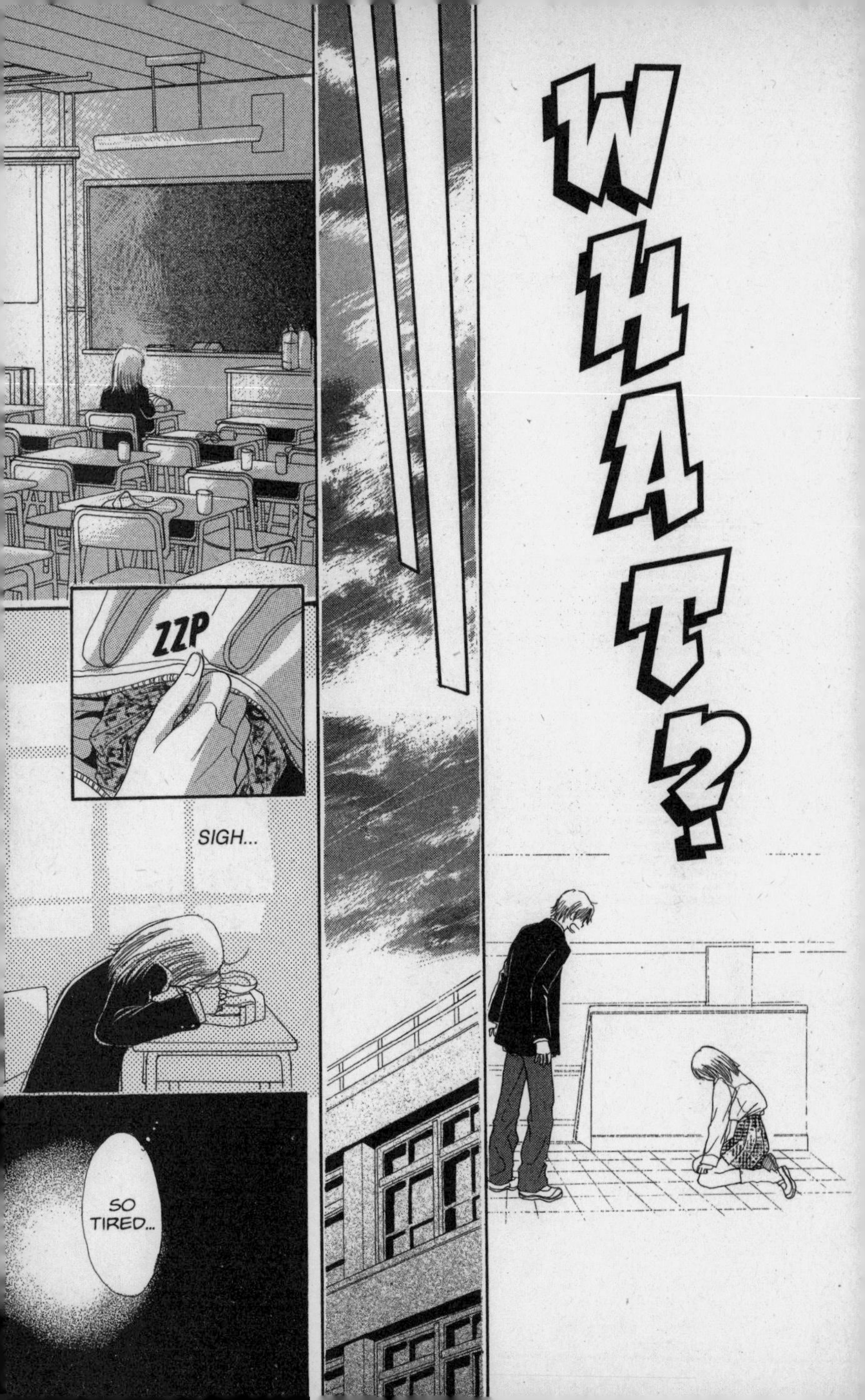
WHAT?
ZZP
SIGH...
SO TIRED...

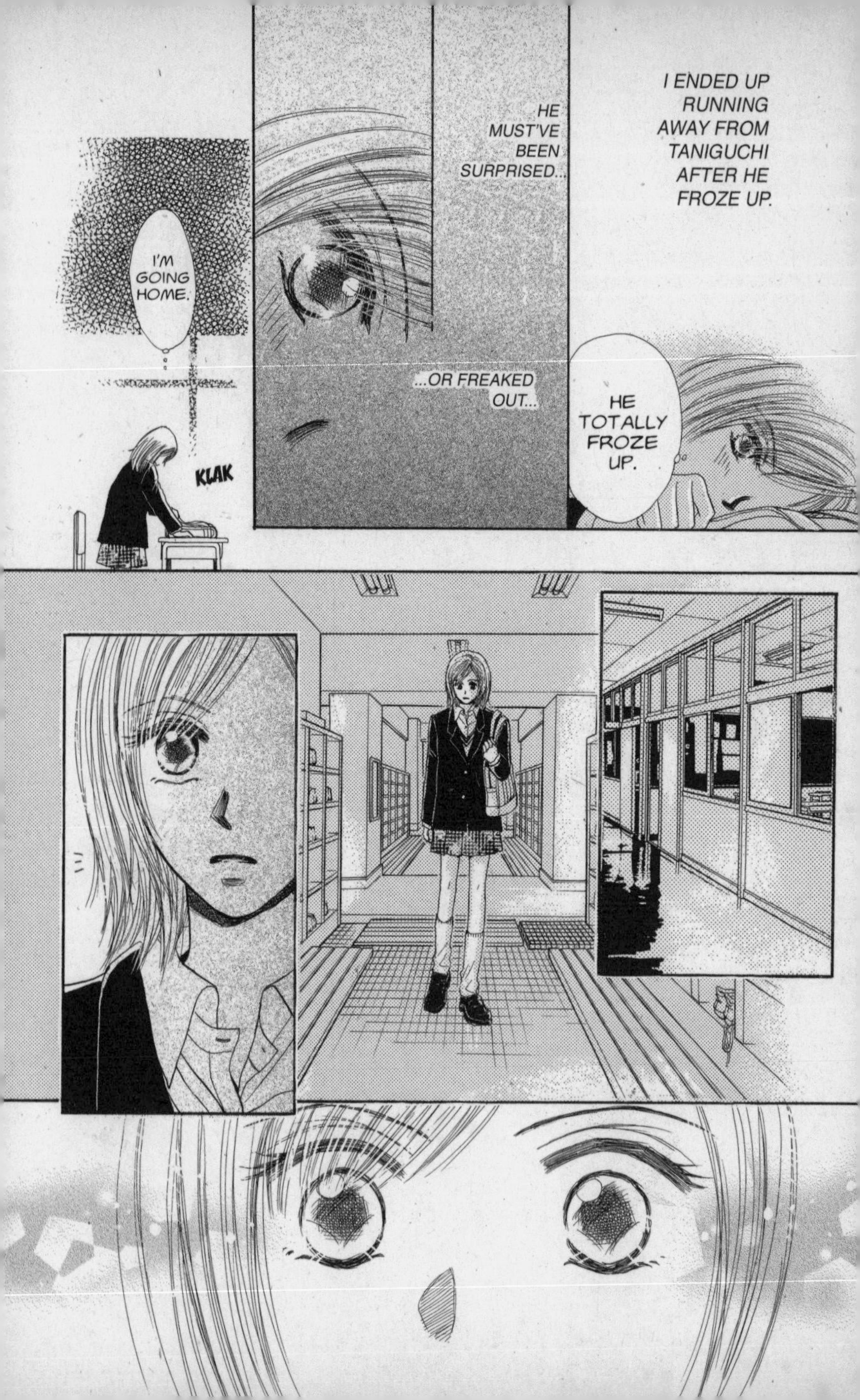
I ENDED UP RUNNING AWAY FROM TANIGUCHI AFTER HE FROZE UP.
HE TOTALLY FROZE UP.
HE MUST'VE BEEN SURPRISED...
...OR FREAKED OUT...
I'M GOING HOME.
KLAK

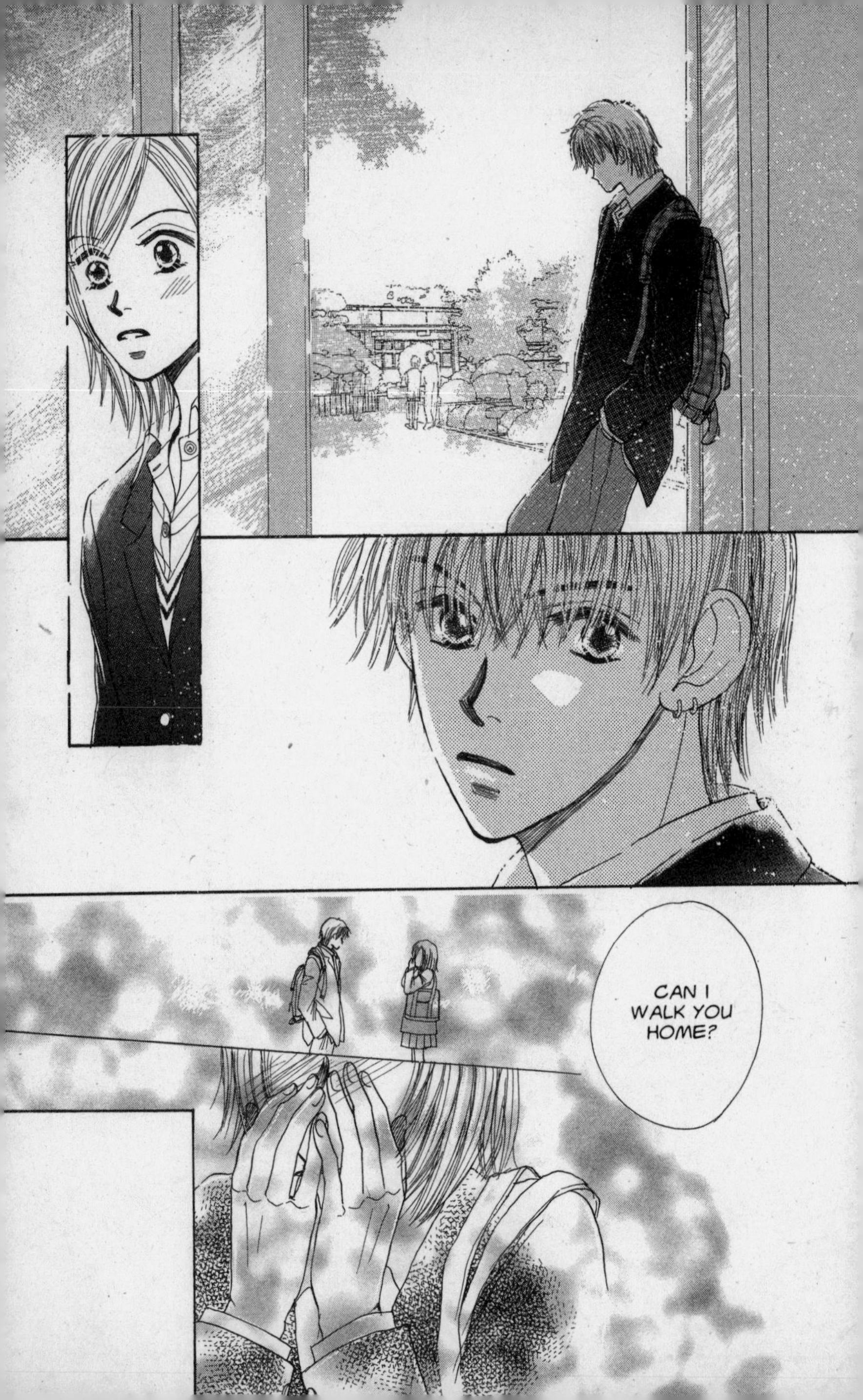
CAN I WALK YOU HOME?

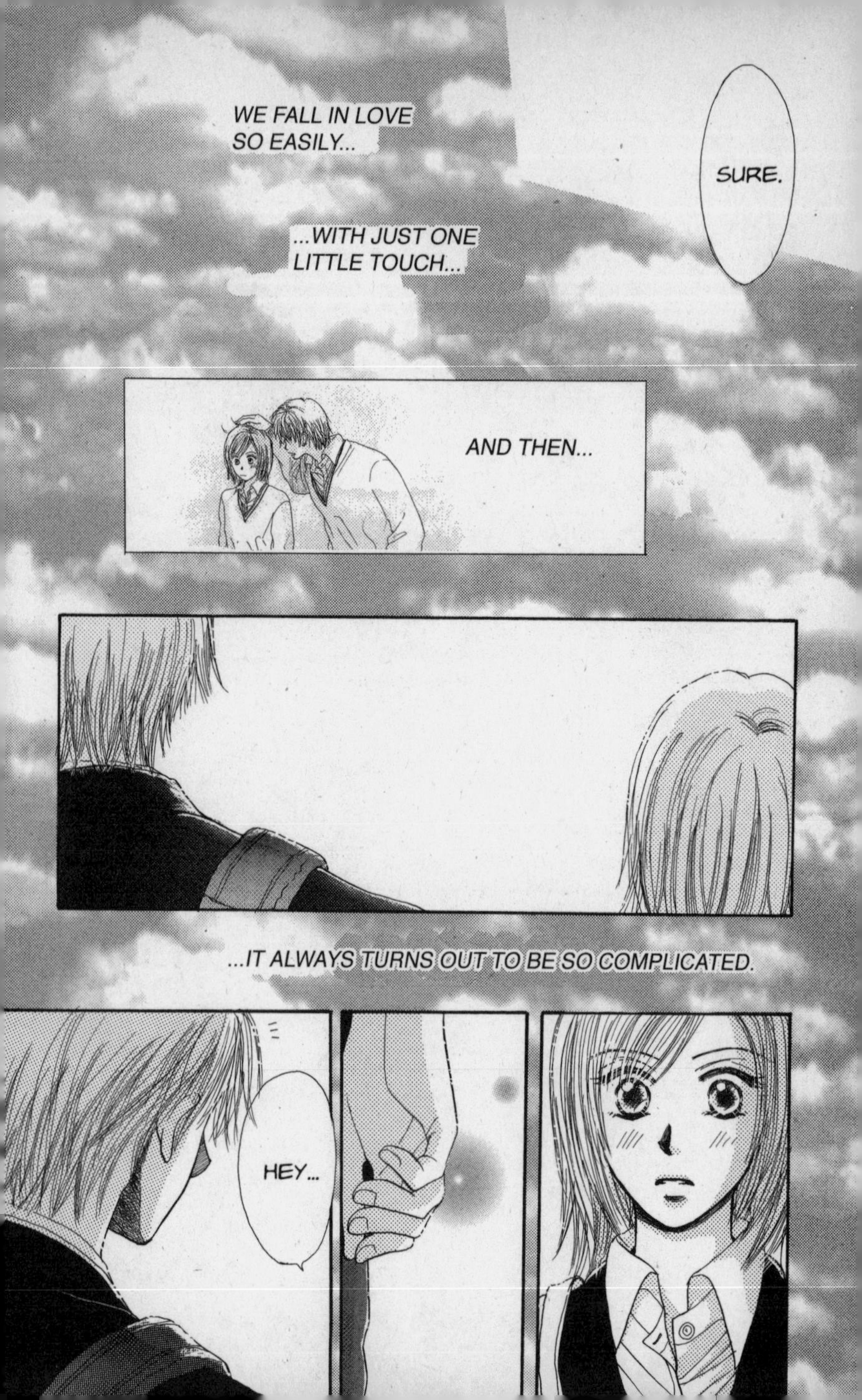
SURE.
WE FALL IN LOVE SO EASILY...
...WITH JUST ONE LITTLE TOUCH...
AND THEN...
...IT ALWAYS TURNS OUT TO BE SO COMPLICATED.
HEY...

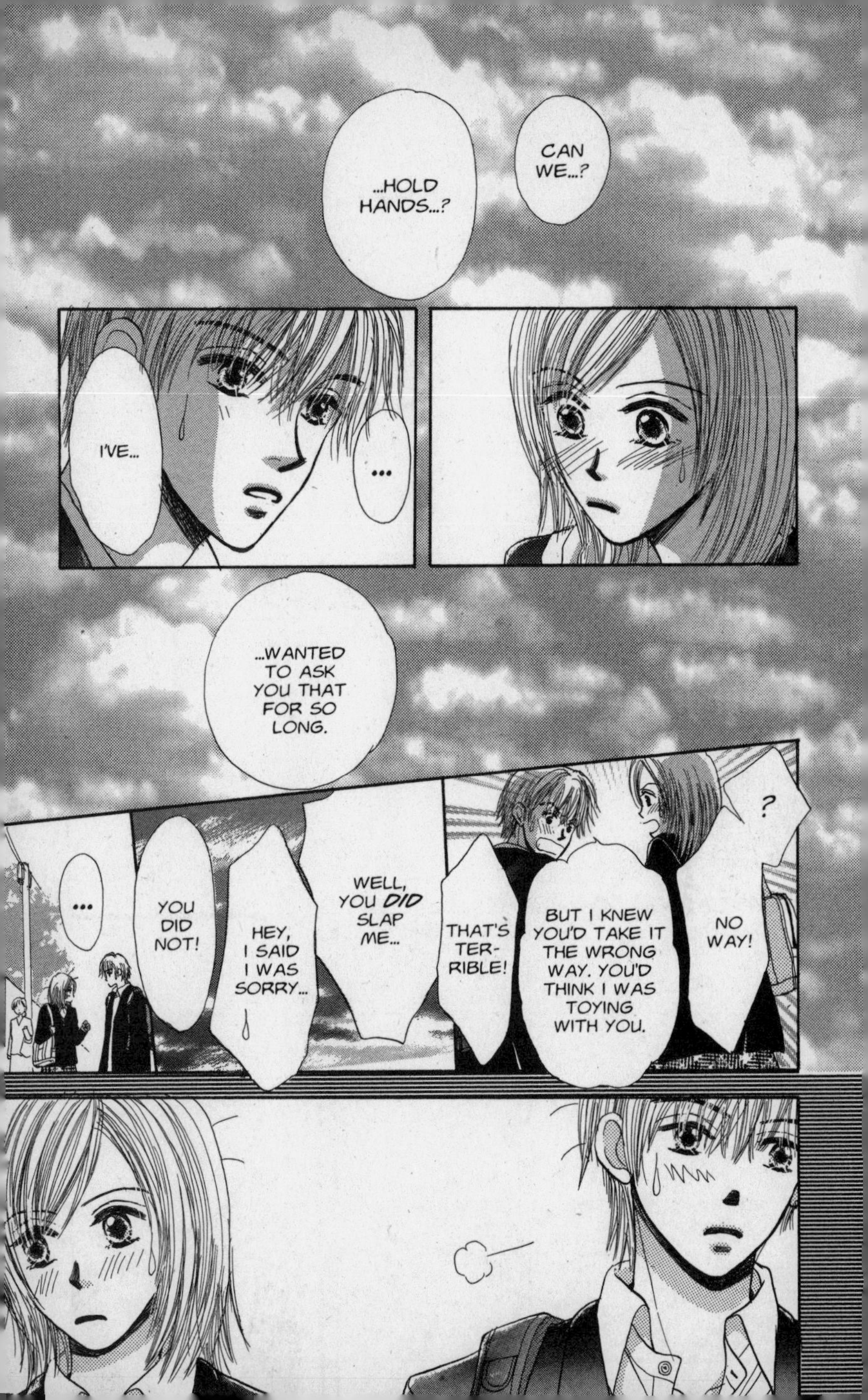
CAN WE...?
...HOLD HANDS...?
...
I'VE...
...WANTED TO ASK YOU THAT FOR SO LONG.
?
NO WAY!
BUT I KNEW YOU'D TAKE IT THE WRONG WAY. YOU'D THINK I WAS TOYING WITH YOU.
THAT'S TER-RIBLE!
WELL, YOU *DID* SLAP ME...
HEY, I SAID I WAS SORRY...
YOU DID NOT!
...

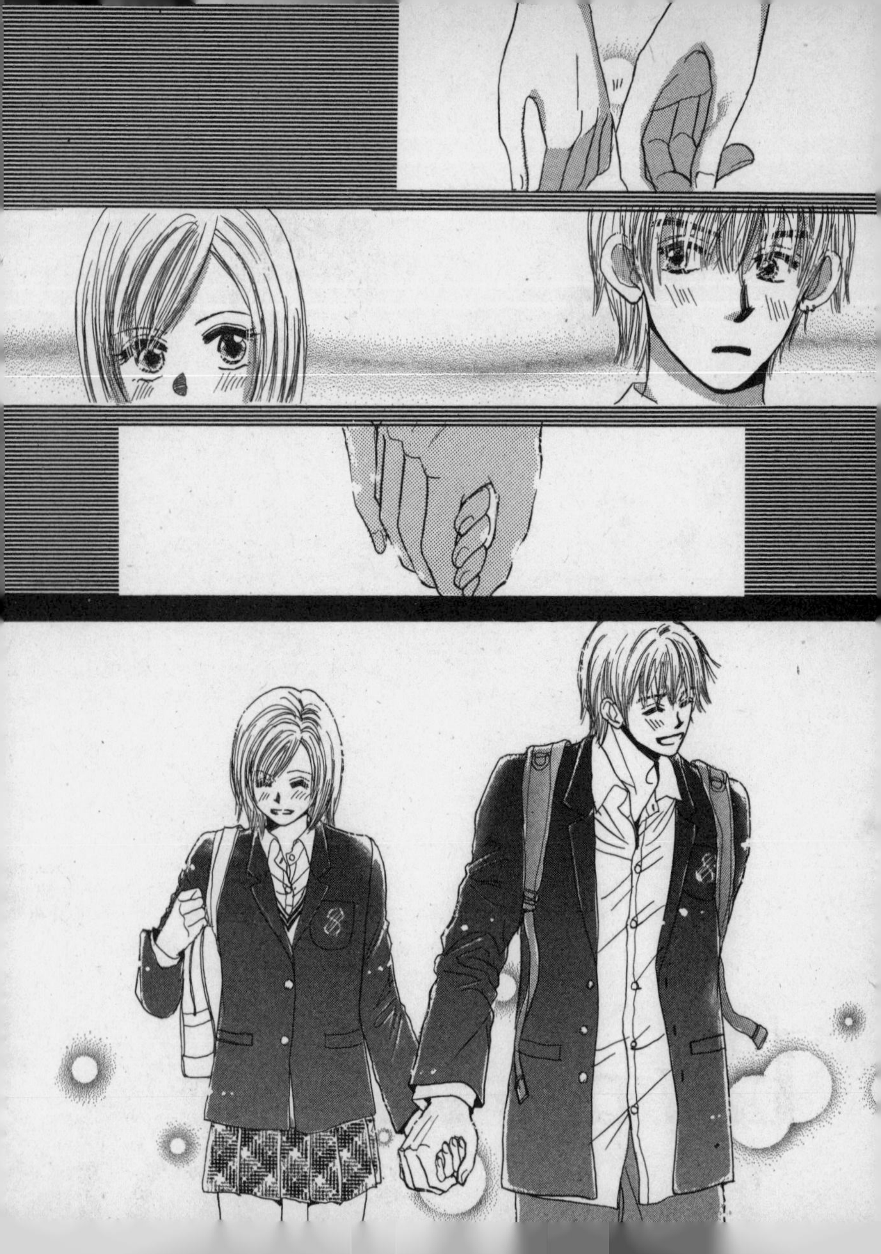

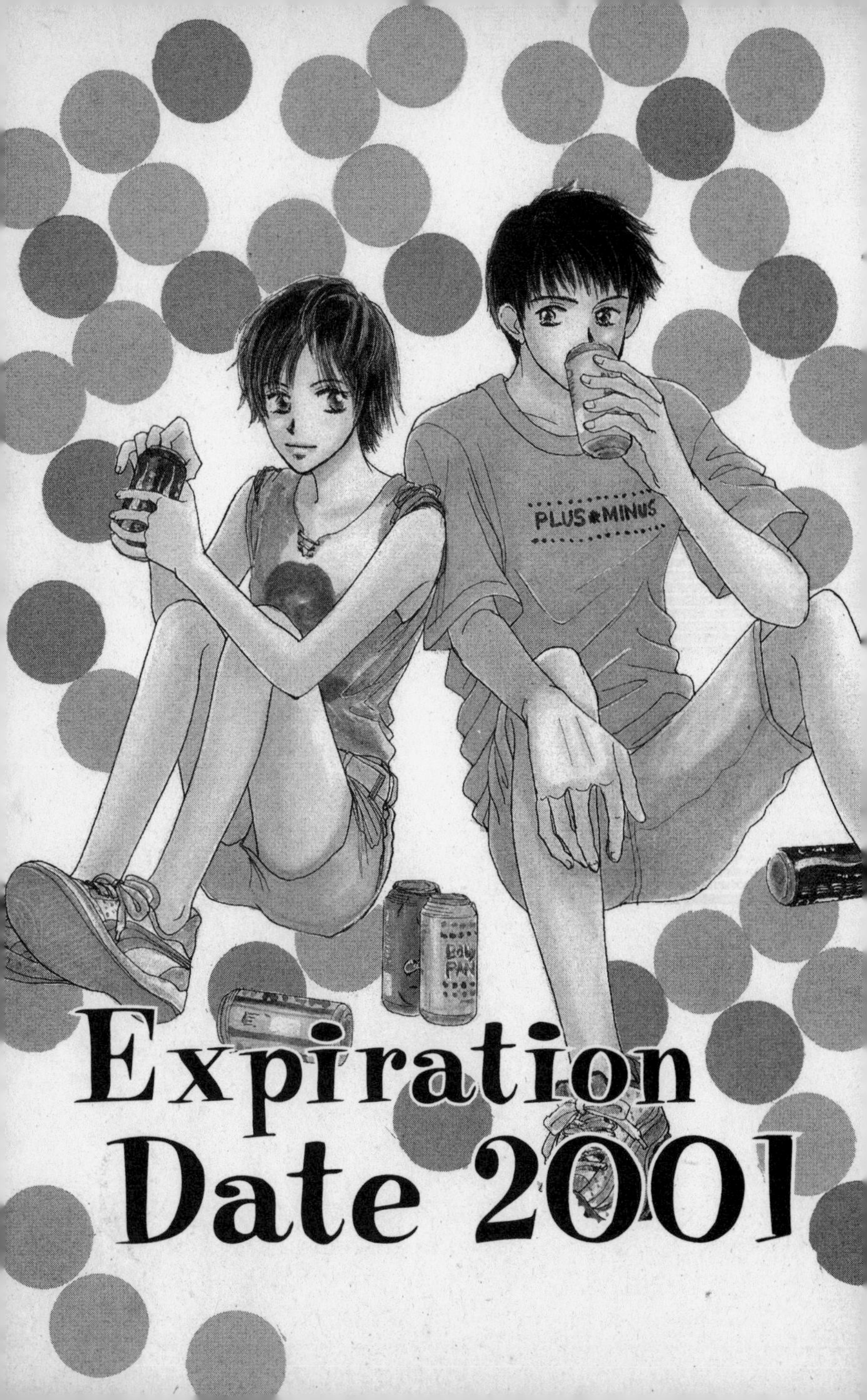
PLUS MINUS
Expiration Date 2001

Expiration Date
2001

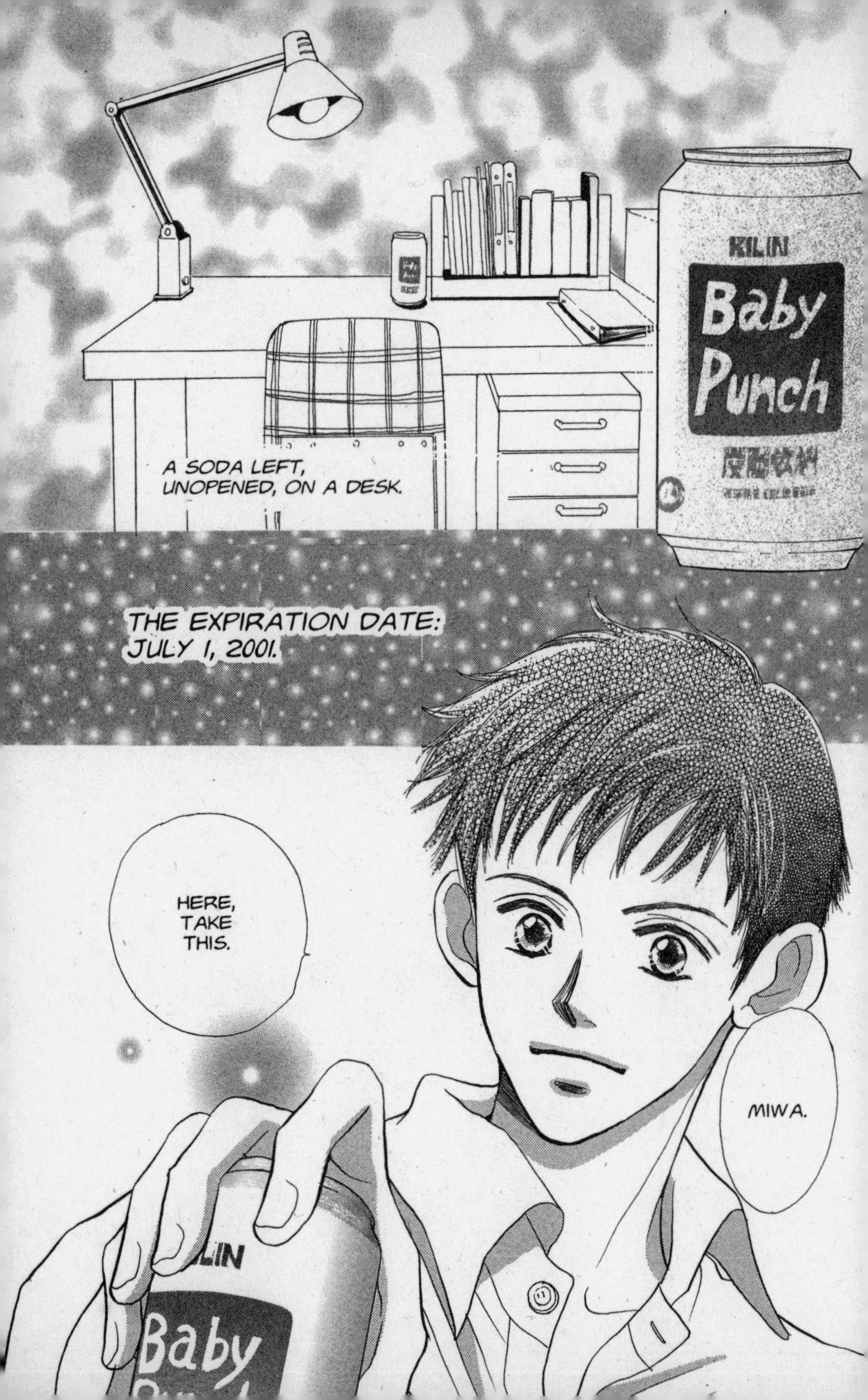
KILIN
Baby Punch
A SODA LEFT, UNOPENED, ON A DESK.
THE EXPIRATION DATE: JULY 1, 2001.
MIWA.
HERE, TAKE THIS.
KILIN
Baby

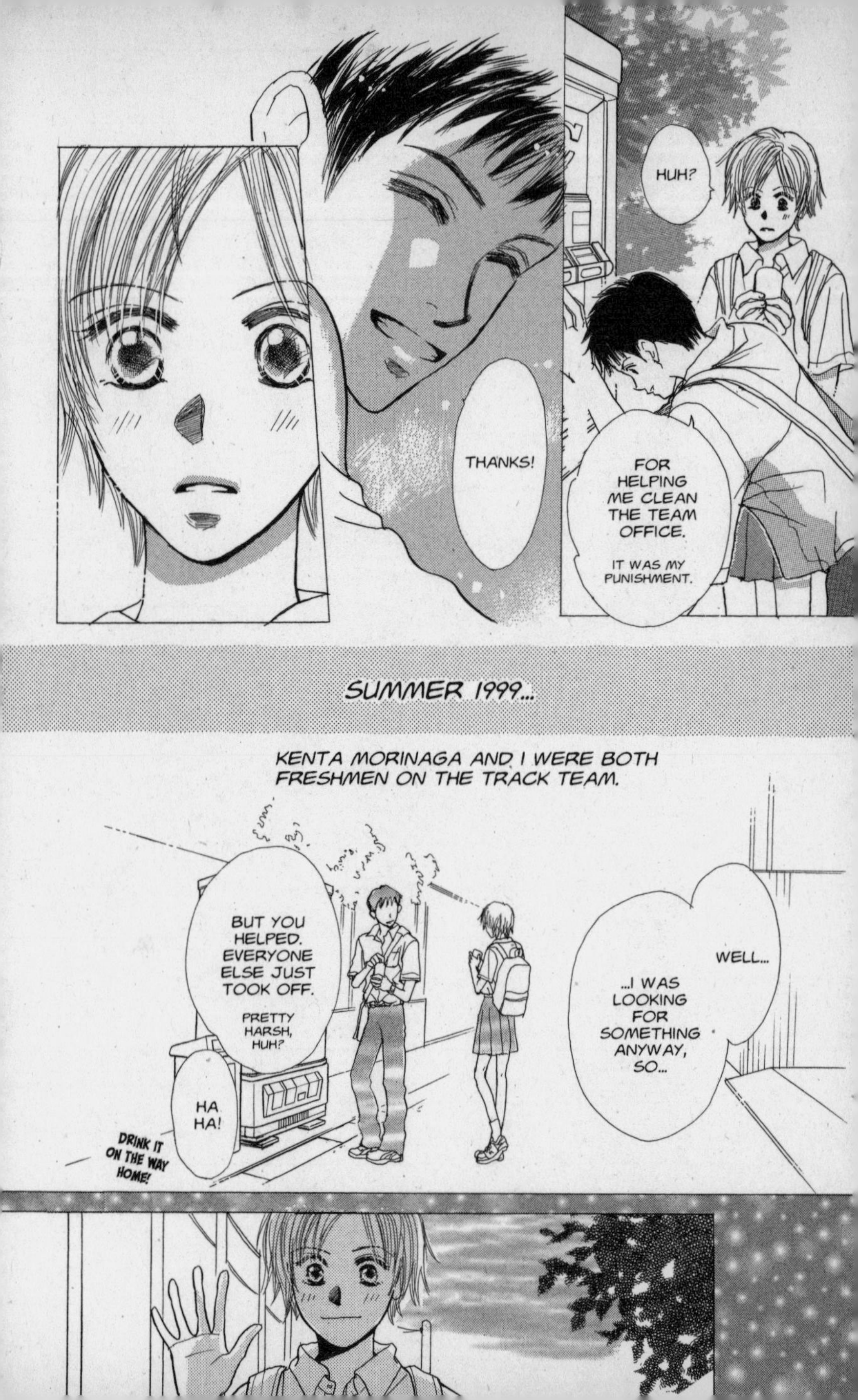
HUH?
FOR HELPING ME CLEAN THE TEAM OFFICE.
IT WAS MY PUNISHMENT.
THANKS!
SUMMER 1999...
KENTA MORINAGA AND I WERE BOTH FRESHMEN ON THE TRACK TEAM.
WELL...
...I WAS LOOKING FOR SOMETHING ANYWAY, SO...
BUT YOU HELPED. EVERYONE ELSE JUST TOOK OFF.
PRETTY HARSH, HUH?
HA HA!
DRINK IT ON THE WAY HOME!

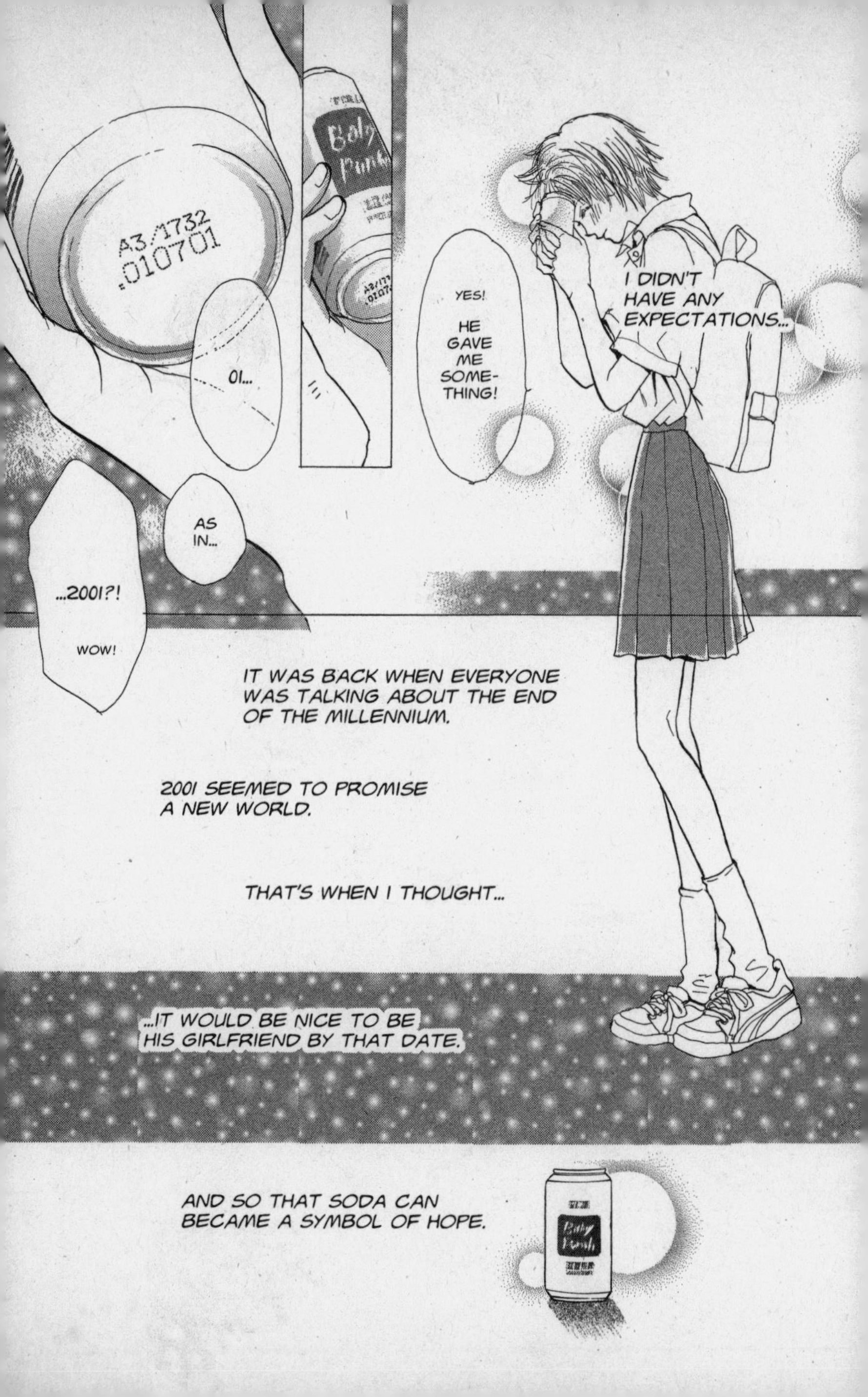
YES!
HE GAVE ME SOMETHING!
A3/1732 .010701
01...
AS IN...
...2001?!
WOW!
I DIDN'T HAVE ANY EXPECTATIONS...
IT WAS BACK WHEN EVERYONE WAS TALKING ABOUT THE END OF THE MILLENNIUM.
2001 SEEMED TO PROMISE A NEW WORLD.
THAT'S WHEN I THOUGHT...
...IT WOULD BE NICE TO BE HIS GIRLFRIEND BY THAT DATE.
AND SO THAT SODA CAN BECAME A SYMBOL OF HOPE.

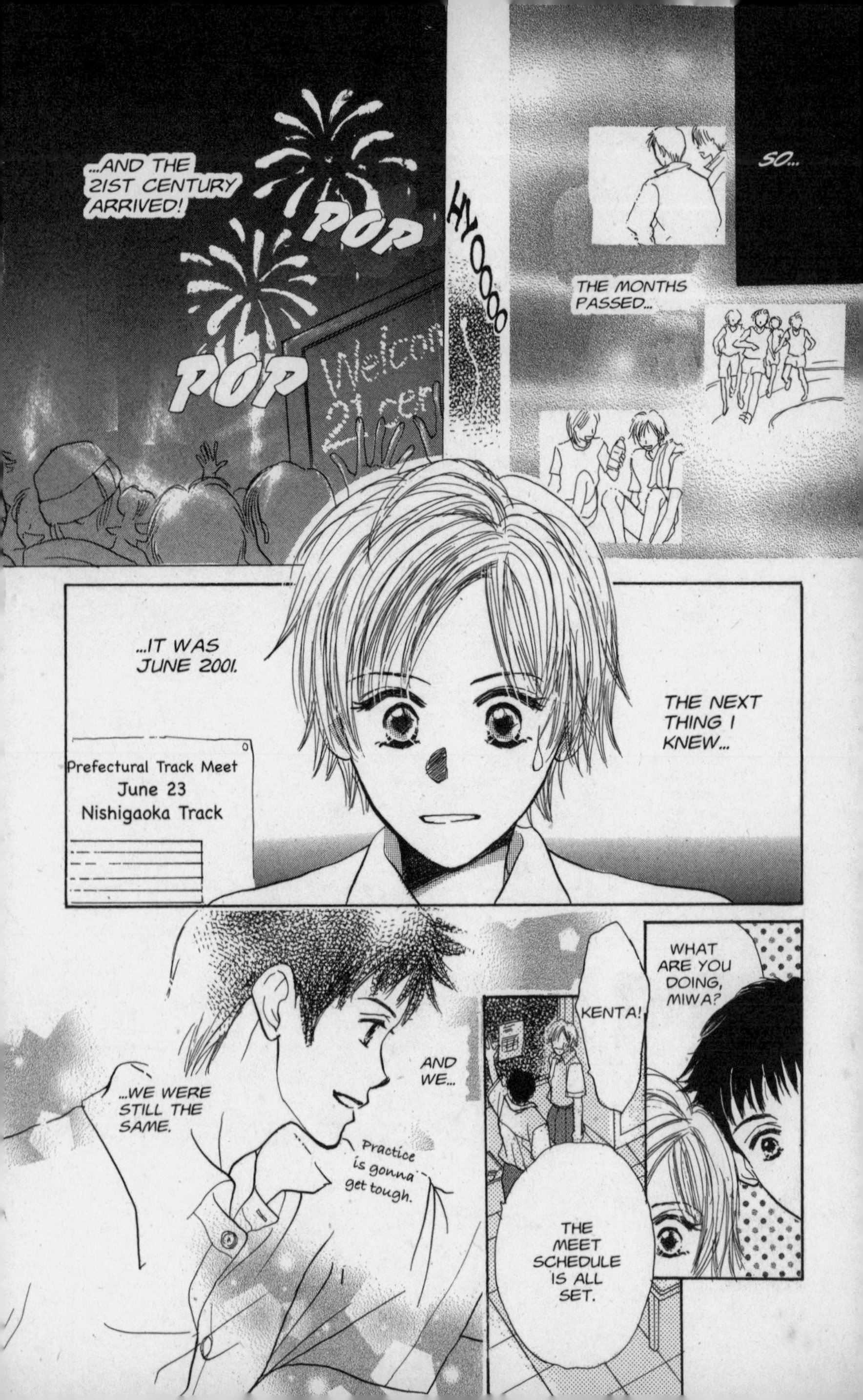
SO...
THE MONTHS PASSED...
HYOOOO
...AND THE 21ST CENTURY ARRIVED!
POP
POP
Welco
21 cen
THE NEXT THING I KNEW...
...IT WAS JUNE 2001.
Prefectural Track Meet
June 23
Nishigaoka Track
WHAT ARE YOU DOING, MIWA?
KENTA!
THE MEET SCHEDULE IS ALL SET.
AND WE...
...WE WERE STILL THE SAME.
Practice is gonna get tough.

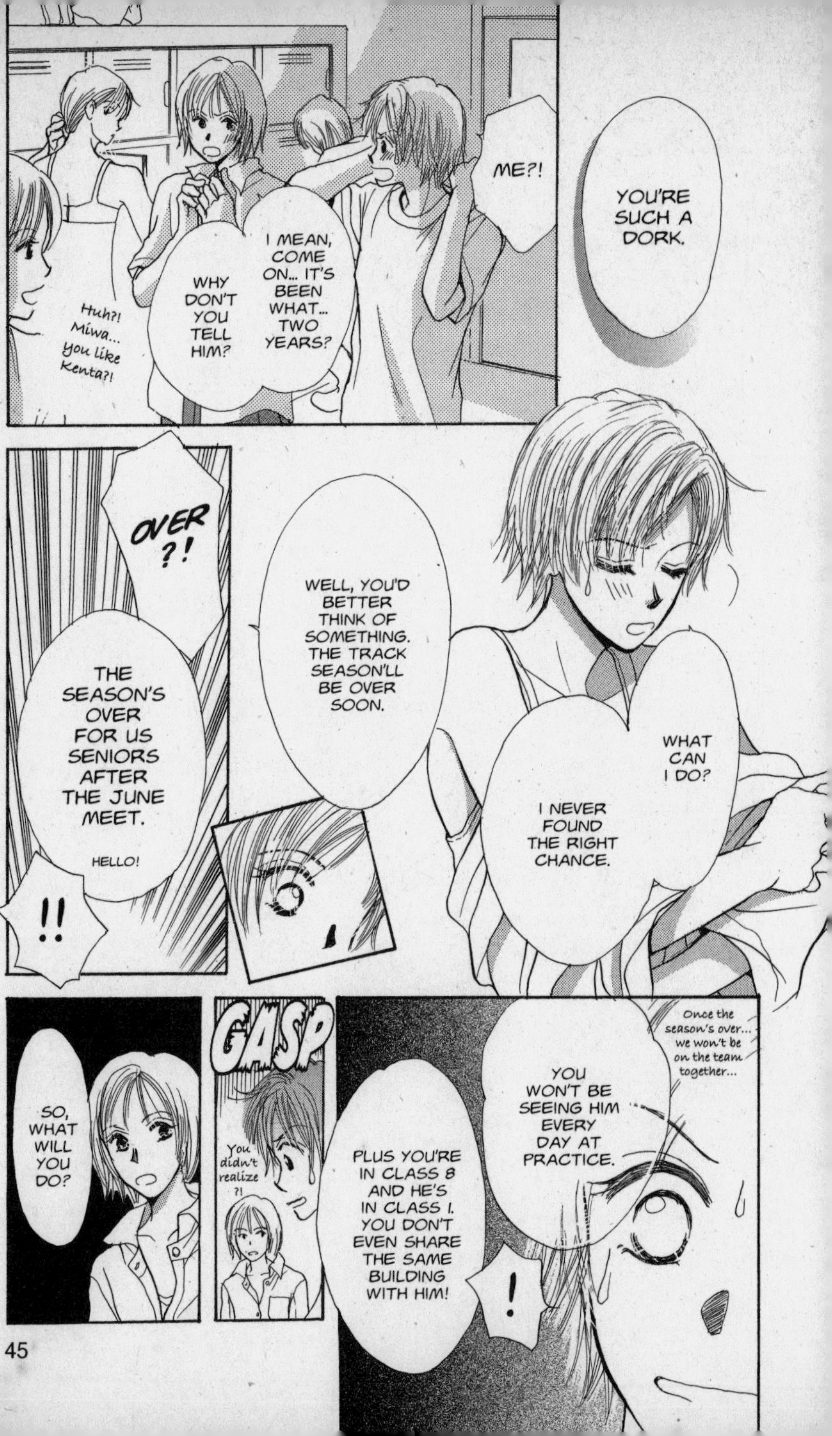
YOU'RE SUCH A DORK.
ME?!
I MEAN, COME ON... IT'S BEEN WHAT... TWO YEARS?
WHY DON'T YOU TELL HIM?
Huh?! Miwa... you like Kenta?!
WHAT CAN I DO?
I NEVER FOUND THE RIGHT CHANCE.
WELL, YOU'D BETTER THINK OF SOMETHING. THE TRACK SEASON'LL BE OVER SOON.
OVER ?!
THE SEASON'S OVER FOR US SENIORS AFTER THE JUNE MEET.
HELLO!
!!
Once the season's over... we won't be on the team together...
YOU WON'T BE SEEING HIM EVERY DAY AT PRACTICE.
PLUS YOU'RE IN CLASS 8 AND HE'S IN CLASS 1. YOU DON'T EVEN SHARE THE SAME BUILDING WITH HIM!
!
GASP
You didn't realize ?!
SO, WHAT WILL YOU DO?

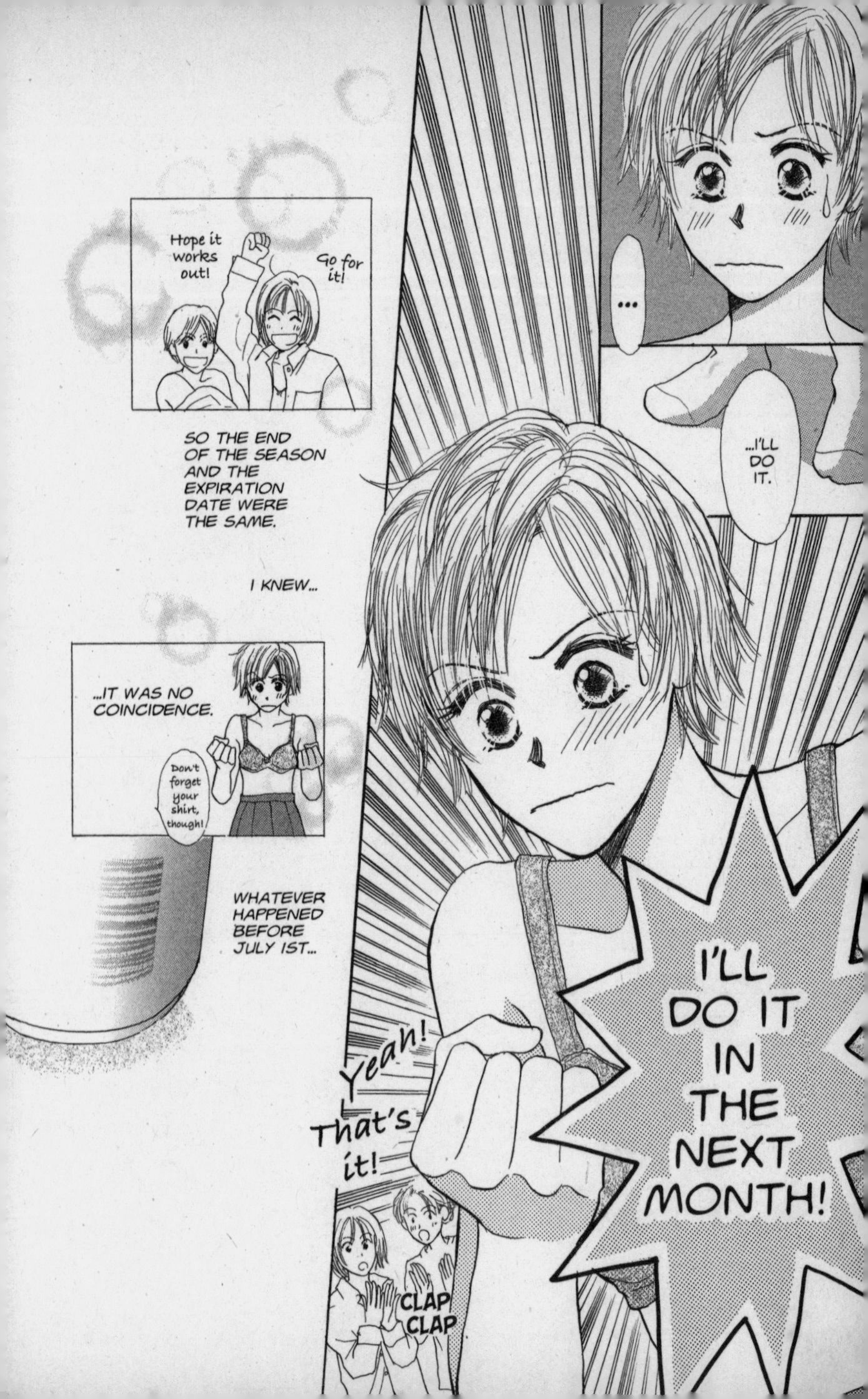
...
...I'LL DO IT.
I'LL DO IT IN THE NEXT MONTH!
Yeah! That's it!
CLAP CLAP
Go for it!
Hope it works out!
SO THE END OF THE SEASON AND THE EXPIRATION DATE WERE THE SAME.
I KNEW...
...IT WAS NO COINCIDENCE.
Don't forget your shirt, though!
WHATEVER HAPPENED BEFORE JULY 1ST...

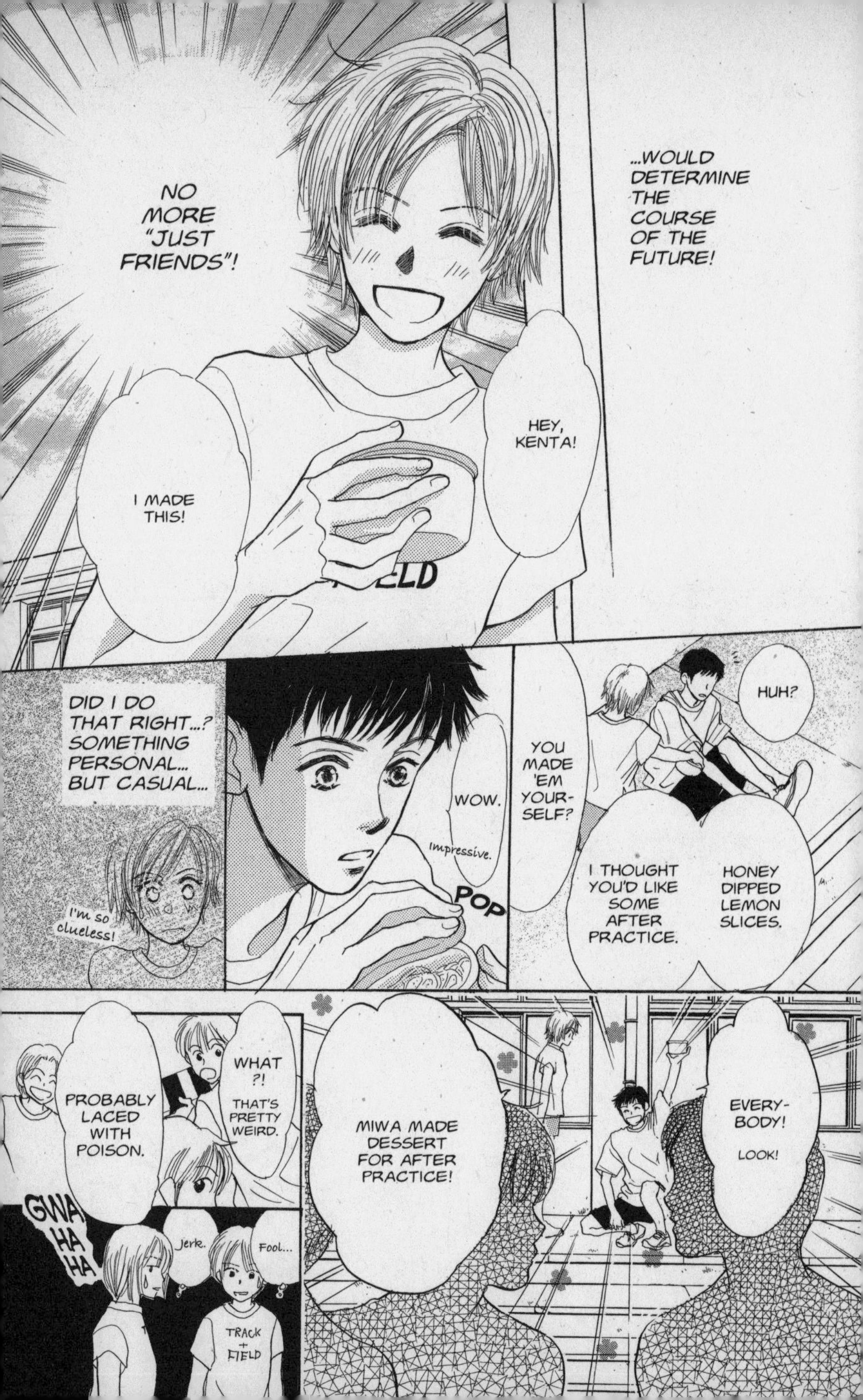
...WOULD DETERMINE THE COURSE OF THE FUTURE!
NO MORE "JUST FRIENDS"!
HEY, KENTA!
I MADE THIS!
HUH?
YOU MADE 'EM YOUR-SELF?
HONEY DIPPED LEMON SLICES.
I THOUGHT YOU'D LIKE SOME AFTER PRACTICE.
WOW.
Impressive.
POP
DID I DO THAT RIGHT...? SOMETHING PERSONAL... BUT CASUAL...
I'm so clueless!
EVERY-BODY!
LOOK!
MIWA MADE DESSERT FOR AFTER PRACTICE!
WHAT ?!
THAT'S PRETTY WEIRD.
PROBABLY LACED WITH POISON.
GWA HA HA HA
Fool...
Jerk.
TRACK + FIELD

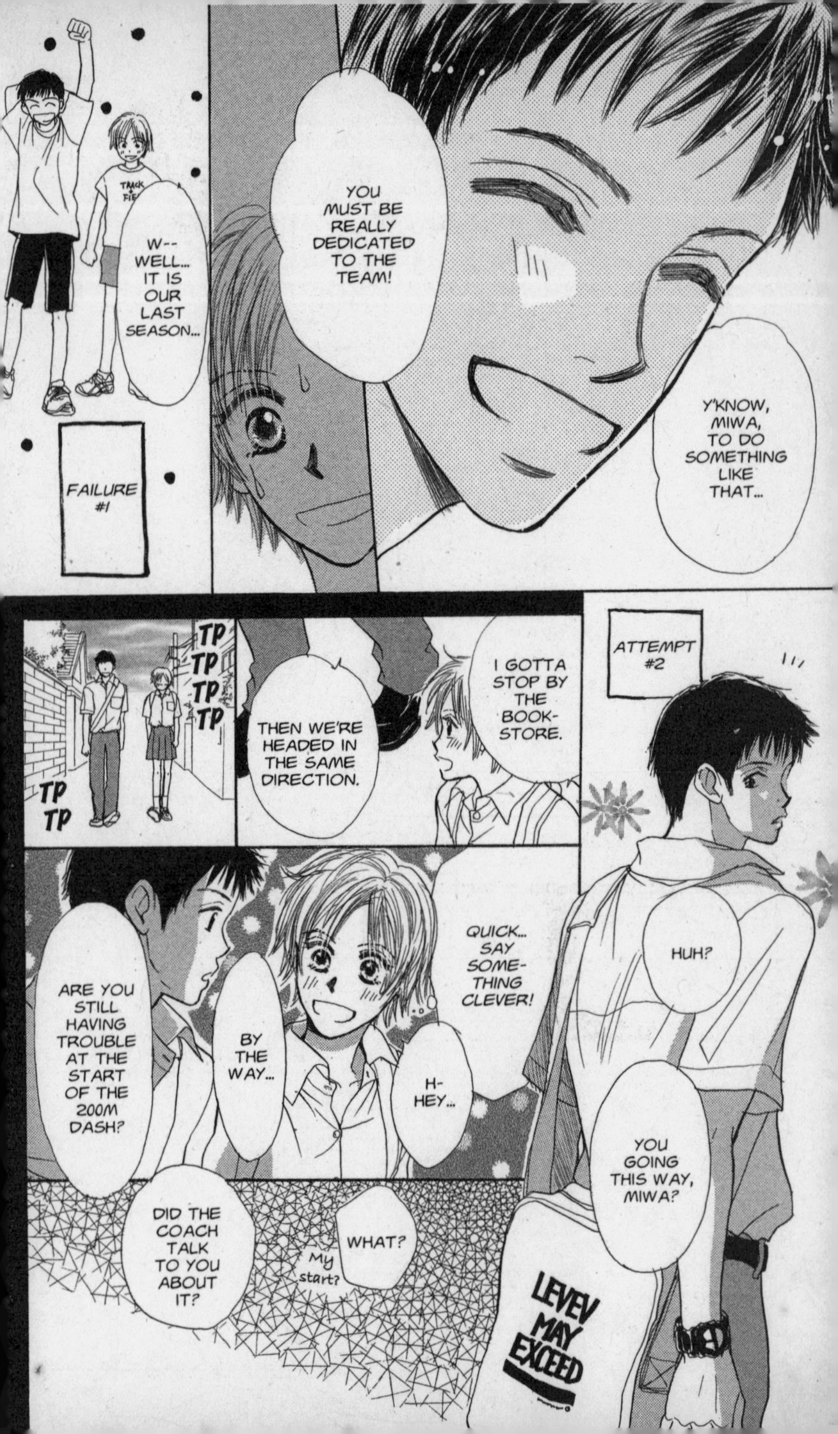
Y'KNOW, MIWA, TO DO SOMETHING LIKE THAT...
YOU MUST BE REALLY DEDICATED TO THE TEAM!
W--WELL... IT IS OUR LAST SEASON...
FAILURE #1
ATTEMPT #2
HUH?
YOU GOING THIS WAY, MIWA?
LEVEV MAY EXCEED
I GOTTA STOP BY THE BOOK-STORE.
THEN WE'RE HEADED IN THE SAME DIRECTION.
TP TP TP TP
TP TP
QUICK... SAY SOME-THING CLEVER!
H-HEY...
BY THE WAY...
ARE YOU STILL HAVING TROUBLE AT THE START OF THE 200M DASH?
WHAT?
My start?
DID THE COACH TALK TO YOU ABOUT IT?

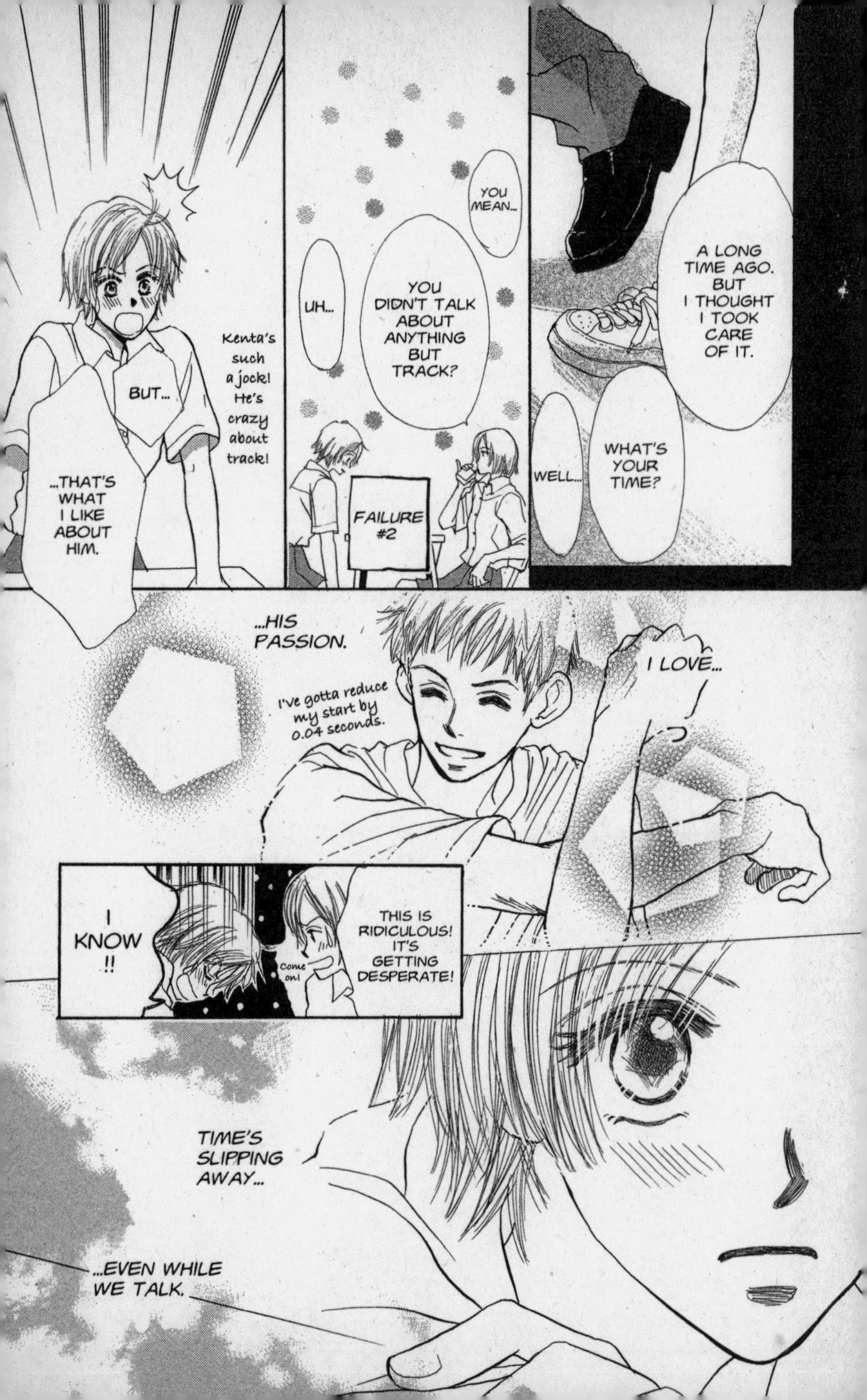
A LONG TIME AGO. BUT I THOUGHT I TOOK CARE OF IT.
WHAT'S YOUR TIME?
WELL...
YOU MEAN...
YOU DIDN'T TALK ABOUT ANYTHING BUT TRACK?
UH...
FAILURE #2
Kenta's such a jock! He's crazy about track!
BUT...
...THAT'S WHAT I LIKE ABOUT HIM.
I LOVE...
...HIS PASSION.
I've gotta reduce my start by 0.04 seconds.
THIS IS RIDICULOUS! IT'S GETTING DESPERATE!
Come on!
I KNOW!!
TIME'S SLIPPING AWAY...
...EVEN WHILE WE TALK.

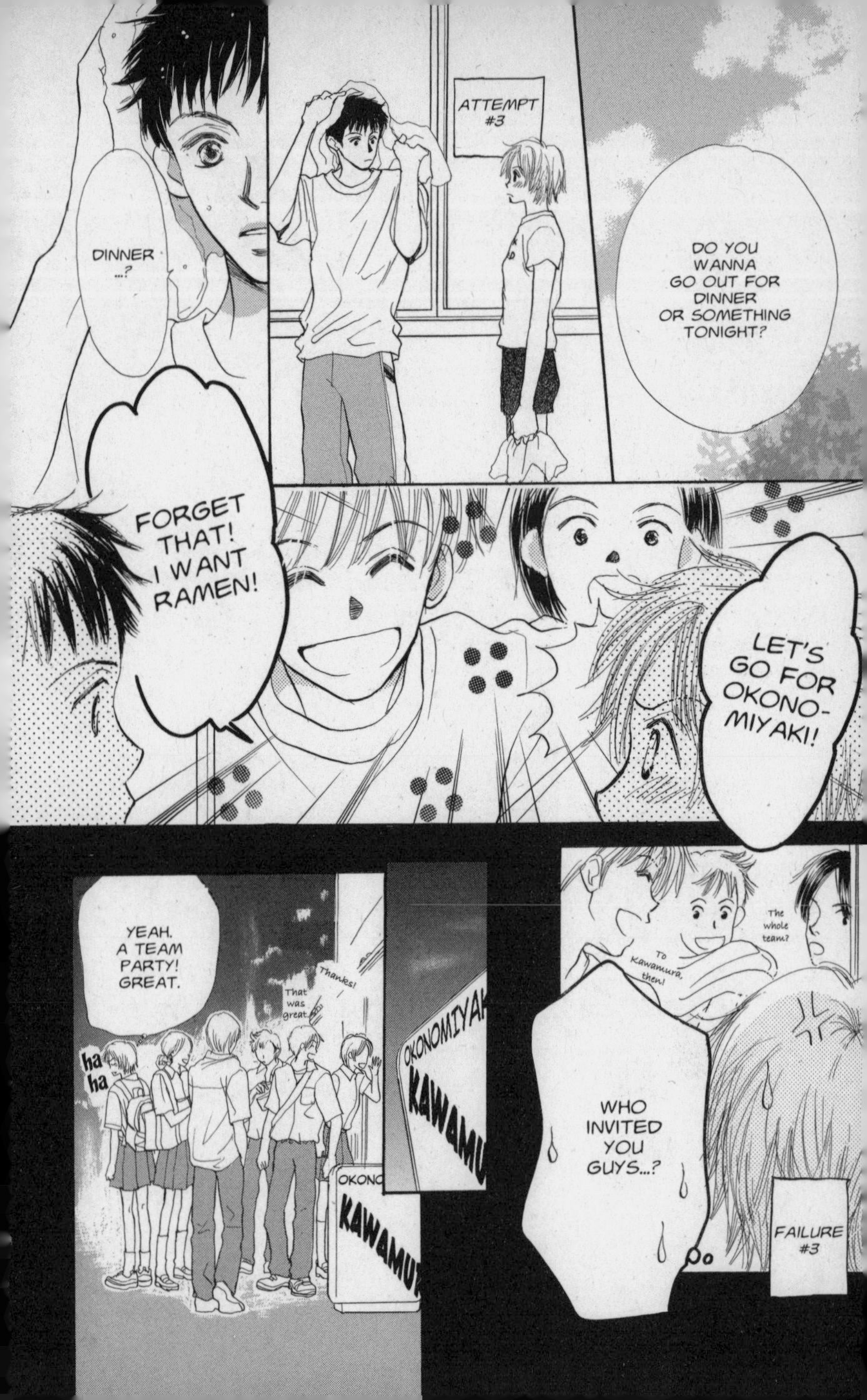
DO YOU WANNA GO OUT FOR DINNER OR SOMETHING TONIGHT?
ATTEMPT #3
DINNER ...?
LET'S GO FOR OKONOMI-YAKI!
FORGET THAT! I WANT RAMEN!
The whole team?
To Kawamura, then!
WHO INVITED YOU GUYS...?
FAILURE #3
OKONOMIYAK
KAWAMU
YEAH. A TEAM PARTY! GREAT.
Thanks!
That was great.
ha ha
OKONO
KAWAMU

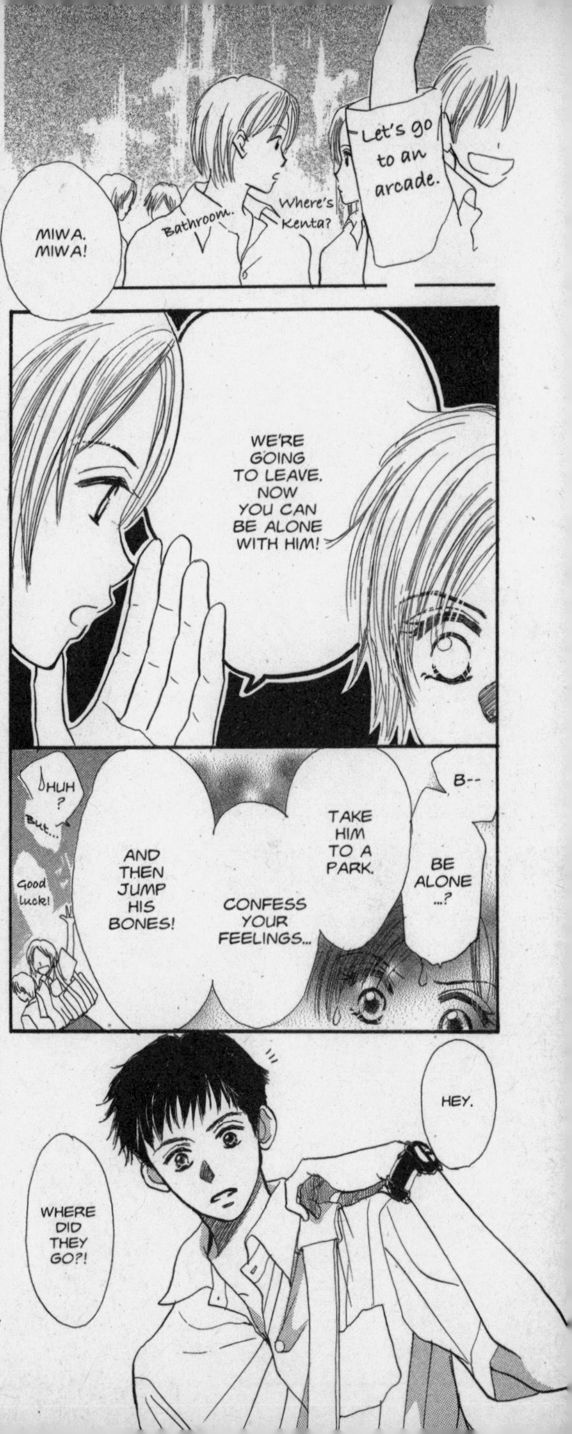
Let's go to an arcade.
Where's Kenta?
Bathroom.
MIWA. MIWA!
WE'RE GOING TO LEAVE. NOW YOU CAN BE ALONE WITH HIM!
B--
BE ALONE ...?
TAKE HIM TO A PARK.
CONFESS YOUR FEELINGS...
AND THEN JUMP HIS BONES!
HUH?
But...
Good luck!
HEY.
WHERE DID THEY GO?!

02

✖✖

"Expiration Date 2001":

I came up with the title and the rough concept for this story a long time ago. It took me this long to get to it, but I'm glad I did. Time moves too fast...

✖

The drink in the story is made-up, of course, but I think of it as being similar to Calpico Soda.

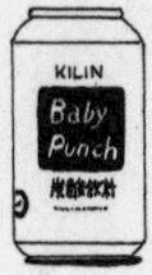
KILIN
Baby Punch

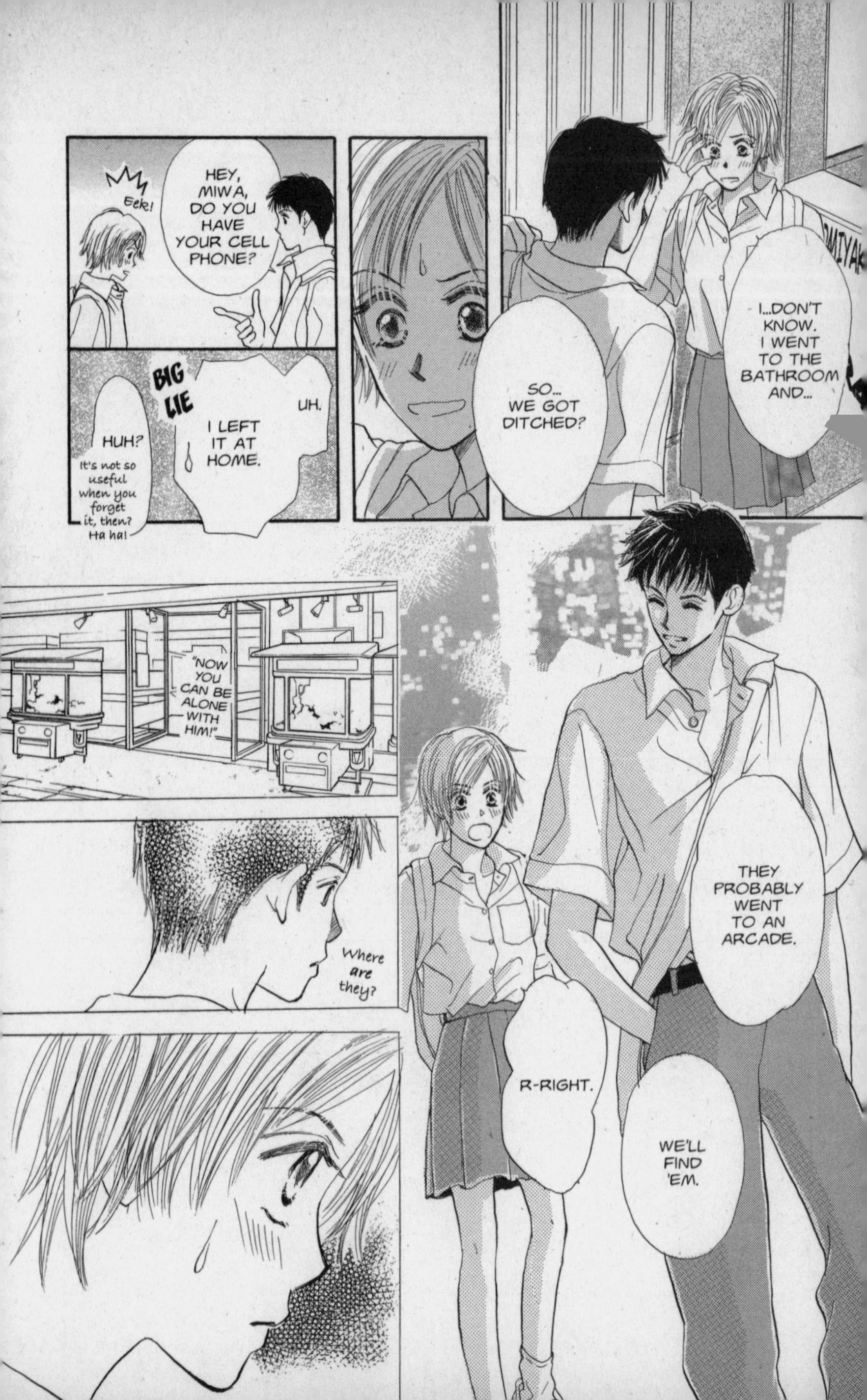
I...DON'T KNOW. I WENT TO THE BATHROOM AND...
SO... WE GOT DITCHED?
HEY, MIWA, DO YOU HAVE YOUR CELL PHONE?
Eek!
UH.
I LEFT IT AT HOME.
BIG LIE
HUH?
It's not so useful when you forget it, then? Ha ha!
THEY PROBABLY WENT TO AN ARCADE.
R-RIGHT.
WE'LL FIND 'EM.
"NOW YOU CAN BE ALONE WITH HIM!"
Where are they?

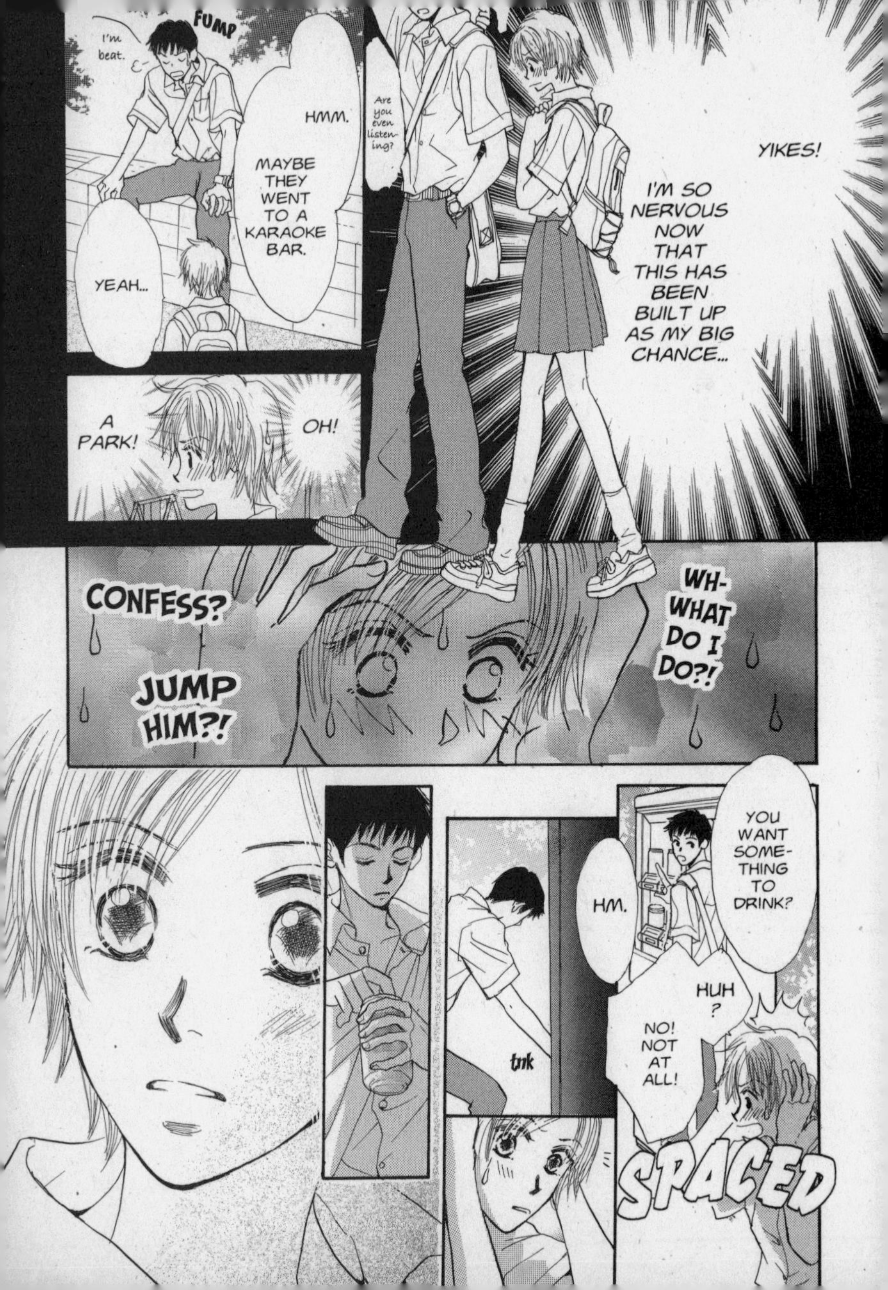
YIKES!
I'M SO NERVOUS NOW THAT THIS HAS BEEN BUILT UP AS MY BIG CHANCE...
Are you even listening?
FUMP
I'm beat.
HMM.
MAYBE THEY WENT TO A KARAOKE BAR.
YEAH...
OH!
A PARK!
WH-WHAT DO I DO?!
CONFESS?
JUMP HIM?!
YOU WANT SOMETHING TO DRINK?
HM.
HUH?
NO! NOT AT ALL!
SPACED
tnk

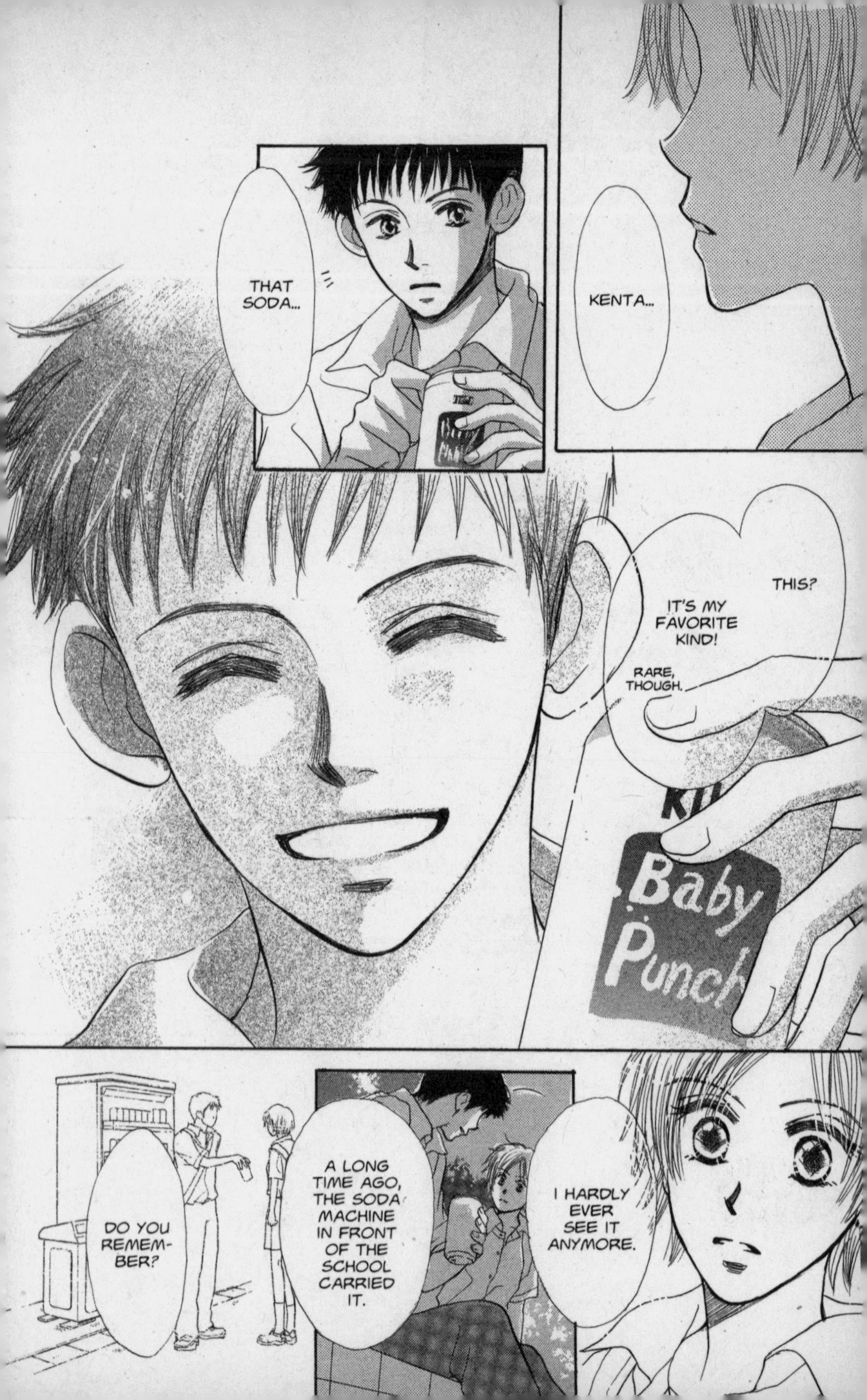
KENTA...
THAT SODA...
THIS?
IT'S MY FAVORITE KIND!
RARE, THOUGH.
Baby Punch
I HARDLY EVER SEE IT ANYMORE.
A LONG TIME AGO, THE SODA MACHINE IN FRONT OF THE SCHOOL CARRIED IT.
DO YOU REMEM-BER?

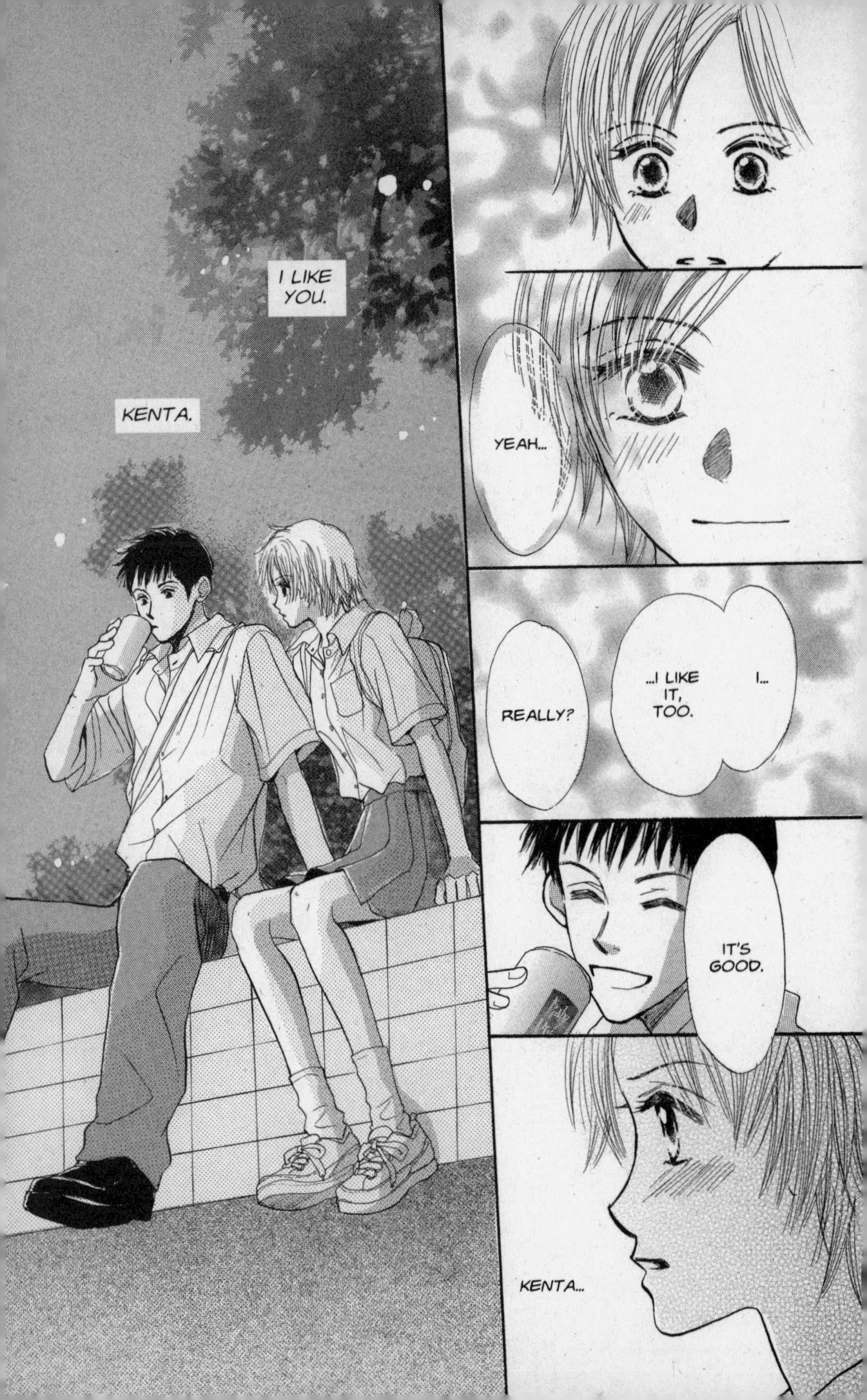
YEAH...
I...
...I LIKE IT, TOO.
REALLY?
IT'S GOOD.
KENTA...
I LIKE YOU.
KENTA.

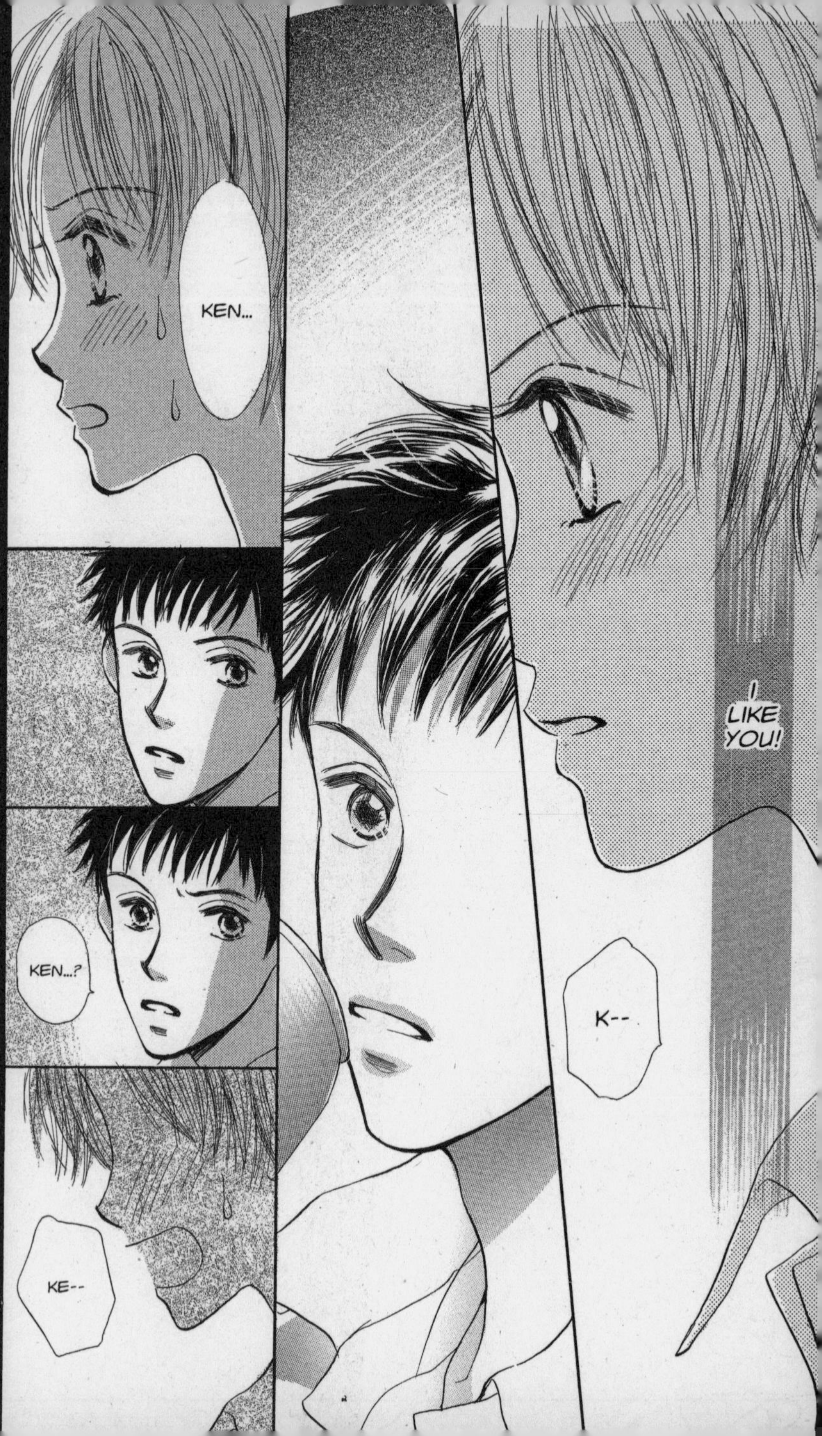
I LIKE YOU!
K--.
KEN...
KEN...?
KE--

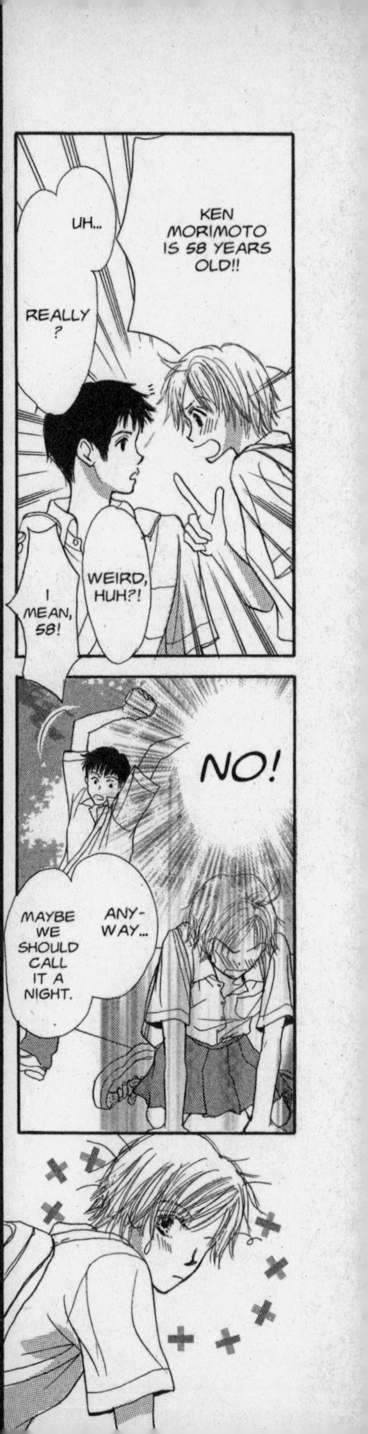
KEN MORIMOTO IS 58 YEARS OLD!!
UH...
REALLY?
WEIRD, HUH?!
I MEAN, 58!
NO!
ANY-WAY...
MAYBE WE SHOULD CALL IT A NIGHT.

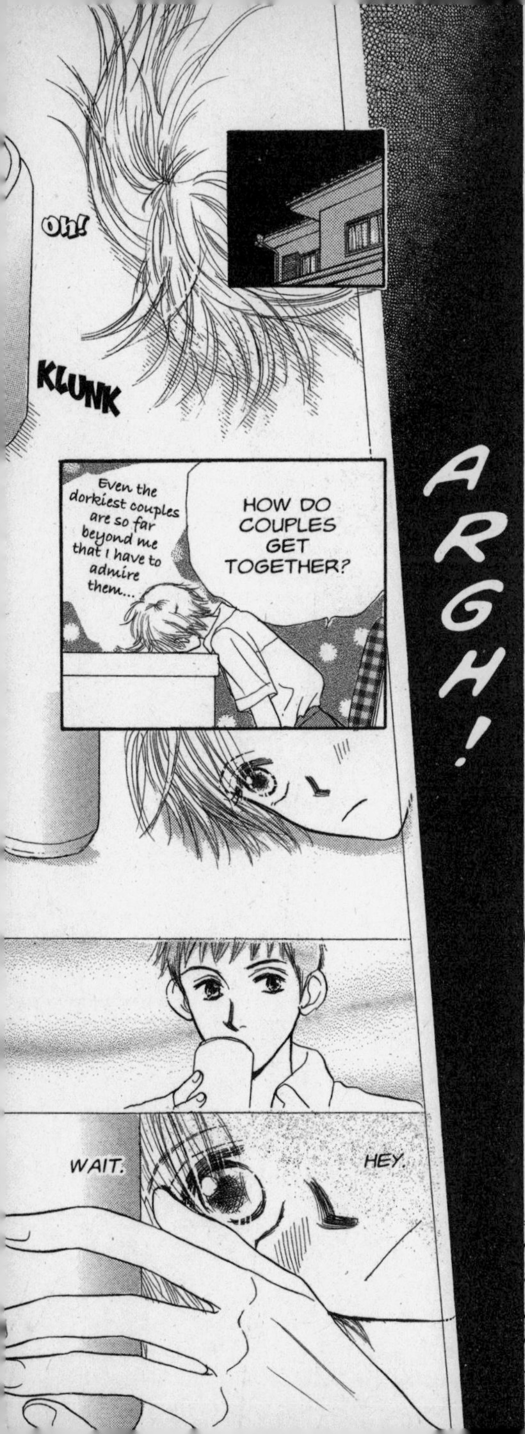
Oh!
KLUNK
HOW DO COUPLES GET TOGETHER?
Even the dorkiest couples are so far beyond me that I have to admire them...
ARGH!
HEY.
WAIT.

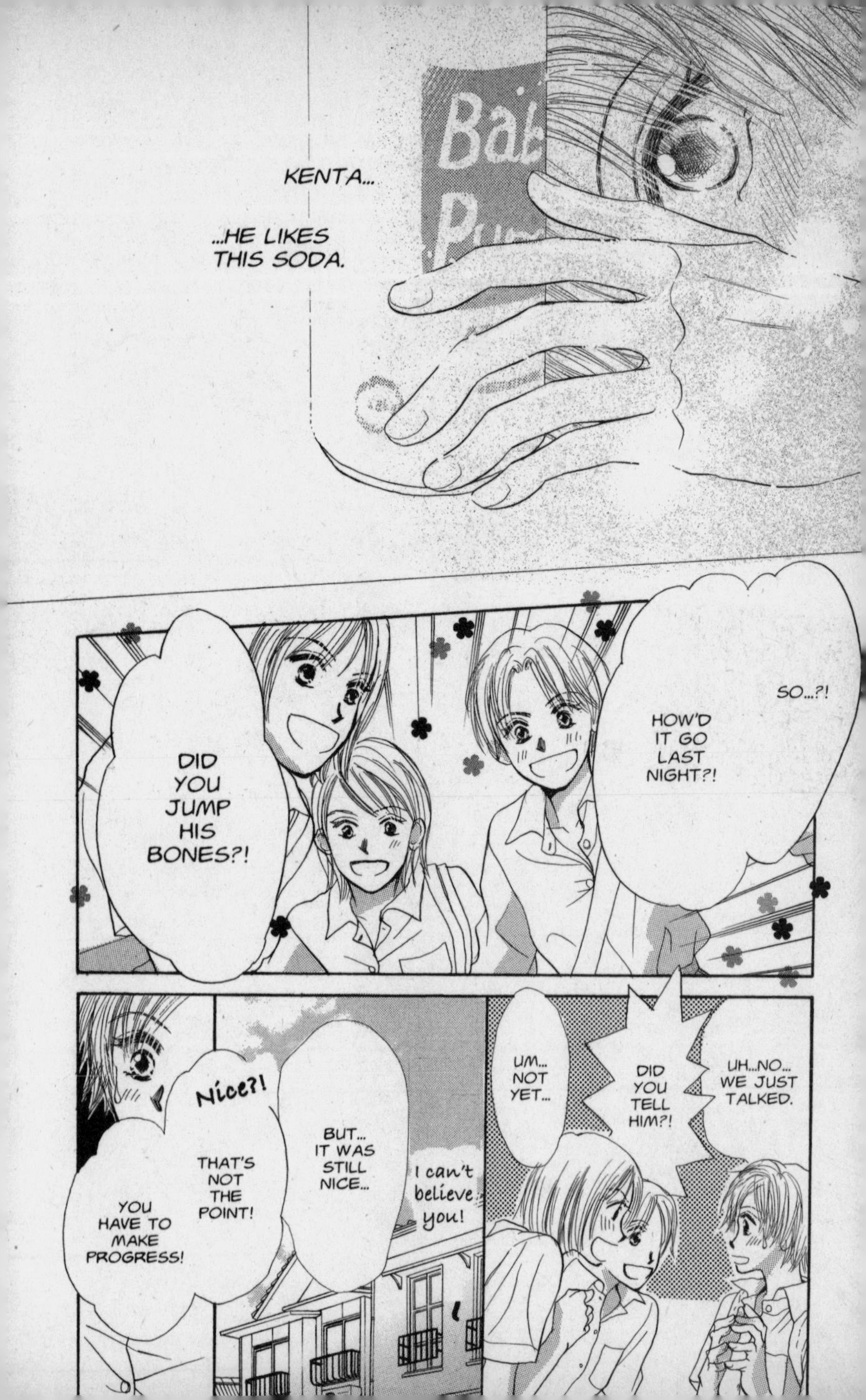
KENTA...
...HE LIKES THIS SODA.
SO...?!
HOW'D IT GO LAST NIGHT?!
DID YOU JUMP HIS BONES?!
UH...NO... WE JUST TALKED.
DID YOU TELL HIM?!
UM... NOT YET...
I can't believe you!
BUT... IT WAS STILL NICE...
Nice?!
THAT'S NOT THE POINT!
YOU HAVE TO MAKE PROGRESS!

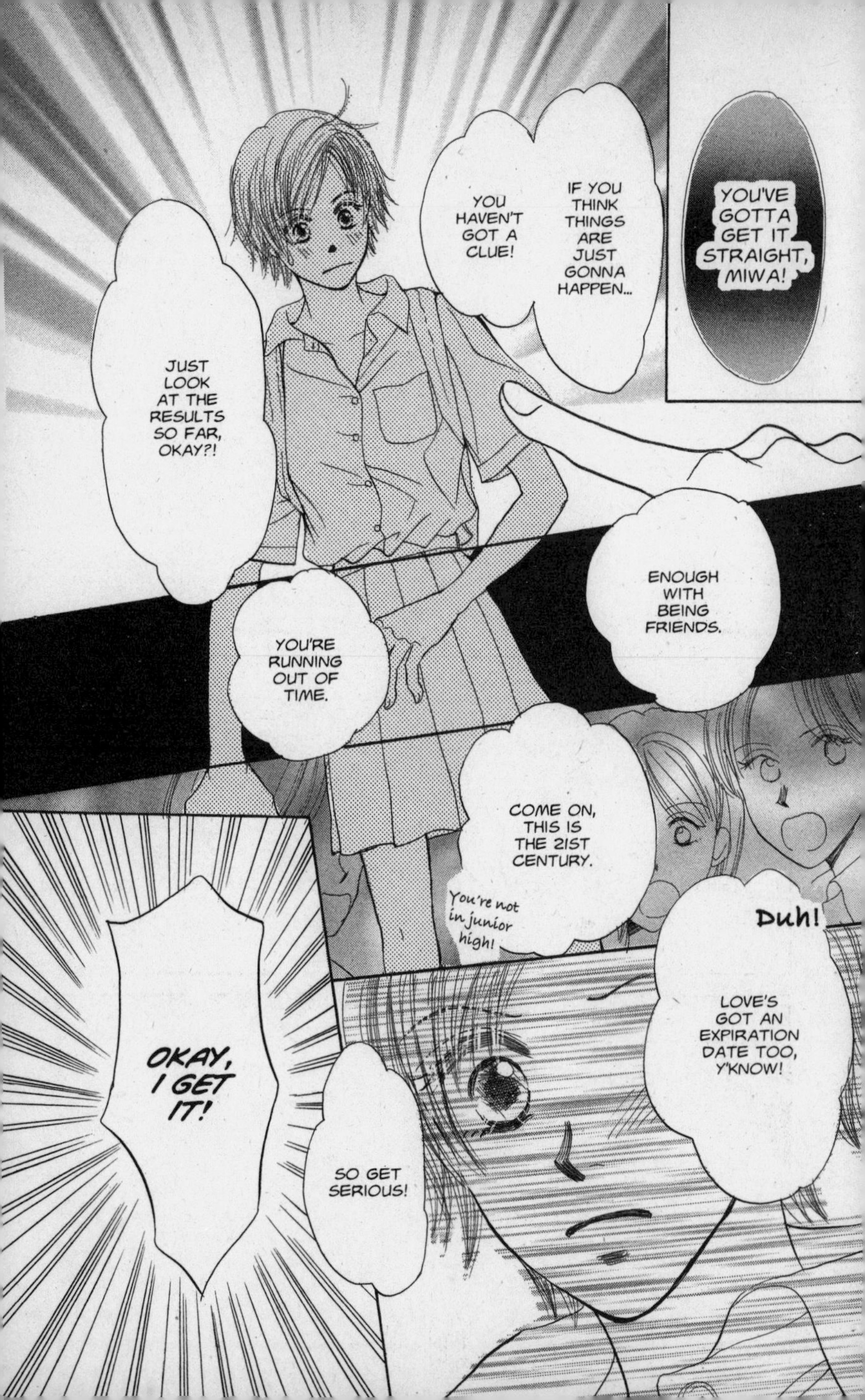

YOU'VE GOTTA GET IT STRAIGHT, MIWA!
IF YOU THINK THINGS ARE JUST GONNA HAPPEN...
YOU HAVEN'T GOT A CLUE!
JUST LOOK AT THE RESULTS SO FAR, OKAY?!
ENOUGH WITH BEING FRIENDS.
YOU'RE RUNNING OUT OF TIME.
COME ON, THIS IS THE 21ST CENTURY.
You're not in junior high!
Duh!
LOVE'S GOT AN EXPIRATION DATE TOO, Y'KNOW!
SO GET SERIOUS!
OKAY, I GET IT!

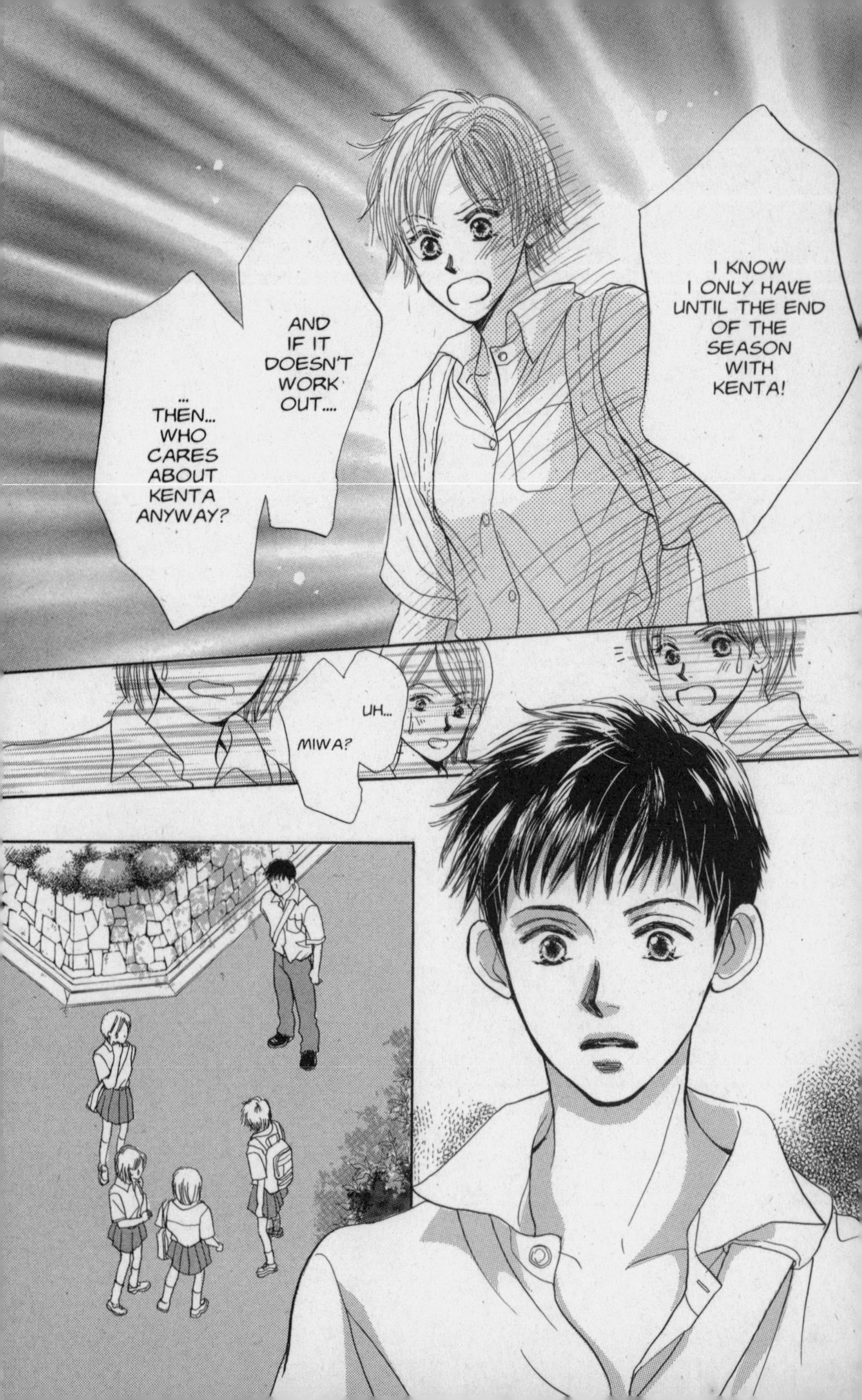
I KNOW I ONLY HAVE UNTIL THE END OF THE SEASON WITH KENTA!
AND IF IT DOESN'T WORK OUT....
... THEN... WHO CARES ABOUT KENTA ANYWAY?
UH... MIWA?

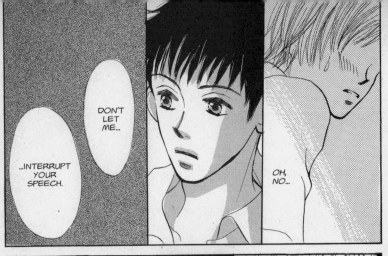

DON'T LET ME...

...INTERRUPT YOUR SPEECH.

OH, NO...

KENTA...

SAVE YOUR BREATH.

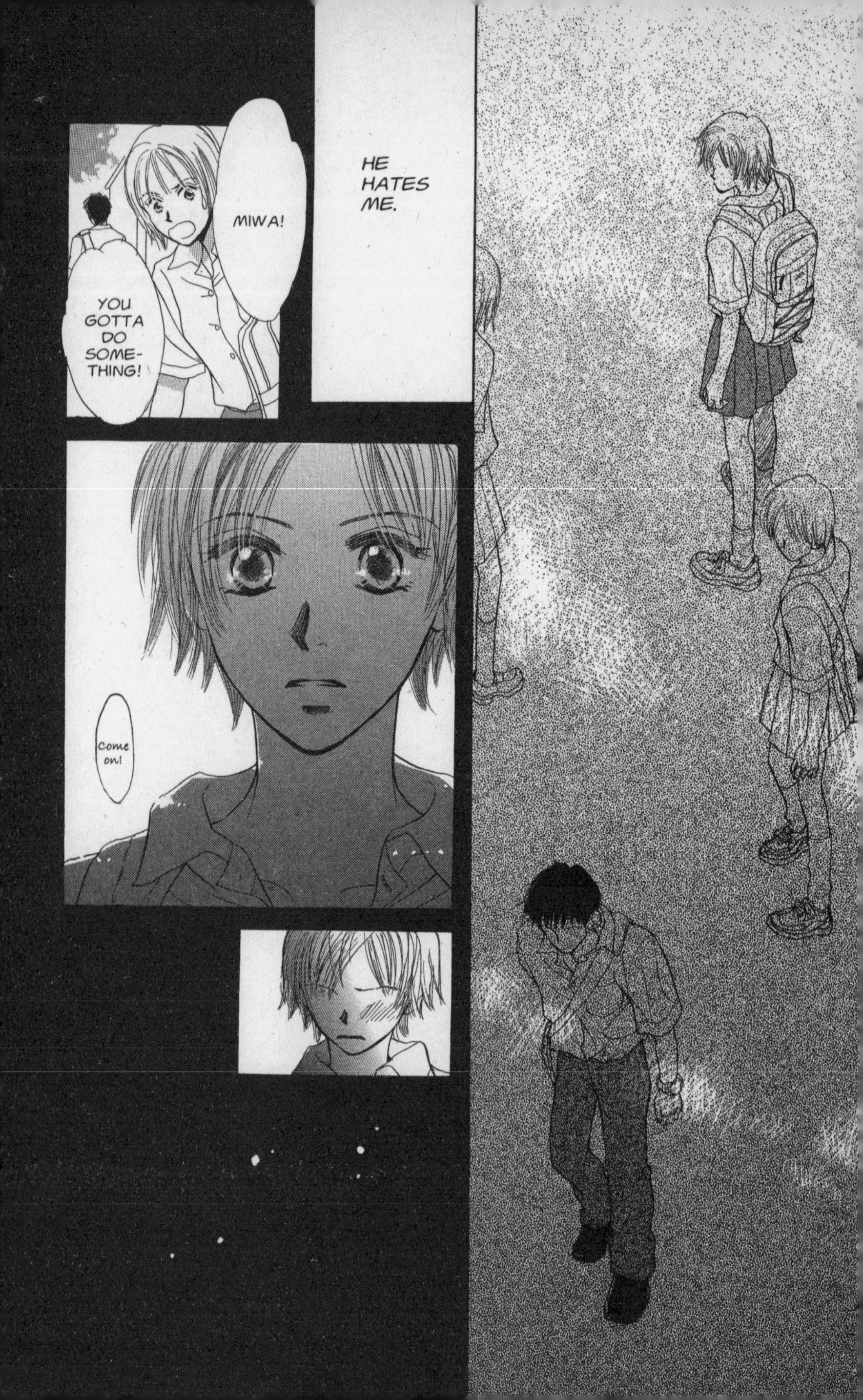
HE HATES ME.
MIWA!
YOU GOTTA DO SOME-THING!
Come on!

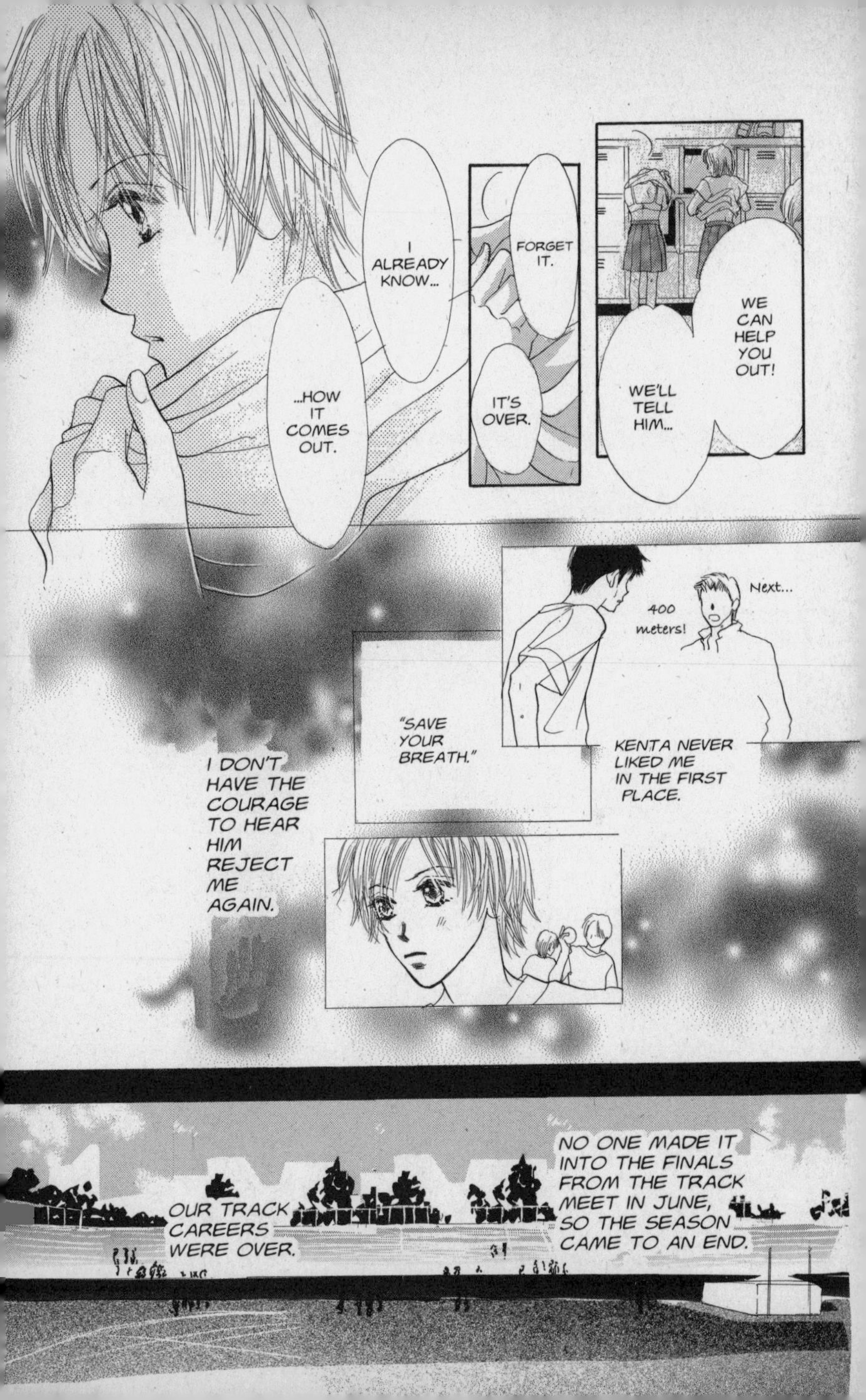
WE CAN HELP YOU OUT!
WE'LL TELL HIM...
FORGET IT.
IT'S OVER.
I ALREADY KNOW...
...HOW IT COMES OUT.
Next... 400 meters!
KENTA NEVER LIKED ME IN THE FIRST PLACE.
"SAVE YOUR BREATH."
I DON'T HAVE THE COURAGE TO HEAR HIM REJECT ME AGAIN.
NO ONE MADE IT INTO THE FINALS FROM THE TRACK MEET IN JUNE, SO THE SEASON CAME TO AN END.
OUR TRACK CAREERS WERE OVER.

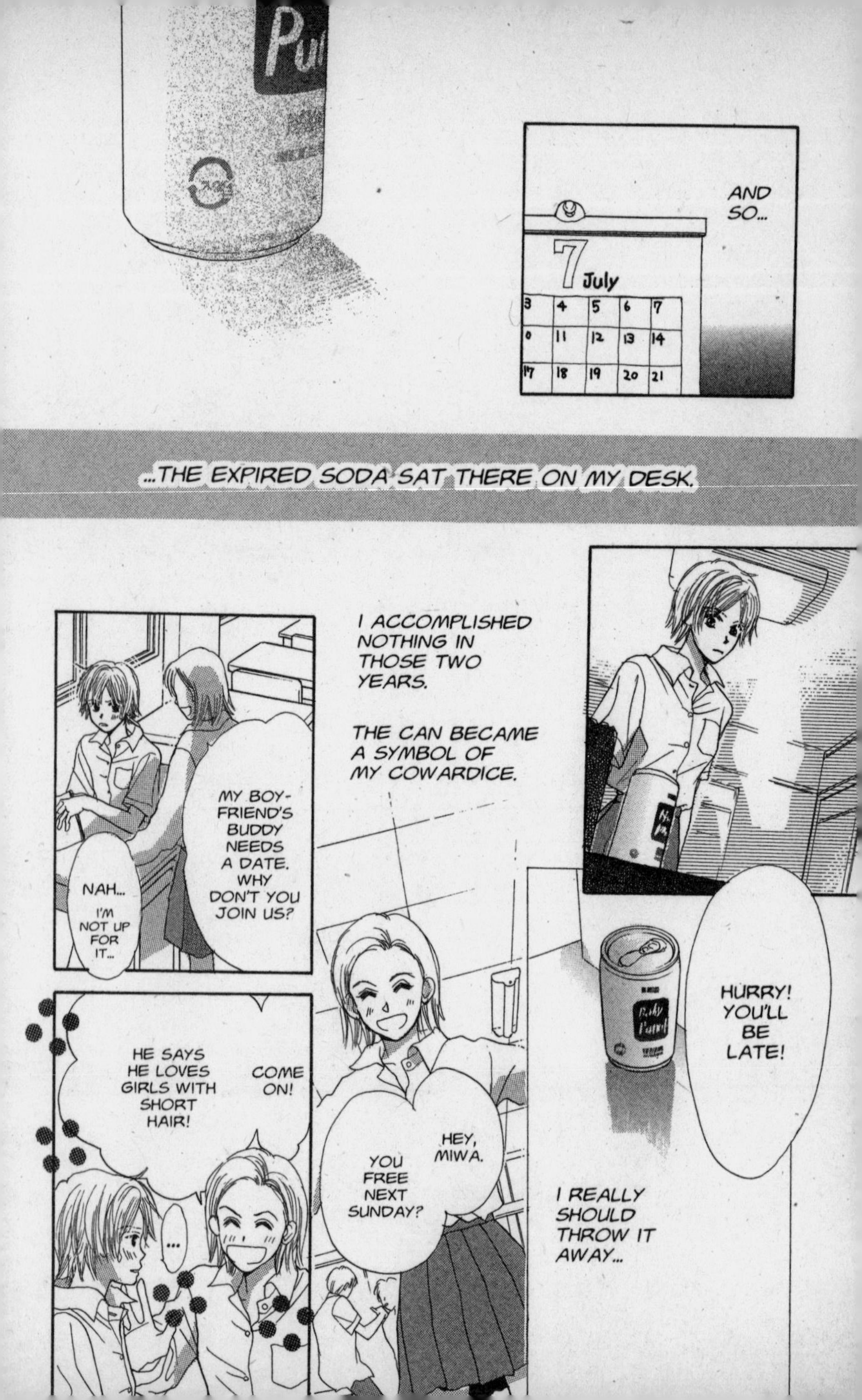
AND SO...
7 July
...THE EXPIRED SODA SAT THERE ON MY DESK.
HURRY! YOU'LL BE LATE!
I REALLY SHOULD THROW IT AWAY...
I ACCOMPLISHED NOTHING IN THOSE TWO YEARS.
THE CAN BECAME A SYMBOL OF MY COWARDICE.
HEY, MIWA.
YOU FREE NEXT SUNDAY?
MY BOY-FRIEND'S BUDDY NEEDS A DATE. WHY DON'T YOU JOIN US?
NAH... I'M NOT UP FOR IT...
COME ON!
HE SAYS HE LOVES GIRLS WITH SHORT HAIR!
...

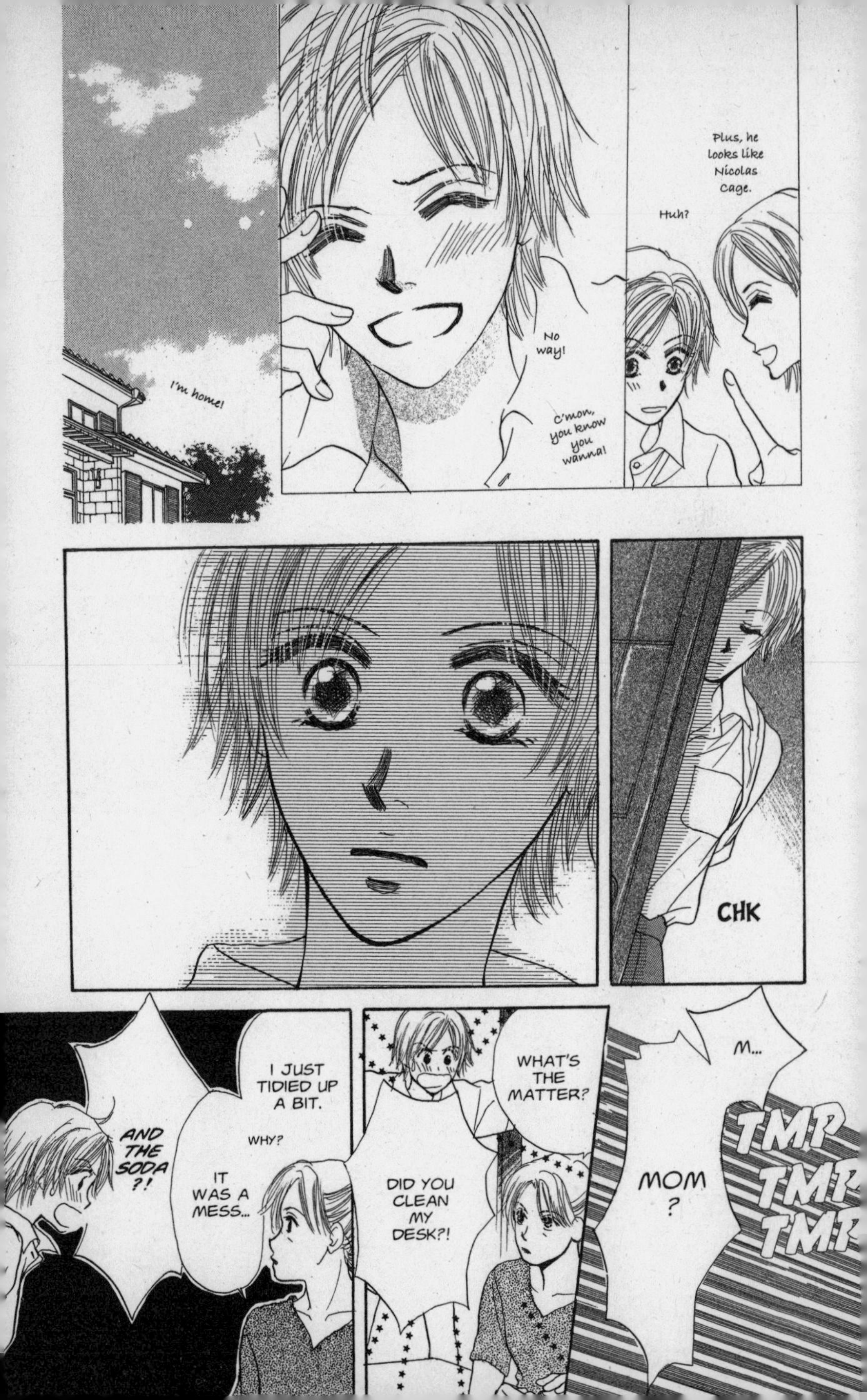
Plus, he looks like Nicolas Cage.
Huh?
No way!
C'mon, you know you wanna!
I'm home!
CHK
M...
TMP TMP TMP
MOM?
WHAT'S THE MATTER?
DID YOU CLEAN MY DESK?!
WHY?
IT WAS A MESS...
I JUST TIDIED UP A BIT.
AND THE SODA?!

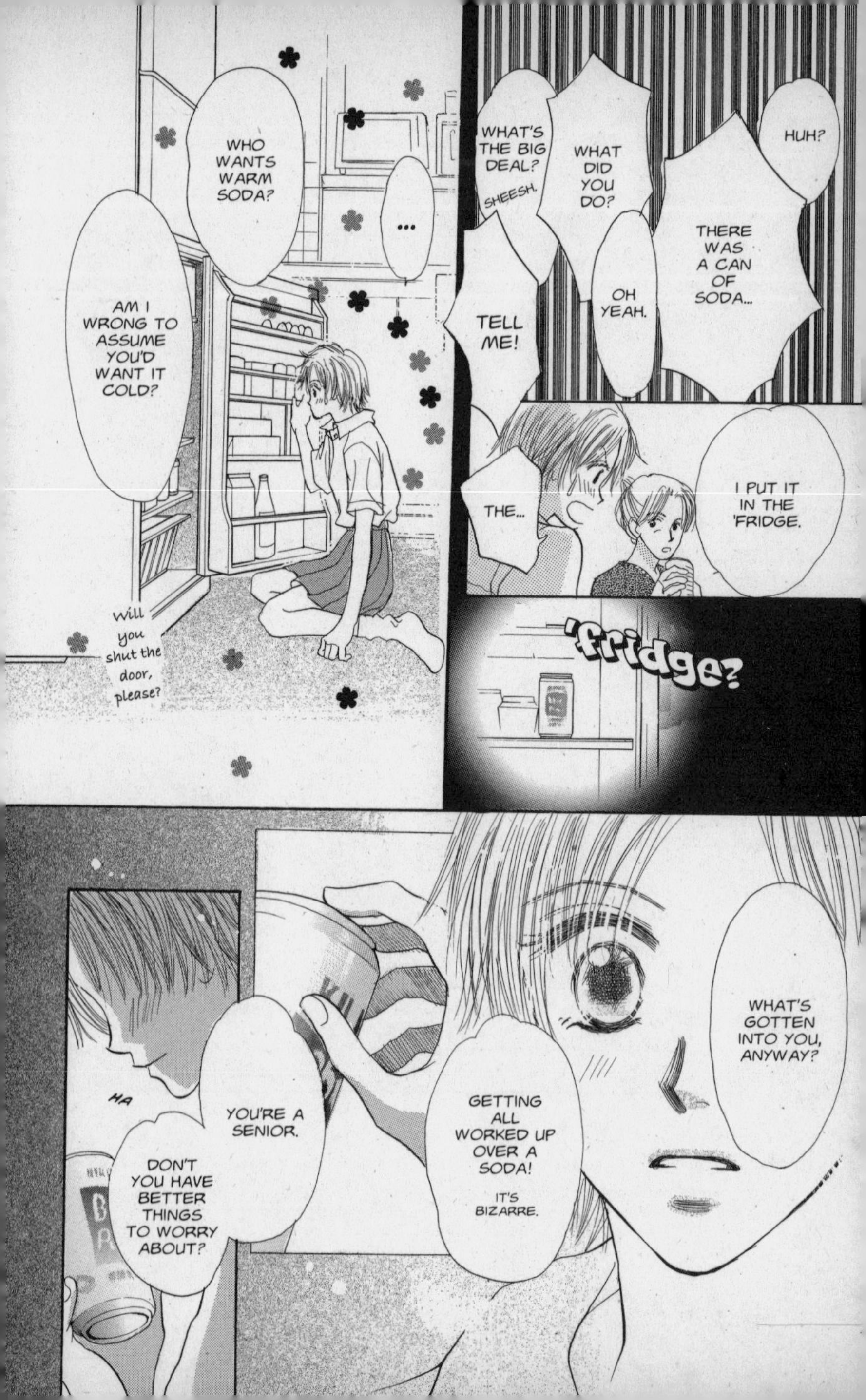
HUH?
THERE WAS A CAN OF SODA...
OH YEAH.
WHAT DID YOU DO?
WHAT'S THE BIG DEAL?
SHEESH.
TELL ME!
I PUT IT IN THE 'FRIDGE.
THE...
'fridge?
...
WHO WANTS WARM SODA?
AM I WRONG TO ASSUME YOU'D WANT IT COLD?
Will you shut the door, please?
WHAT'S GOTTEN INTO YOU, ANYWAY?
GETTING ALL WORKED UP OVER A SODA!
IT'S BIZARRE.
YOU'RE A SENIOR.
DON'T YOU HAVE BETTER THINGS TO WORRY ABOUT?
HA

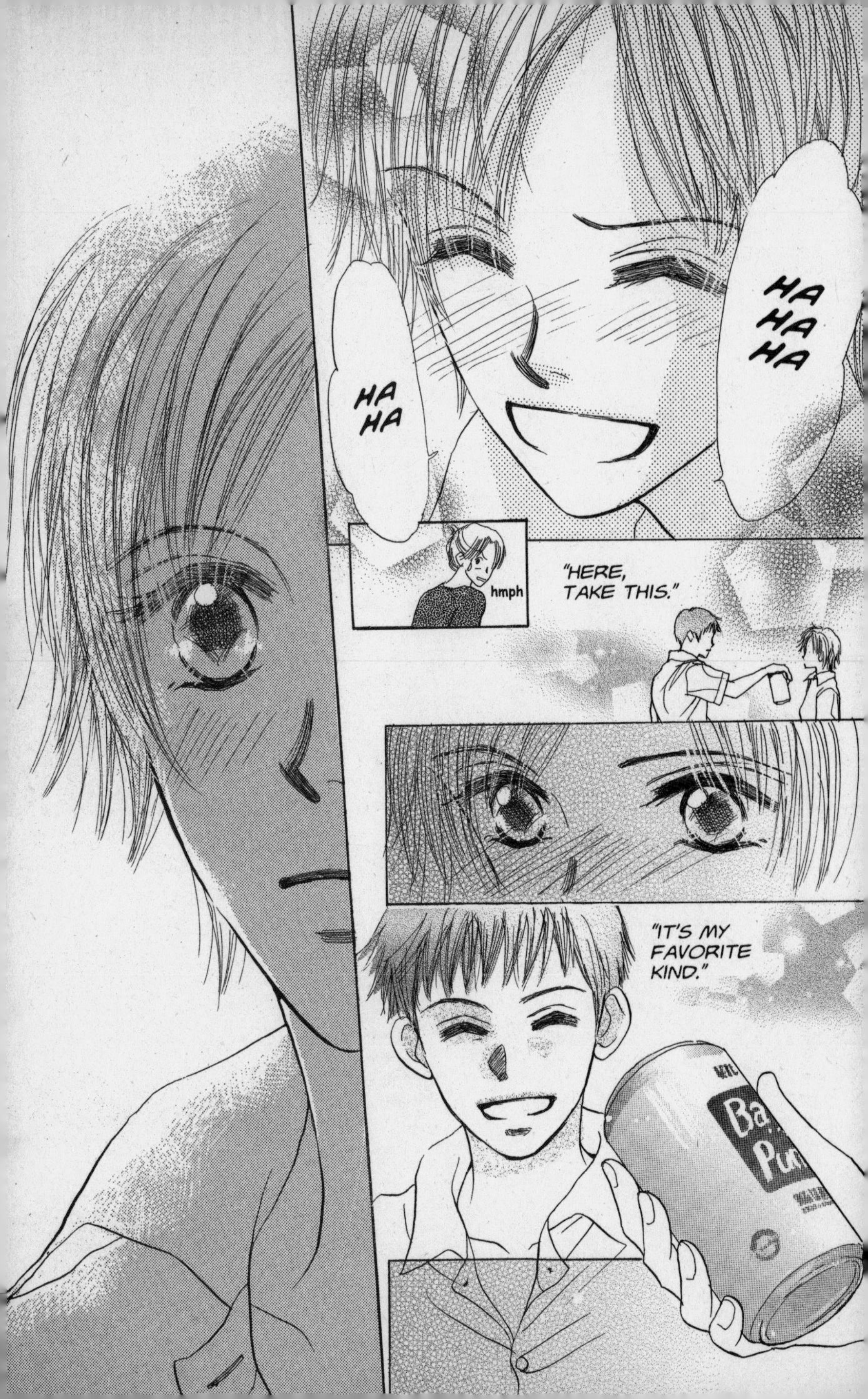
HA HA HA
HA HA
hmph
"HERE, TAKE THIS."
"IT'S MY FAVORITE KIND."

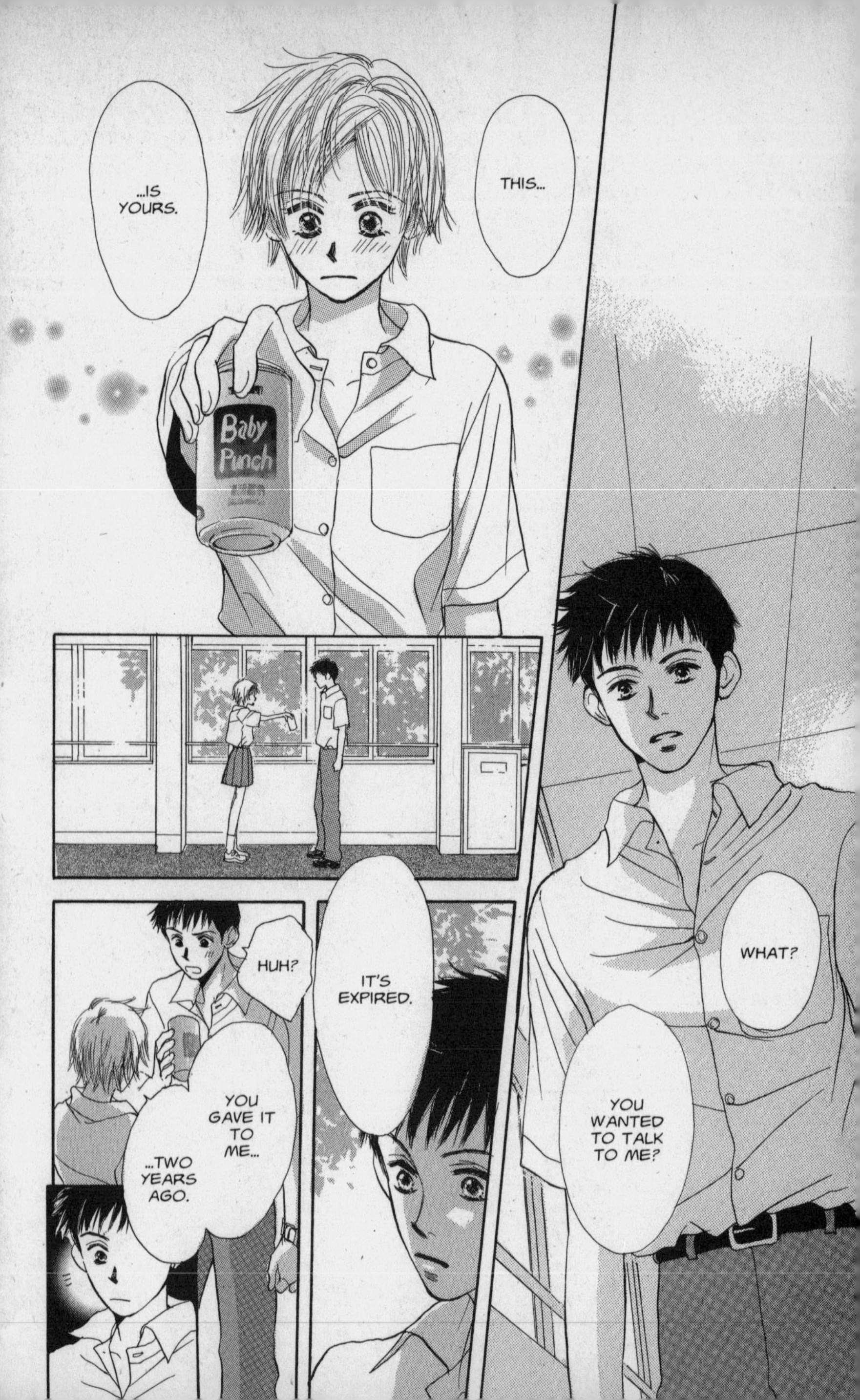
WHAT?
YOU WANTED TO TALK TO ME?
THIS...
...IS YOURS.
Baby Punch
IT'S EXPIRED.
HUH?
YOU GAVE IT TO ME...
...TWO YEARS AGO.

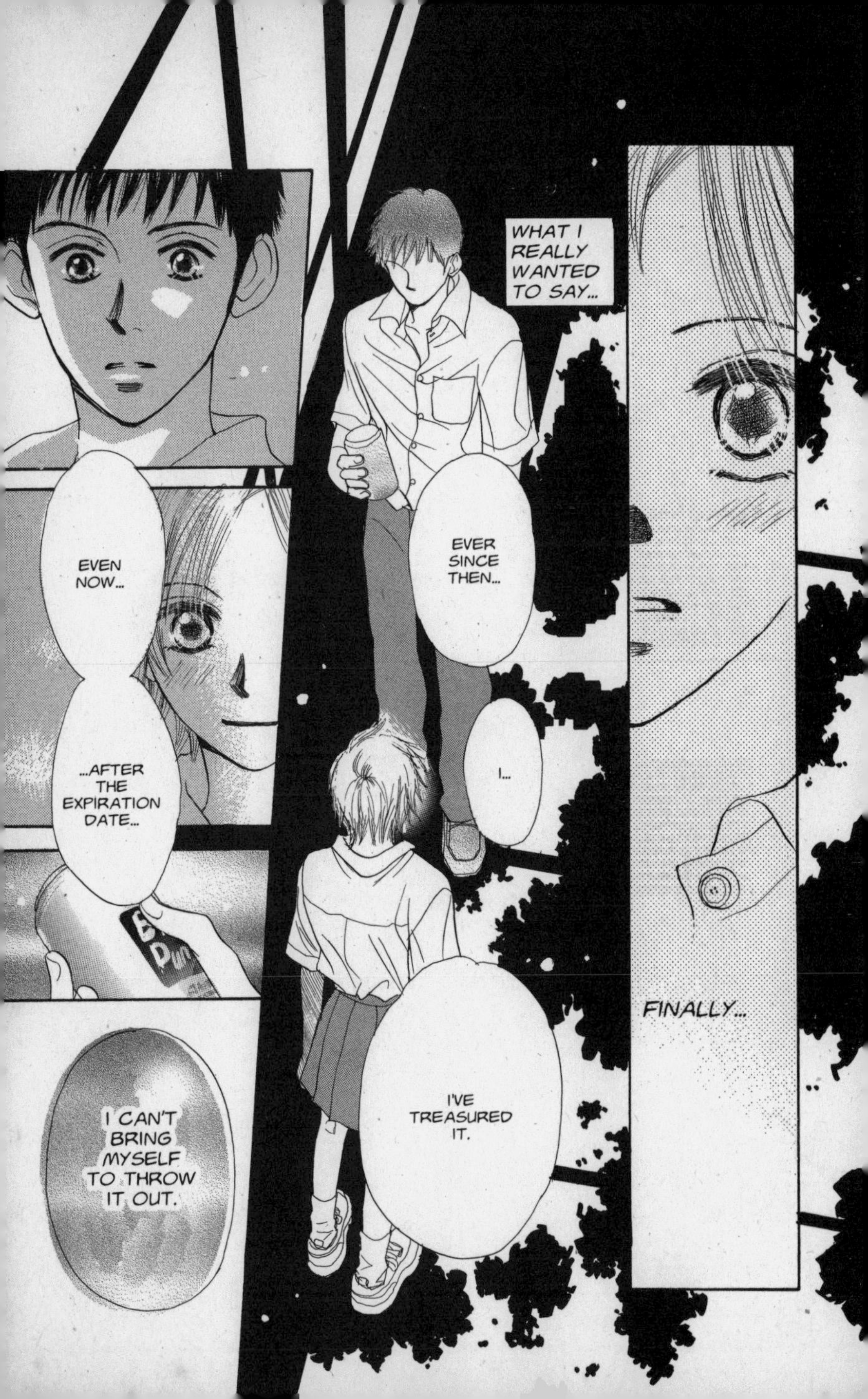
FINALLY...
WHAT I REALLY WANTED TO SAY...
EVER SINCE THEN...
I...
I'VE TREASURED IT.
EVEN NOW...
...AFTER THE EXPIRATION DATE...
I CAN'T BRING MYSELF TO THROW IT OUT.

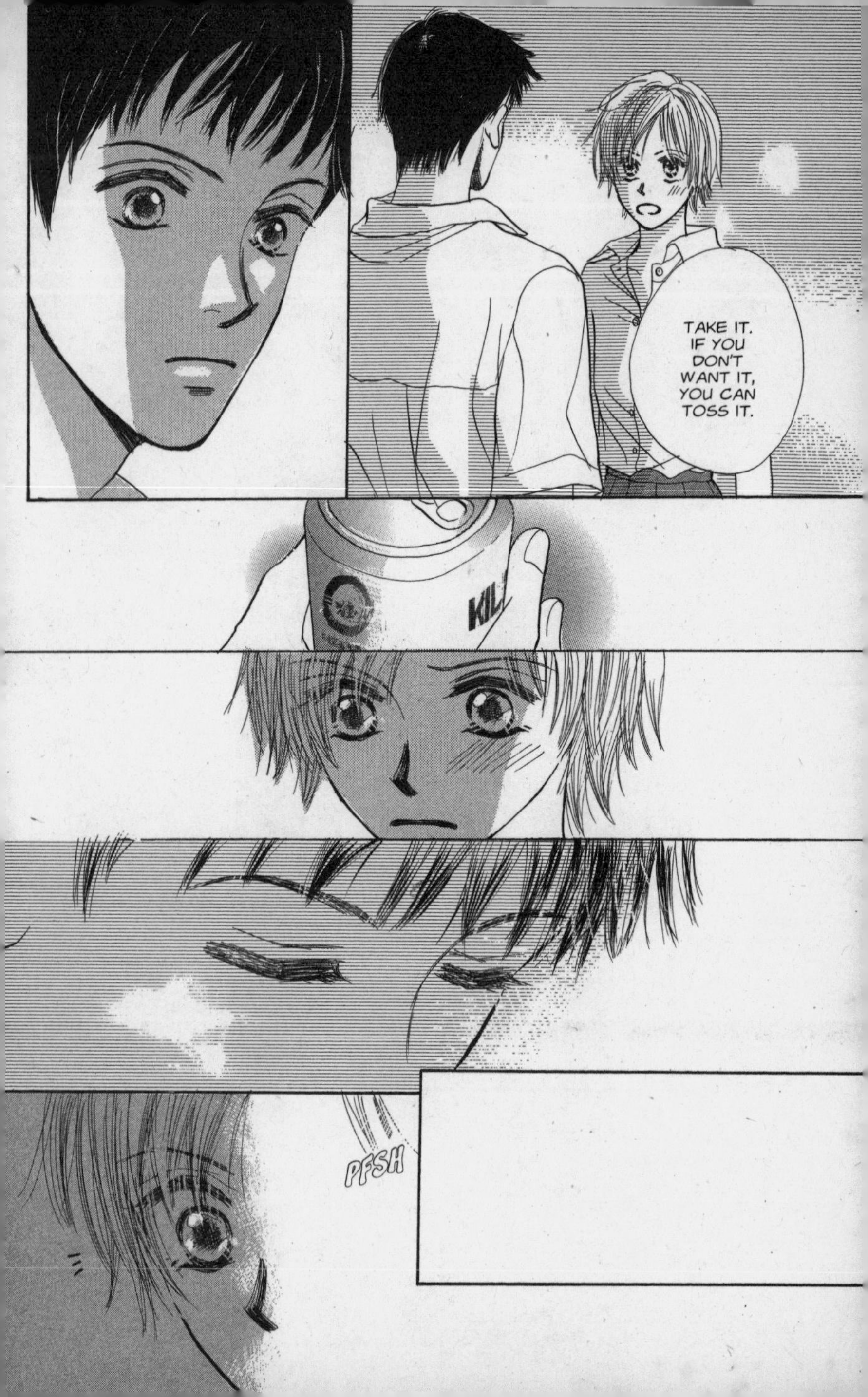
TAKE IT. IF YOU DON'T WANT IT, YOU CAN TOSS IT.
KIL
PFSH

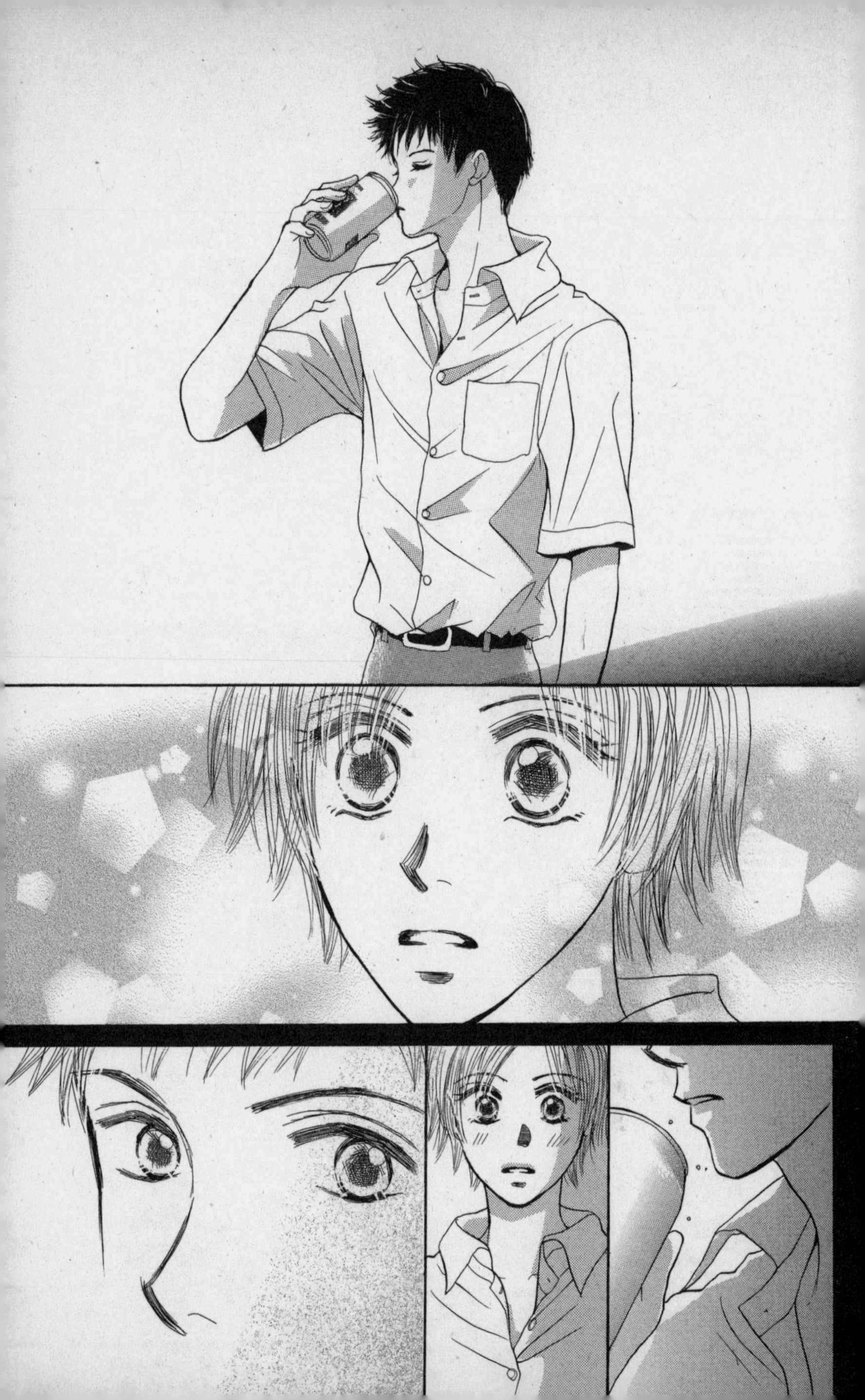

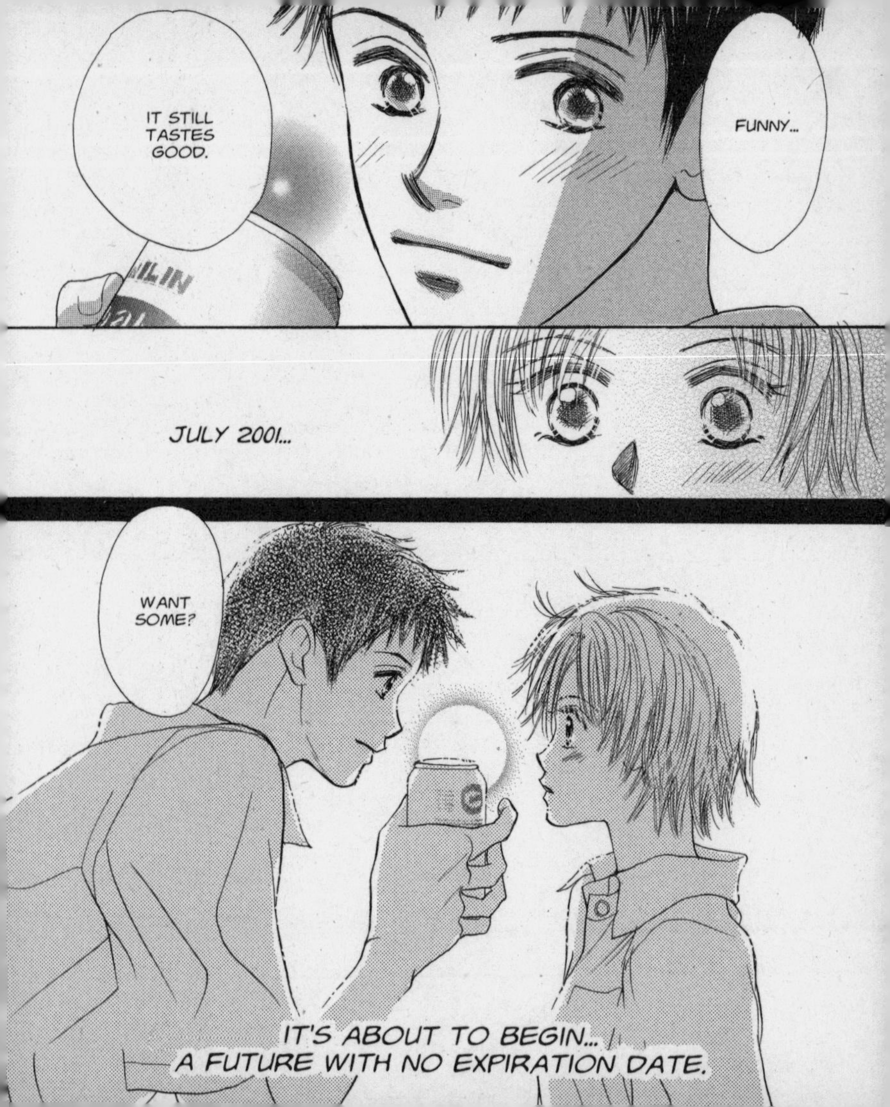
FUNNY...
IT STILL TASTES GOOD.
JULY 2001...
WANT SOME?
IT'S ABOUT TO BEGIN... A FUTURE WITH NO EXPIRATION DATE.

Second Impression

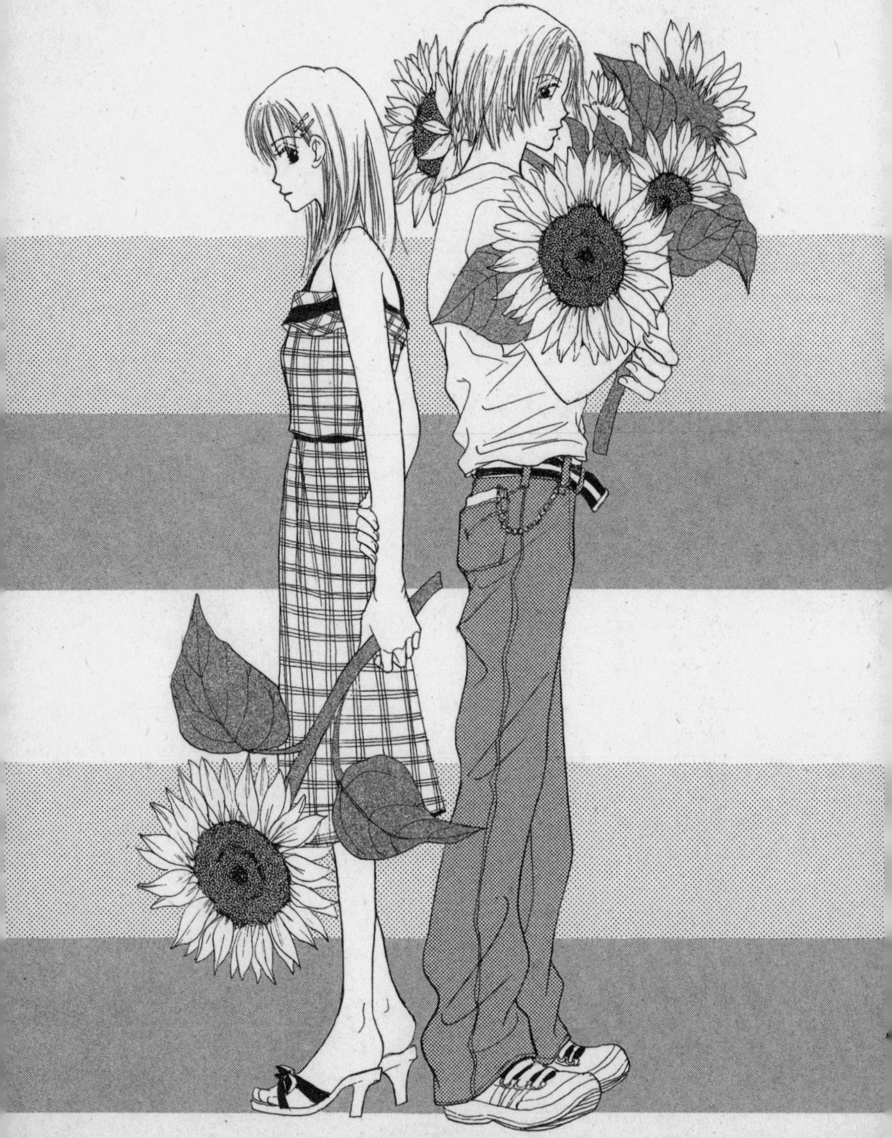

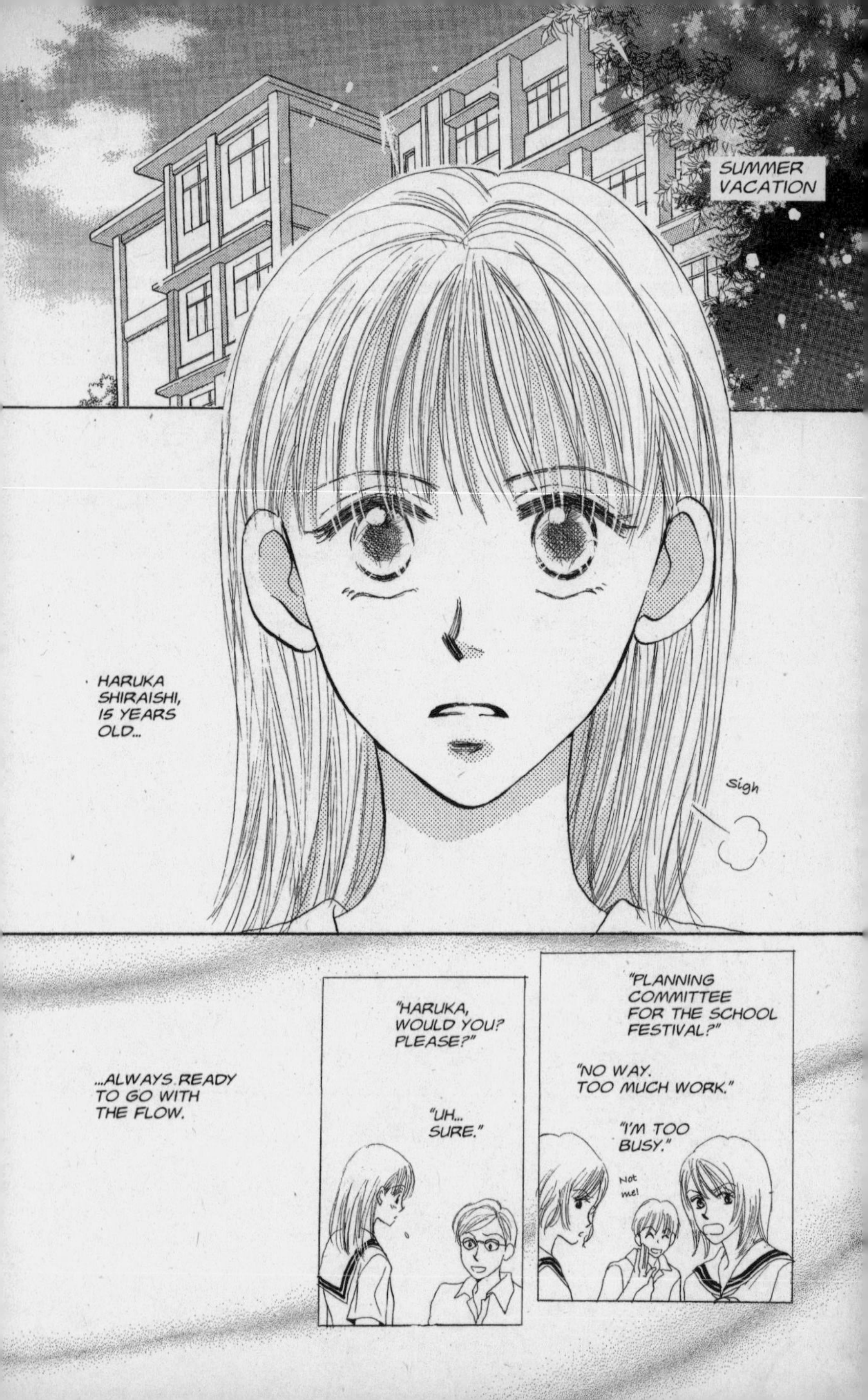
SUMMER VACATION
HARUKA SHIRAISHI, 15 YEARS OLD...
Sigh
"PLANNING COMMITTEE FOR THE SCHOOL FESTIVAL?"
"NO WAY. TOO MUCH WORK."
"I'M TOO BUSY."
Not me!
"HARUKA, WOULD YOU? PLEASE?"
"UH... SURE."
...ALWAYS READY TO GO WITH THE FLOW.

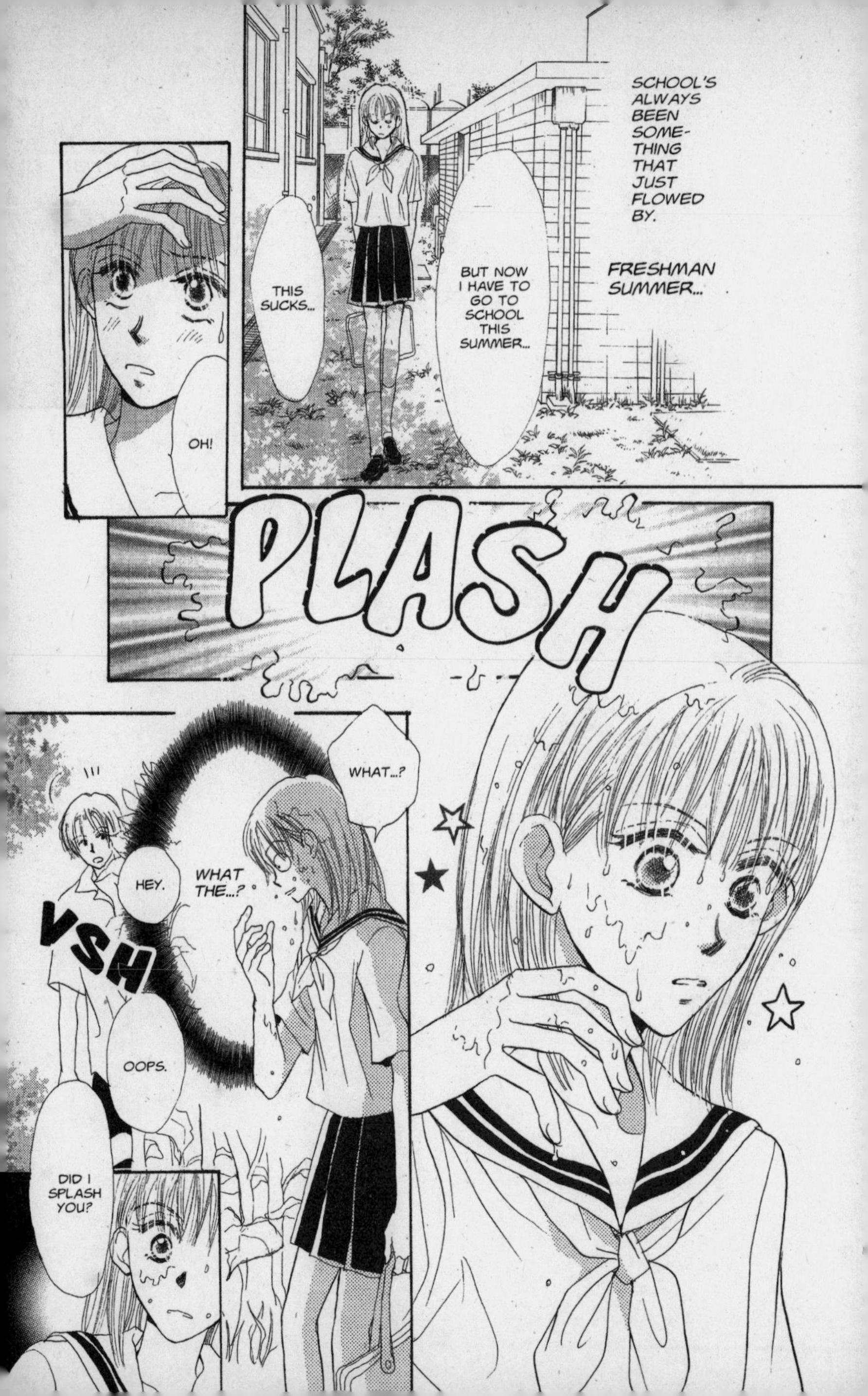
SCHOOL'S ALWAYS BEEN SOME-THING THAT JUST FLOWED BY.
FRESHMAN SUMMER...
BUT NOW I HAVE TO GO TO SCHOOL THIS SUMMER...
THIS SUCKS...
OH!
PLASH
WHAT...?
WHAT THE...?
HEY.
VSH
OOPS.
DID I SPLASH YOU?

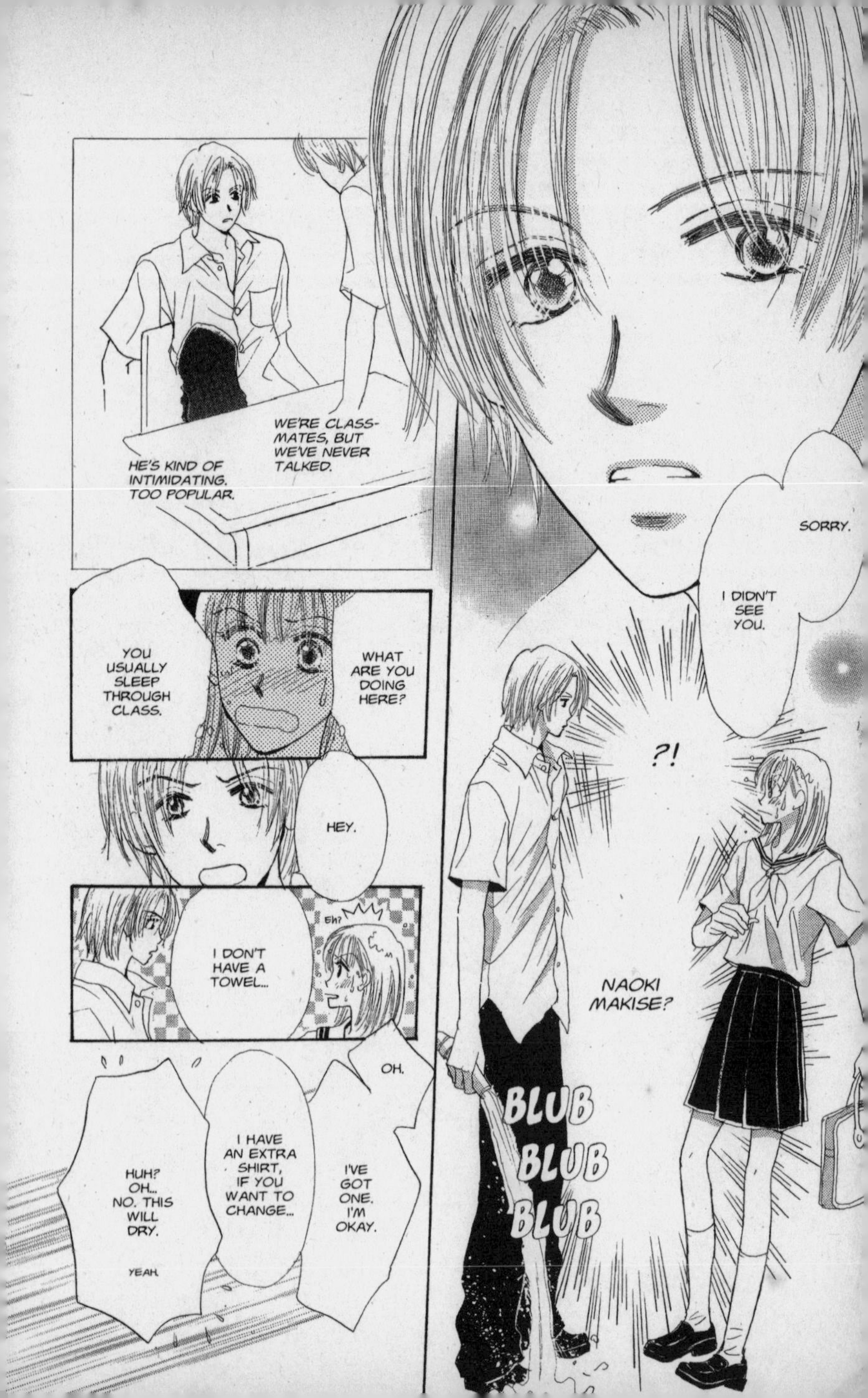
SORRY.
I DIDN'T SEE YOU.
?!
NAOKI MAKISE?
BLUB BLUB BLUB
WE'RE CLASS-MATES, BUT WE'VE NEVER TALKED.
HE'S KIND OF INTIMIDATING. TOO POPULAR.
WHAT ARE YOU DOING HERE?
YOU USUALLY SLEEP THROUGH CLASS.
HEY.
I DON'T HAVE A TOWEL...
Eh?
OH.
I'VE GOT ONE. I'M OKAY.
I HAVE AN EXTRA SHIRT, IF YOU WANT TO CHANGE...
HUH? OH... NO. THIS WILL DRY.
YEAH.

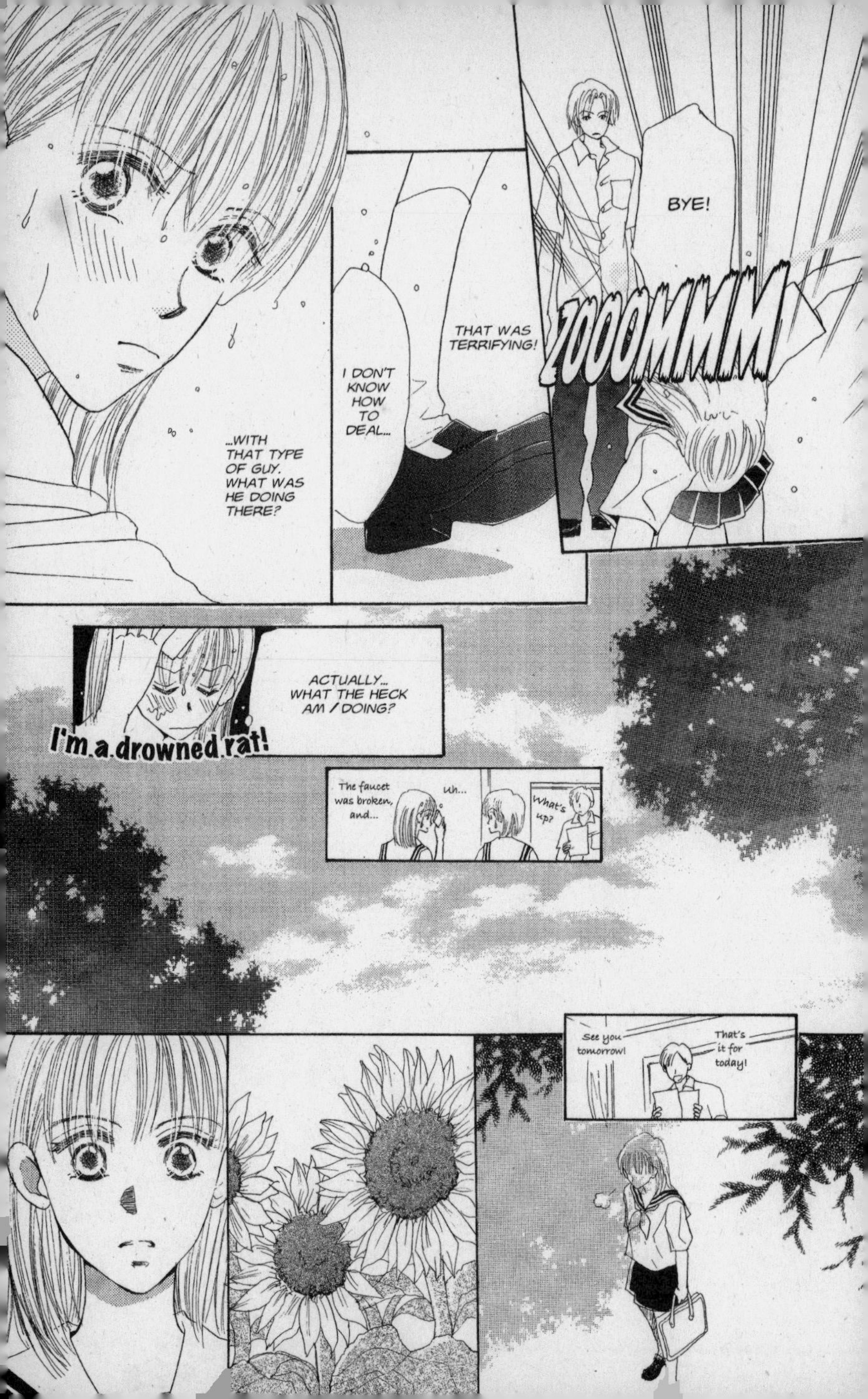
BYE!
ZOOOMMMM
THAT WAS TERRIFYING!
I DON'T KNOW HOW TO DEAL...
...WITH THAT TYPE OF GUY. WHAT WAS HE DOING THERE?
ACTUALLY... WHAT THE HECK AM I DOING?
I'm a drowned rat!
What's up?
Uh...
The faucet was broken, and...
That's it for today!
See you tomorrow!

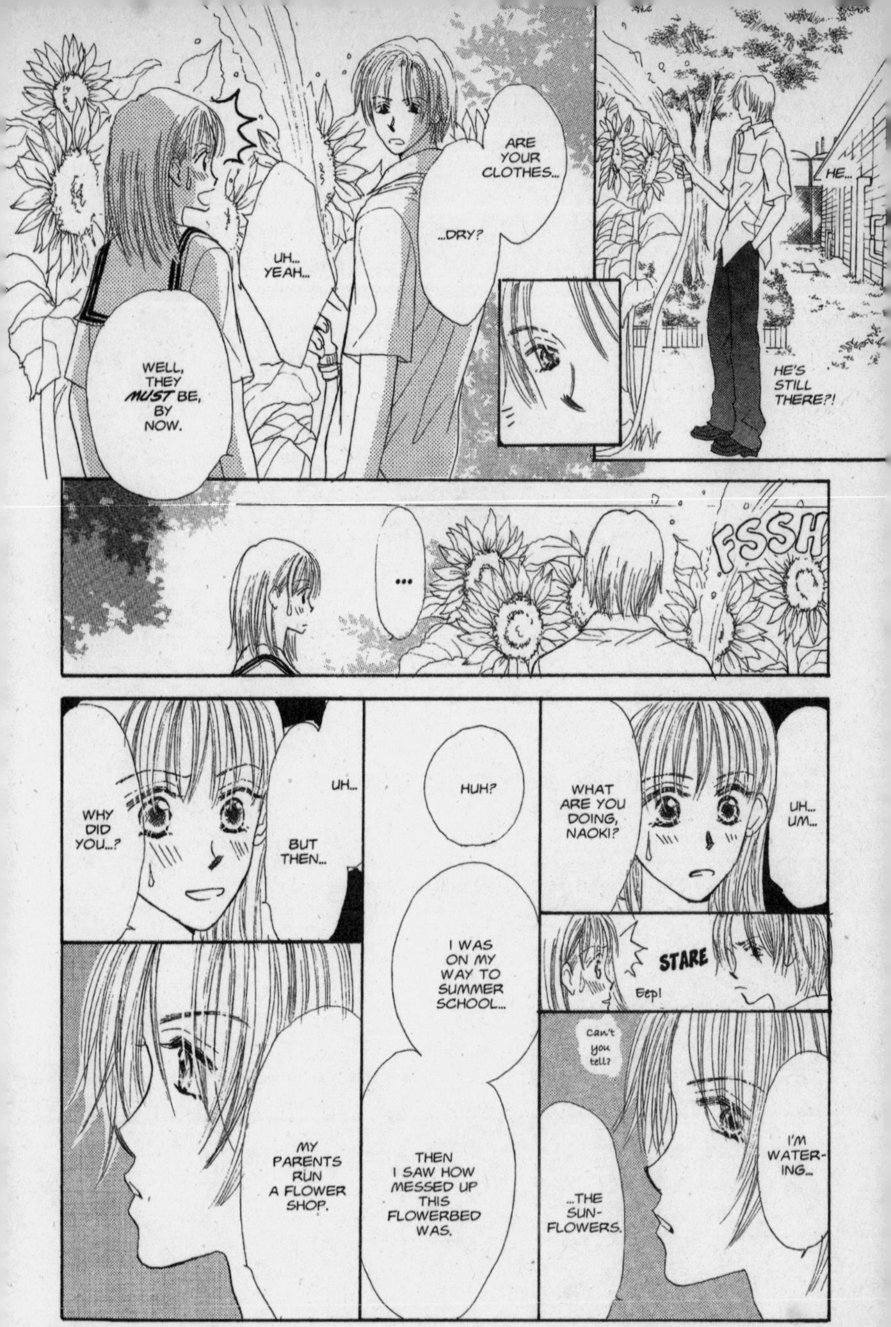
HE...
HE'S STILL THERE?!
ARE YOUR CLOTHES...
...DRY?
UH... YEAH...
WELL, THEY *MUST* BE, BY NOW.
FSSH
...
UH... UM...
WHAT ARE YOU DOING, NAOKI?
STARE
Eep!
I'M WATERING...
...THE SUNFLOWERS.
Can't you tell?
HUH?
I WAS ON MY WAY TO SUMMER SCHOOL...
THEN I SAW HOW MESSED UP THIS FLOWERBED WAS.
UH...
BUT THEN...
WHY DID YOU...?
MY PARENTS RUN A FLOWER SHOP.

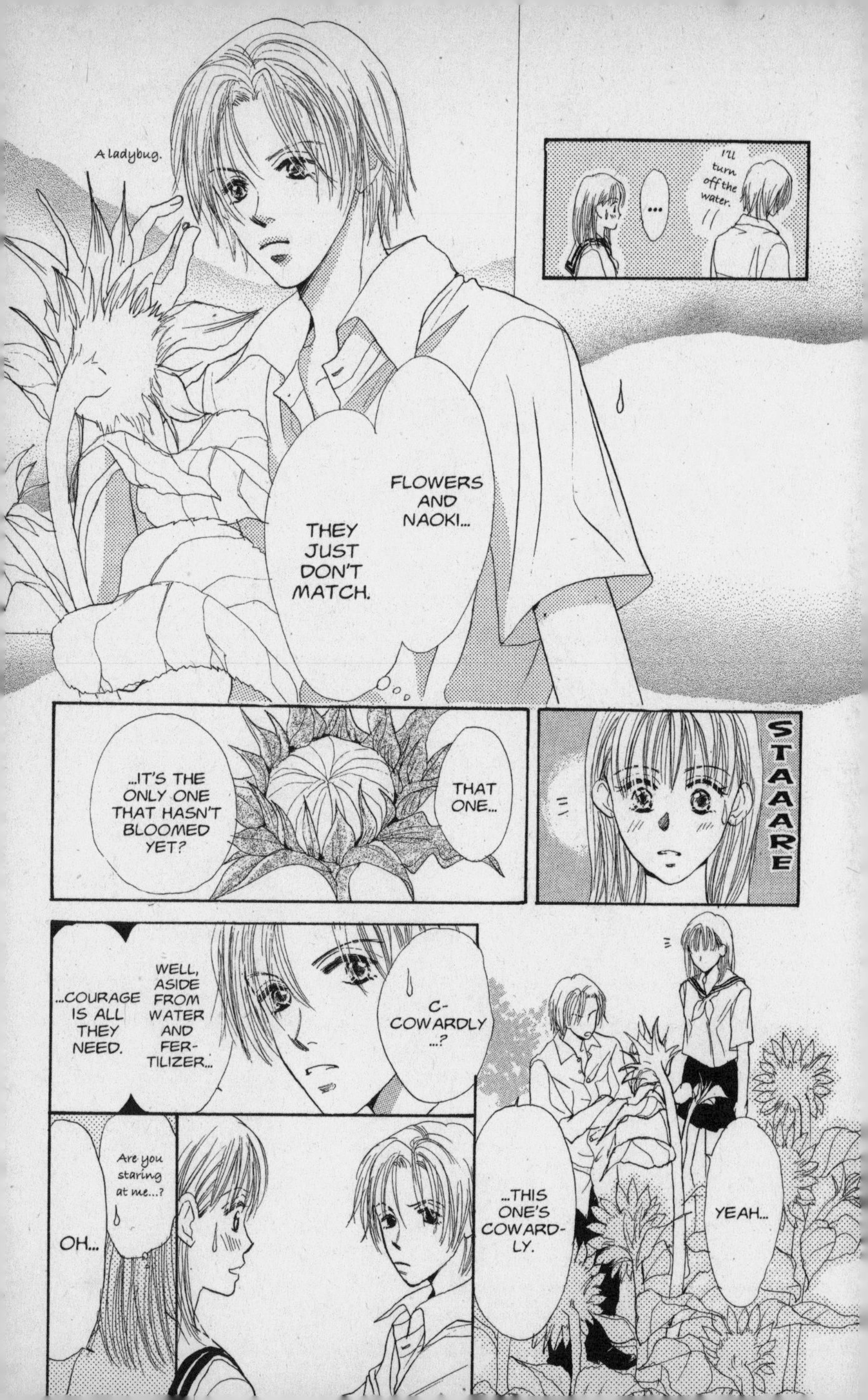
I'll turn off the water.
...
A ladybug.
FLOWERS AND NAOKI...
THEY JUST DON'T MATCH.
STAAAARE
THAT ONE...
...IT'S THE ONLY ONE THAT HASN'T BLOOMED YET?
YEAH...
...THIS ONE'S COWARD-LY.
C-COWARDLY...?
WELL, ASIDE FROM WATER AND FER-TILIZER...
...COURAGE IS ALL THEY NEED.
Are you staring at me...?
OH...

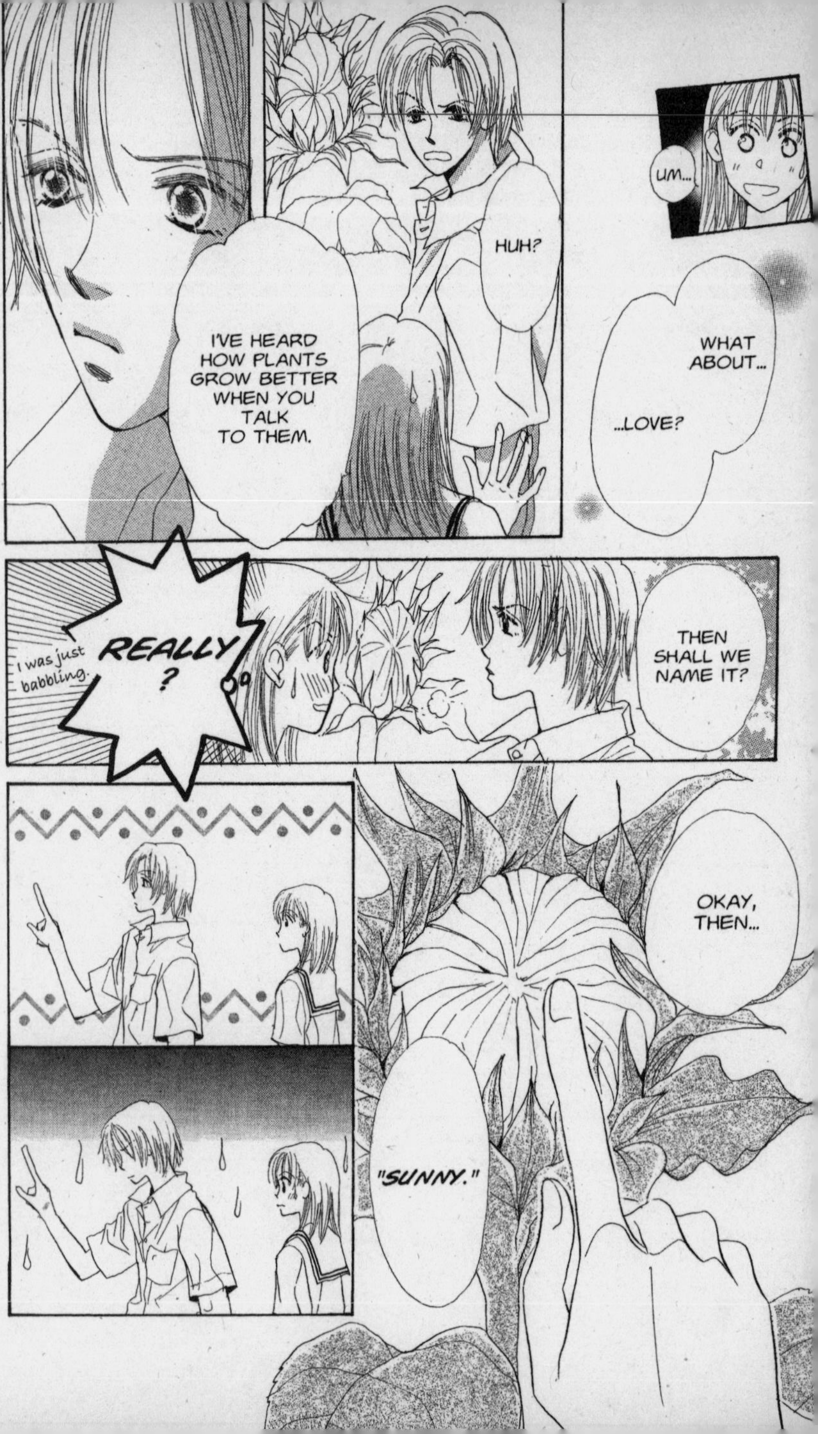
UM...
WHAT ABOUT... ...LOVE?
HUH?
I'VE HEARD HOW PLANTS GROW BETTER WHEN YOU TALK TO THEM.
THEN SHALL WE NAME IT?
REALLY?
I was just babbling.
OKAY, THEN...
"SUNNY."

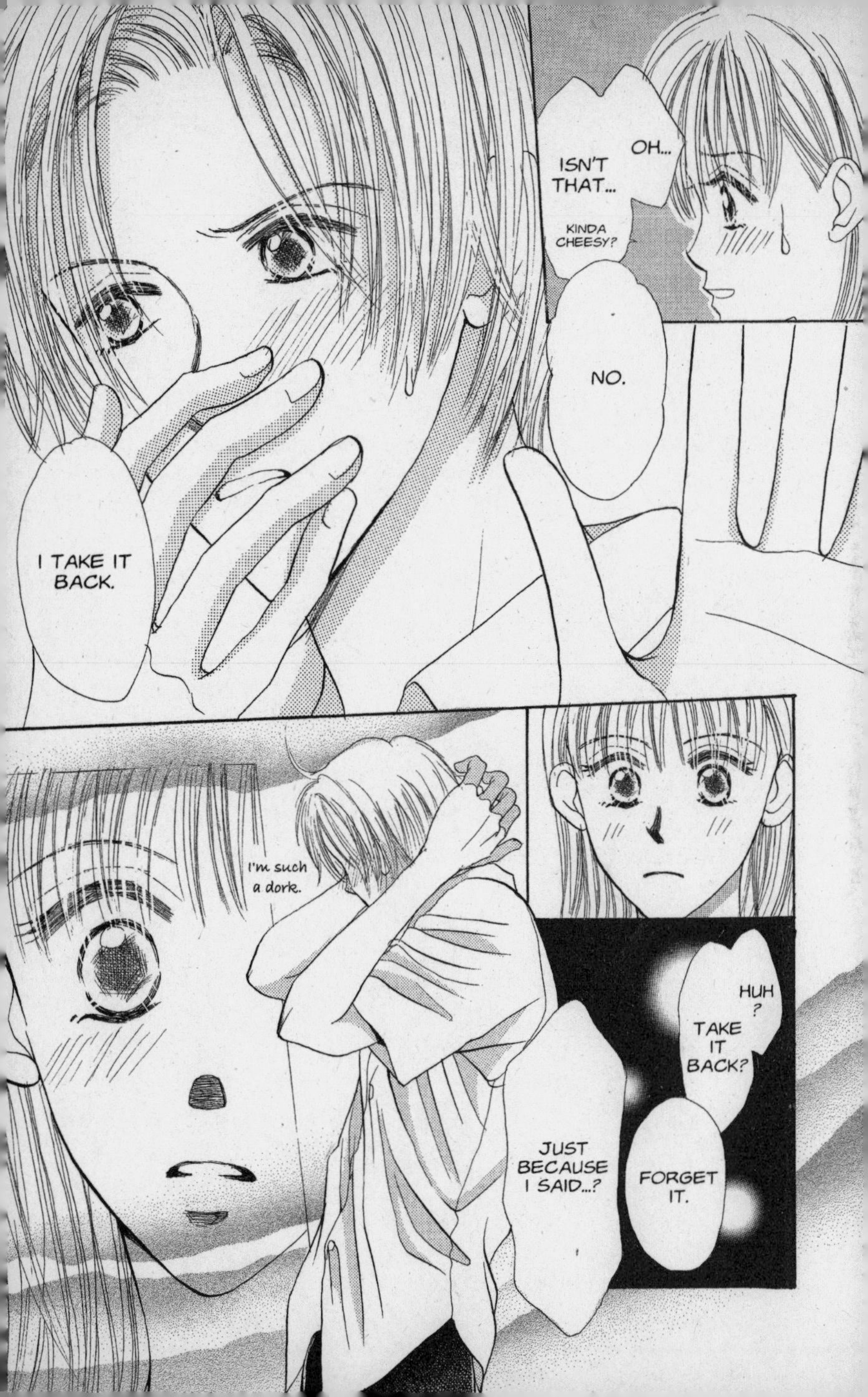

OH...
ISN'T THAT...
KINDA CHEESY?
NO.
I TAKE IT BACK.
HUH? TAKE IT BACK?
JUST BECAUSE I SAID...?
FORGET IT.
I'm such a dork.

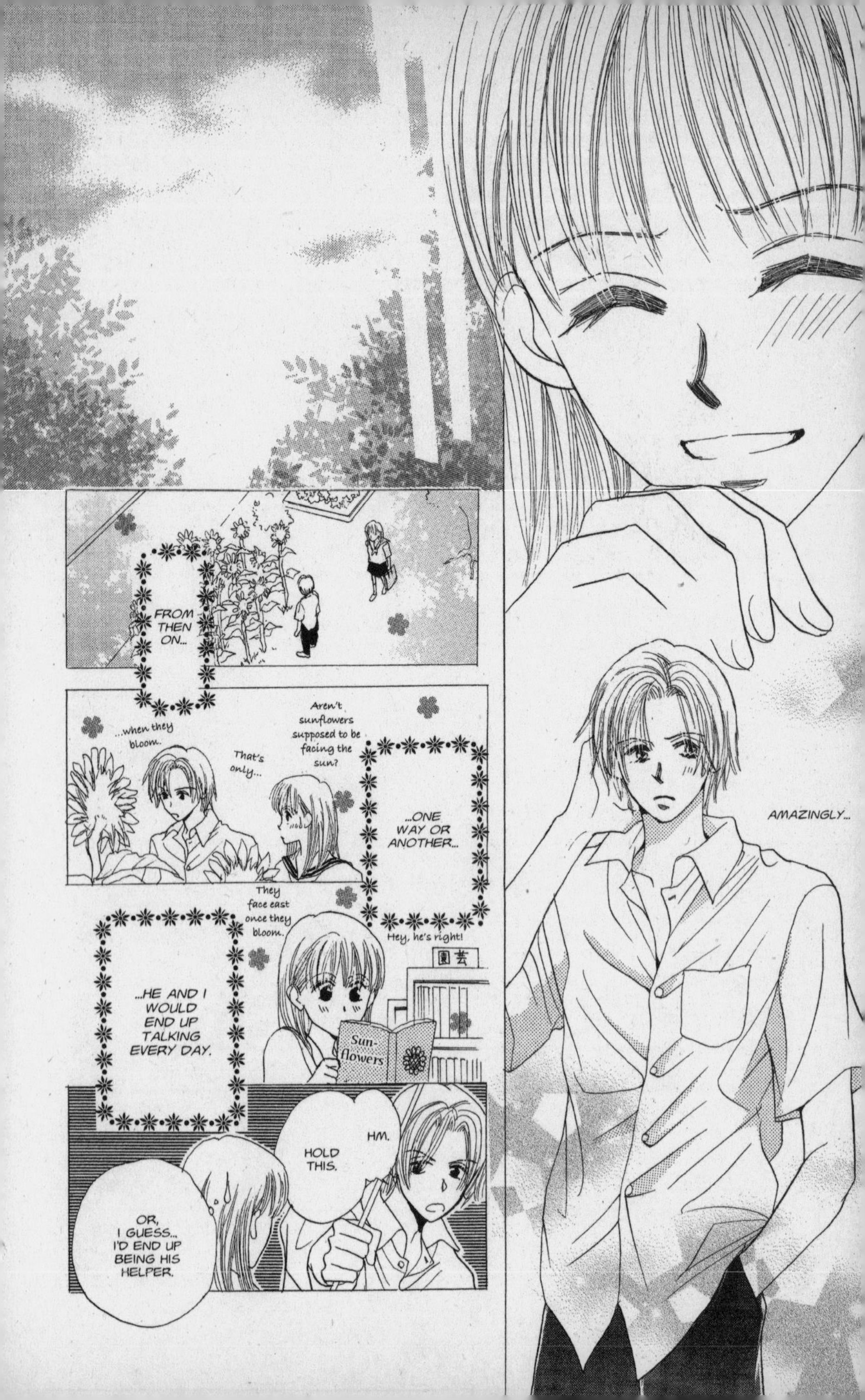
AMAZINGLY...
FROM THEN ON...
...ONE WAY OR ANOTHER...
Aren't sunflowers supposed to be facing the sun?
That's only...
...when they bloom.
They face east once they bloom.
Hey, he's right!
園芸
Sun-flowers
...HE AND I WOULD END UP TALKING EVERY DAY.
HM.
HOLD THIS.
OR, I GUESS... I'D END UP BEING HIS HELPER.

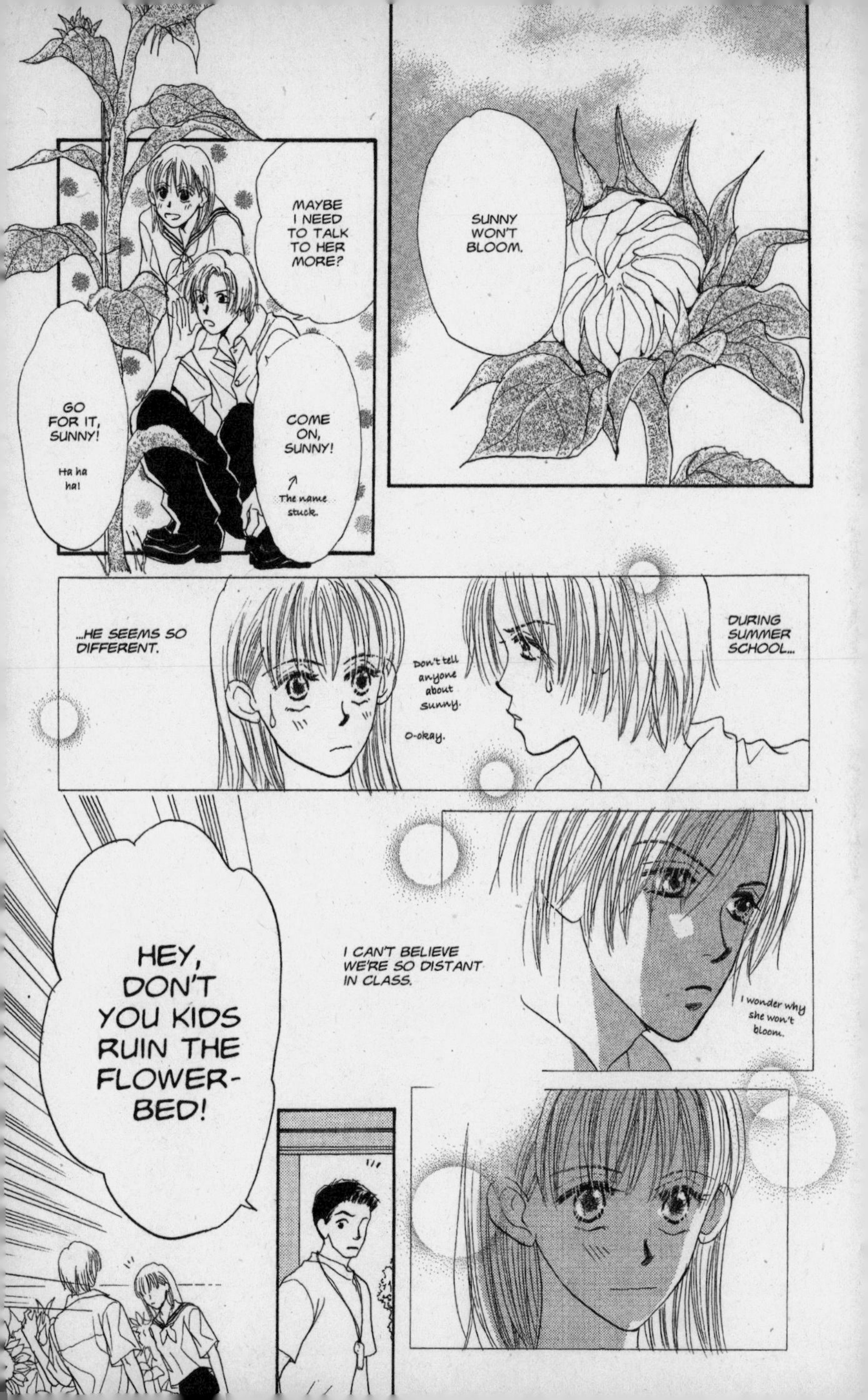
SUNNY WON'T BLOOM.
MAYBE I NEED TO TALK TO HER MORE?
COME ON, SUNNY!
The name stuck.
GO FOR IT, SUNNY!
Ha ha ha!
DURING SUMMER SCHOOL...
Don't tell anyone about Sunny.
O-okay.
...HE SEEMS SO DIFFERENT.
I wonder why she won't bloom.
I CAN'T BELIEVE WE'RE SO DISTANT IN CLASS.
HEY, DON'T YOU KIDS RUIN THE FLOWER-BED!

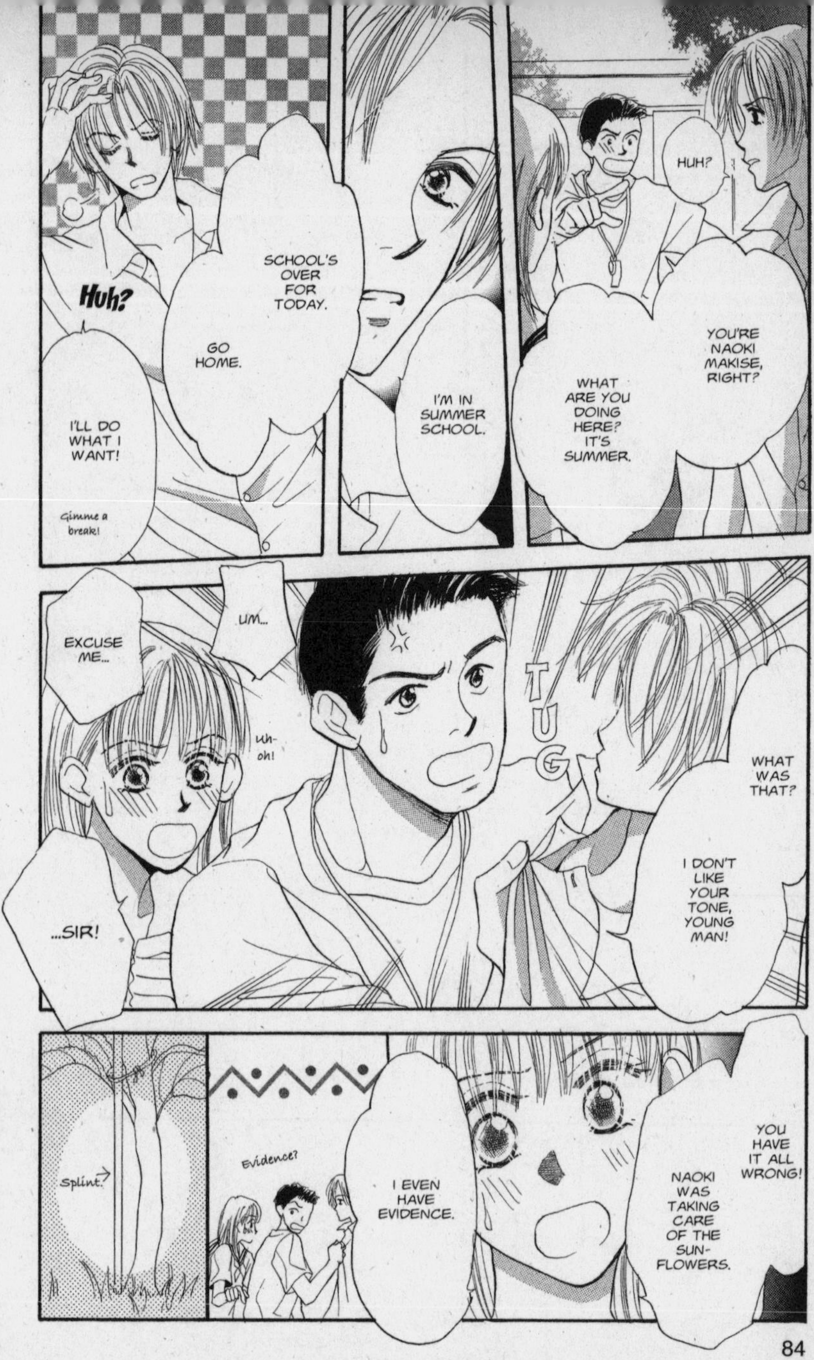
HUH?
YOU'RE NAOKI MAKISE, RIGHT?
WHAT ARE YOU DOING HERE? IT'S SUMMER.
I'M IN SUMMER SCHOOL.
SCHOOL'S OVER FOR TODAY.
GO HOME.
Huh?
I'LL DO WHAT I WANT!
Gimme a break!
WHAT WAS THAT?
I DON'T LIKE YOUR TONE, YOUNG MAN!
TUG
UM...
EXCUSE ME...
Uh-oh!
...SIR!
YOU HAVE IT ALL WRONG!
NAOKI WAS TAKING CARE OF THE SUN-FLOWERS.
I EVEN HAVE EVIDENCE.
Evidence?
Splint.

03

✖✖

"Second Impression":

I began with the idea of drawing a boy with doe eyes. It turned out be challenging. (Although I don't think I've ever done a story that wasn't challenging...)

I was terrible in elementary and junior high school when it came to caring for plants. They just wouldn't grow right... Maybe they needed more love.

✖

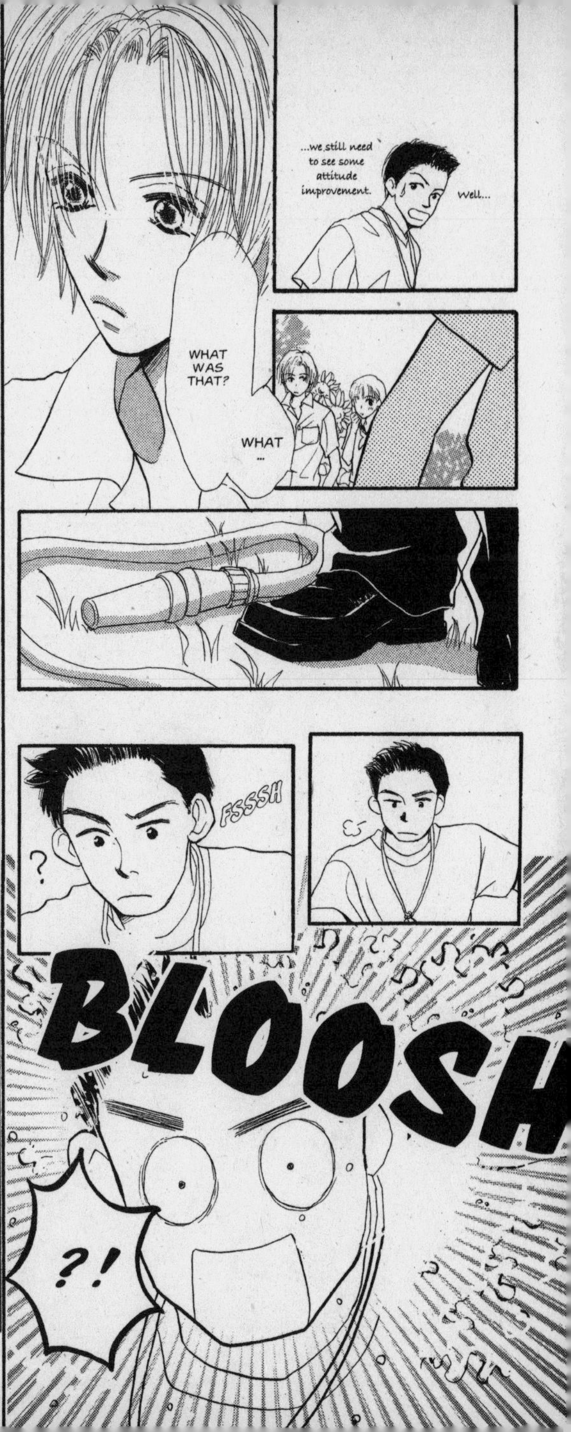

Well...
...we still need to see some attitude improvement.
WHAT WAS THAT?
WHAT ...
FSSSH
?
BLOOSH
?!

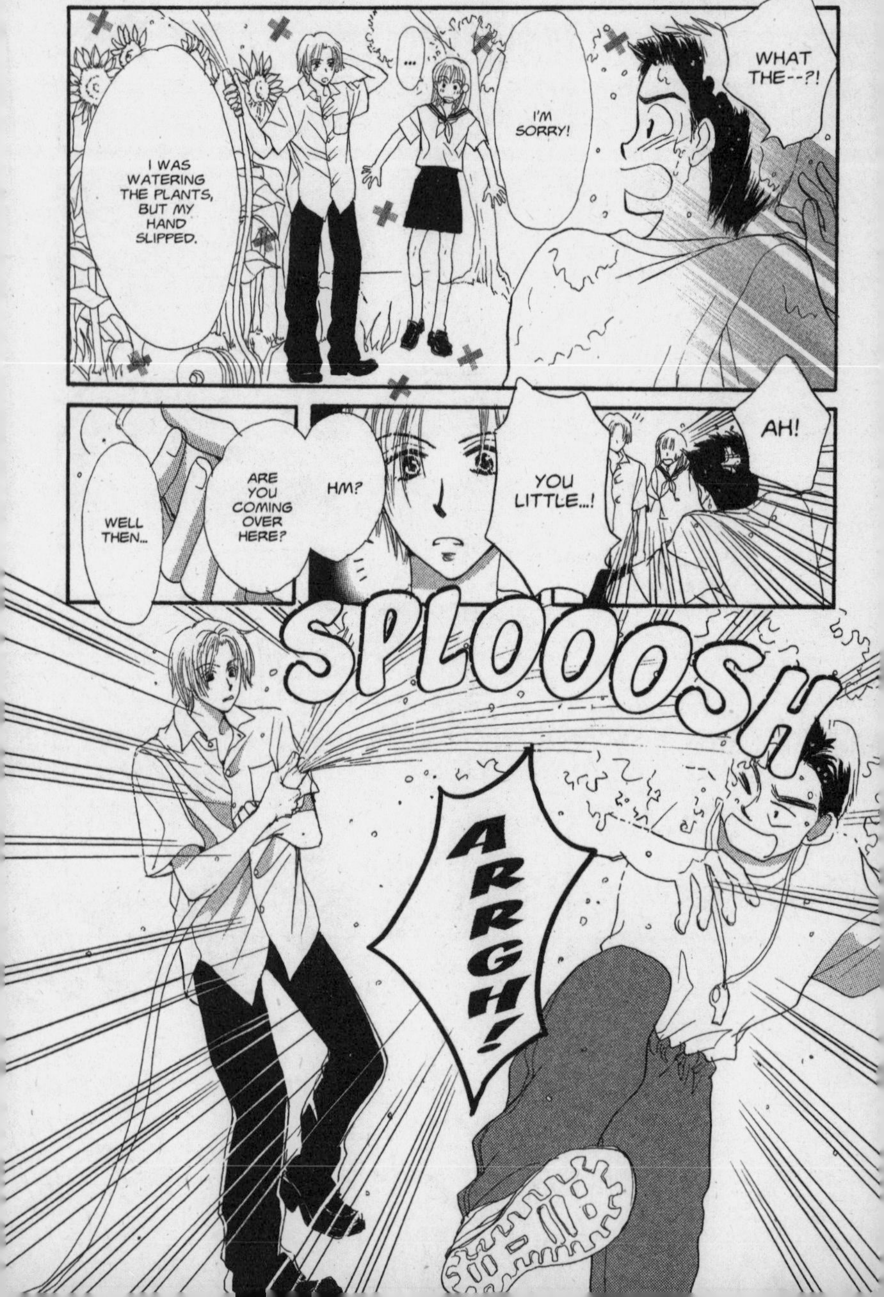
WHAT THE--?!
I'M SORRY!
...
I WAS WATERING THE PLANTS, BUT MY HAND SLIPPED.
AH!
YOU LITTLE...!
HM?
ARE YOU COMING OVER HERE?
WELL THEN...
SPLOOOSH
ARRGH!

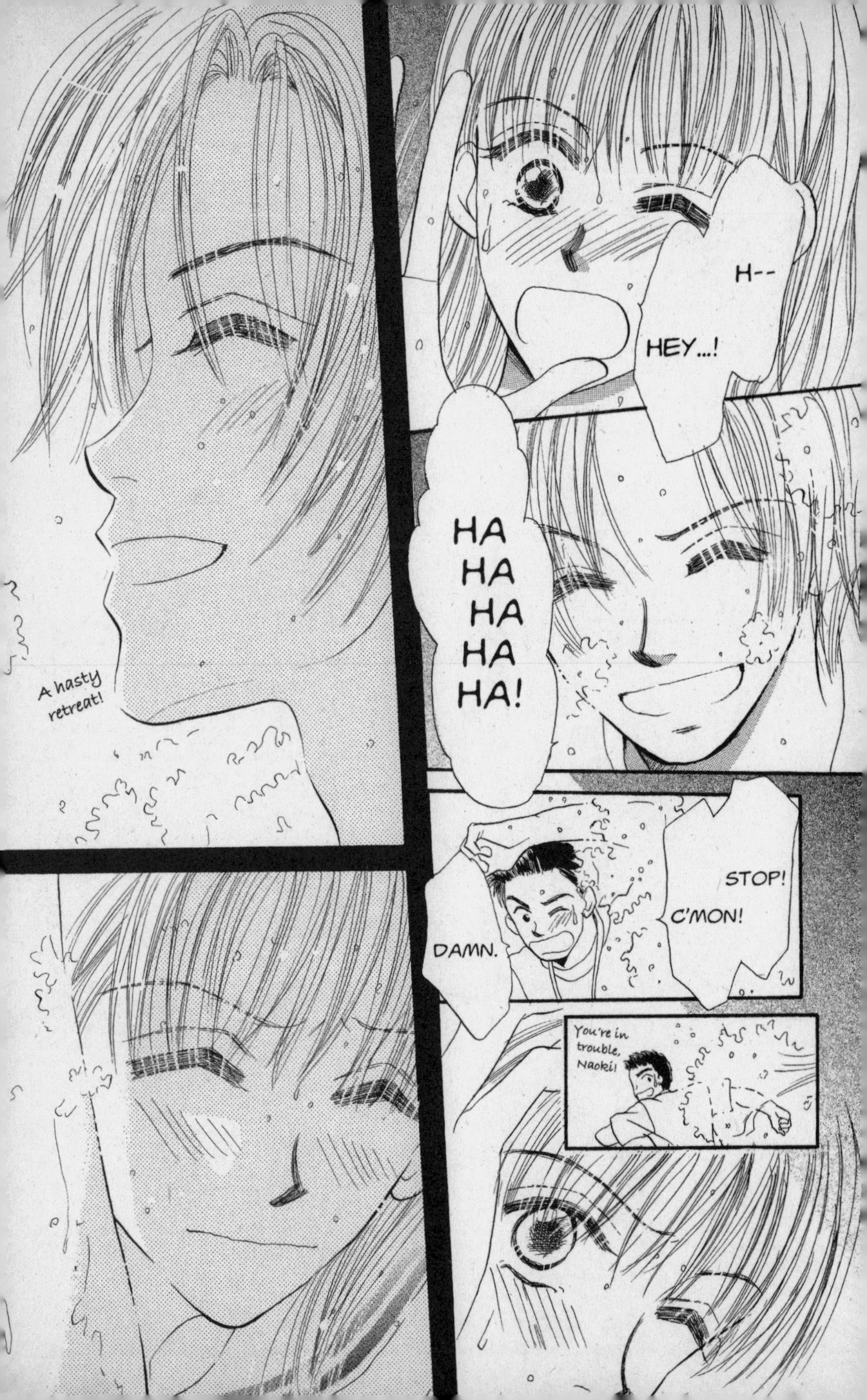
H--
HEY...!
HA HA HA HA HA!
STOP!
C'MON!
DAMN.
You're in trouble, Naoki!
A hasty retreat!

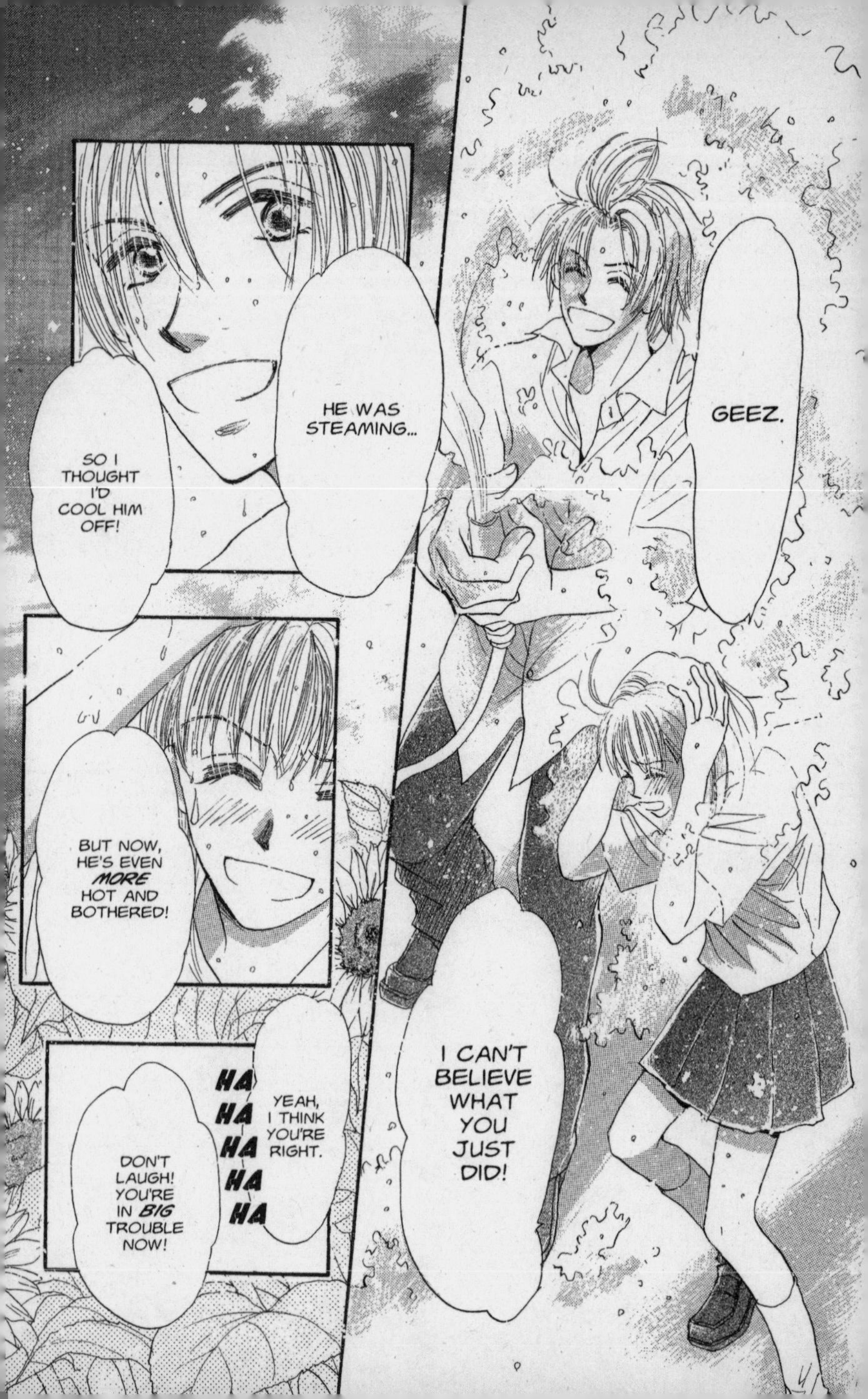
GEEZ.
I CAN'T BELIEVE WHAT YOU JUST DID!
HE WAS STEAMING...
SO I THOUGHT I'D COOL HIM OFF!
BUT NOW, HE'S EVEN *MORE* HOT AND BOTHERED!
YEAH, I THINK YOU'RE RIGHT.
HA HA HA HA HA
DON'T LAUGH! YOU'RE IN *BIG* TROUBLE NOW!

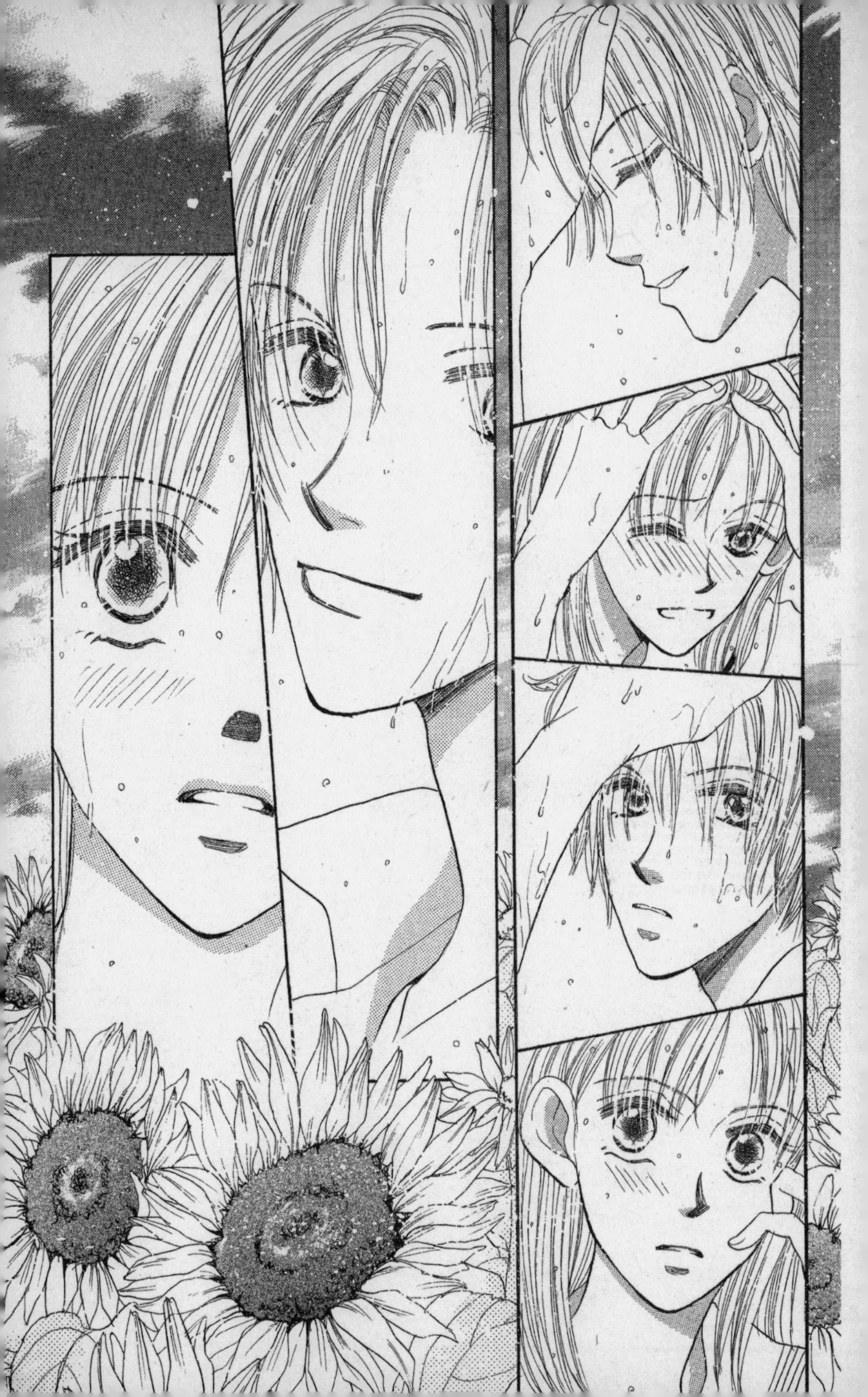

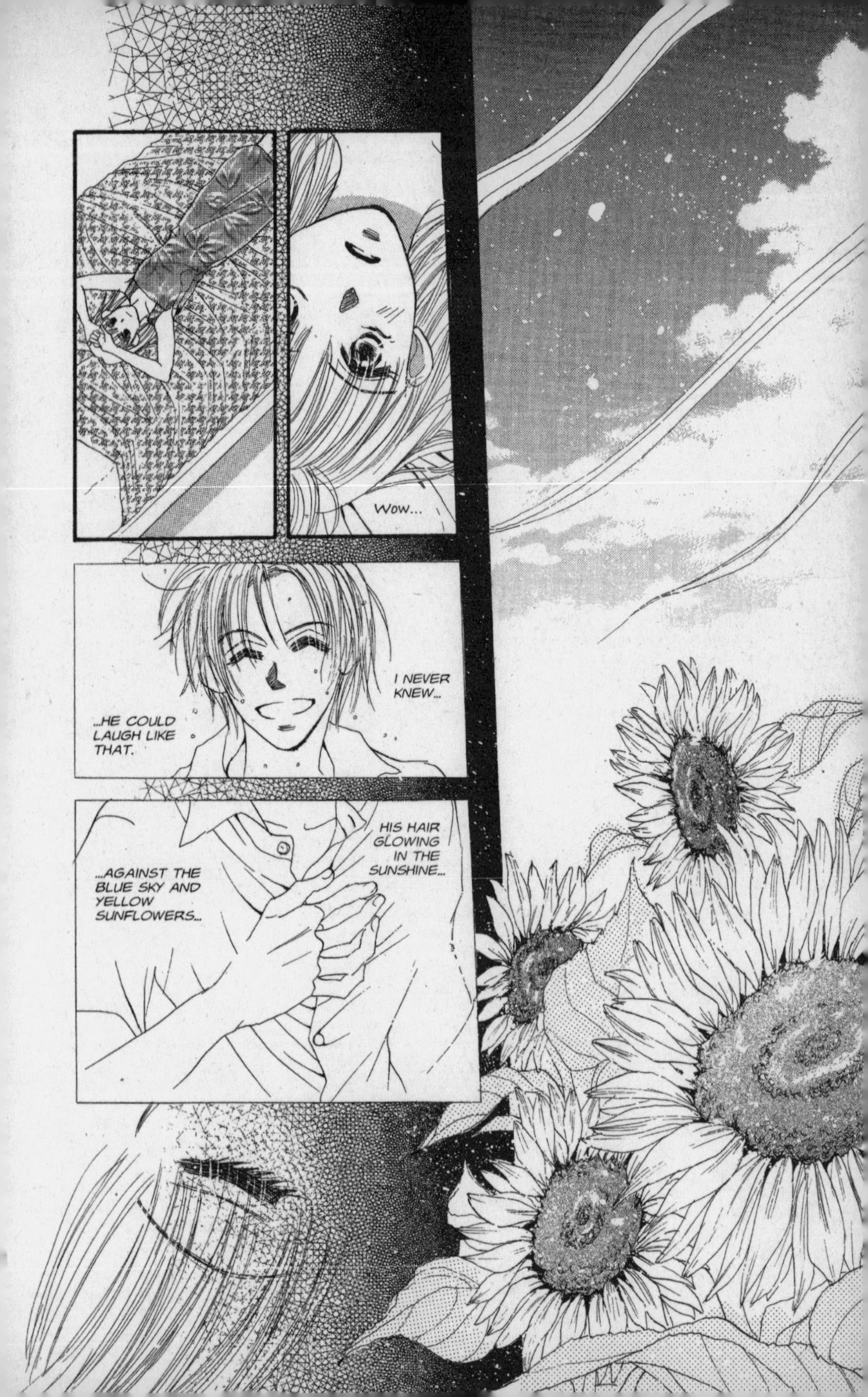
WOW...
I NEVER KNEW...
...HE COULD LAUGH LIKE THAT.
HIS HAIR GLOWING IN THE SUNSHINE...
...AGAINST THE BLUE SKY AND YELLOW SUNFLOWERS...

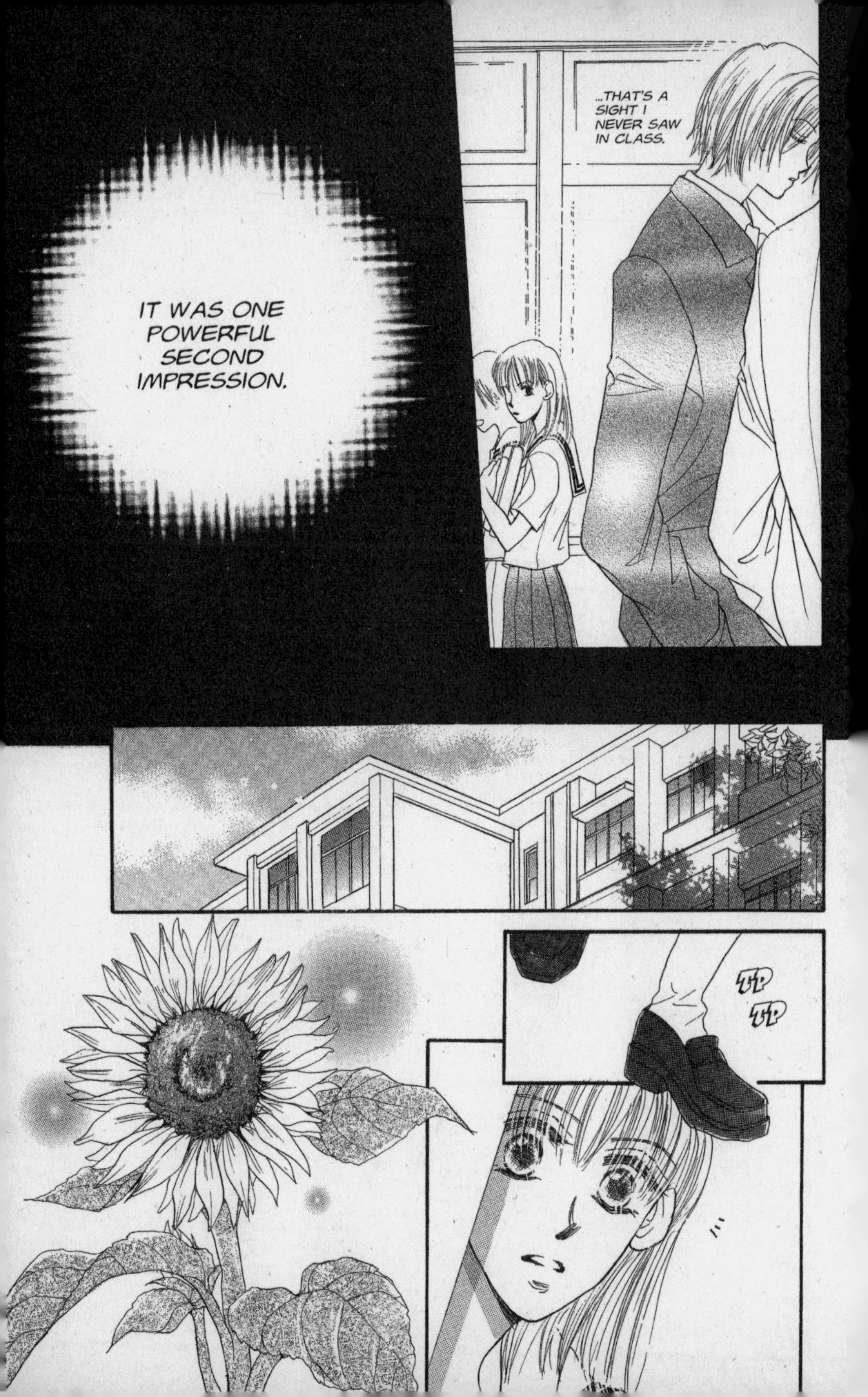
...THAT'S A SIGHT I NEVER SAW IN CLASS.
IT WAS ONE POWERFUL SECOND IMPRESSION.
TP TP

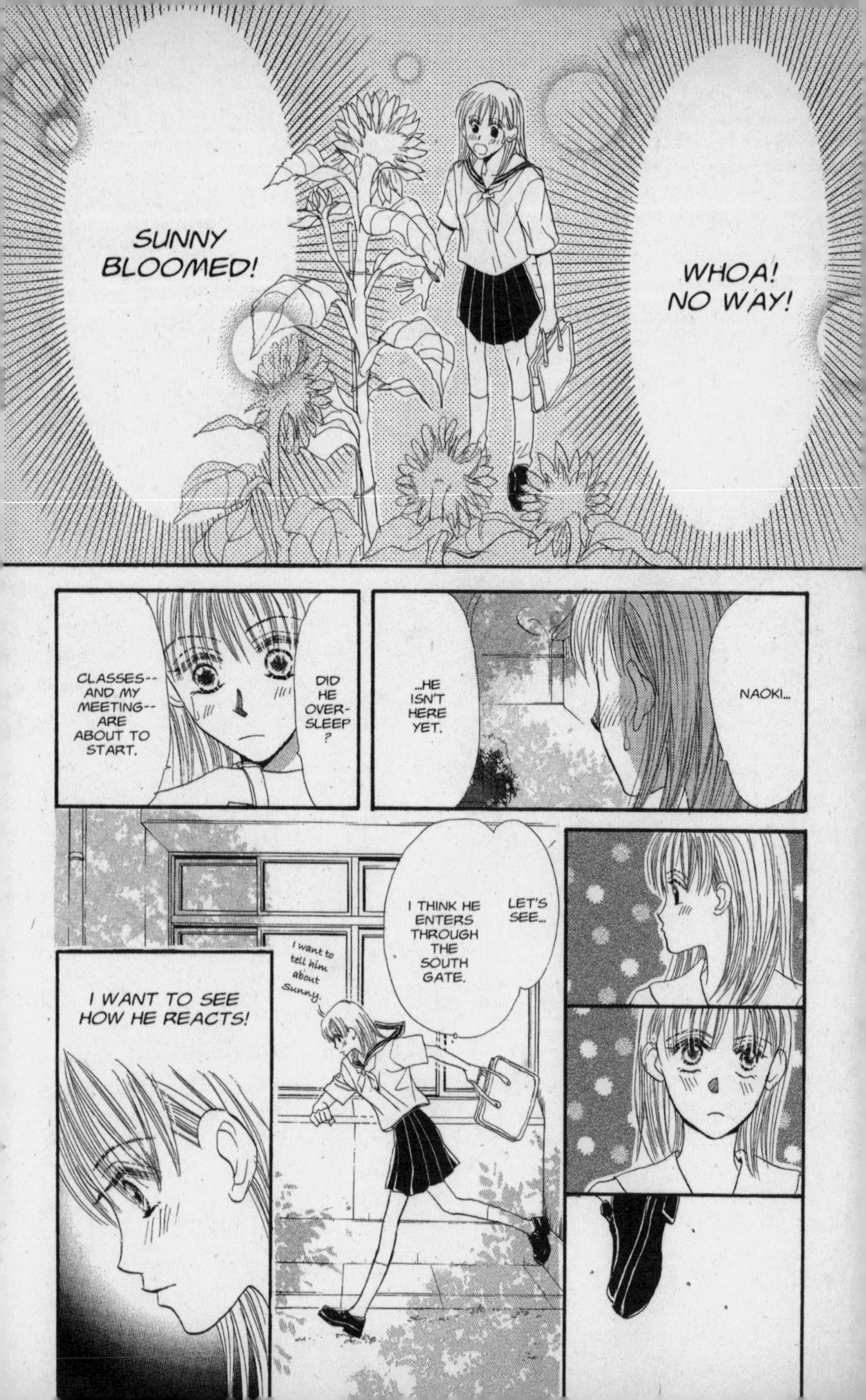
WHOA! NO WAY!
SUNNY BLOOMED!
NAOKI...
...HE ISN'T HERE YET.
DID HE OVERSLEEP?
CLASSES--AND MY MEETING--ARE ABOUT TO START.
LET'S SEE...
I THINK HE ENTERS THROUGH THE SOUTH GATE.
I want to tell him about Sunny.
I WANT TO SEE HOW HE REACTS!

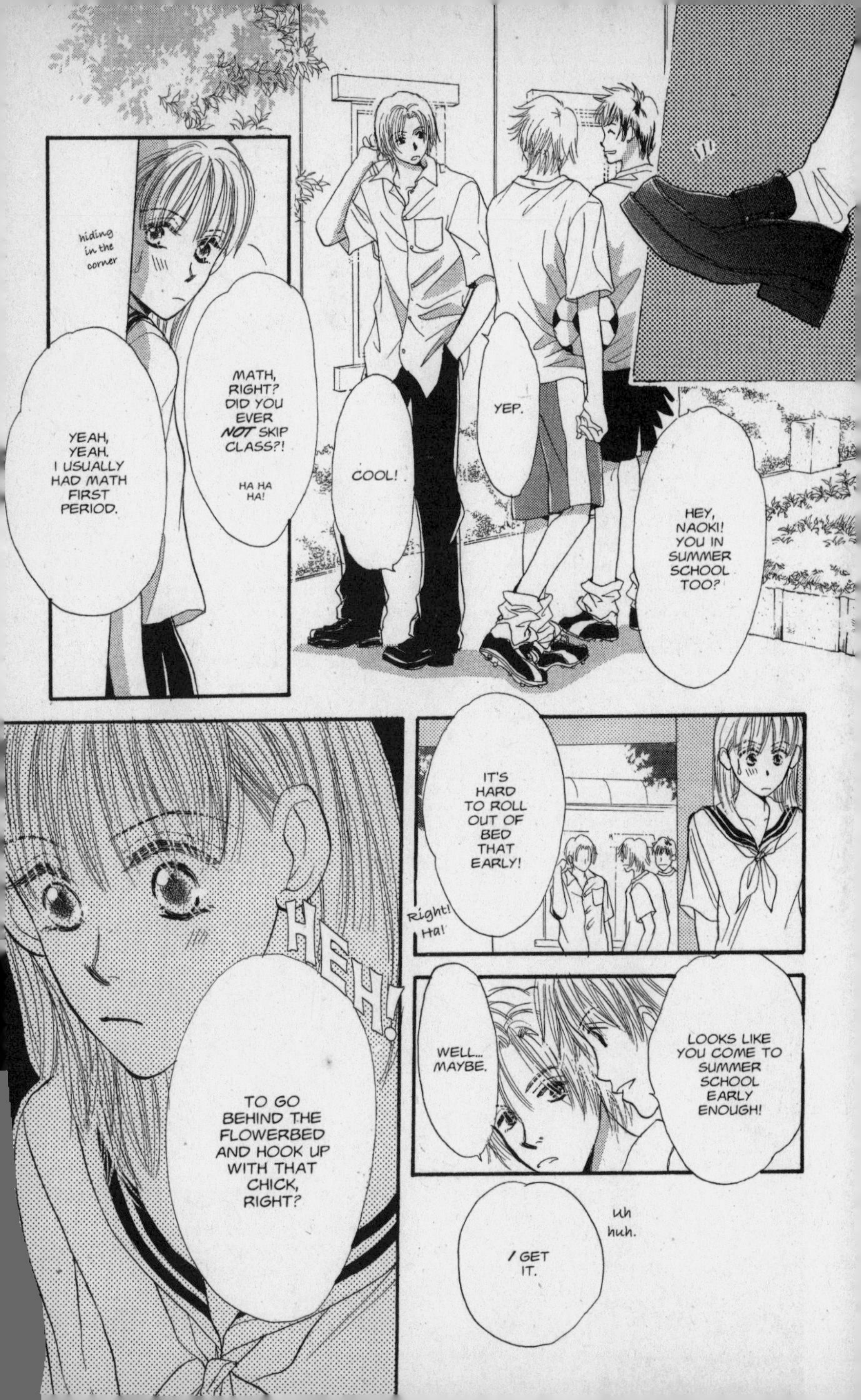
HEY, NAOKI! YOU IN SUMMER SCHOOL TOO?
YEP.
COOL!
MATH, RIGHT? DID YOU EVER NOT SKIP CLASS?!
HA HA HA!
hiding in the corner
YEAH, YEAH. I USUALLY HAD MATH FIRST PERIOD.
IT'S HARD TO ROLL OUT OF BED THAT EARLY!
Right! Ha!
LOOKS LIKE YOU COME TO SUMMER SCHOOL EARLY ENOUGH!
WELL... MAYBE.
Uh huh.
I GET IT.
HEH!
TO GO BEHIND THE FLOWERBED AND HOOK UP WITH THAT CHICK, RIGHT?

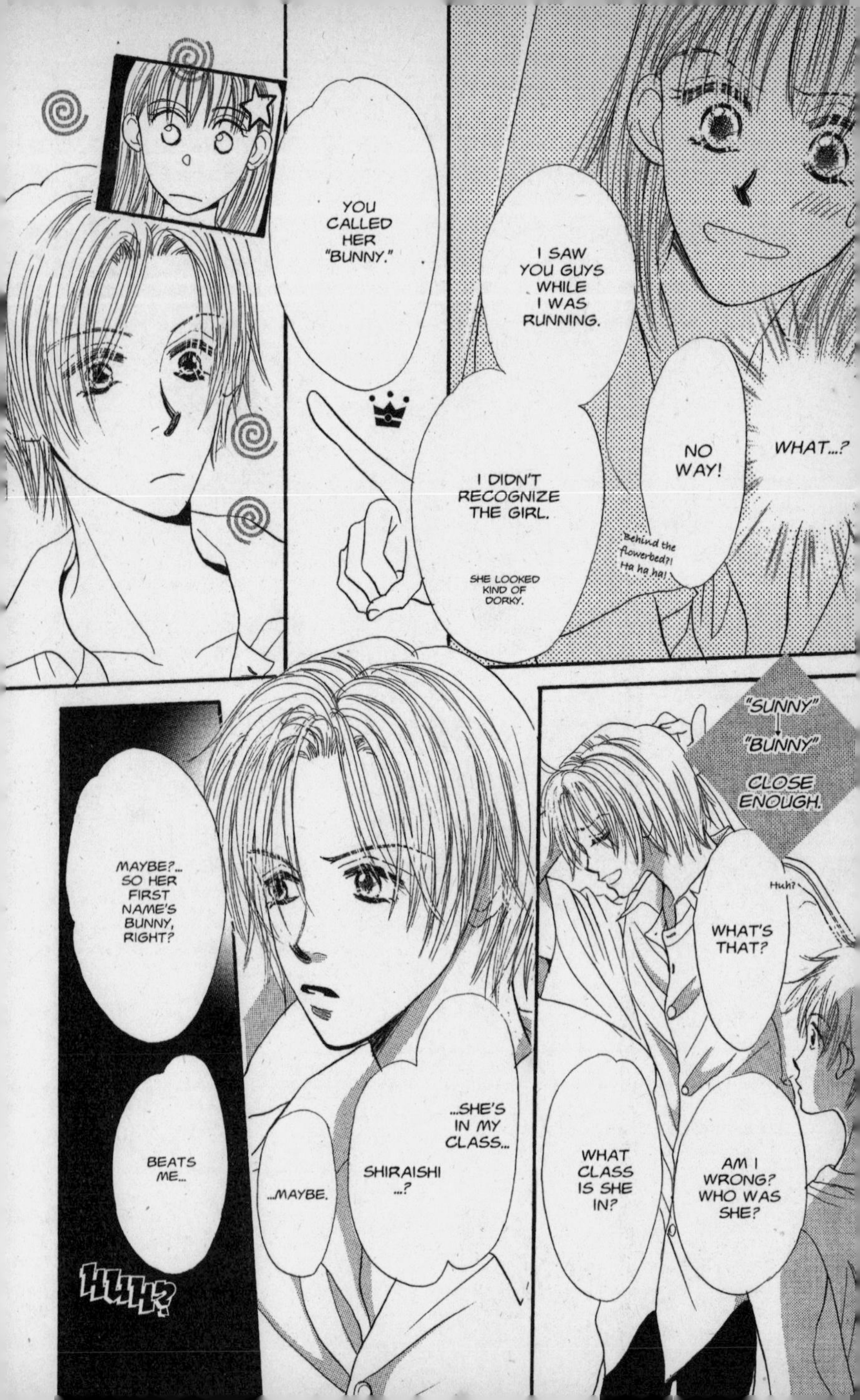
WHAT...?
NO WAY!
Behind the flowerbed?! Ha ha ha!
I SAW YOU GUYS WHILE I WAS RUNNING.
I DIDN'T RECOGNIZE THE GIRL.
SHE LOOKED KIND OF DORKY.
YOU CALLED HER "BUNNY."
"SUNNY" → "BUNNY" CLOSE ENOUGH.
Huh?
WHAT'S THAT?
AM I WRONG? WHO WAS SHE?
WHAT CLASS IS SHE IN?
...SHE'S IN MY CLASS...
SHIRAISHI ...?
...MAYBE.
MAYBE?... SO HER FIRST NAME'S BUNNY, RIGHT?
BEATS ME...
HUH?

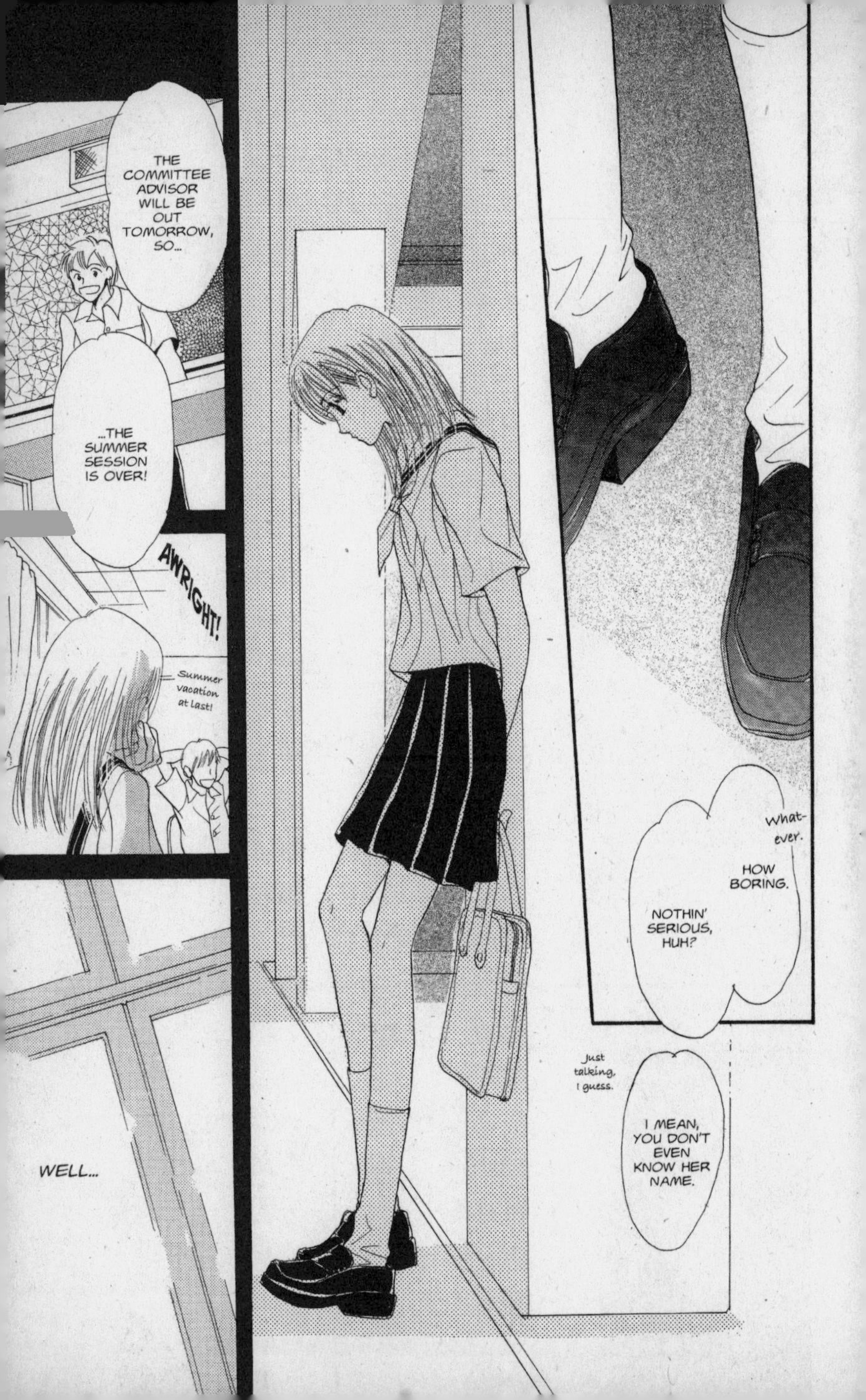
What-ever.
HOW BORING.
NOTHIN' SERIOUS, HUH?
Just talking, I guess.
I MEAN, YOU DON'T EVEN KNOW HER NAME.
THE COMMITTEE ADVISOR WILL BE OUT TOMORROW, SO...
...THE SUMMER SESSION IS OVER!
AWRIGHT!
Summer vacation at last!
WELL...

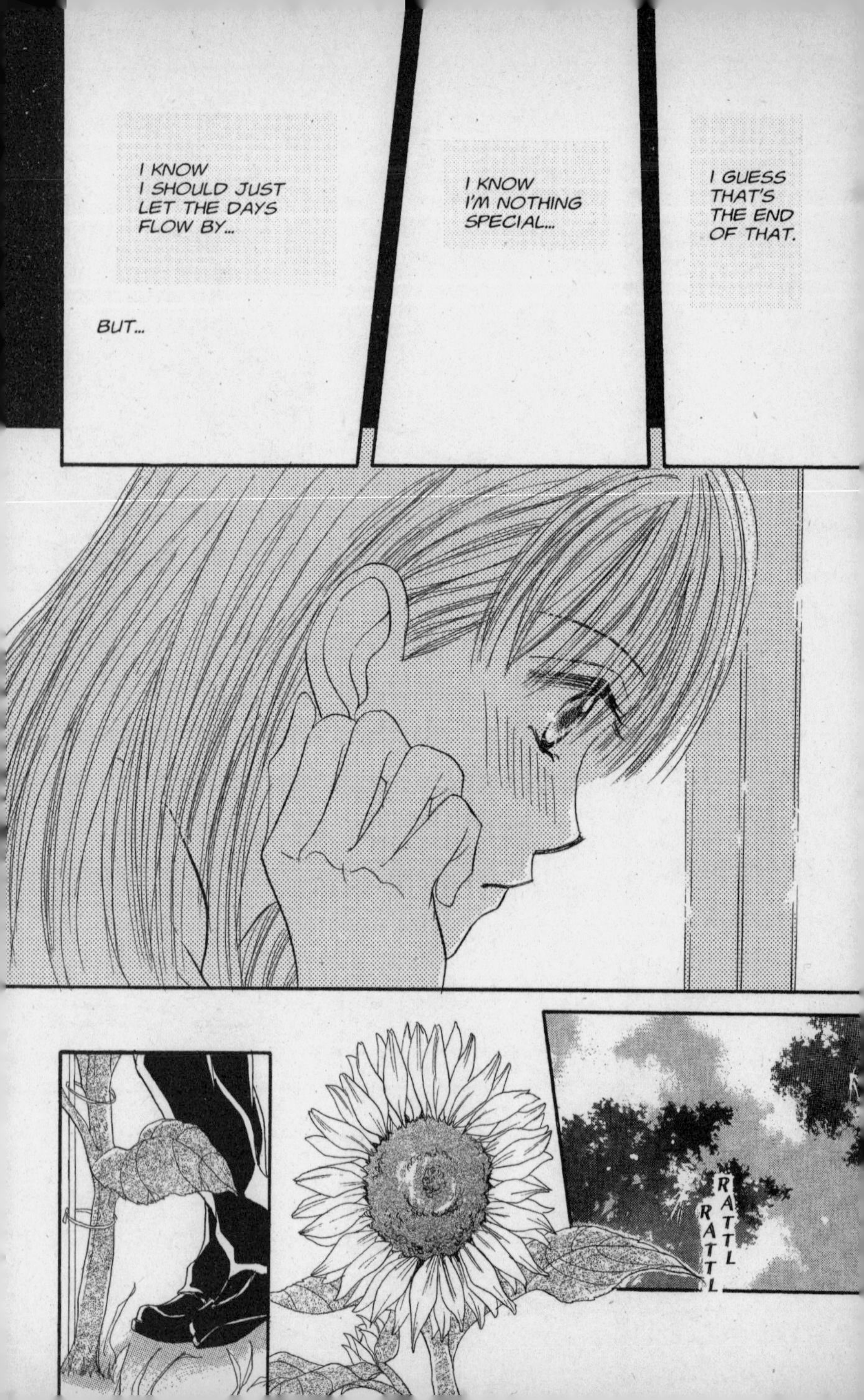
I GUESS THAT'S THE END OF THAT.
I KNOW I'M NOTHING SPECIAL...
I KNOW I SHOULD JUST LET THE DAYS FLOW BY...
BUT...
RATTL
RATTL

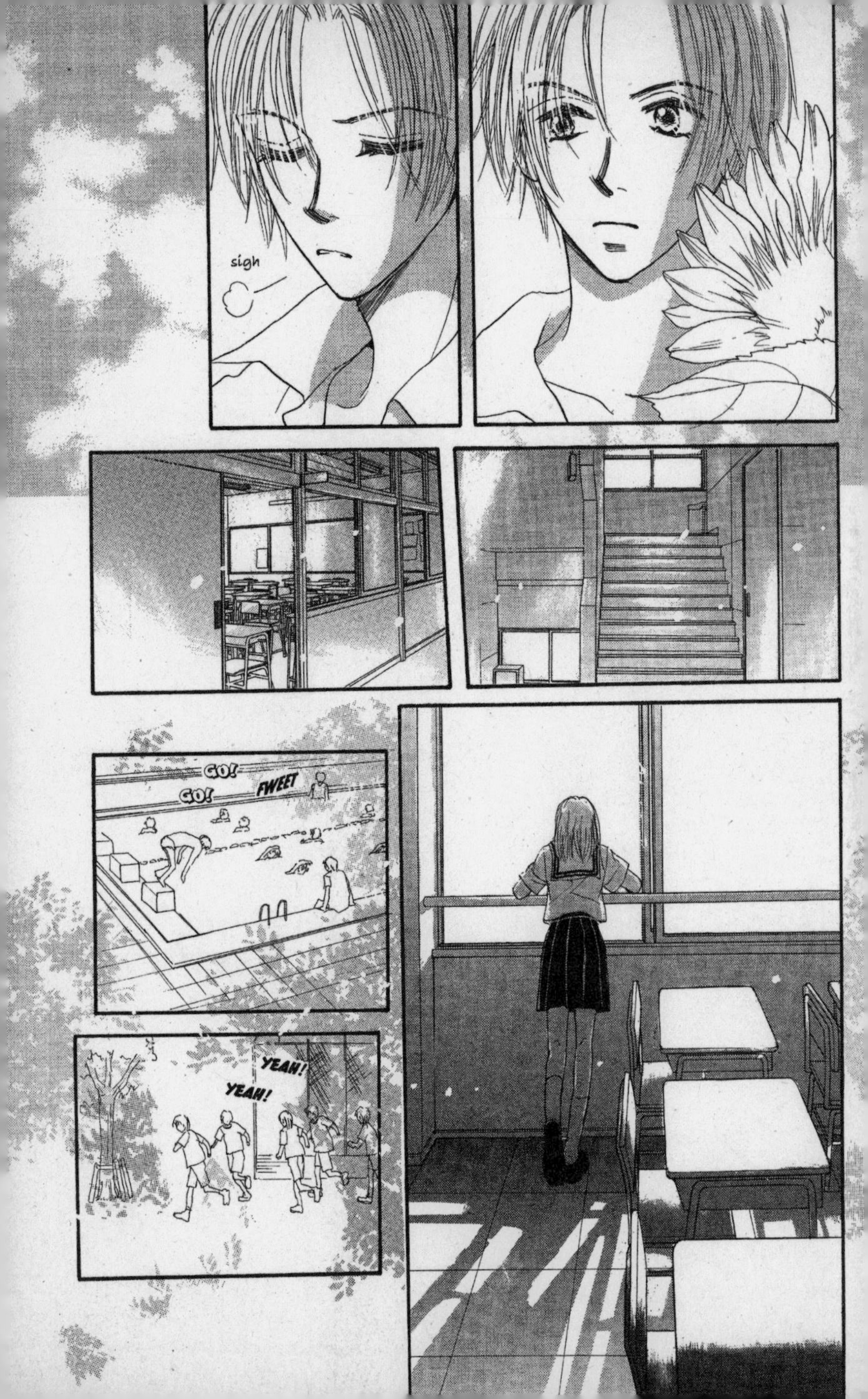
sigh
GO!
GO!
FWEET
YEAH!
YEAH!

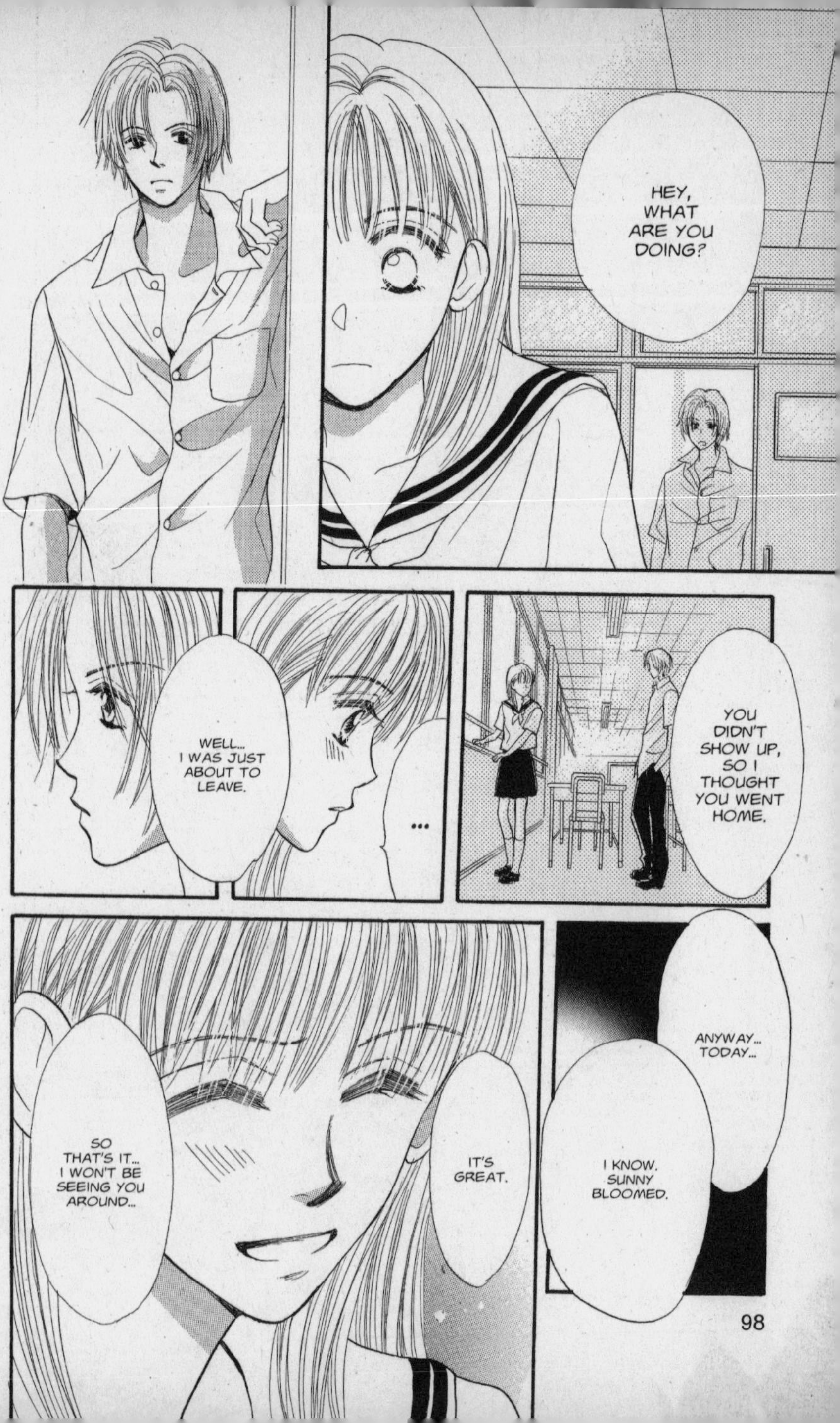
HEY, WHAT ARE YOU DOING?
YOU DIDN'T SHOW UP, SO I THOUGHT YOU WENT HOME.
...
WELL... I WAS JUST ABOUT TO LEAVE.
ANYWAY... TODAY...
I KNOW. SUNNY BLOOMED.
IT'S GREAT.
SO THAT'S IT... I WON'T BE SEEING YOU AROUND...

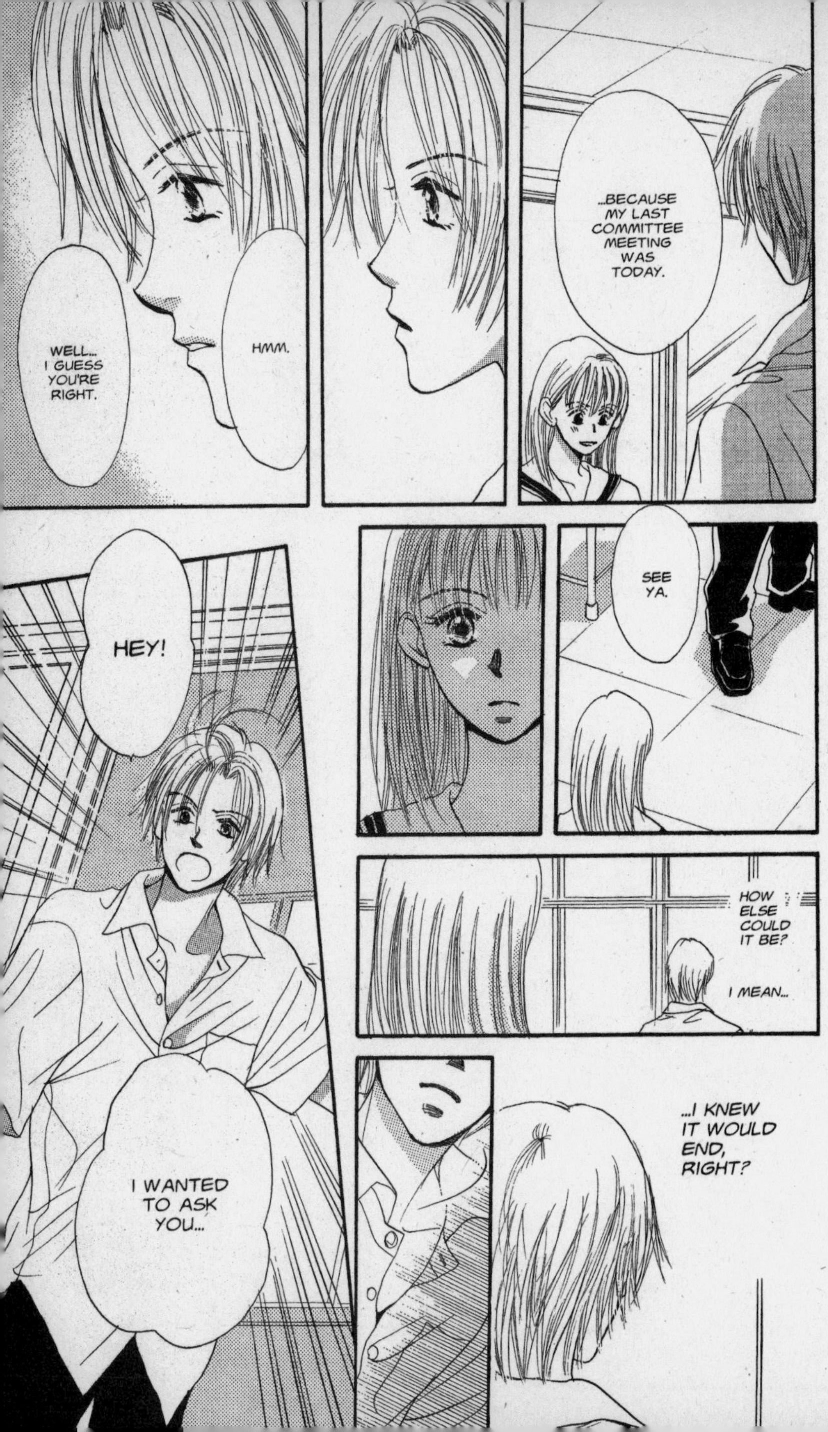
...BECAUSE MY LAST COMMITTEE MEETING WAS TODAY.
HMM.
WELL... I GUESS YOU'RE RIGHT.
SEE YA.
HOW ELSE COULD IT BE?
I MEAN...
...I KNEW IT WOULD END, RIGHT?
HEY!
I WANTED TO ASK YOU...

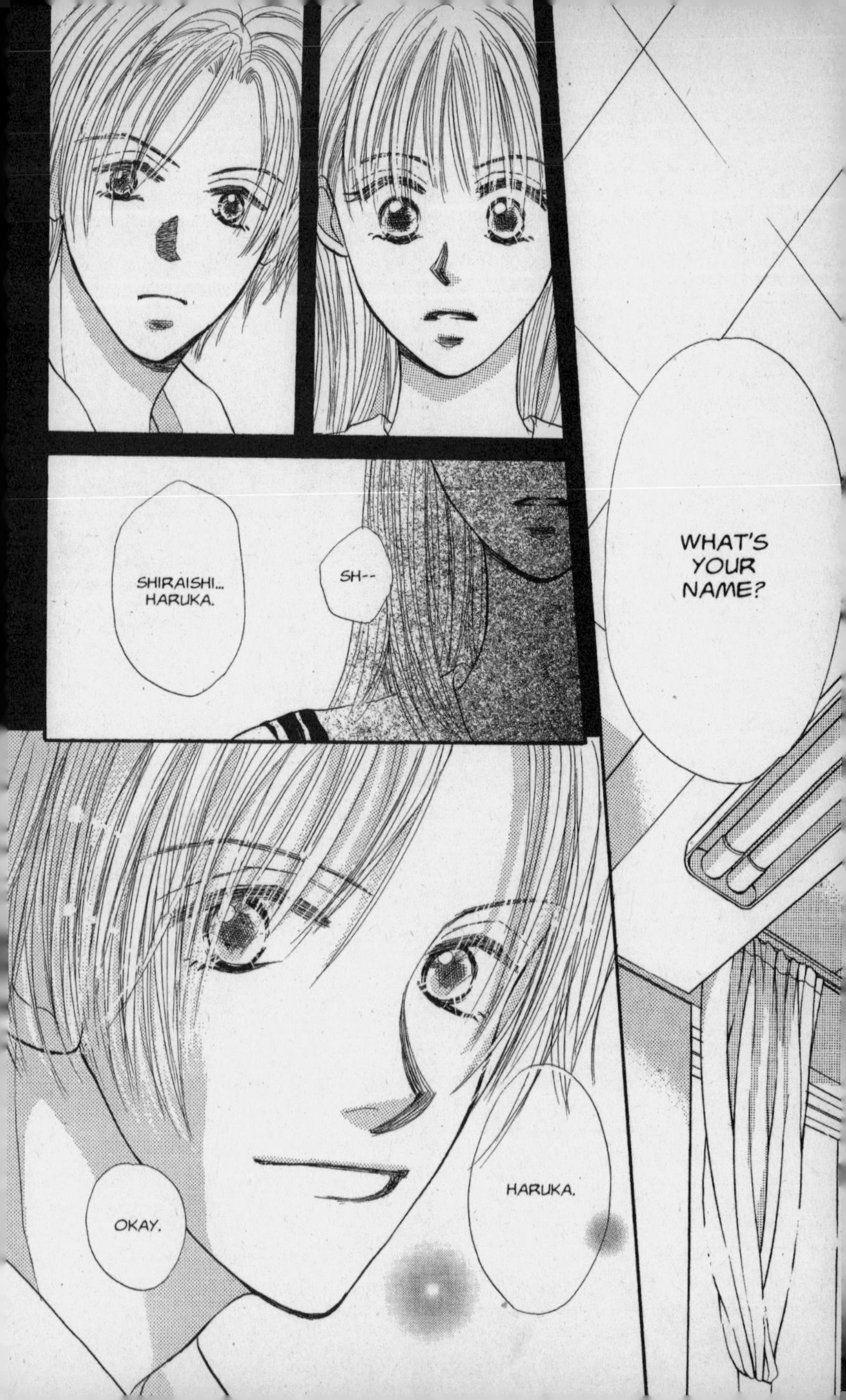
WHAT'S YOUR NAME?
SH--
SHIRAISHI... HARUKA.
HARUKA.
OKAY.

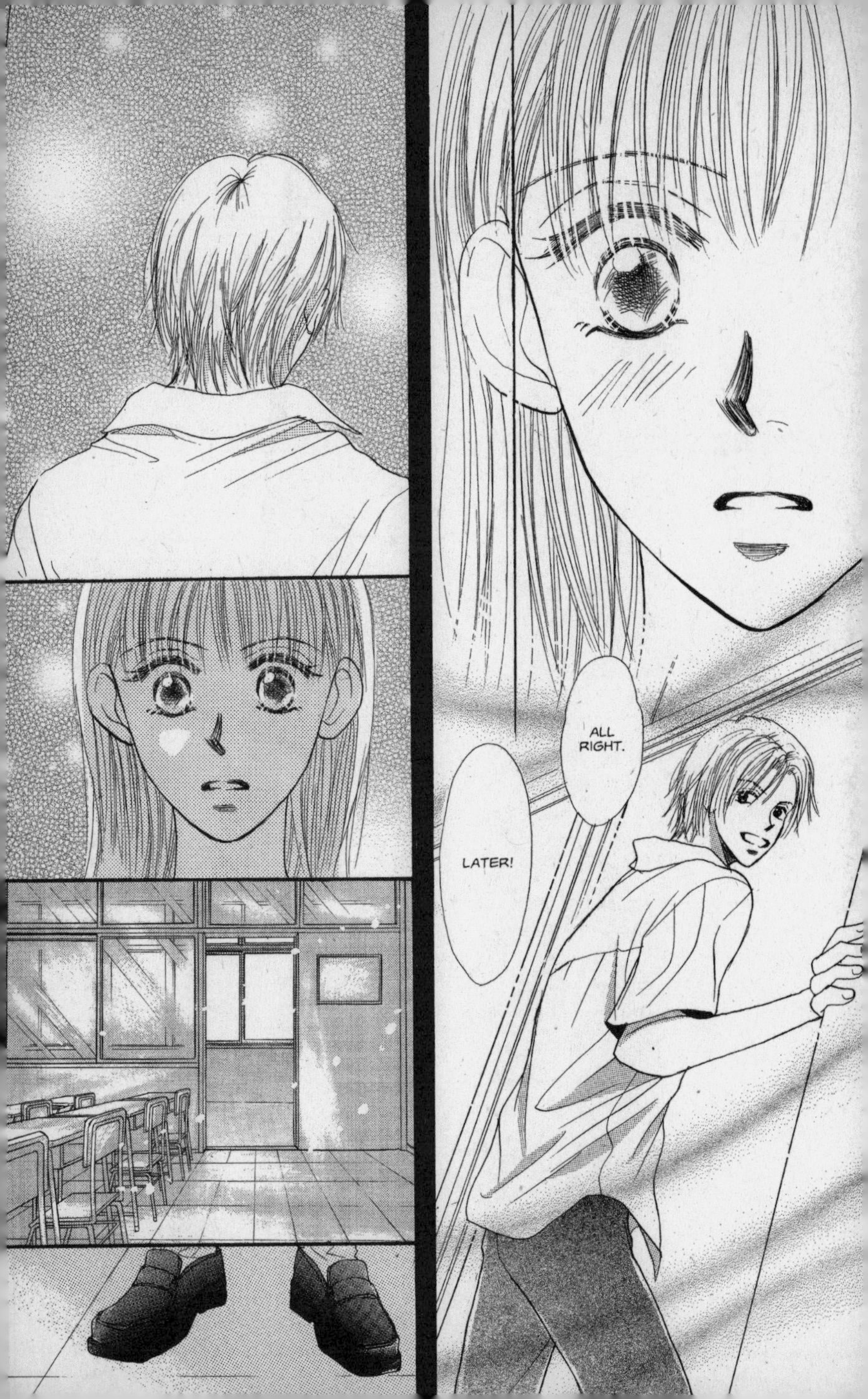
ALL RIGHT.
LATER!

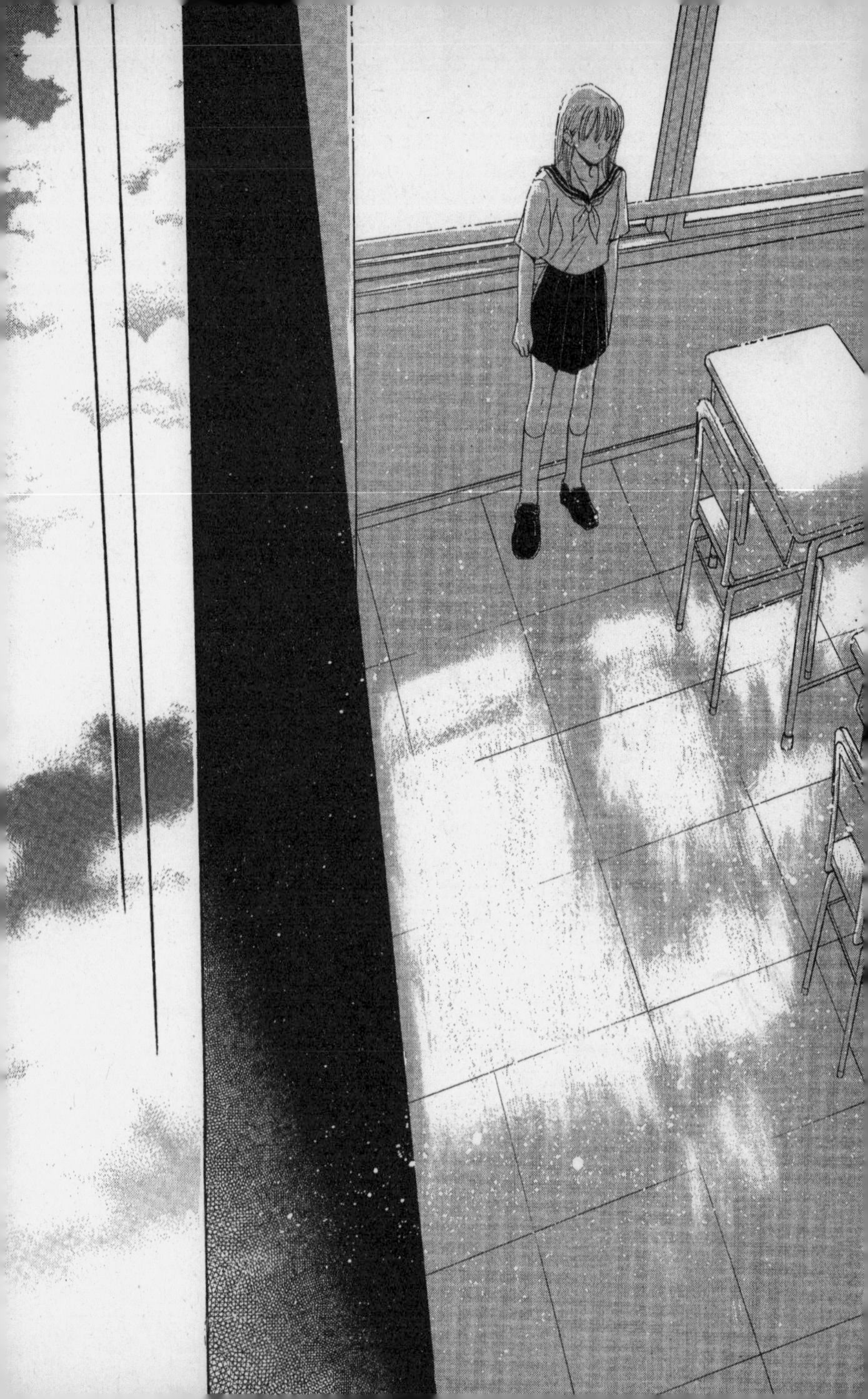

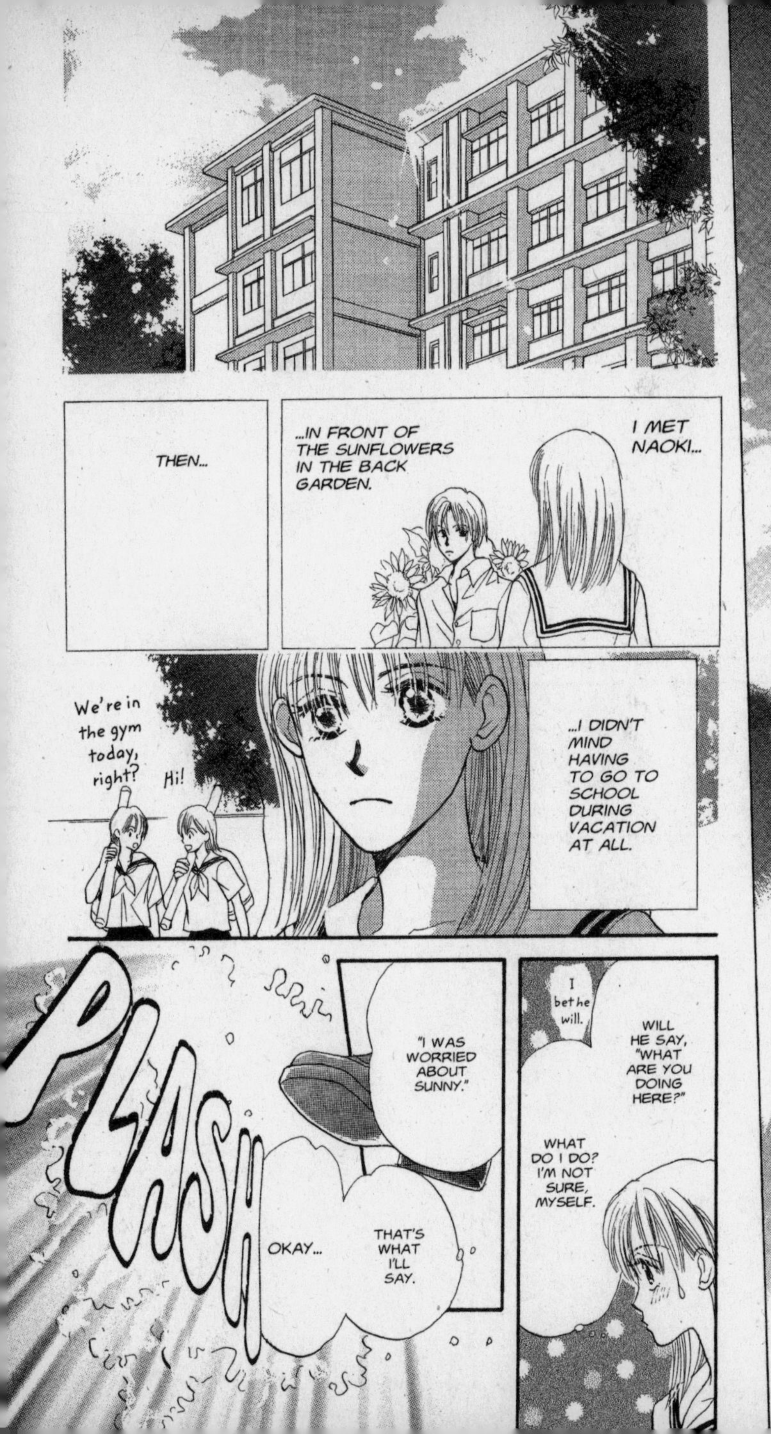
I MET NAOKI...
...IN FRONT OF THE SUNFLOWERS IN THE BACK GARDEN.
THEN...
...I DIDN'T MIND HAVING TO GO TO SCHOOL DURING VACATION AT ALL.
We're in the gym today, right?
Hi!
WILL HE SAY, "WHAT ARE YOU DOING HERE?"
I bet he will.
WHAT DO I DO? I'M NOT SURE, MYSELF.
"I WAS WORRIED ABOUT SUNNY."
THAT'S WHAT I'LL SAY.
OKAY...
PLASH

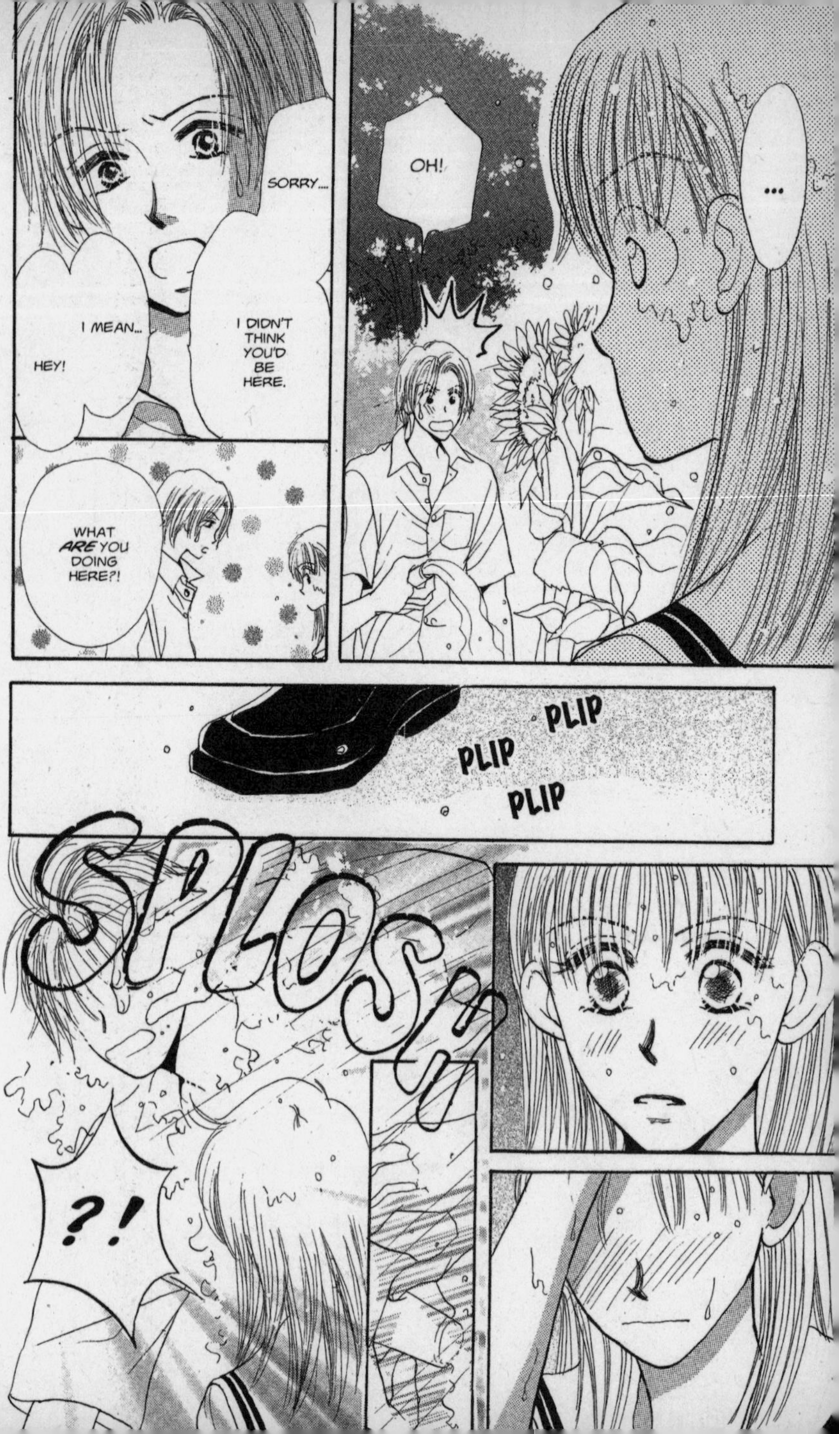
...
OH!
SORRY....
I DIDN'T THINK YOU'D BE HERE.
I MEAN...
HEY!
WHAT ARE YOU DOING HERE?!
PLIP
PLIP
PLIP
SPLOSH
?!

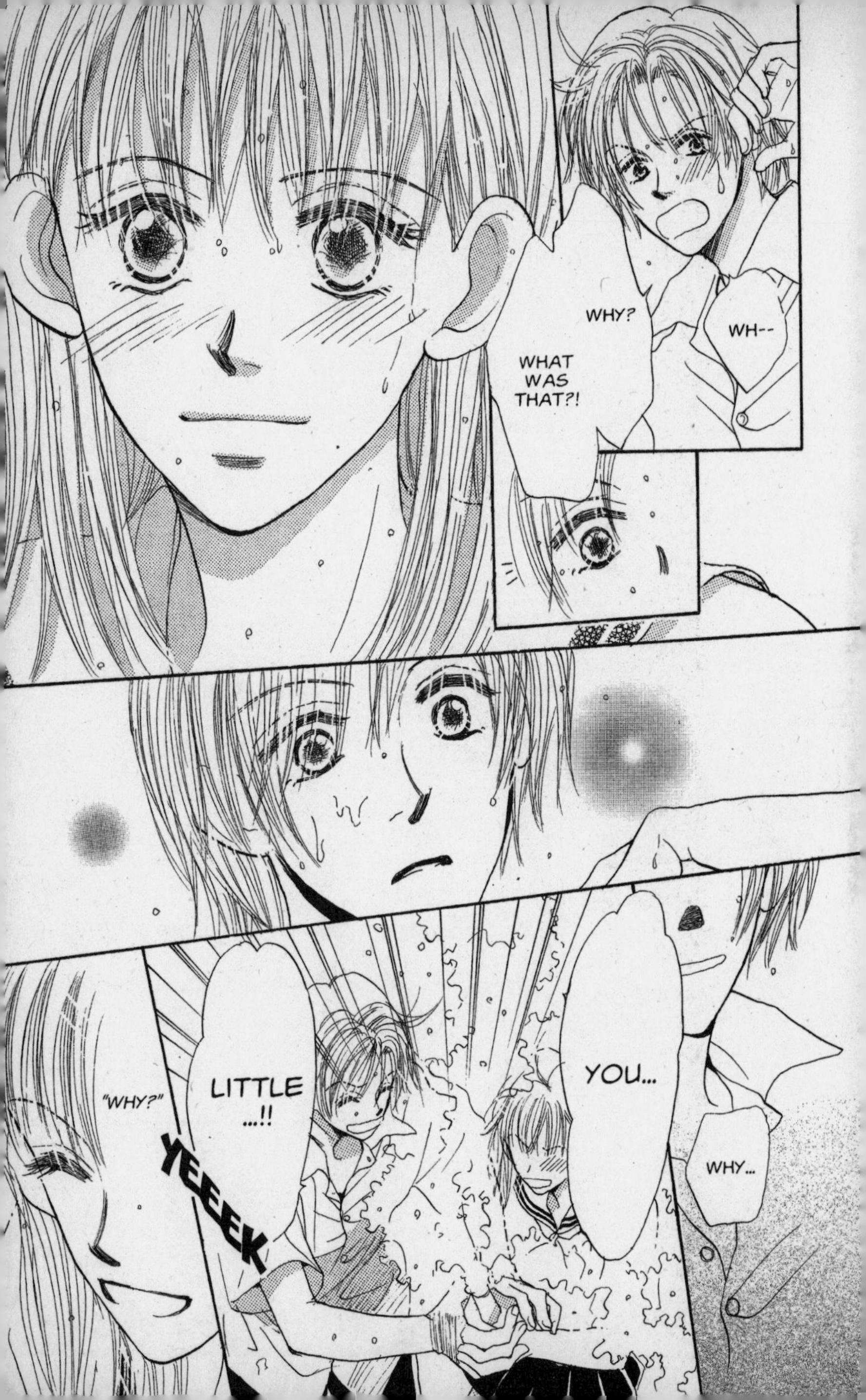
WH--
WHY?
WHAT WAS THAT?!
WHY...
YOU...
LITTLE ...!!
"WHY?"
YEEEK

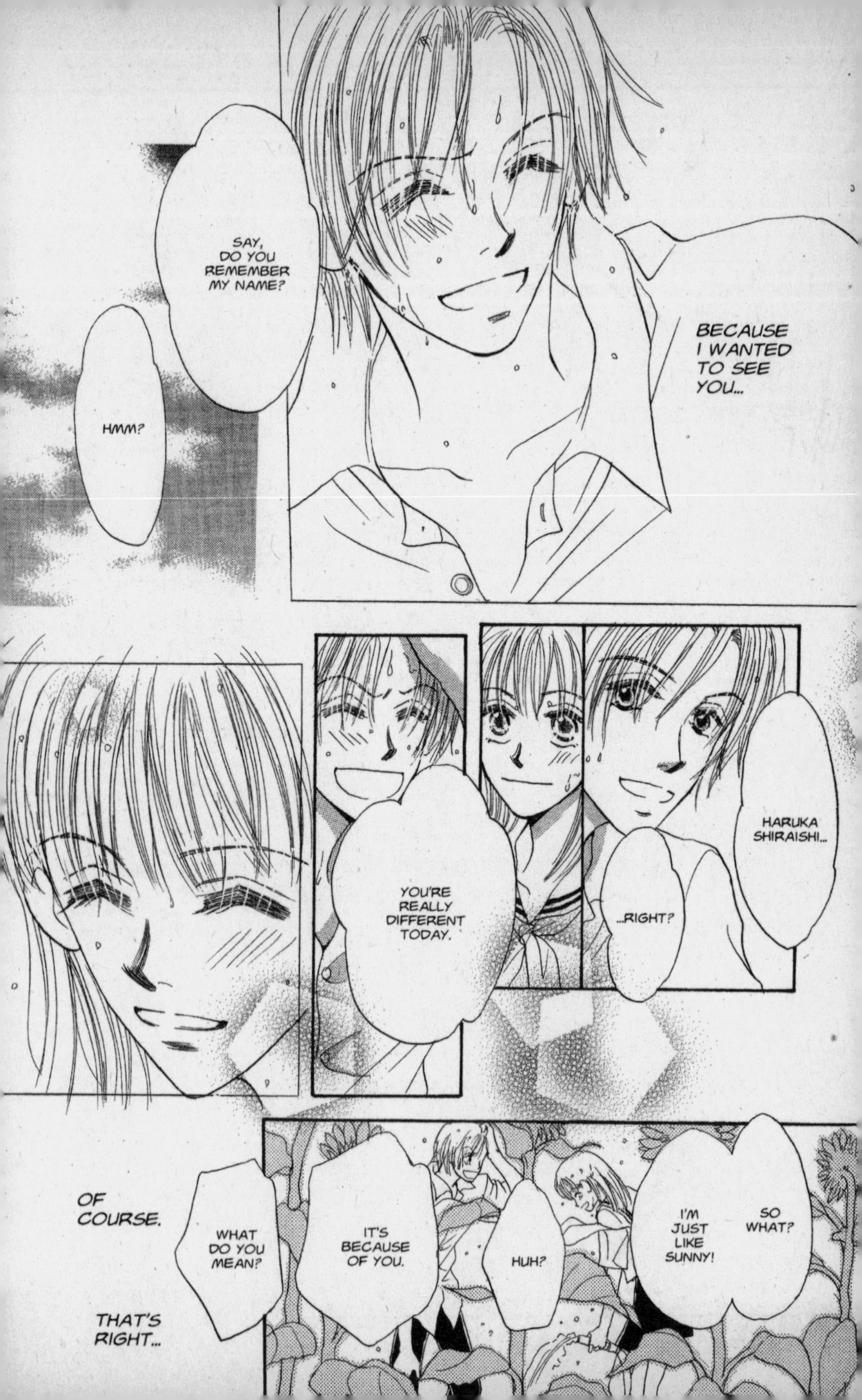
BECAUSE I WANTED TO SEE YOU...
SAY, DO YOU REMEMBER MY NAME?
HMM?
HARUKA SHIRAISHI...
...RIGHT?
YOU'RE REALLY DIFFERENT TODAY.
SO WHAT?
I'M JUST LIKE SUNNY!
HUH?
IT'S BECAUSE OF YOU.
WHAT DO YOU MEAN?
OF COURSE.
THAT'S RIGHT...

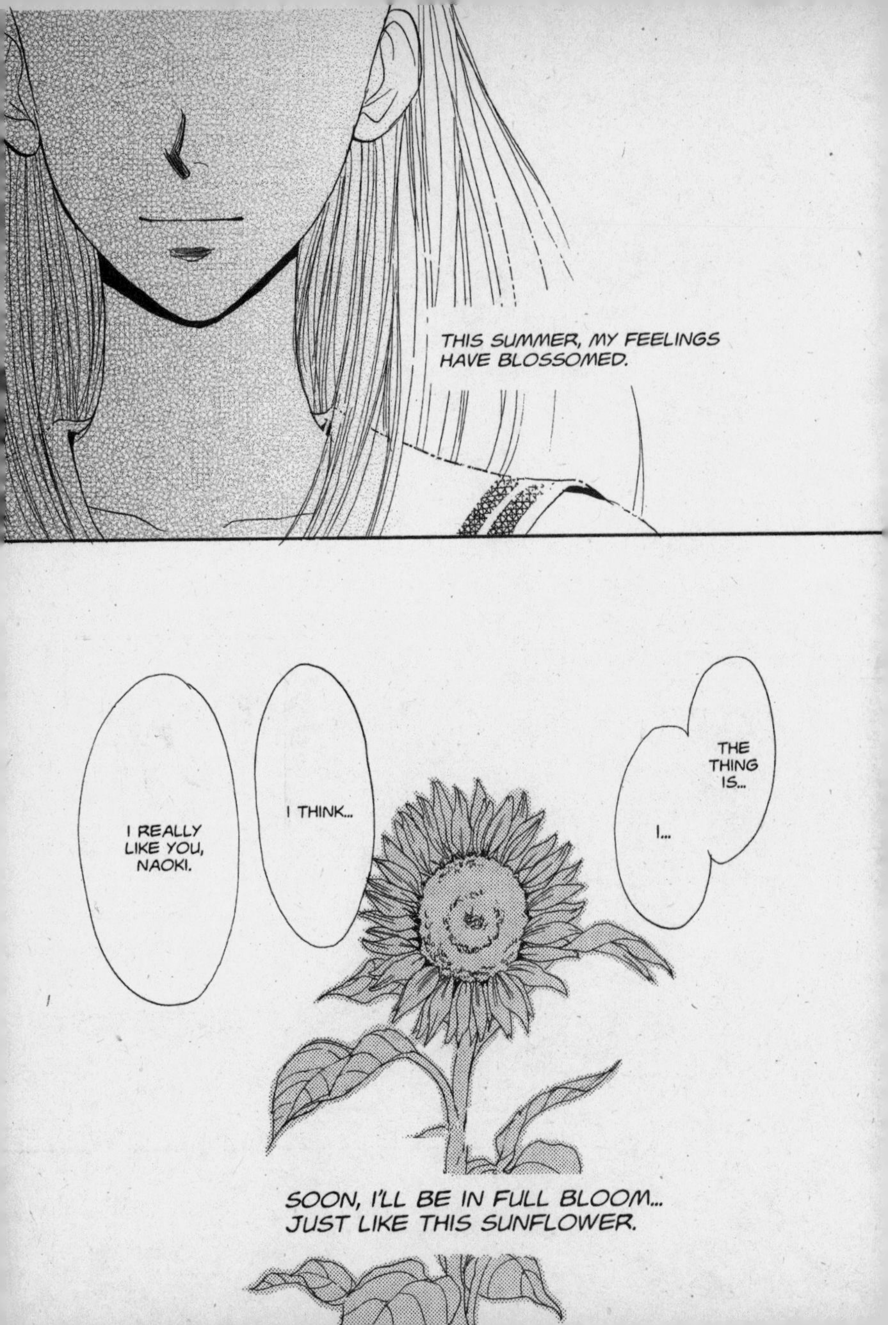
THIS SUMMER, MY FEELINGS HAVE BLOSSOMED.
THE THING IS...
I...
I THINK...
I REALLY LIKE YOU, NAOKI.
SOON, I'LL BE IN FULL BLOOM... JUST LIKE THIS SUNFLOWER.

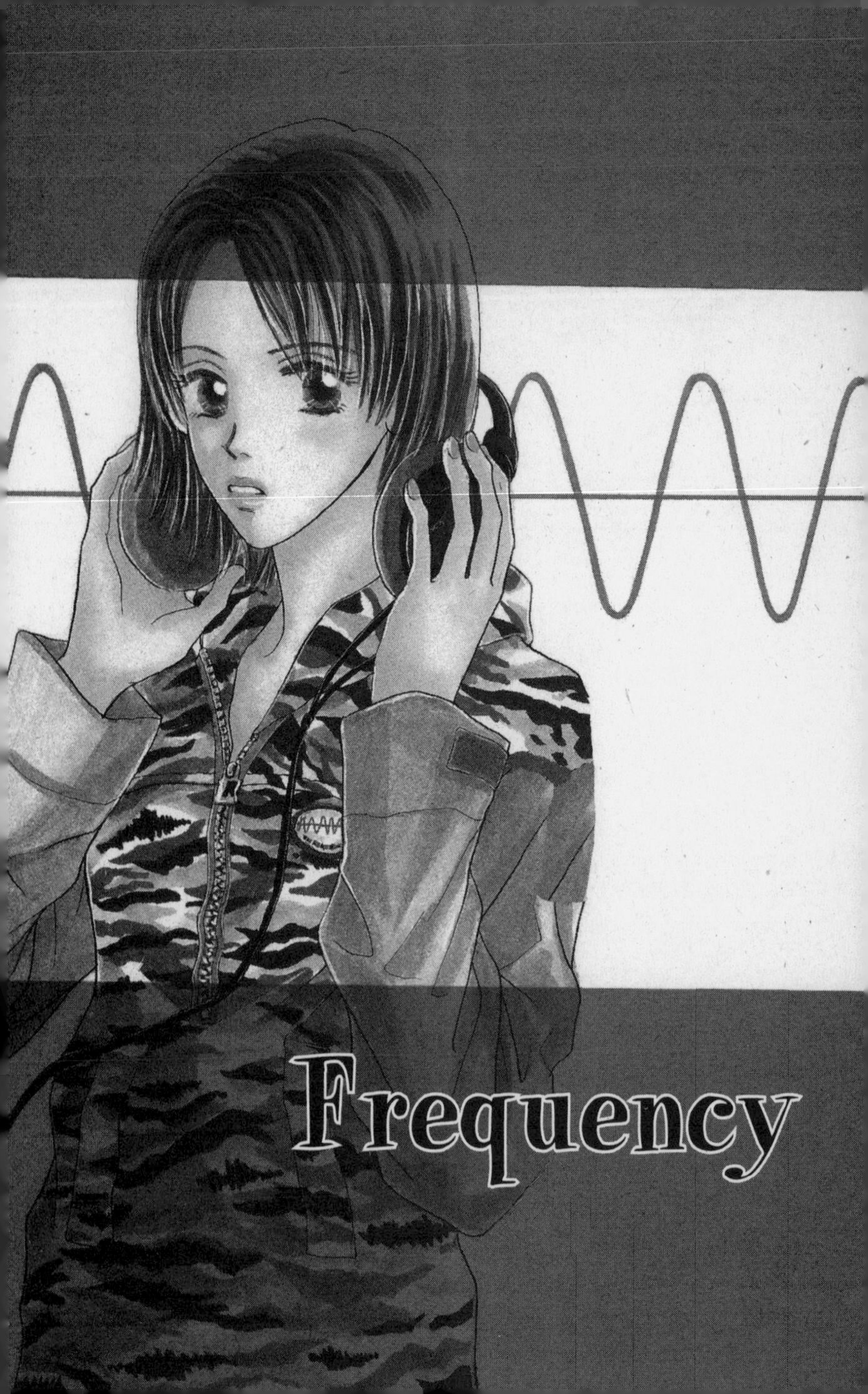
Frequency

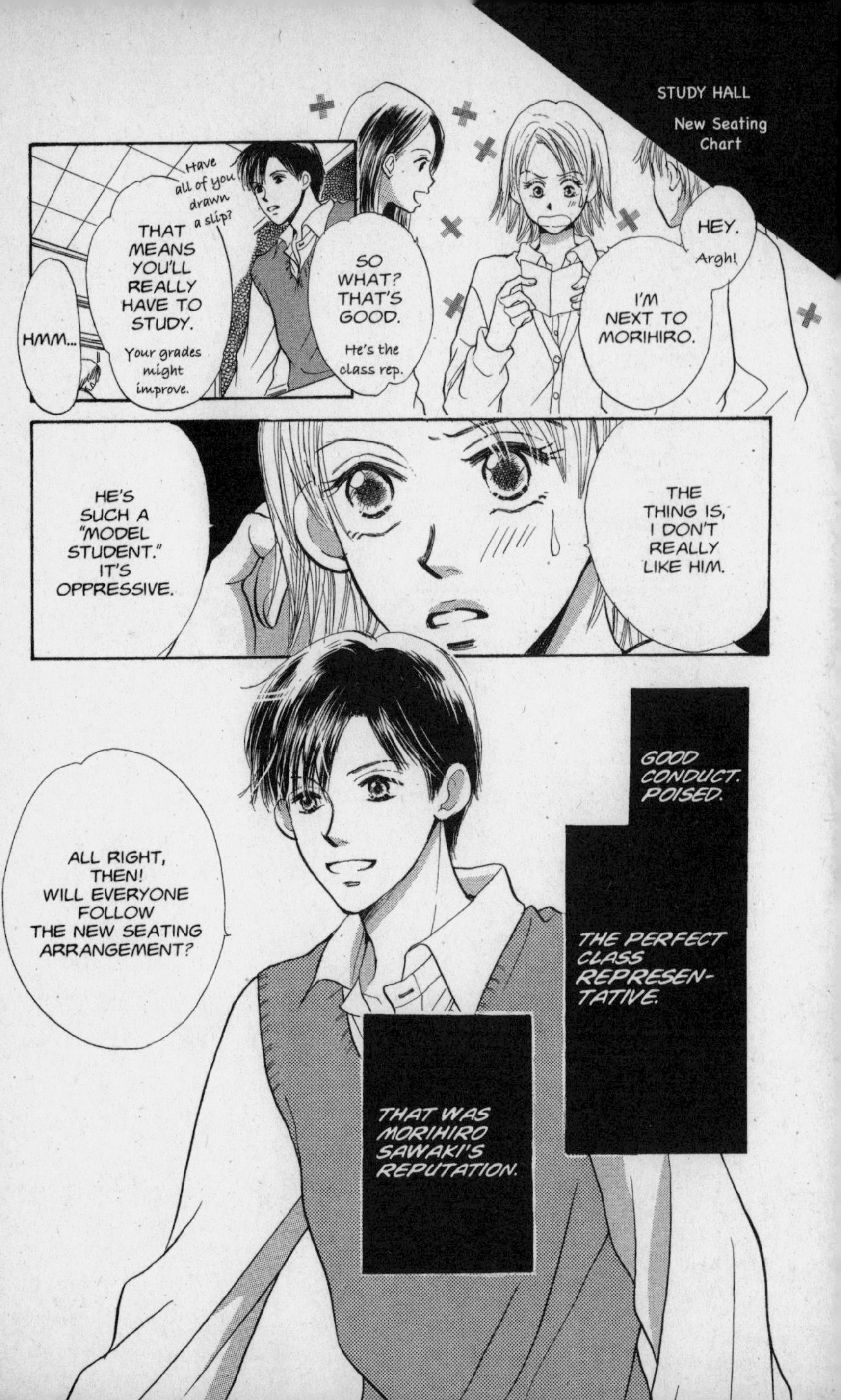
STUDY HALL
New Seating Chart
HEY.
Argh!
I'M NEXT TO MORIHIRO.
SO WHAT? THAT'S GOOD.
He's the class rep.
Have all of you drawn a slip?
THAT MEANS YOU'LL REALLY HAVE TO STUDY.
Your grades might improve.
HMM...
THE THING IS, I DON'T REALLY LIKE HIM.
HE'S SUCH A "MODEL STUDENT." IT'S OPPRESSIVE.
GOOD CONDUCT. POISED.
THE PERFECT CLASS REPRESEN-TATIVE.
ALL RIGHT, THEN! WILL EVERYONE FOLLOW THE NEW SEATING ARRANGEMENT?
THAT WAS MORIHIRO SAWAKI'S REPUTATION.

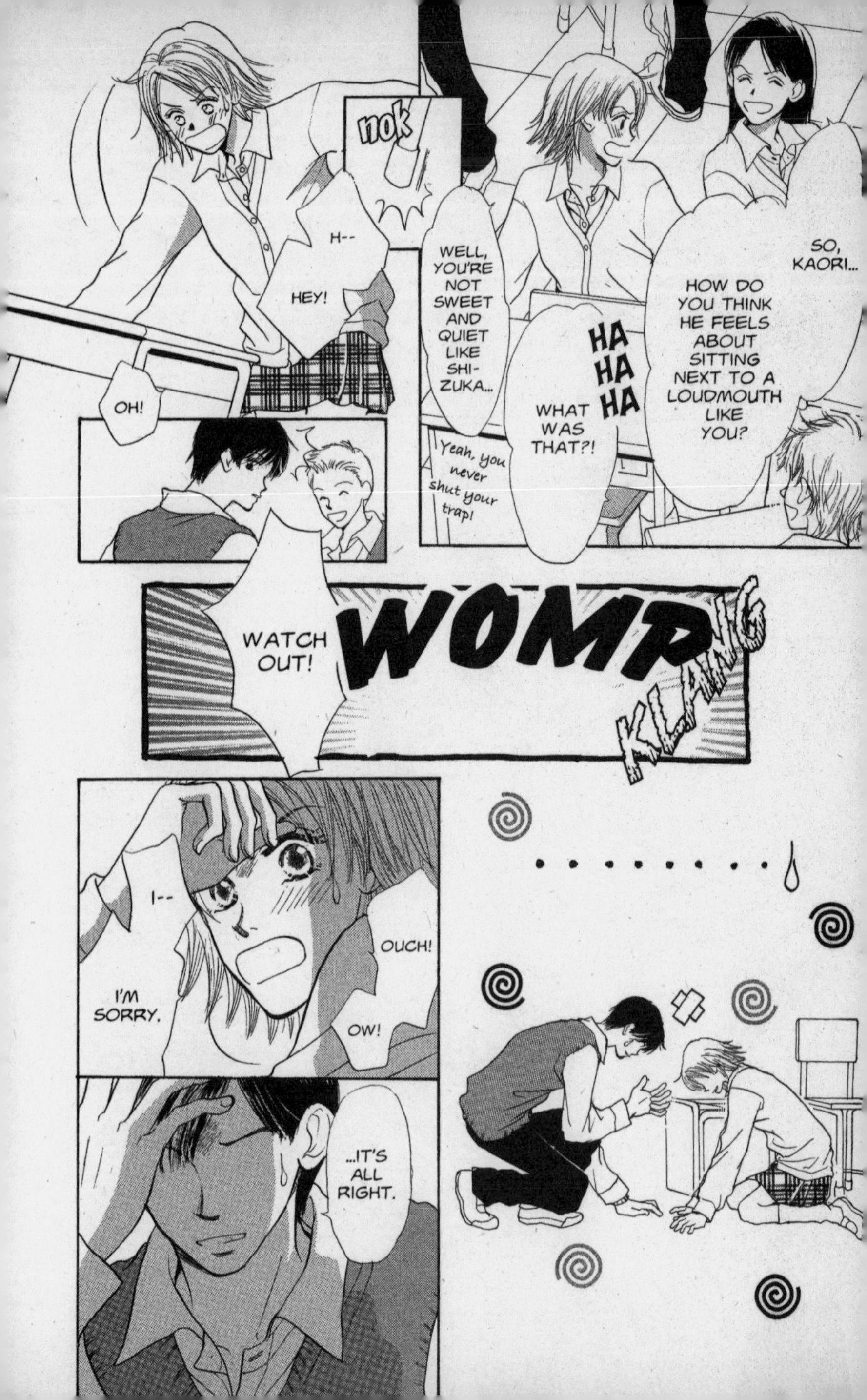
SO, KAORI...
HOW DO YOU THINK HE FEELS ABOUT SITTING NEXT TO A LOUDMOUTH LIKE YOU?
HA HA HA
WHAT WAS THAT?!
WELL, YOU'RE NOT SWEET AND QUIET LIKE SHI-ZUKA...
Yeah, you never shut your trap!
nok
H--
HEY!
OH!
WATCH OUT!
WOMP
KLANG
....
OUCH!
I--
OW!
I'M SORRY.
...IT'S ALL RIGHT.

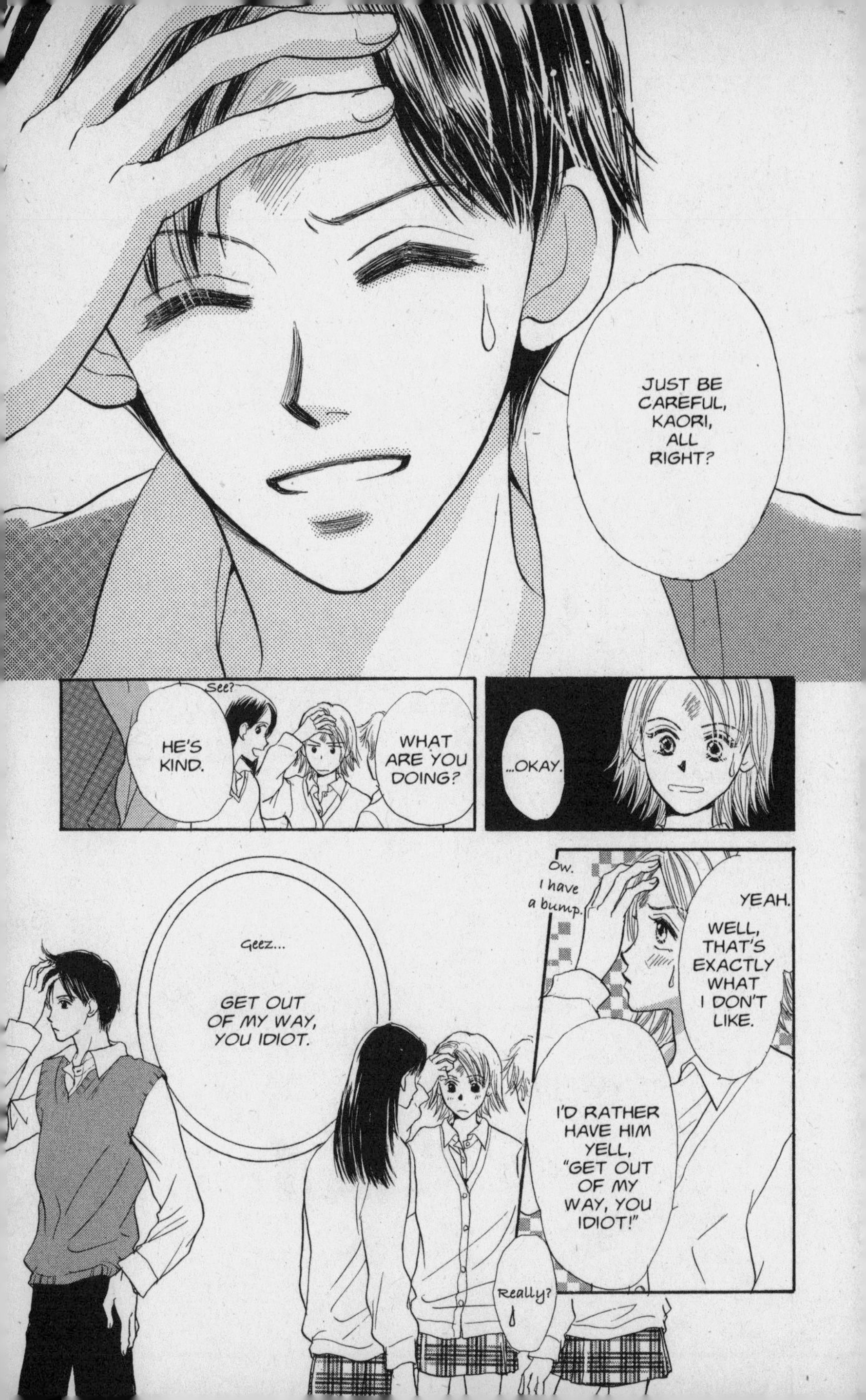
JUST BE CAREFUL, KAORI, ALL RIGHT?
...OKAY.
WHAT ARE YOU DOING?
See?
HE'S KIND.
YEAH.
WELL, THAT'S EXACTLY WHAT I DON'T LIKE.
Ow. I have a bump.
I'D RATHER HAVE HIM YELL, "GET OUT OF MY WAY, YOU IDIOT!"
Geez...
GET OUT OF MY WAY, YOU IDIOT.
Really?

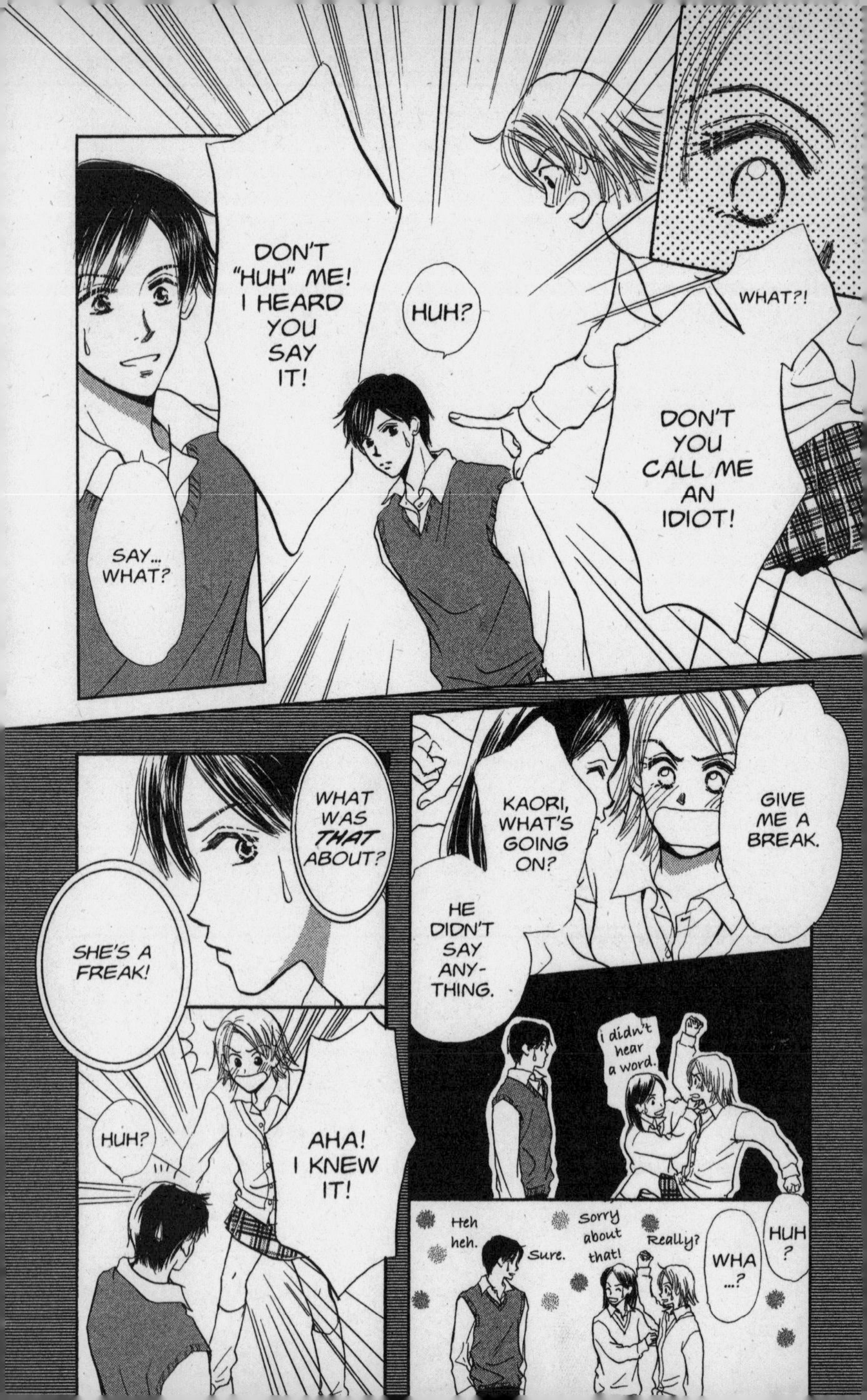
WHAT?!
DON'T YOU CALL ME AN IDIOT!
HUH?
DON'T "HUH" ME! I HEARD YOU SAY IT!
SAY... WHAT?
GIVE ME A BREAK.
KAORI, WHAT'S GOING ON?
HE DIDN'T SAY ANY-THING.
WHAT WAS *THAT* ABOUT?
SHE'S A FREAK!
I didn't hear a word.
AHA! I KNEW IT!
HUH?
HUH?
WHA ...?
Really?
Sorry about that!
Sure.
Heh heh.

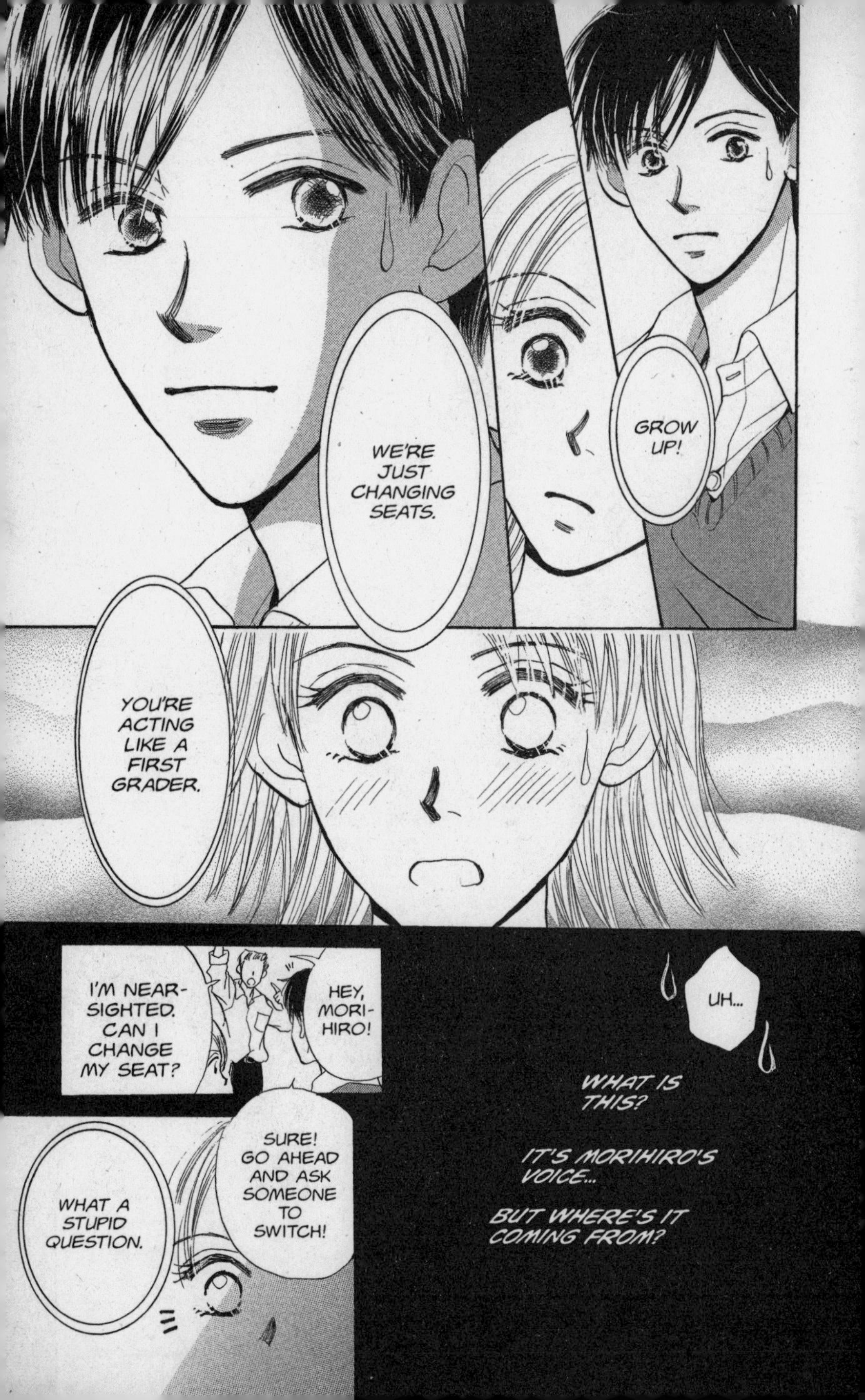
GROW UP!
WE'RE JUST CHANGING SEATS.
YOU'RE ACTING LIKE A FIRST GRADER.
UH...
WHAT IS THIS?
IT'S MORIHIRO'S VOICE...
BUT WHERE'S IT COMING FROM?
HEY, MORIHIRO!
I'M NEAR-SIGHTED. CAN I CHANGE MY SEAT?
SURE! GO AHEAD AND ASK SOMEONE TO SWITCH!
WHAT A STUPID QUESTION.

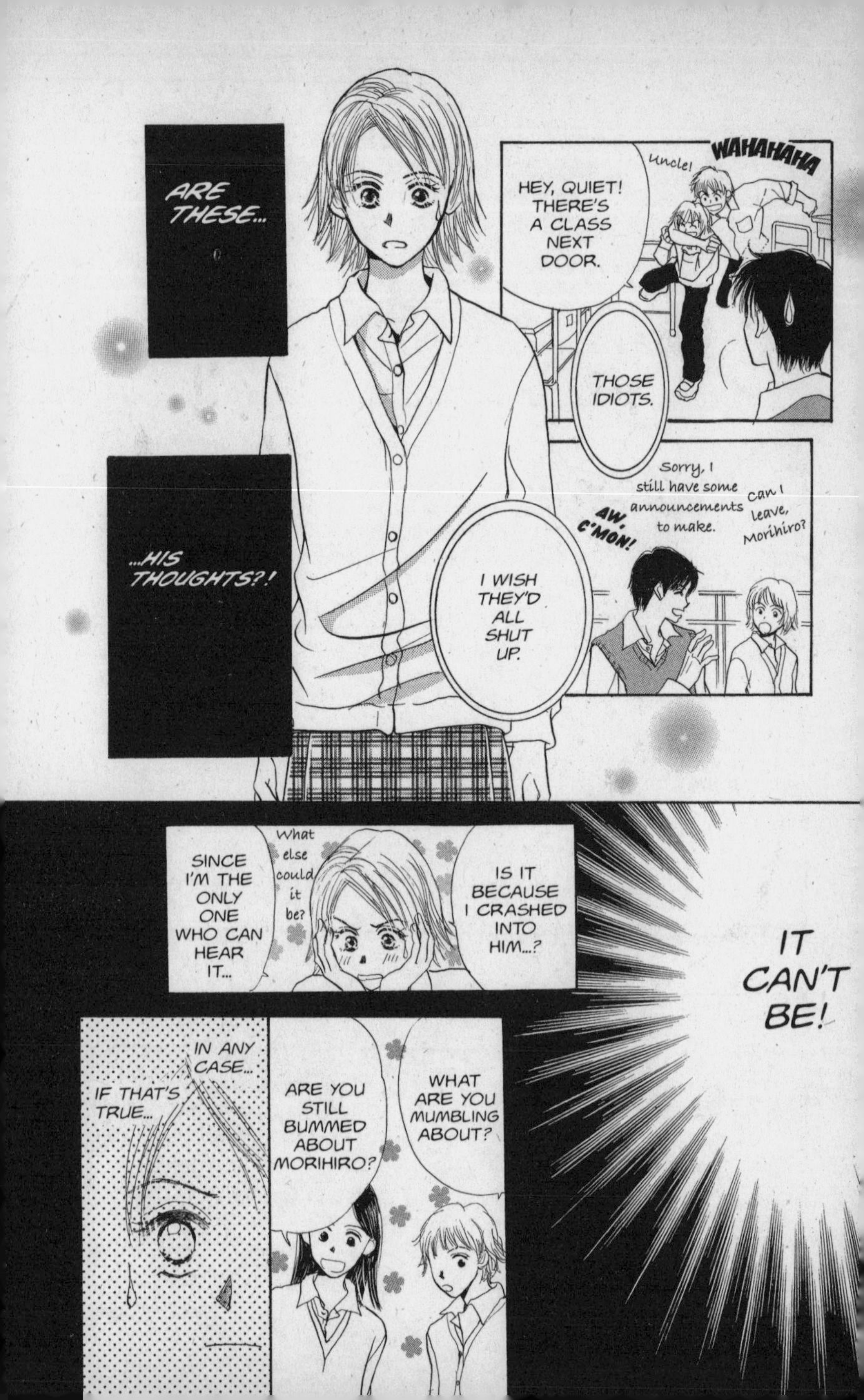
WAHAHAHA
Uncle!
HEY, QUIET! THERE'S A CLASS NEXT DOOR.
THOSE IDIOTS.
Can I leave, Morihiro?
Sorry, I still have some announcements to make.
AW, C'MON!
I WISH THEY'D ALL SHUT UP.
ARE THESE...
...HIS THOUGHTS?!
IT CAN'T BE!
IS IT BECAUSE I CRASHED INTO HIM...?
What else could it be?
SINCE I'M THE ONLY ONE WHO CAN HEAR IT...
WHAT ARE YOU MUMBLING ABOUT?
ARE YOU STILL BUMMED ABOUT MORIHIRO?
IN ANY CASE...
IF THAT'S TRUE...

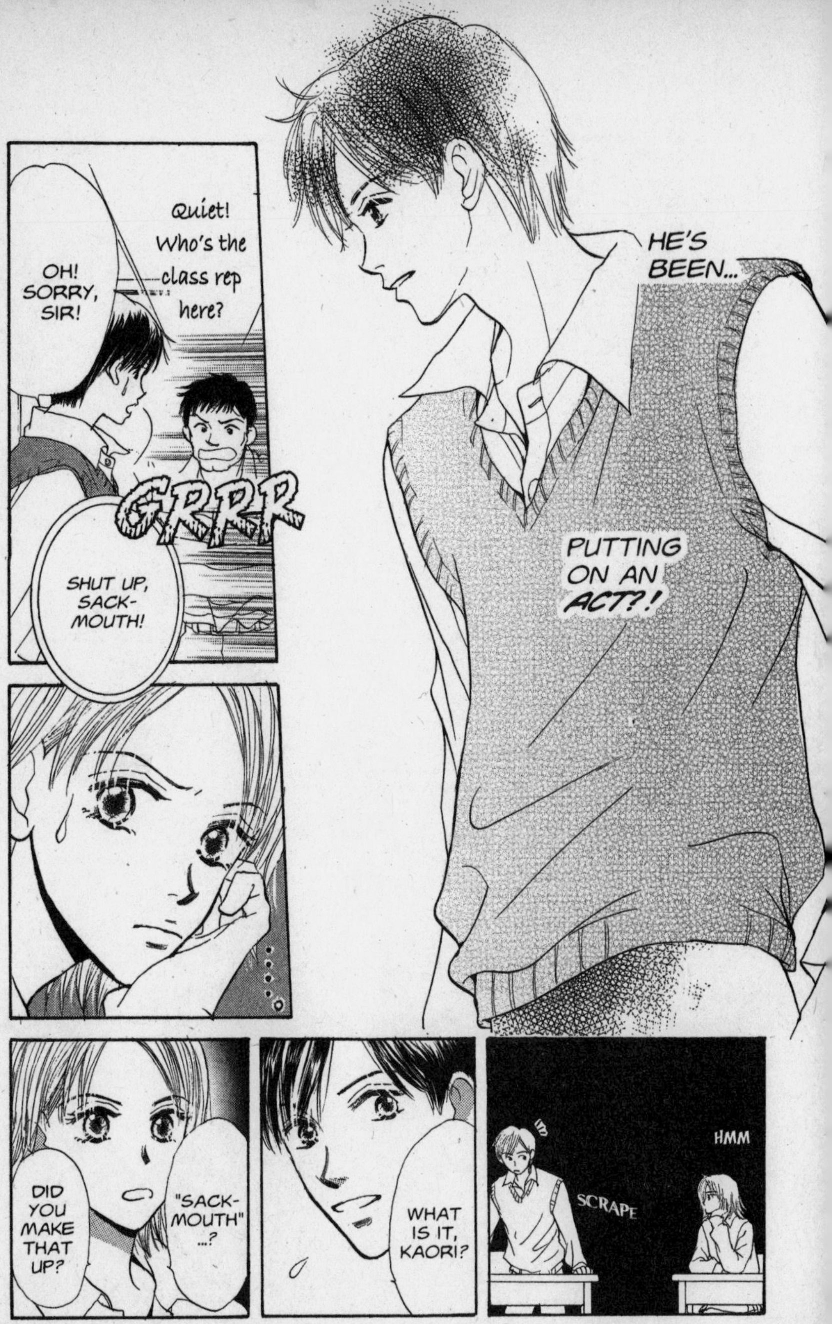
HE'S BEEN...
PUTTING ON AN ACT?!
Quiet! Who's the class rep here?
OH! SORRY, SIR!
GRRR
SHUT UP, SACK-MOUTH!
HMM
SCRAPE
WHAT IS IT, KAORI?
"SACK-MOUTH" ...?
DID YOU MAKE THAT UP?

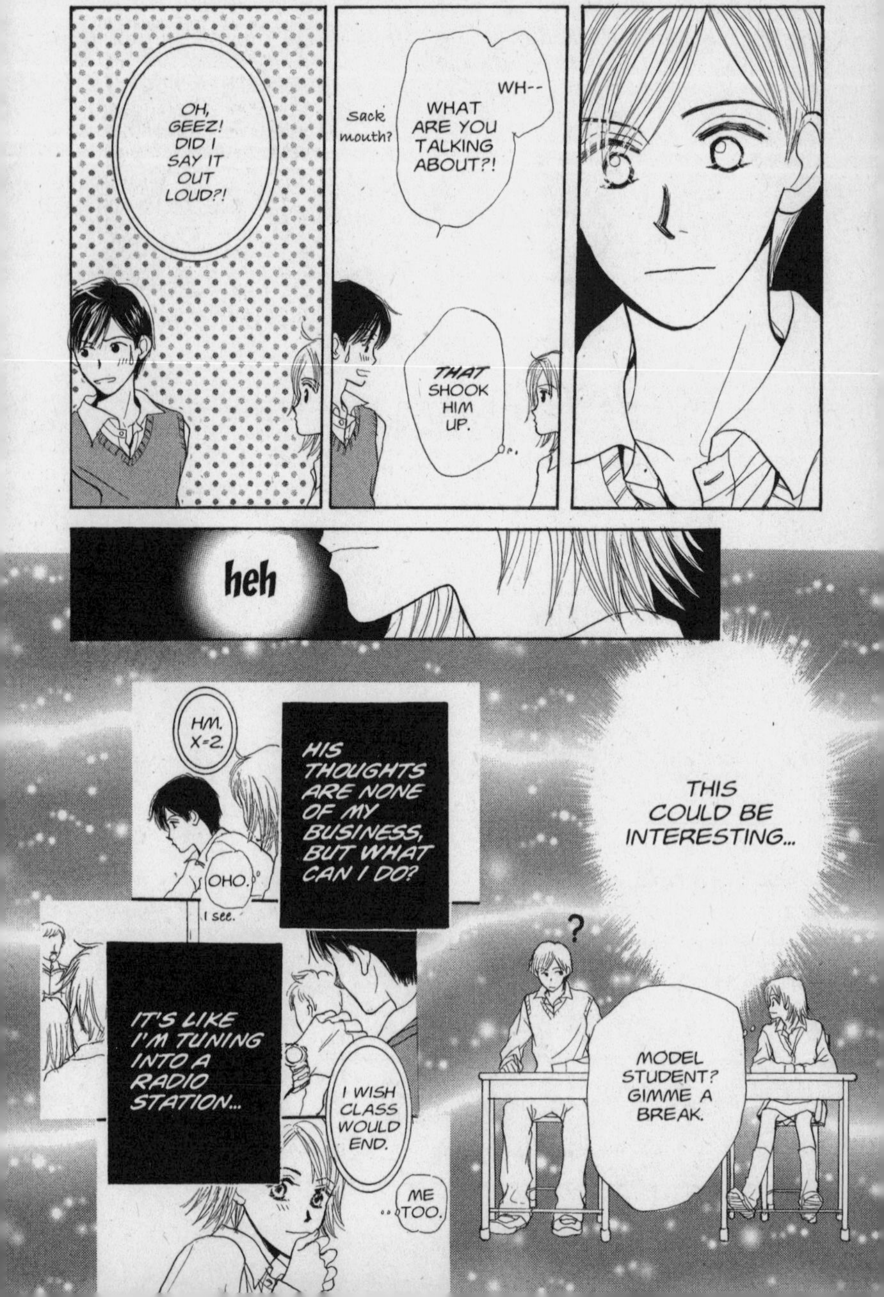
WH--
WHAT ARE YOU TALKING ABOUT?!
Sack mouth?
THAT SHOOK HIM UP.
OH, GEEZ! DID I SAY IT OUT LOUD?!
heh
THIS COULD BE INTERESTING...
?
MODEL STUDENT? GIMME A BREAK.
HIS THOUGHTS ARE NONE OF MY BUSINESS, BUT WHAT CAN I DO?
HM. X=2.
OHO.
I see.
IT'S LIKE I'M TUNING INTO A RADIO STATION...
I WISH CLASS WOULD END.
ME TOO.

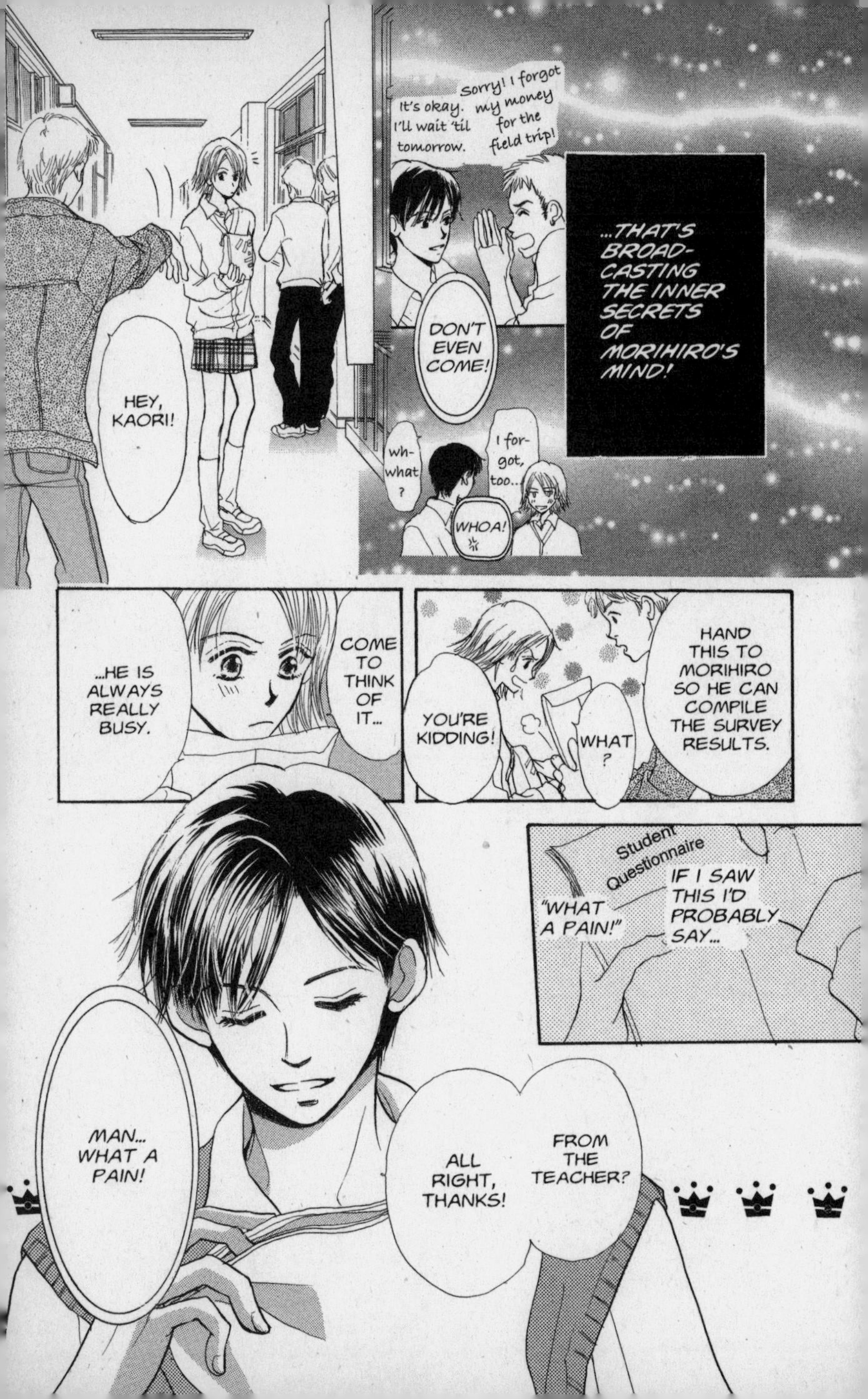
...THAT'S BROADCASTING THE INNER SECRETS OF MORIHIRO'S MIND!
Sorry! I forgot my money for the field trip!
It's okay. I'll wait 'til tomorrow.
DON'T EVEN COME!
I forgot, too...
wh-what?
WHOA!
HEY, KAORI!
HAND THIS TO MORIHIRO SO HE CAN COMPILE THE SURVEY RESULTS.
WHAT?
YOU'RE KIDDING!
COME TO THINK OF IT...
...HE IS ALWAYS REALLY BUSY.
Student Questionnaire
IF I SAW THIS I'D PROBABLY SAY...
"WHAT A PAIN!"
FROM THE TEACHER?
ALL RIGHT, THANKS!
MAN... WHAT A PAIN!

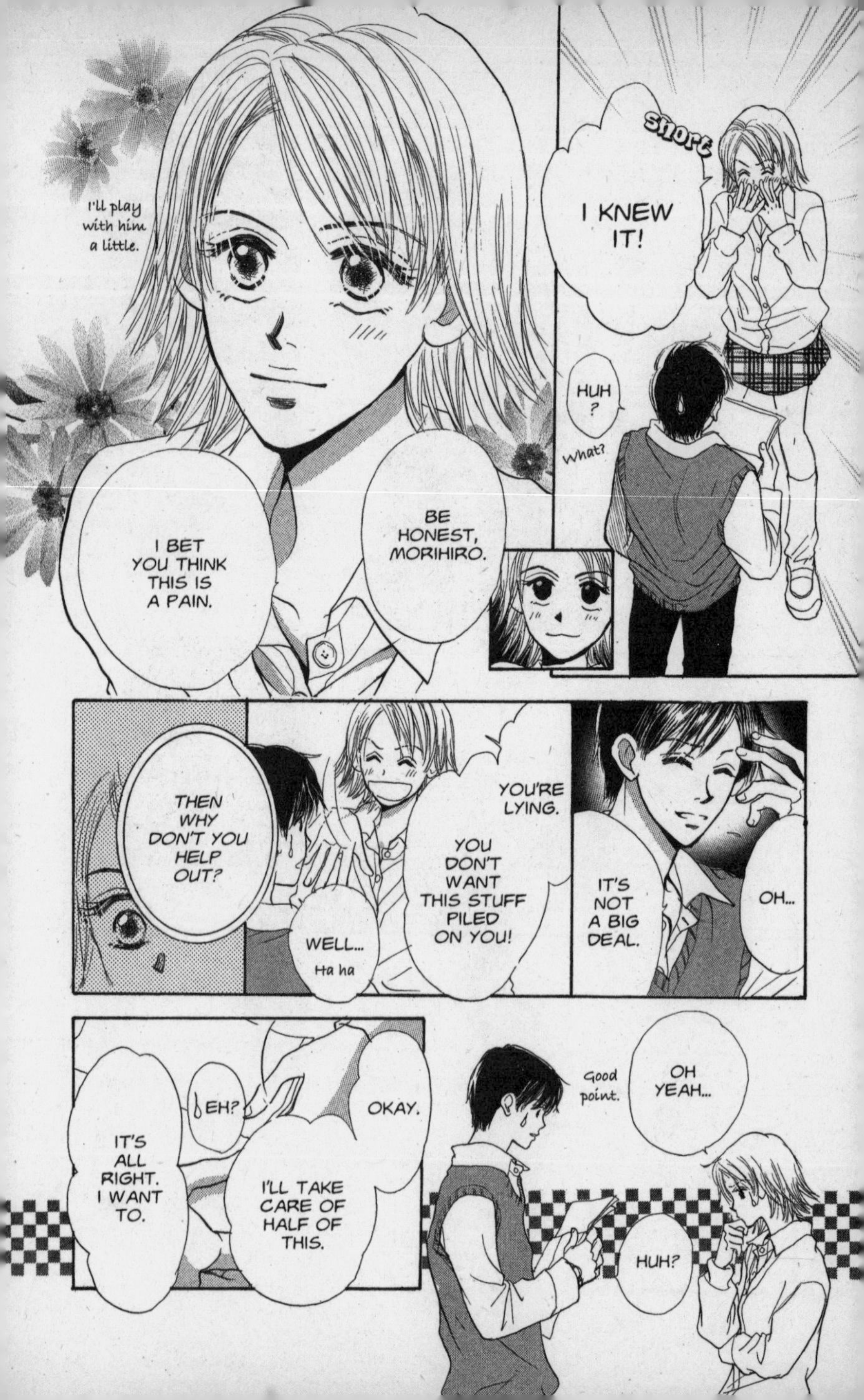
snort
I KNEW IT!
HUH?
What?
I'll play with him a little.
BE HONEST, MORIHIRO.
I BET YOU THINK THIS IS A PAIN.
OH...
IT'S NOT A BIG DEAL.
YOU'RE LYING.
YOU DON'T WANT THIS STUFF PILED ON YOU!
WELL...
Ha ha
THEN WHY DON'T YOU HELP OUT?
OH YEAH...
Good point.
HUH?
OKAY.
EH?
I'LL TAKE CARE OF HALF OF THIS.
IT'S ALL RIGHT. I WANT TO.

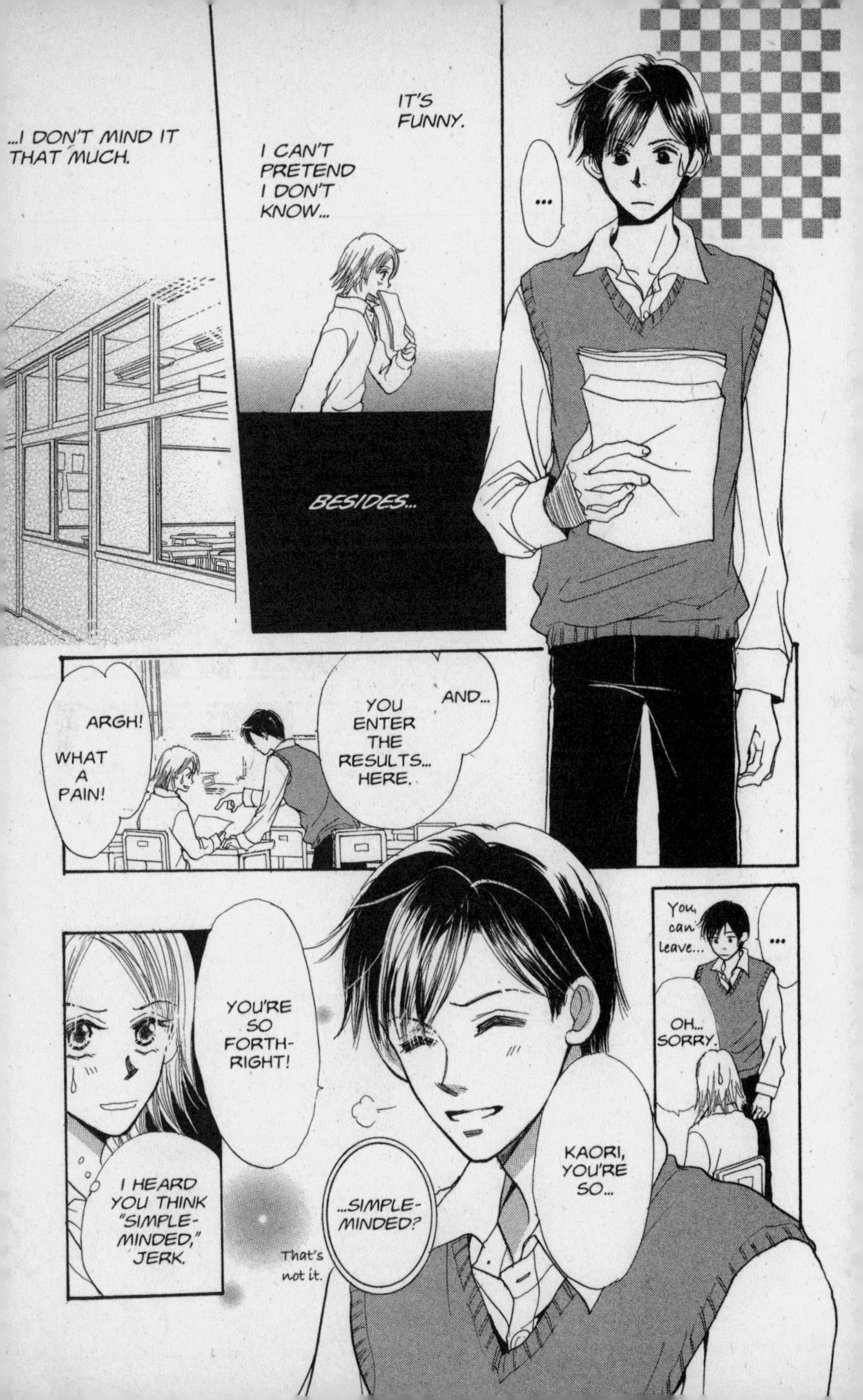
...
IT'S FUNNY.
I CAN'T PRETEND I DON'T KNOW...
BESIDES...
...I DON'T MIND IT THAT MUCH.
AND... YOU ENTER THE RESULTS... HERE.
ARGH! WHAT A PAIN!
You can leave...
...
OH... SORRY.
KAORI, YOU'RE SO...
...SIMPLE-MINDED?
That's not it.
YOU'RE SO FORTH-RIGHT!
I HEARD YOU THINK "SIMPLE-MINDED," JERK.

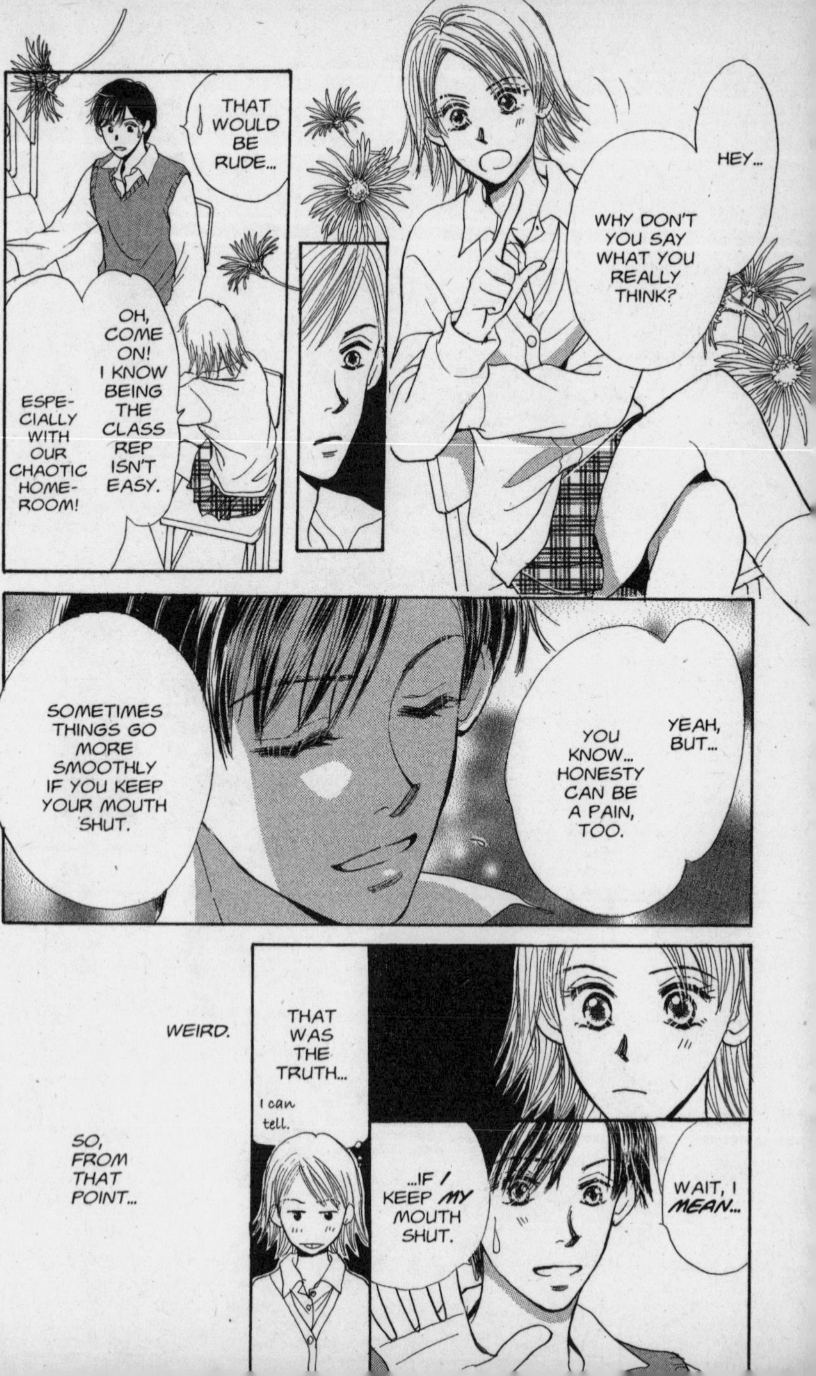
HEY...
WHY DON'T YOU SAY WHAT YOU REALLY THINK?
THAT WOULD BE RUDE...
OH, COME ON! I KNOW BEING THE CLASS REP ISN'T EASY.
ESPE-CIALLY WITH OUR CHAOTIC HOME-ROOM!
YEAH, BUT...
YOU KNOW... HONESTY CAN BE A PAIN, TOO.
SOMETIMES THINGS GO MORE SMOOTHLY IF YOU KEEP YOUR MOUTH SHUT.
THAT WAS THE TRUTH...
WEIRD.
WAIT, I MEAN...
...IF I KEEP MY MOUTH SHUT.
I can tell.
SO, FROM THAT POINT...

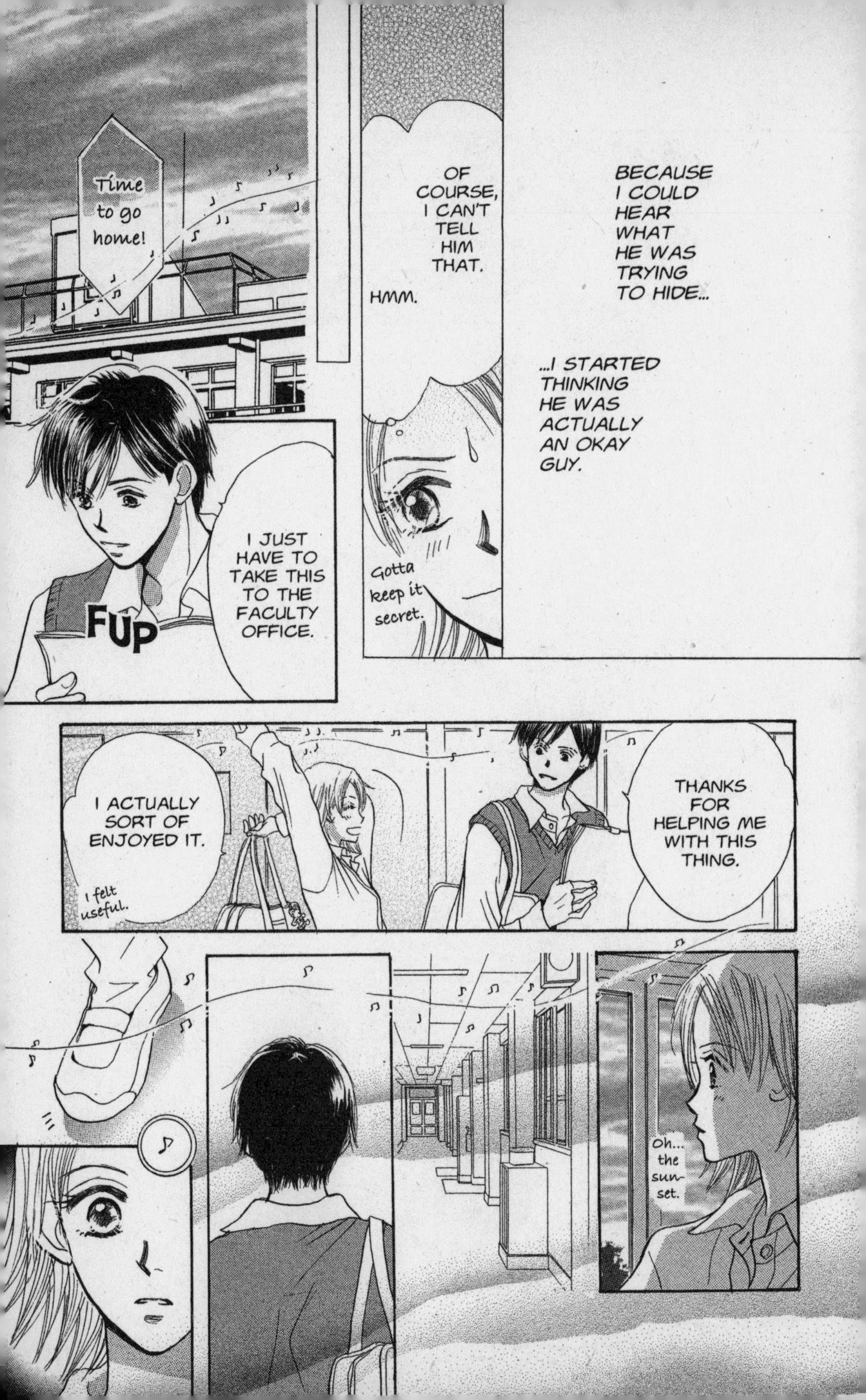
BECAUSE I COULD HEAR WHAT HE WAS TRYING TO HIDE...
...I STARTED THINKING HE WAS ACTUALLY AN OKAY GUY.
OF COURSE, I CAN'T TELL HIM THAT.
HMM.
Gotta keep it secret.
Time to go home!
I JUST HAVE TO TAKE THIS TO THE FACULTY OFFICE.
FUP
THANKS FOR HELPING ME WITH THIS THING.
I ACTUALLY SORT OF ENJOYED IT.
I felt useful.
Oh... the sun-set.

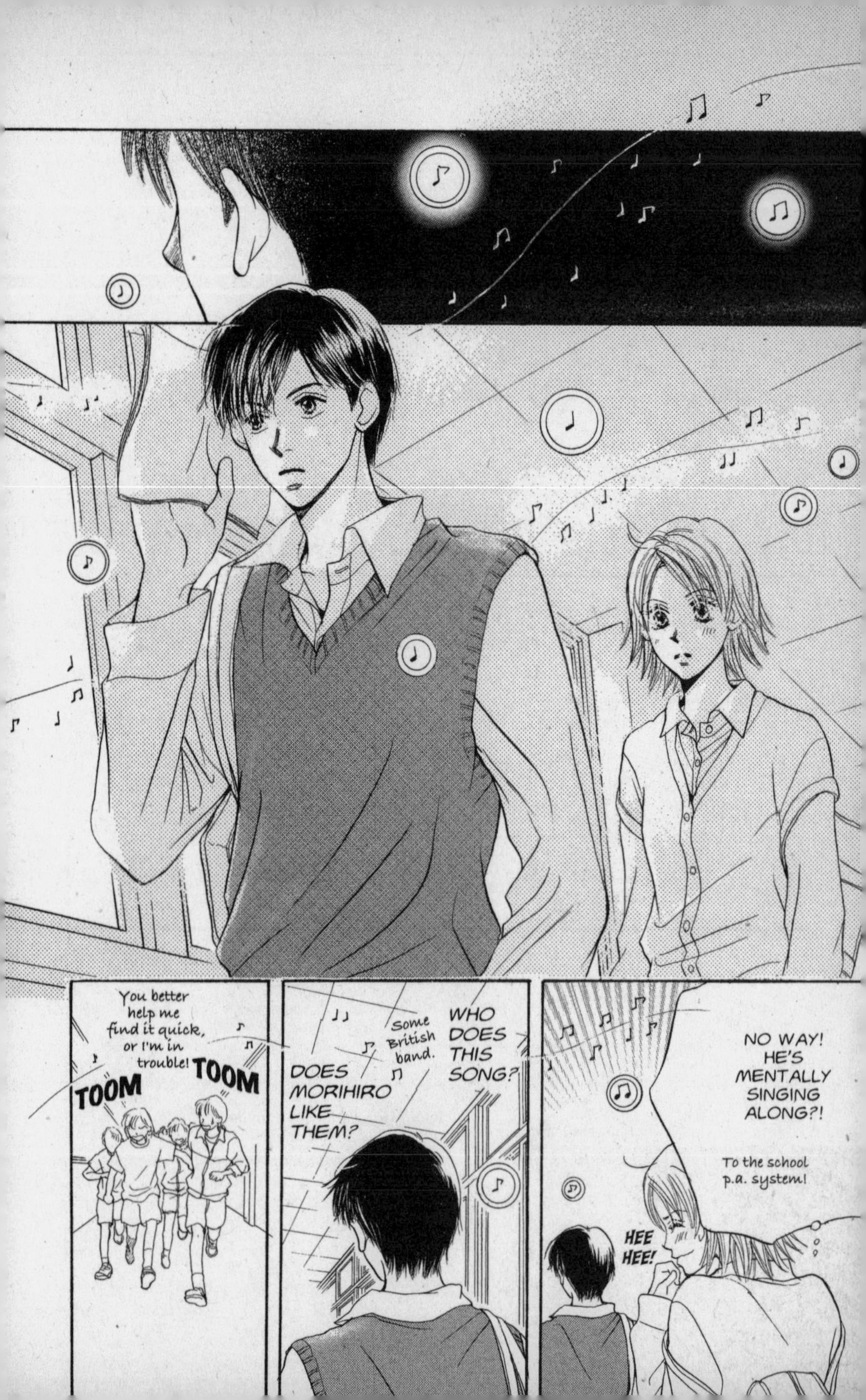
You better help me find it quick, or I'm in trouble!
TOOM
TOOM
WHO DOES THIS SONG?
Some British band.
DOES MORIHIRO LIKE THEM?
NO WAY! HE'S MENTALLY SINGING ALONG?!
To the school p.a. system!
HEE HEE!

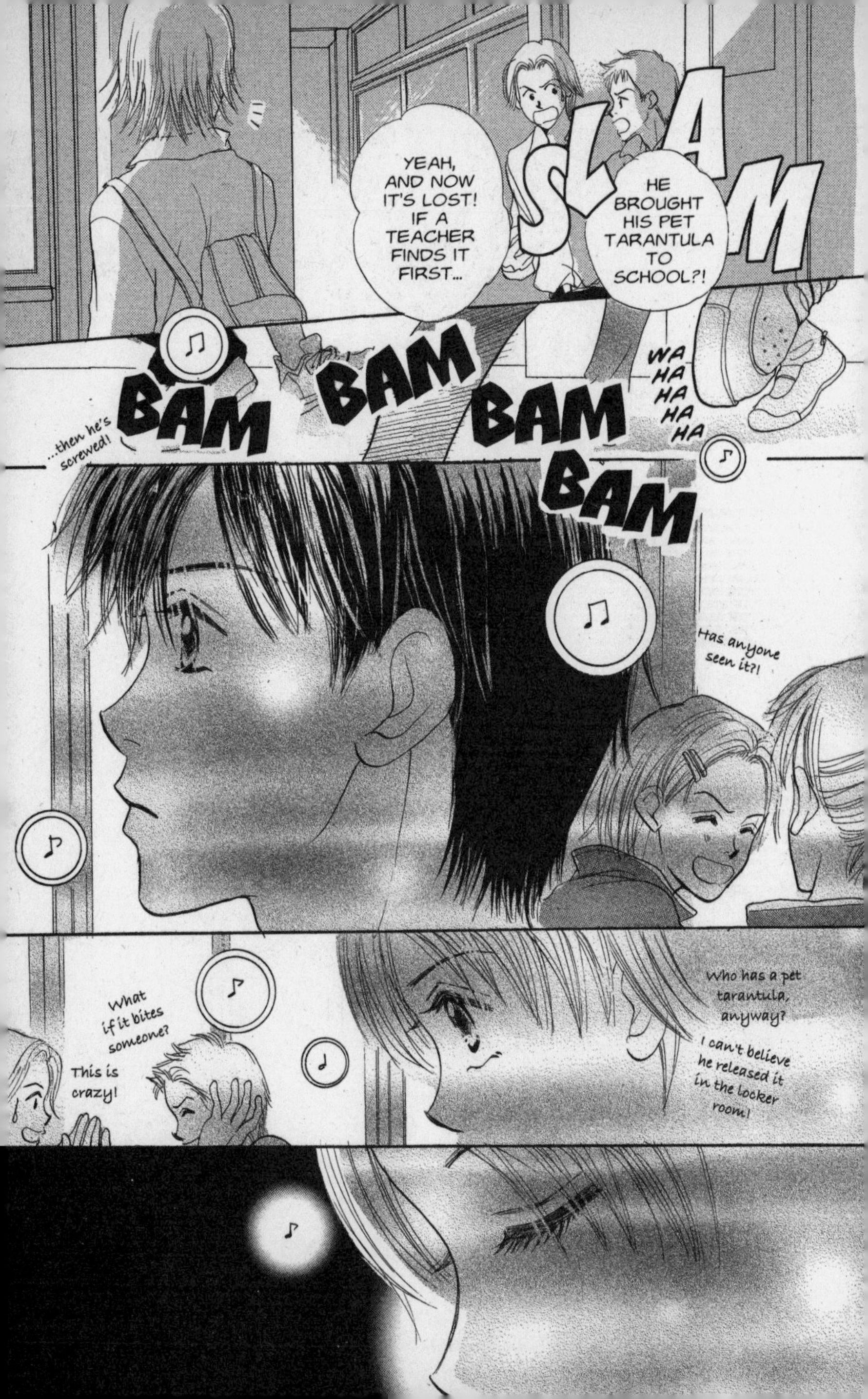
SLAM
HE BROUGHT HIS PET TARANTULA TO SCHOOL?!
YEAH, AND NOW IT'S LOST! IF A TEACHER FINDS IT FIRST...
...then he's screwed!
WA HA HA HA HA
BAM BAM BAM BAM
BAM
Has anyone seen it?!
Who has a pet tarantula, anyway?
I can't believe he released it in the locker room!
What if it bites someone?
This is crazy!

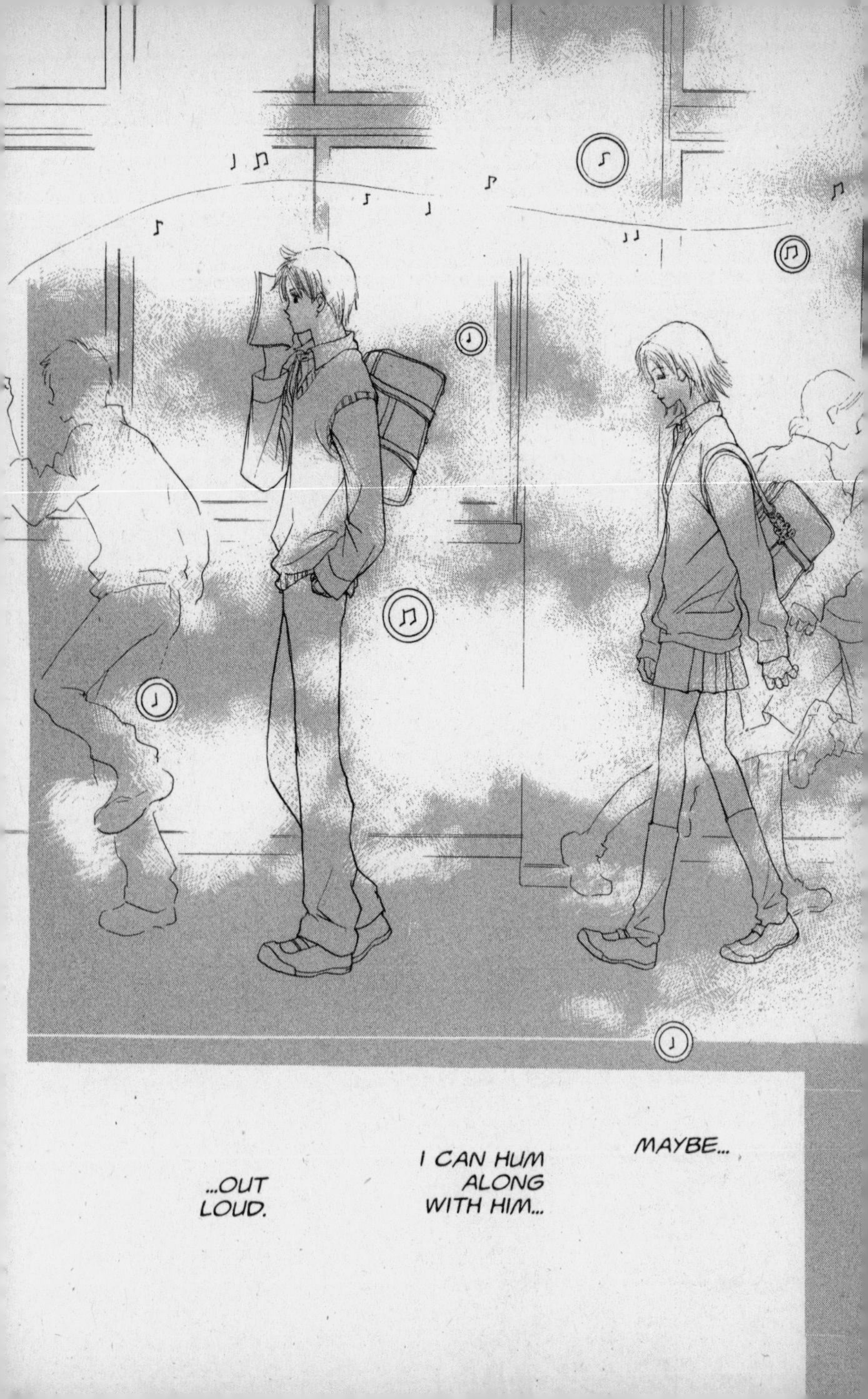
MAYBE...
I CAN HUM ALONG WITH HIM...
...OUT LOUD.

I CAN USE MY VOICE... AND PRIVATELY SHARE HIS.

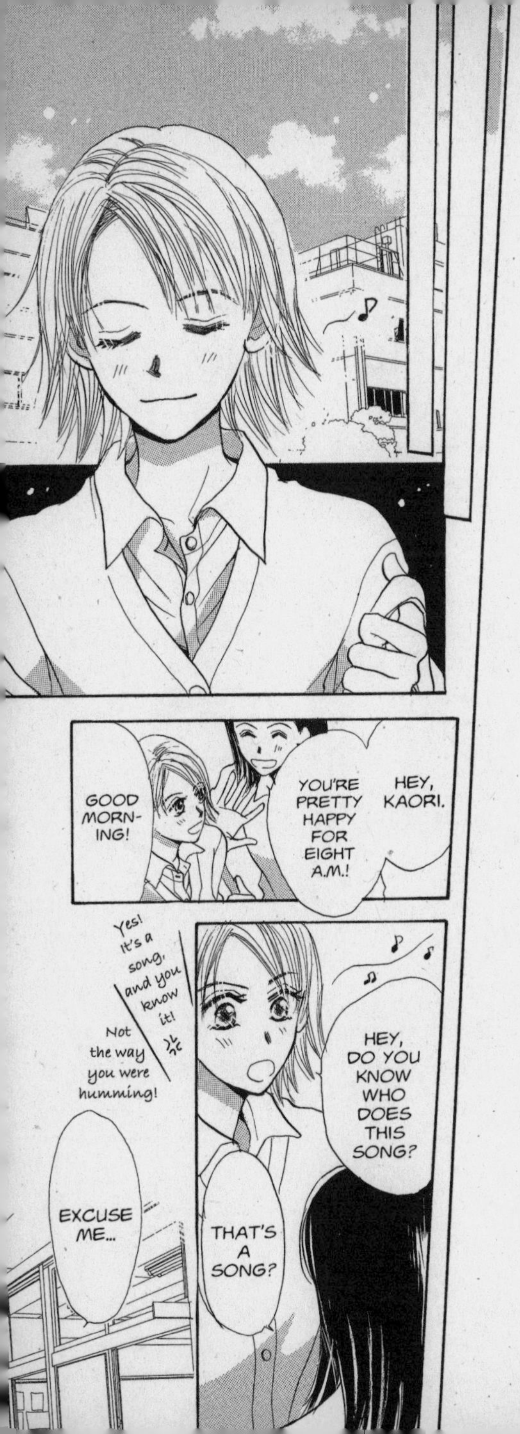
HEY, KAORI.
YOU'RE PRETTY HAPPY FOR EIGHT A.M.!
GOOD MORNING!
HEY, DO YOU KNOW WHO DOES THIS SONG?
Yes! It's a song, and you know it!
Not the way you were humming!
THAT'S A SONG?
EXCUSE ME...

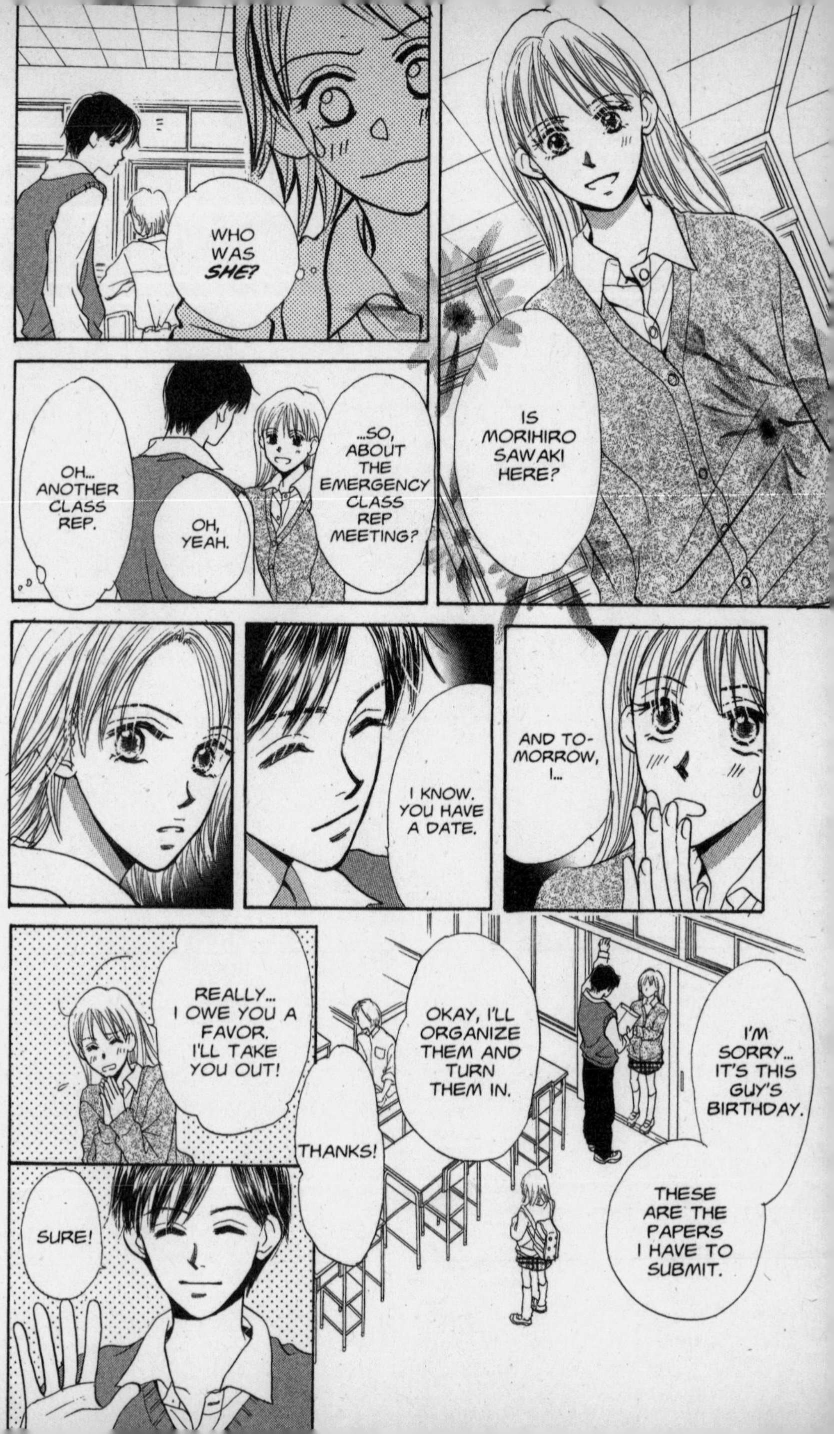
IS MORIHIRO SAWAKI HERE?
WHO WAS *SHE?*
...SO, ABOUT THE EMERGENCY CLASS REP MEETING?
OH, YEAH.
OH... ANOTHER CLASS REP.
AND TO-MORROW, I...
I KNOW. YOU HAVE A DATE.
I'M SORRY... IT'S THIS GUY'S BIRTHDAY.
THESE ARE THE PAPERS I HAVE TO SUBMIT.
OKAY, I'LL ORGANIZE THEM AND TURN THEM IN.
THANKS!
REALLY... I OWE YOU A FAVOR. I'LL TAKE YOU OUT!
SURE!

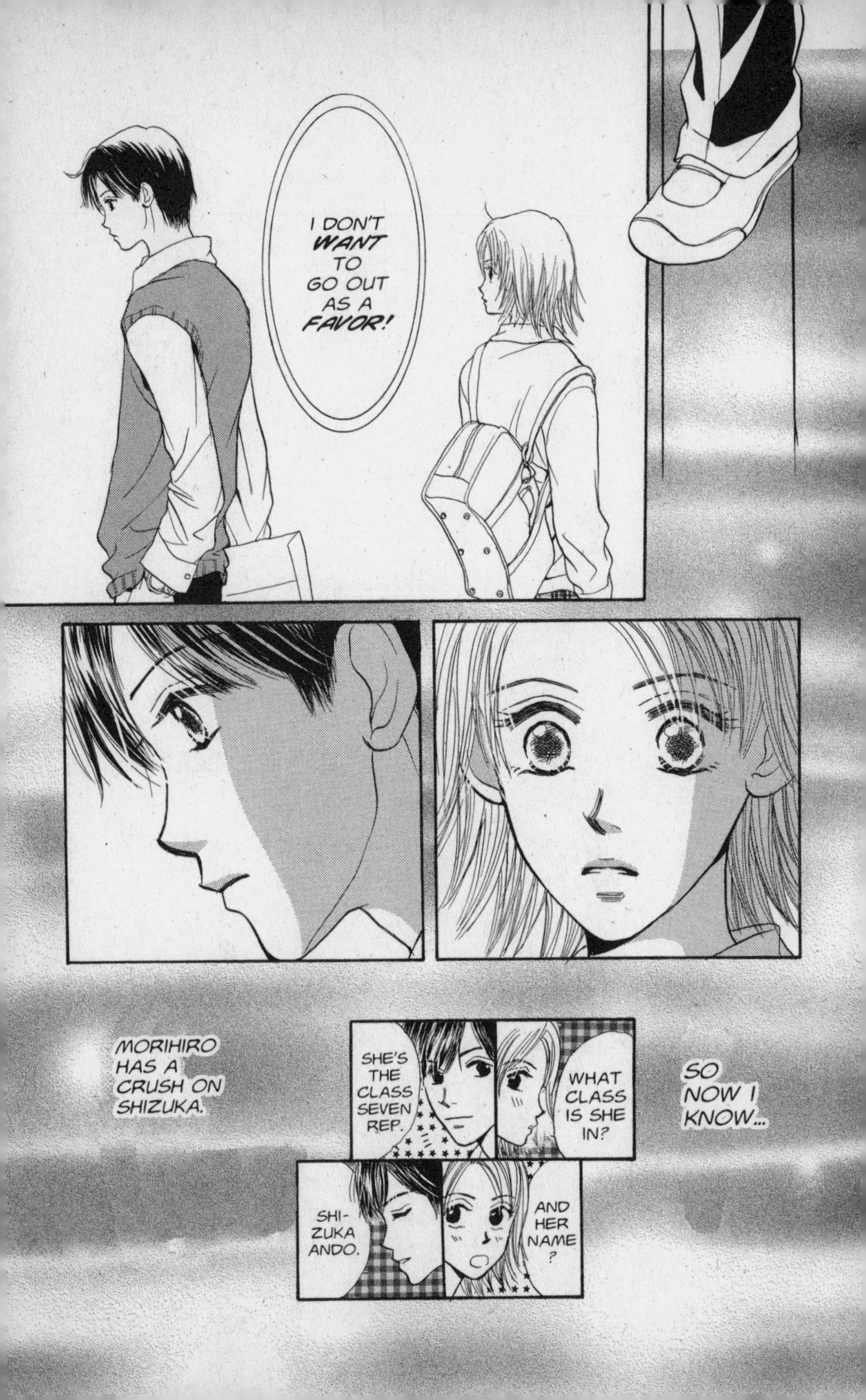
I DON'T WANT TO GO OUT AS A FAVOR!
SO NOW I KNOW...
WHAT CLASS IS SHE IN?
SHE'S THE CLASS SEVEN REP.
AND HER NAME?
SHI-ZUKA ANDO.
MORIHIRO HAS A CRUSH ON SHIZUKA.

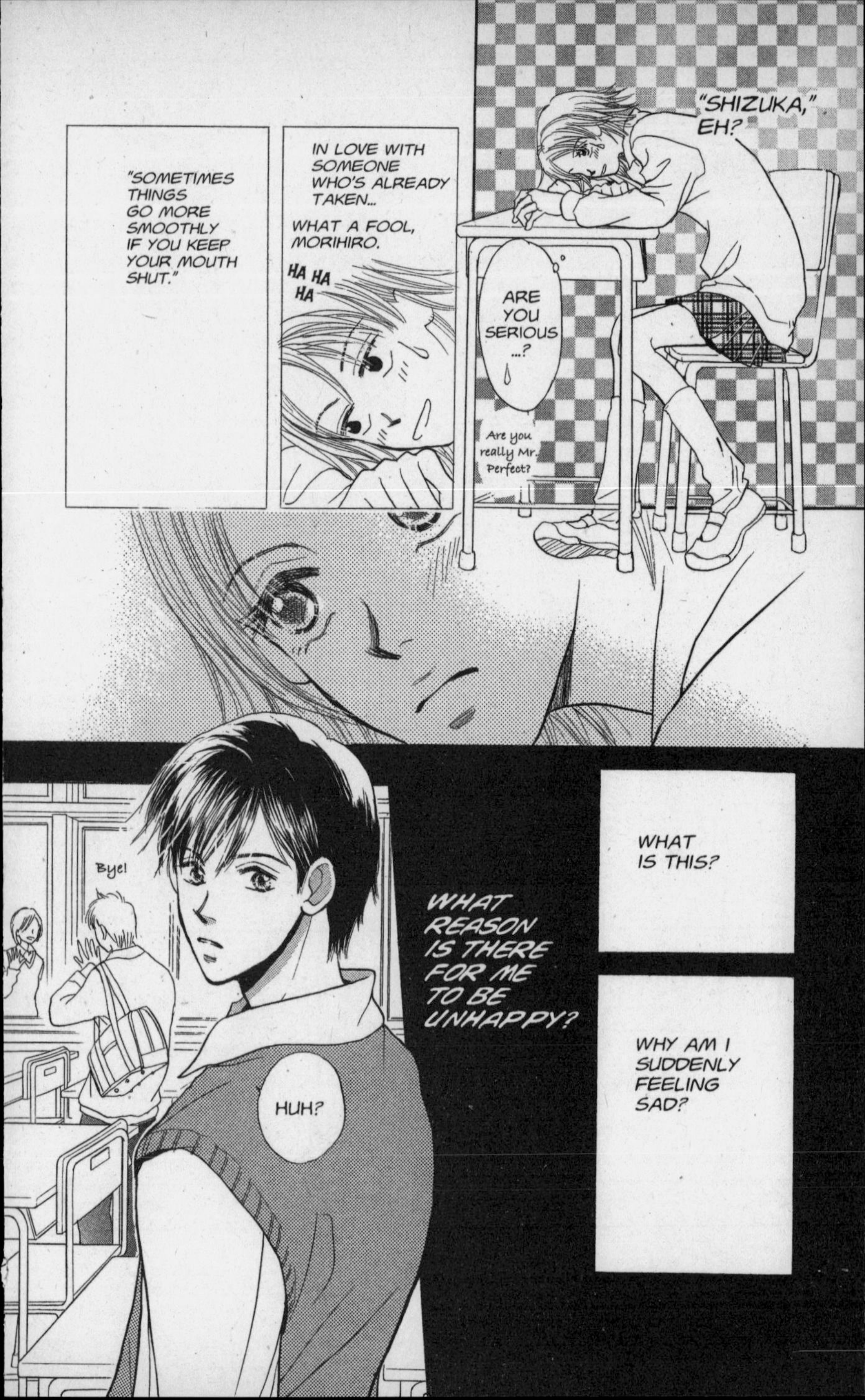
"SHIZUKA," EH?
ARE YOU SERIOUS ...?
Are you really Mr. Perfect?
IN LOVE WITH SOMEONE WHO'S ALREADY TAKEN...
WHAT A FOOL, MORIHIRO.
HA HA HA
"SOMETIMES THINGS GO MORE SMOOTHLY IF YOU KEEP YOUR MOUTH SHUT."
WHAT IS THIS?
WHY AM I SUDDENLY FEELING SAD?
WHAT REASON IS THERE FOR ME TO BE UNHAPPY?
HUH?
Bye!

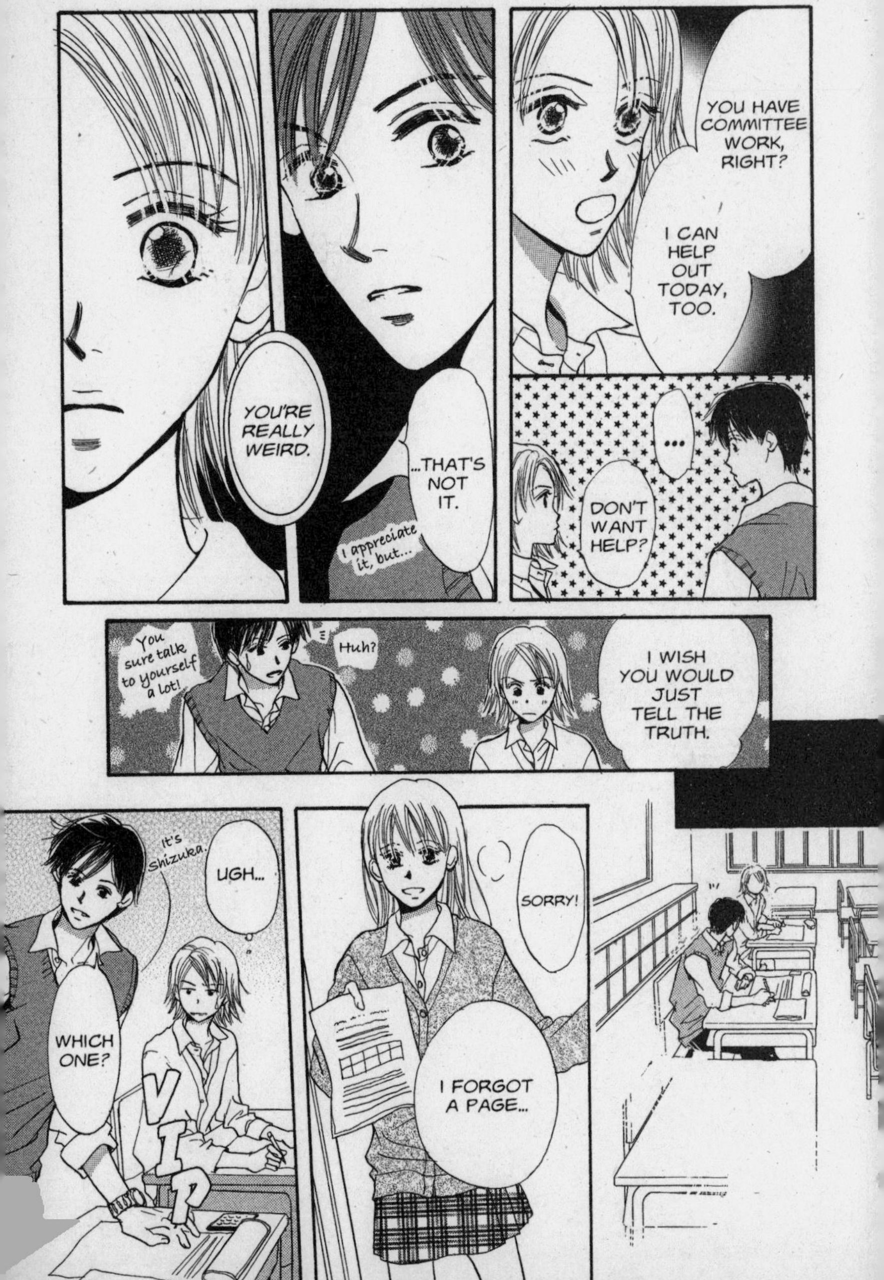
YOU HAVE COMMITTEE WORK, RIGHT?
I CAN HELP OUT TODAY, TOO.
...
DON'T WANT HELP?
...THAT'S NOT IT.
I appreciate it, but...
YOU'RE REALLY WEIRD.
I WISH YOU WOULD JUST TELL THE TRUTH.
Huh?
You sure talk to yourself a lot!
SORRY!
I FORGOT A PAGE...
UGH...
It's Shizuka.
WHICH ONE?
VIP

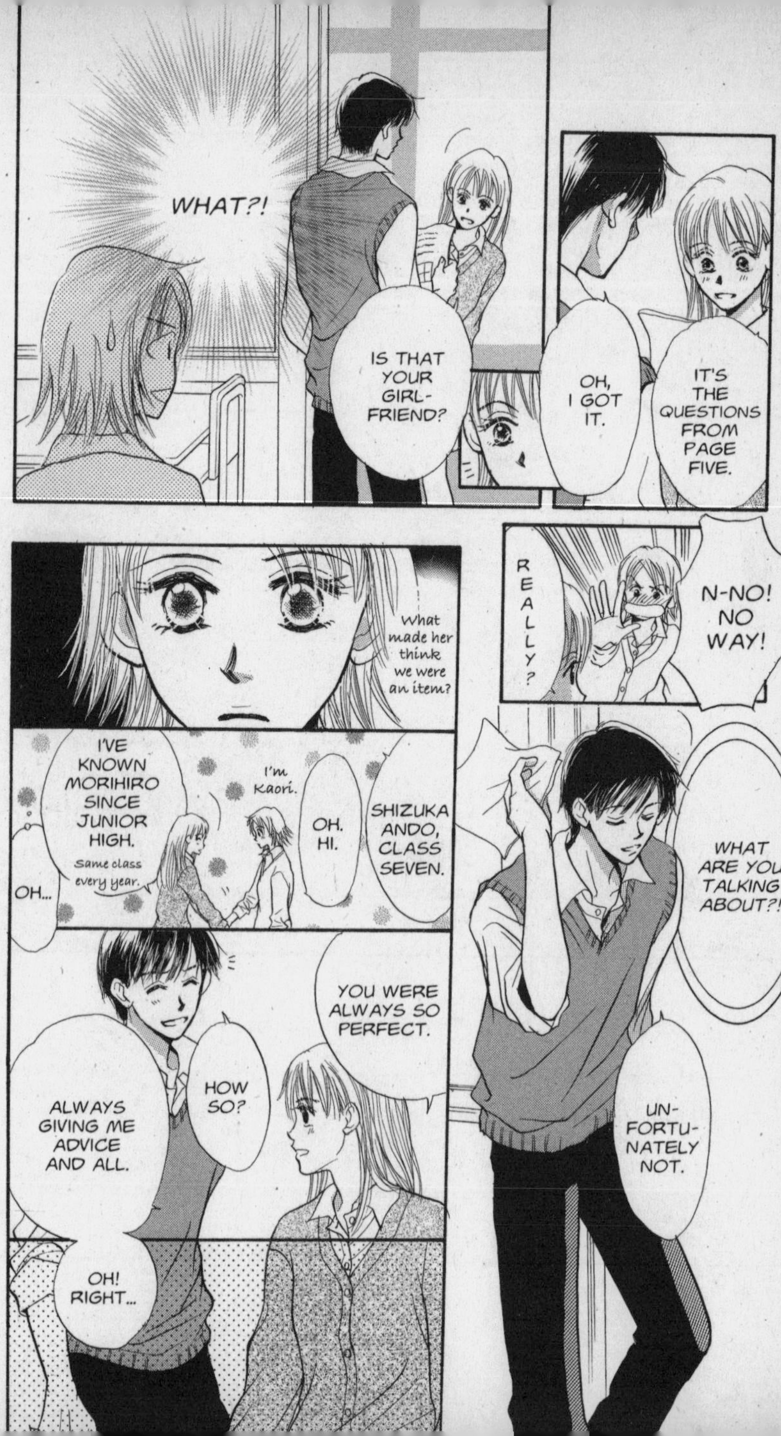
IT'S THE QUESTIONS FROM PAGE FIVE.
OH, I GOT IT.
IS THAT YOUR GIRL-FRIEND?
WHAT?!
N-NO! NO WAY!
REALLY?
WHAT ARE YOU TALKING ABOUT?!
UN-FORTU-NATELY NOT.
What made her think we were an item?
SHIZUKA ANDO, CLASS SEVEN.
OH. HI.
I'm Kaori.
I'VE KNOWN MORIHIRO SINCE JUNIOR HIGH.
Same class every year.
OH...
YOU WERE ALWAYS SO PERFECT.
HOW SO?
ALWAYS GIVING ME ADVICE AND ALL.
OH! RIGHT...

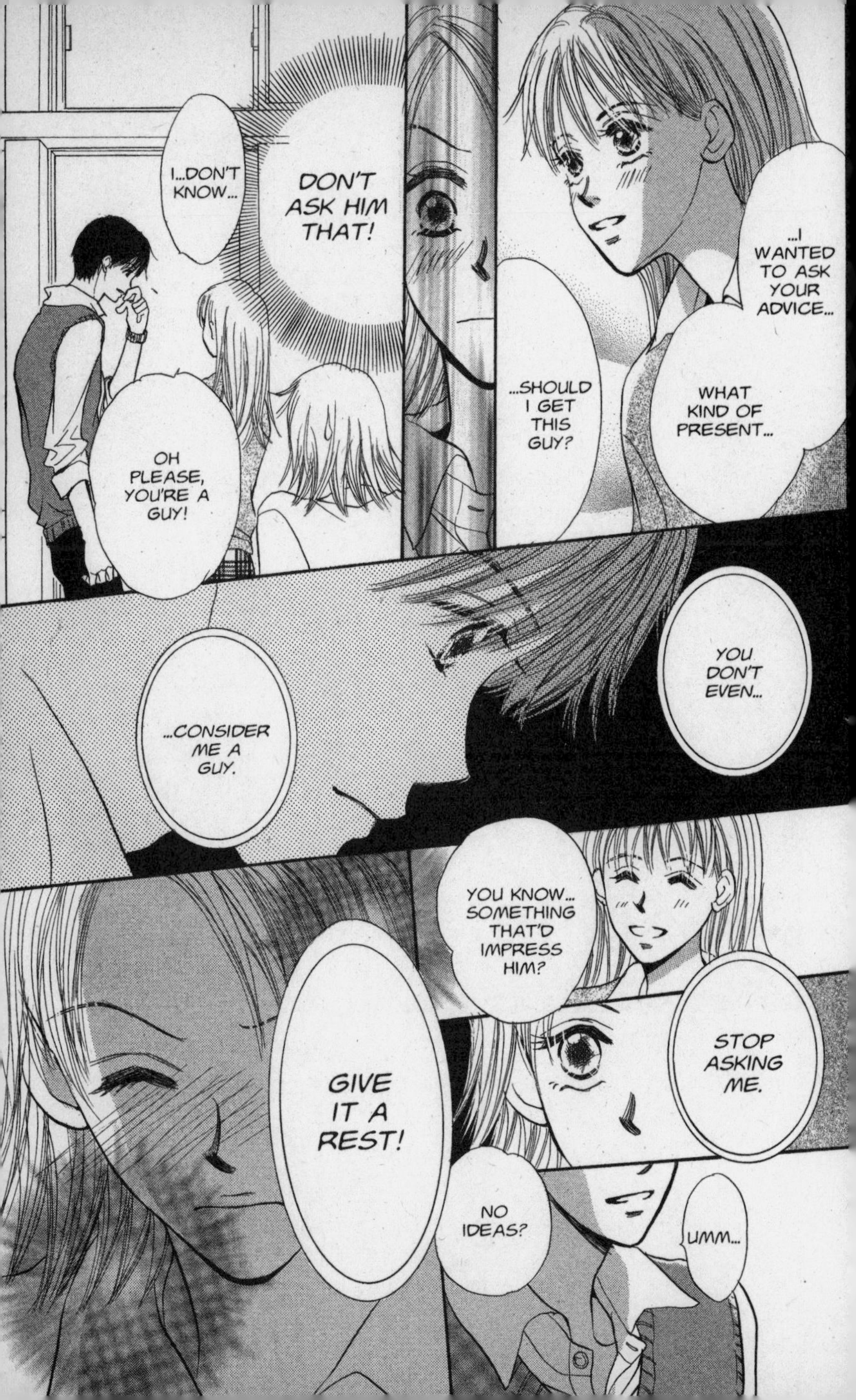
...I WANTED TO ASK YOUR ADVICE...
WHAT KIND OF PRESENT...
...SHOULD I GET THIS GUY?
DON'T ASK HIM THAT!
I...DON'T KNOW...
OH PLEASE, YOU'RE A GUY!
YOU DON'T EVEN...
...CONSIDER ME A GUY.
YOU KNOW... SOMETHING THAT'D IMPRESS HIM?
STOP ASKING ME.
UMM...
NO IDEAS?
GIVE IT A REST!

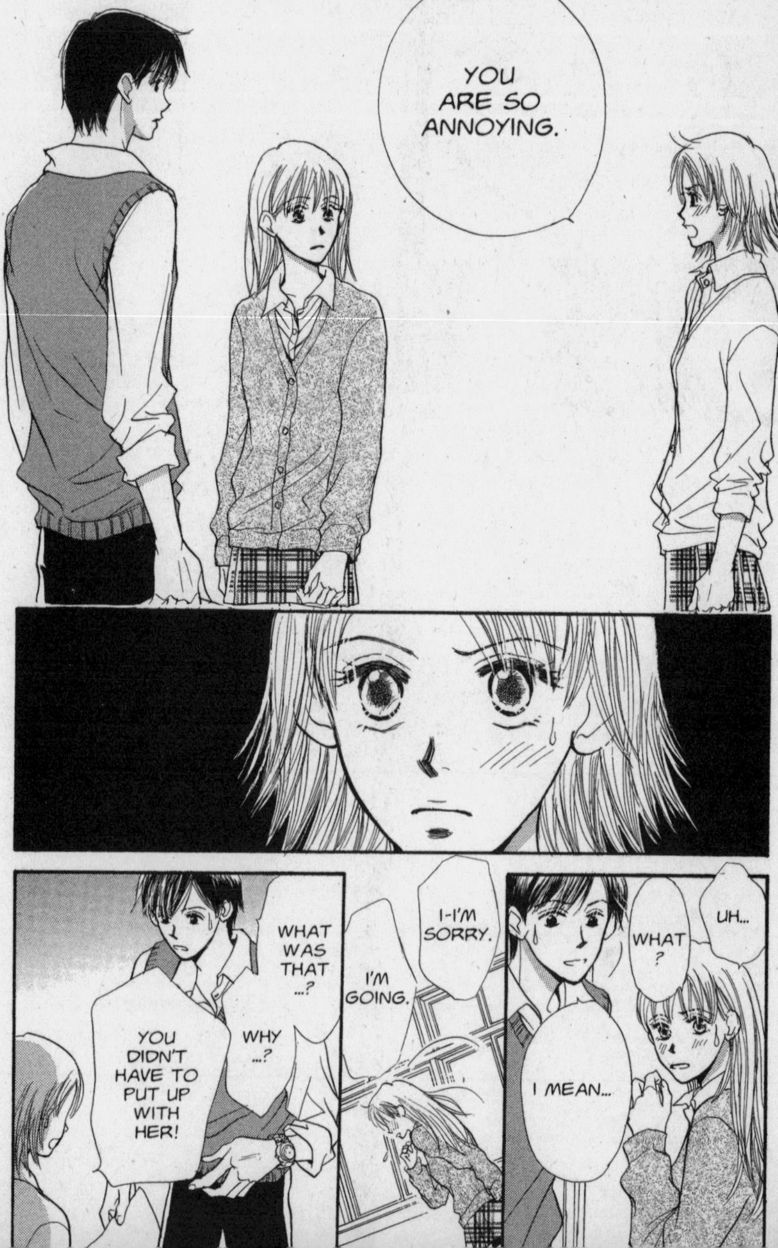
YOU ARE SO ANNOYING.
UH...
WHAT ?
I MEAN...
I-I'M SORRY.
I'M GOING.
WHAT WAS THAT ...?
WHY ...?
YOU DIDN'T HAVE TO PUT UP WITH HER!

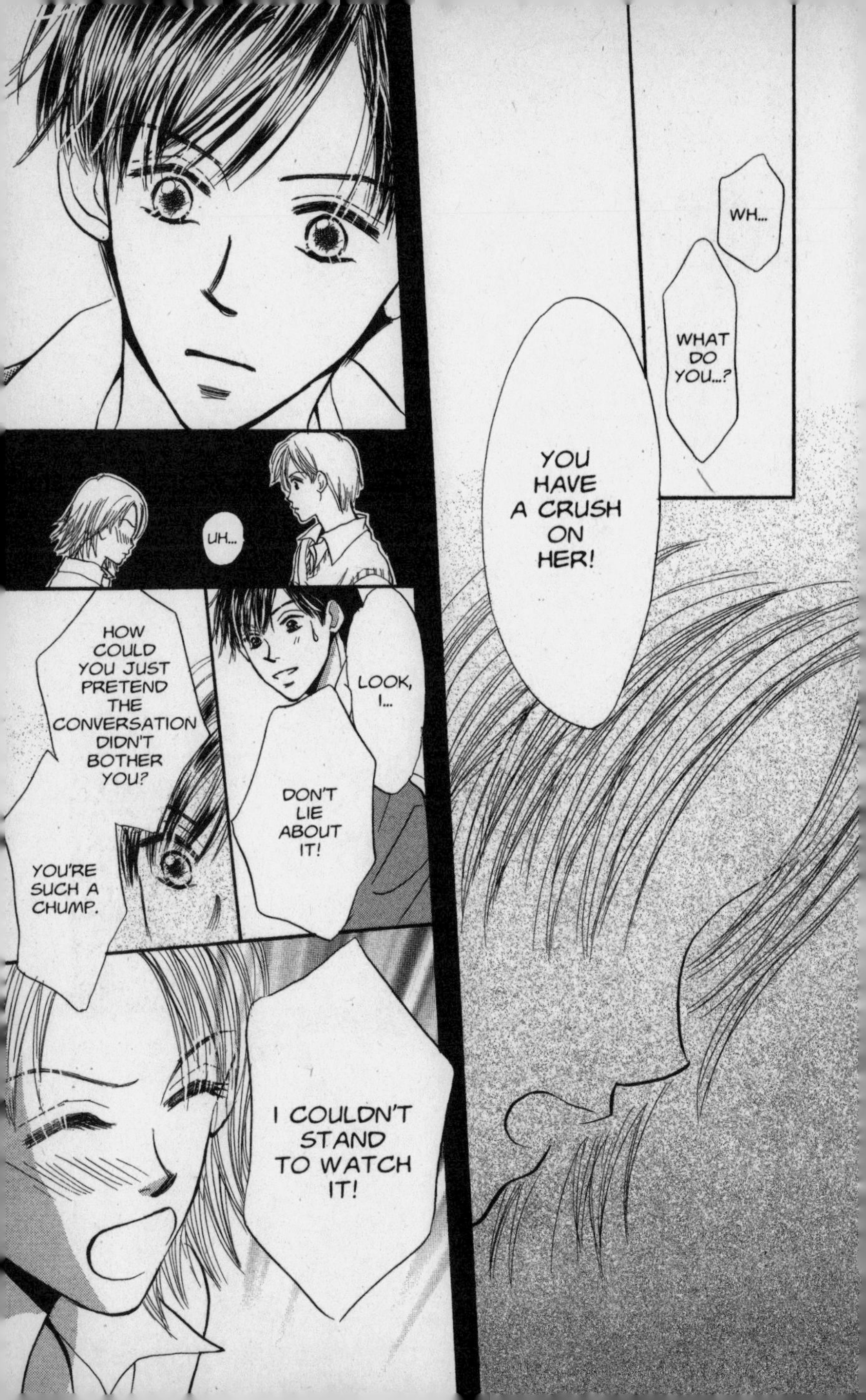
WH...
WHAT DO YOU...?
YOU HAVE A CRUSH ON HER!
UH...
LOOK, I...
DON'T LIE ABOUT IT!
HOW COULD YOU JUST PRETEND THE CONVERSATION DIDN'T BOTHER YOU?
YOU'RE SUCH A CHUMP.
I COULDN'T STAND TO WATCH IT!

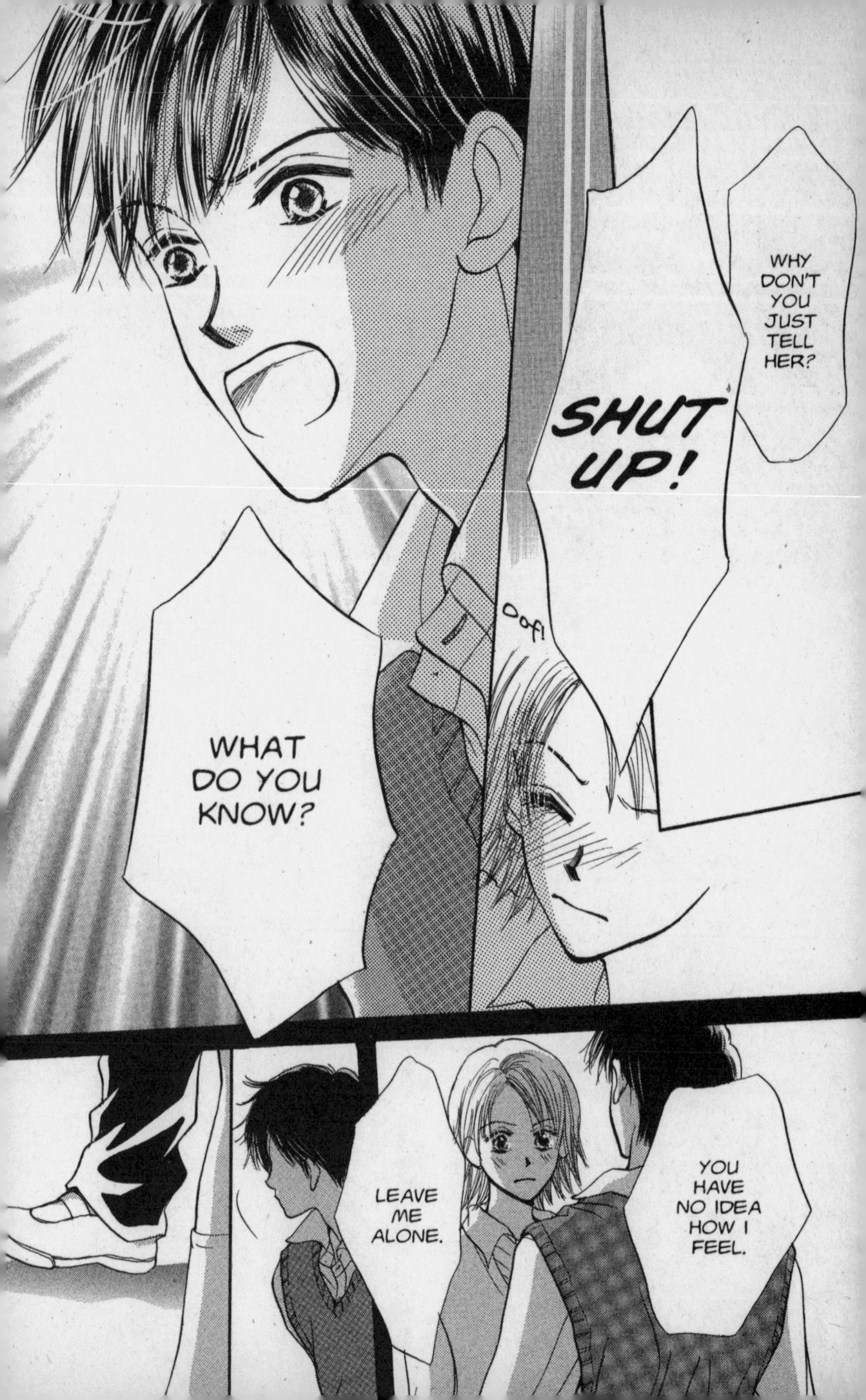
WHY DON'T YOU JUST TELL HER?
SHUT UP!
Oof!
WHAT DO YOU KNOW?
YOU HAVE NO IDEA HOW I FEEL.
LEAVE ME ALONE.

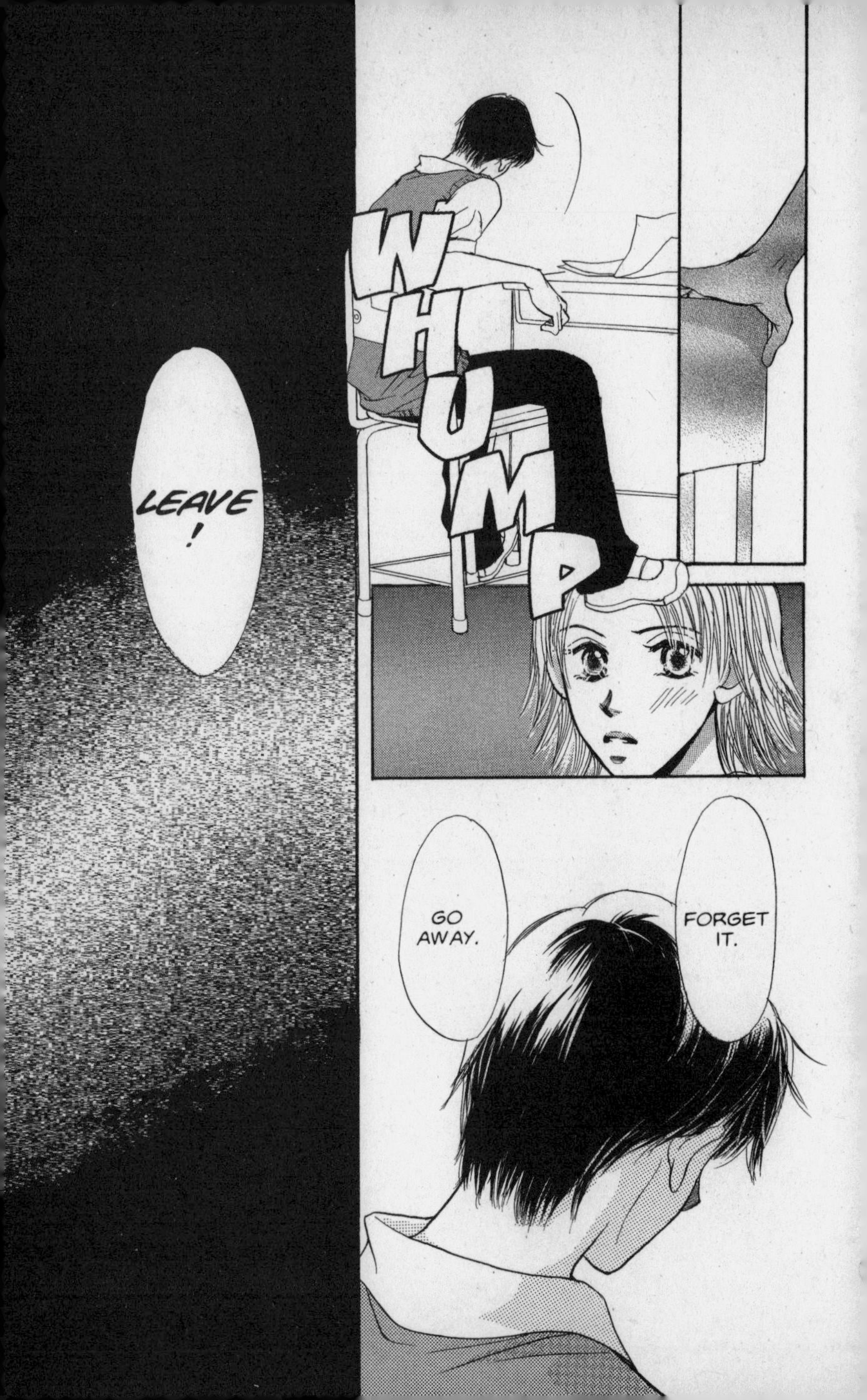
WHUMP
FORGET IT.
GO AWAY.
LEAVE!

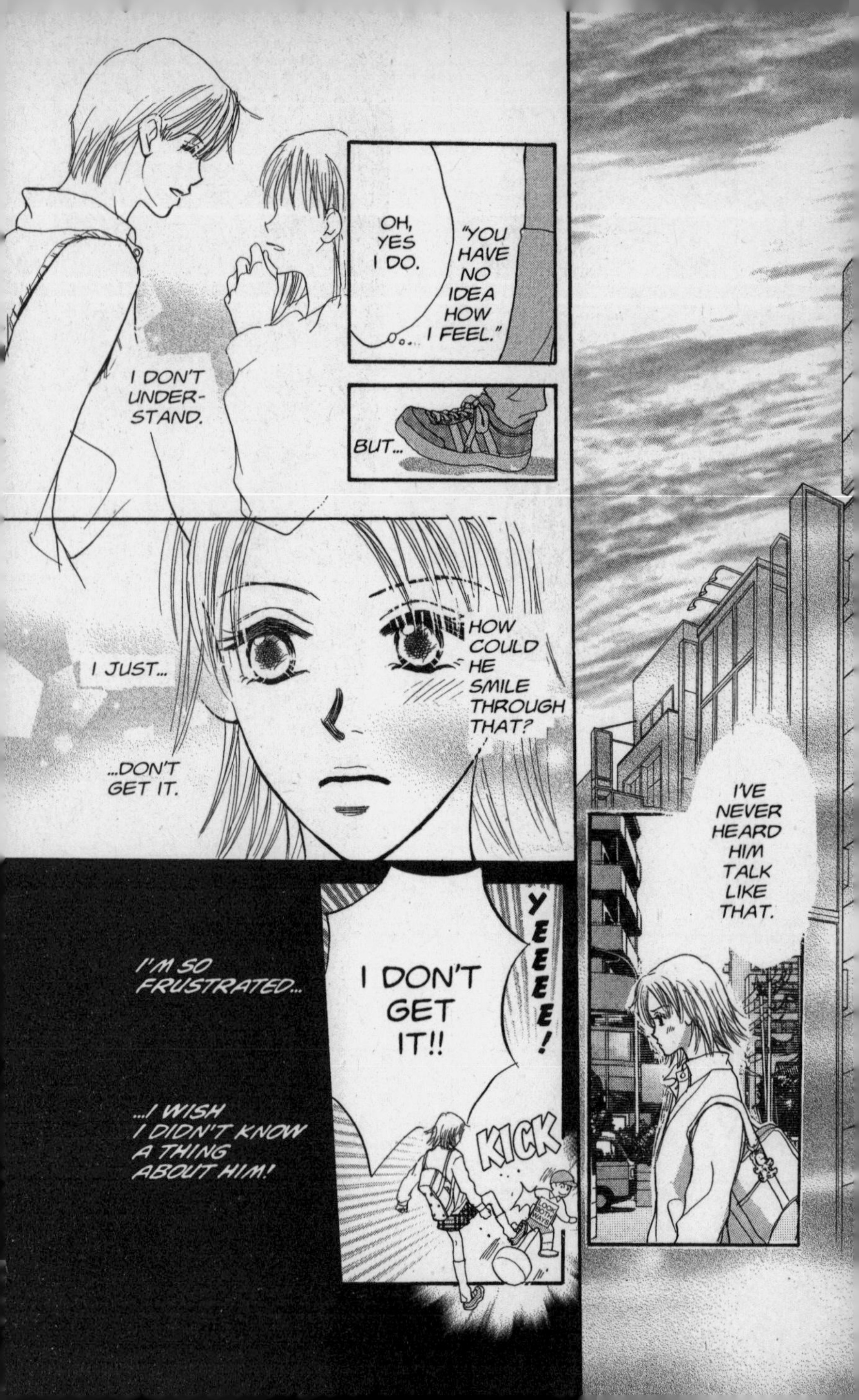
I'VE NEVER HEARD HIM TALK LIKE THAT.
"YOU HAVE NO IDEA HOW I FEEL."
OH, YES I DO.
BUT...
I DON'T UNDERSTAND.
HOW COULD HE SMILE THROUGH THAT?
I JUST...
...DON'T GET IT.
I DON'T GET IT!!
YEEEE!
KICK
LOOK BOTH WAYS
I'M SO FRUSTRATED...
...I WISH I DIDN'T KNOW A THING ABOUT HIM!

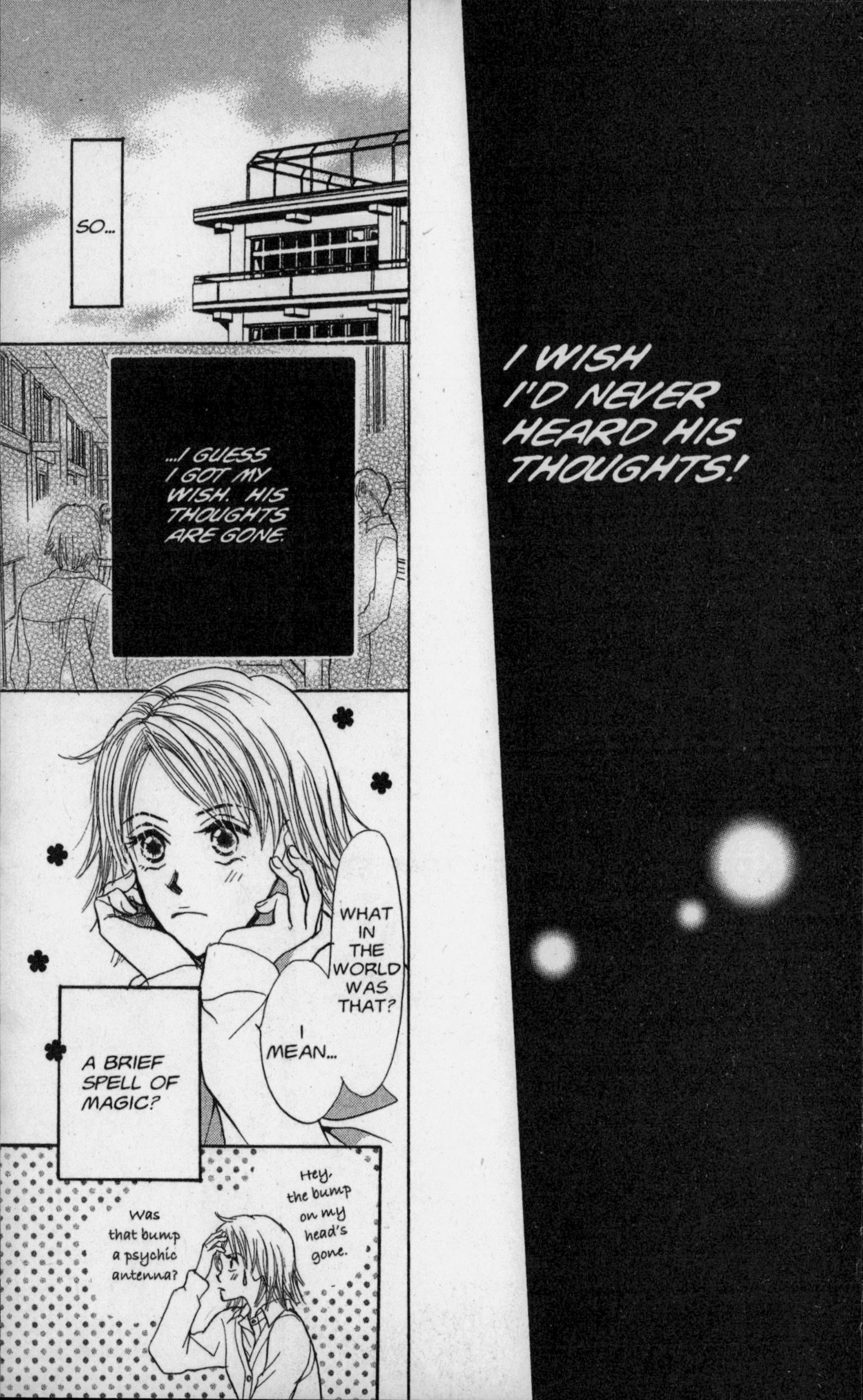
I WISH I'D NEVER HEARD HIS THOUGHTS!
SO...
...I GUESS I GOT MY WISH. HIS THOUGHTS ARE GONE.
WHAT IN THE WORLD WAS THAT?
I MEAN...
A BRIEF SPELL OF MAGIC?
Hey, the bump on my head's gone.
Was that bump a psychic antenna?

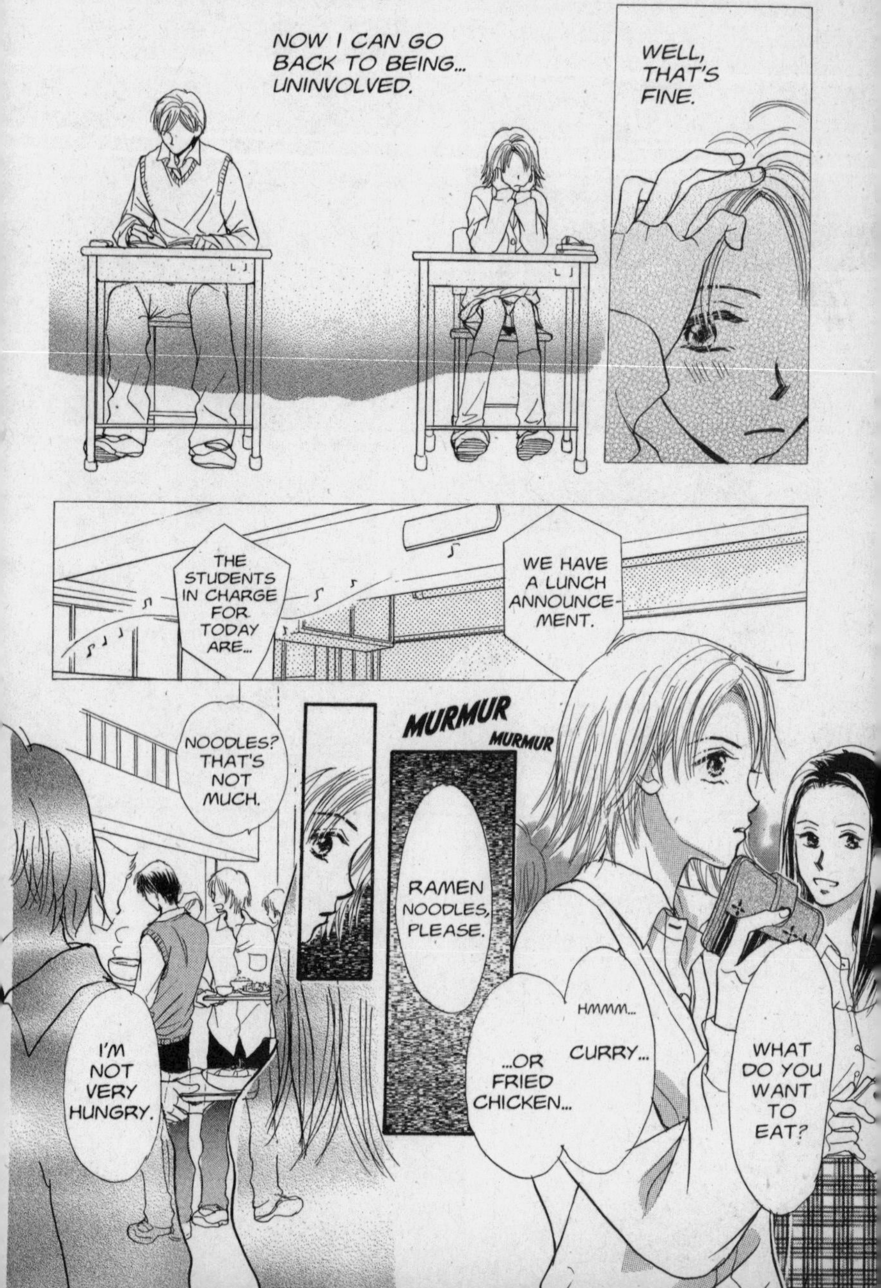
WELL, THAT'S FINE.
NOW I CAN GO BACK TO BEING... UNINVOLVED.
WE HAVE A LUNCH ANNOUNCEMENT.
THE STUDENTS IN CHARGE FOR TODAY ARE...
WHAT DO YOU WANT TO EAT?
HMMM...
CURRY...
...OR FRIED CHICKEN...
MURMUR
MURMUR
RAMEN NOODLES, PLEASE.
NOODLES? THAT'S NOT MUCH.
I'M NOT VERY HUNGRY.

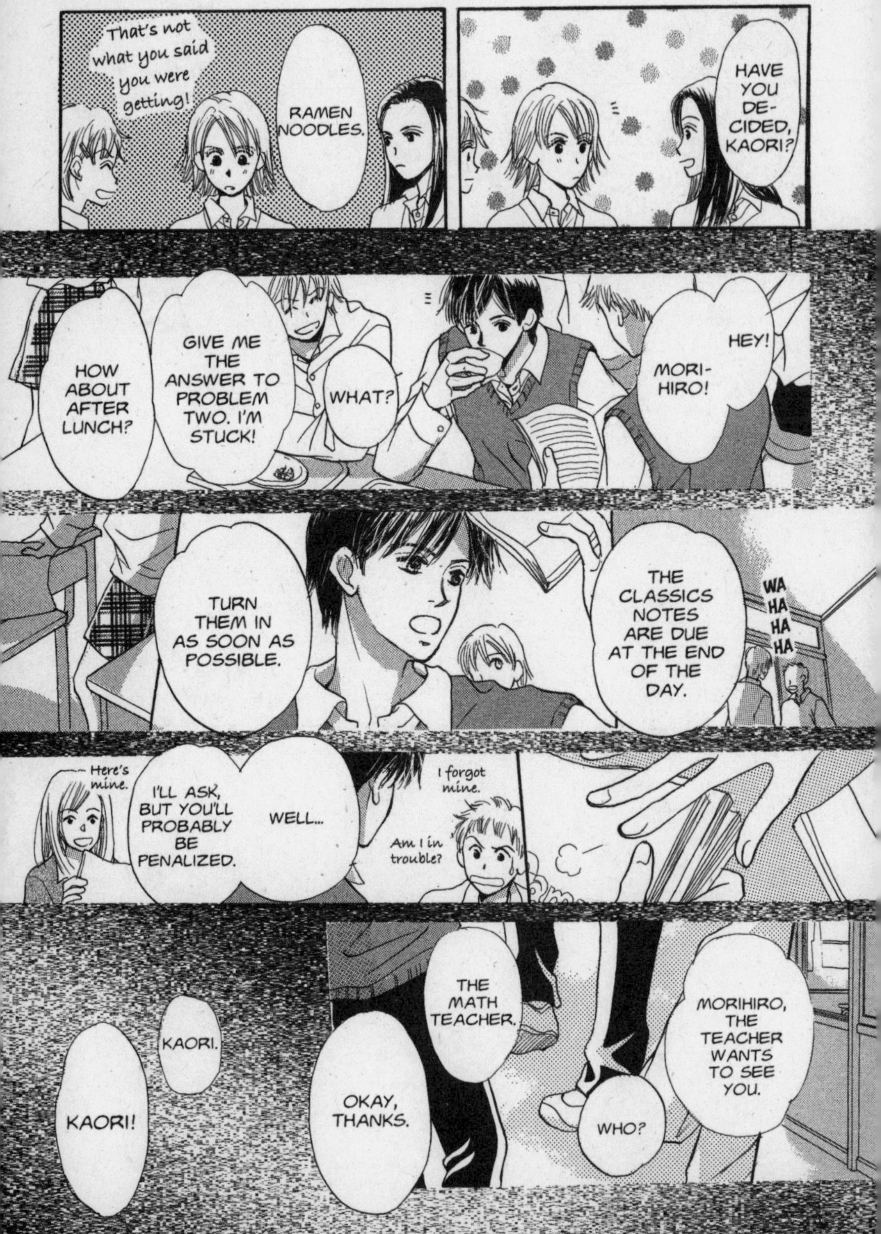
HAVE YOU DE-CIDED, KAORI?
RAMEN NOODLES.
That's not what you said you were getting!
HEY! MORI-HIRO!
WHAT?
GIVE ME THE ANSWER TO PROBLEM TWO. I'M STUCK!
HOW ABOUT AFTER LUNCH?
WA HA HA HA
THE CLASSICS NOTES ARE DUE AT THE END OF THE DAY.
TURN THEM IN AS SOON AS POSSIBLE.
I forgot mine.
Am I in trouble?
WELL...
I'LL ASK, BUT YOU'LL PROBABLY BE PENALIZED.
Here's mine.
MORIHIRO, THE TEACHER WANTS TO SEE YOU.
WHO?
THE MATH TEACHER.
OKAY, THANKS.
KAORI.
KAORI!

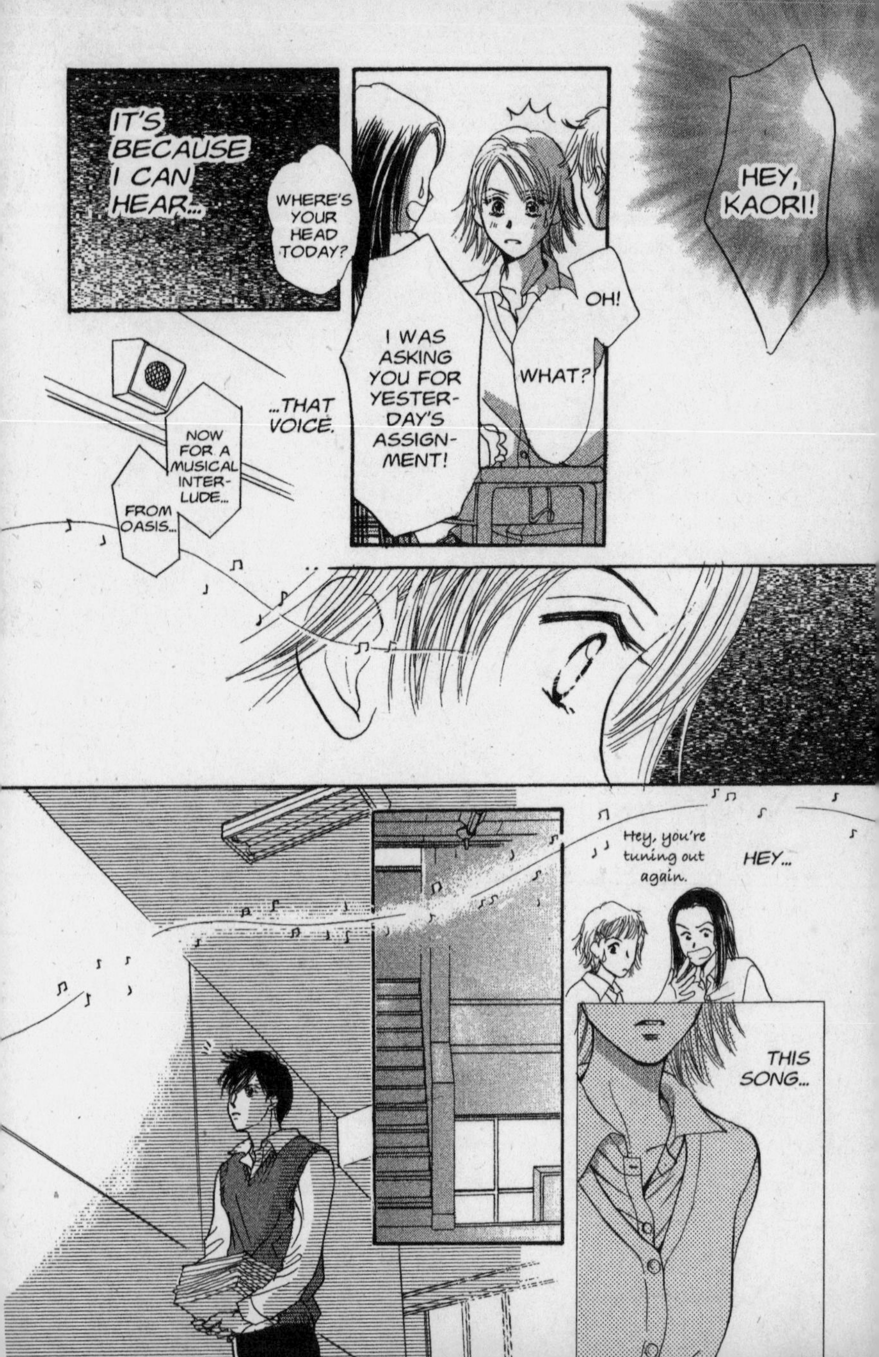
HEY, KAORI!
WHERE'S YOUR HEAD TODAY?
OH!
WHAT?
I WAS ASKING YOU FOR YESTERDAY'S ASSIGNMENT!
IT'S BECAUSE I CAN HEAR...
...THAT VOICE.
NOW FOR A MUSICAL INTERLUDE...
FROM OASIS...
HEY...
Hey, you're tuning out again.
THIS SONG...

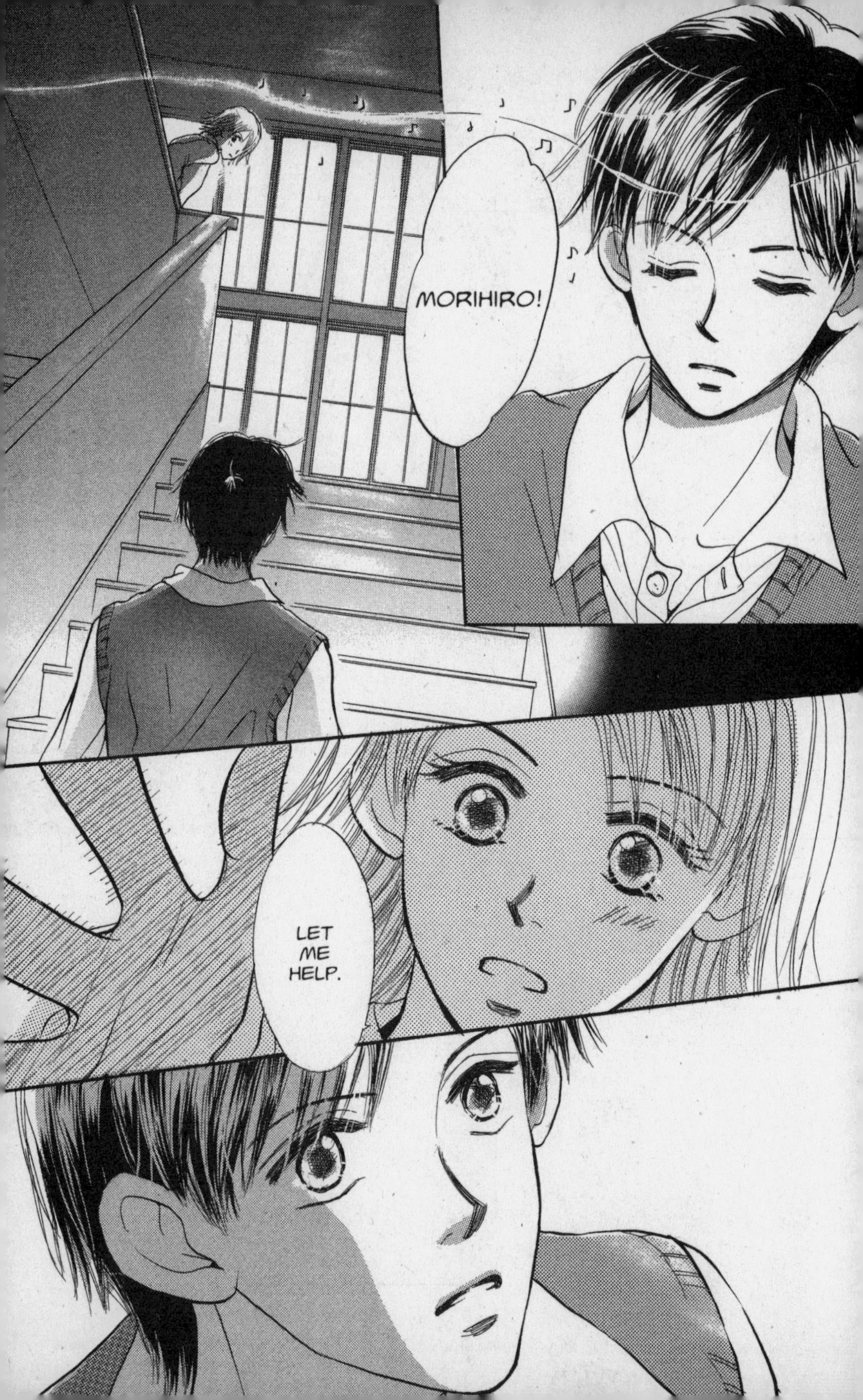
MORIHIRO!
LET ME HELP.

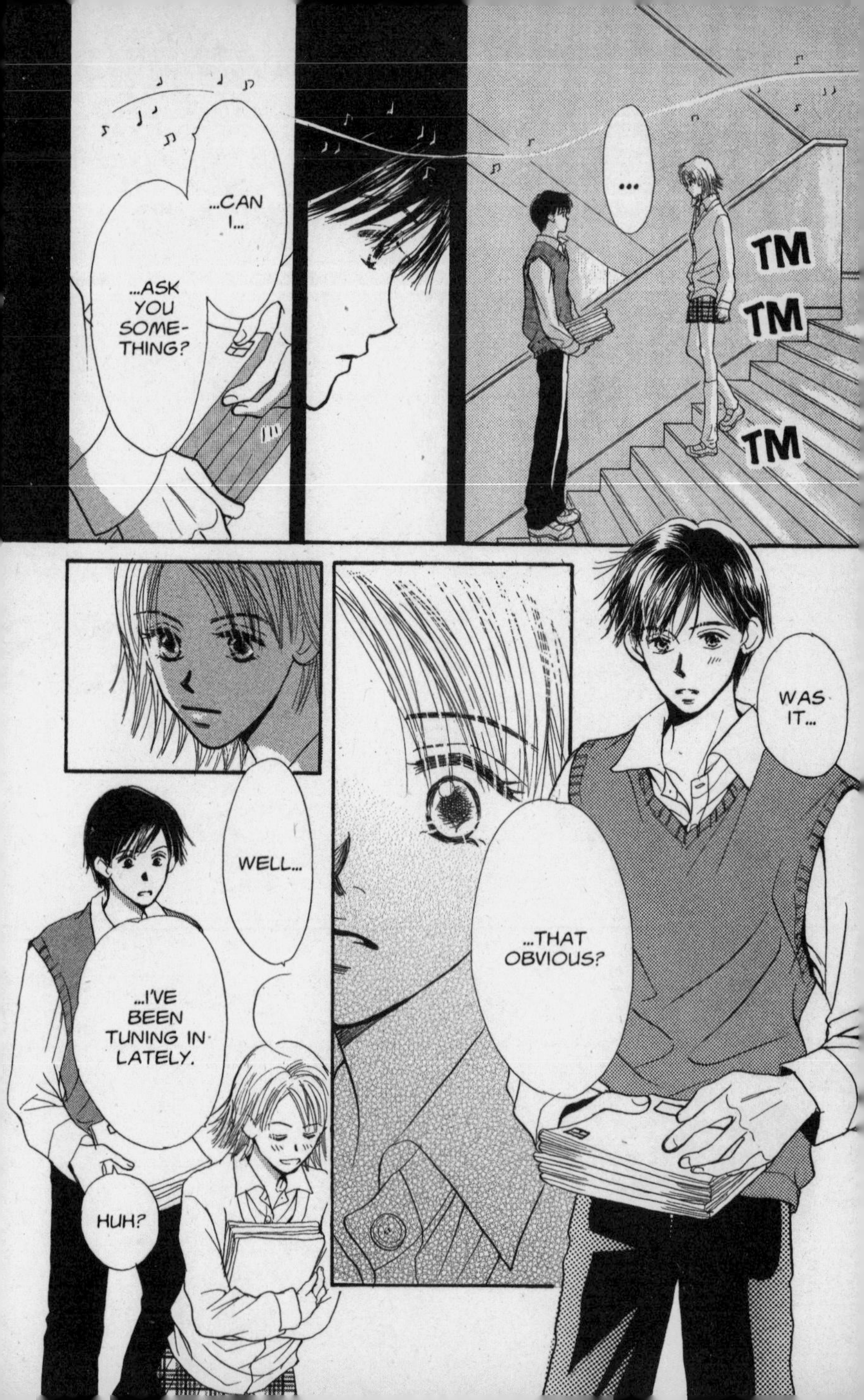
...
TM
TM
TM
...CAN I...
...ASK YOU SOMETHING?
WAS IT...
...THAT OBVIOUS?
WELL...
...I'VE BEEN TUNING IN LATELY.
HUH?

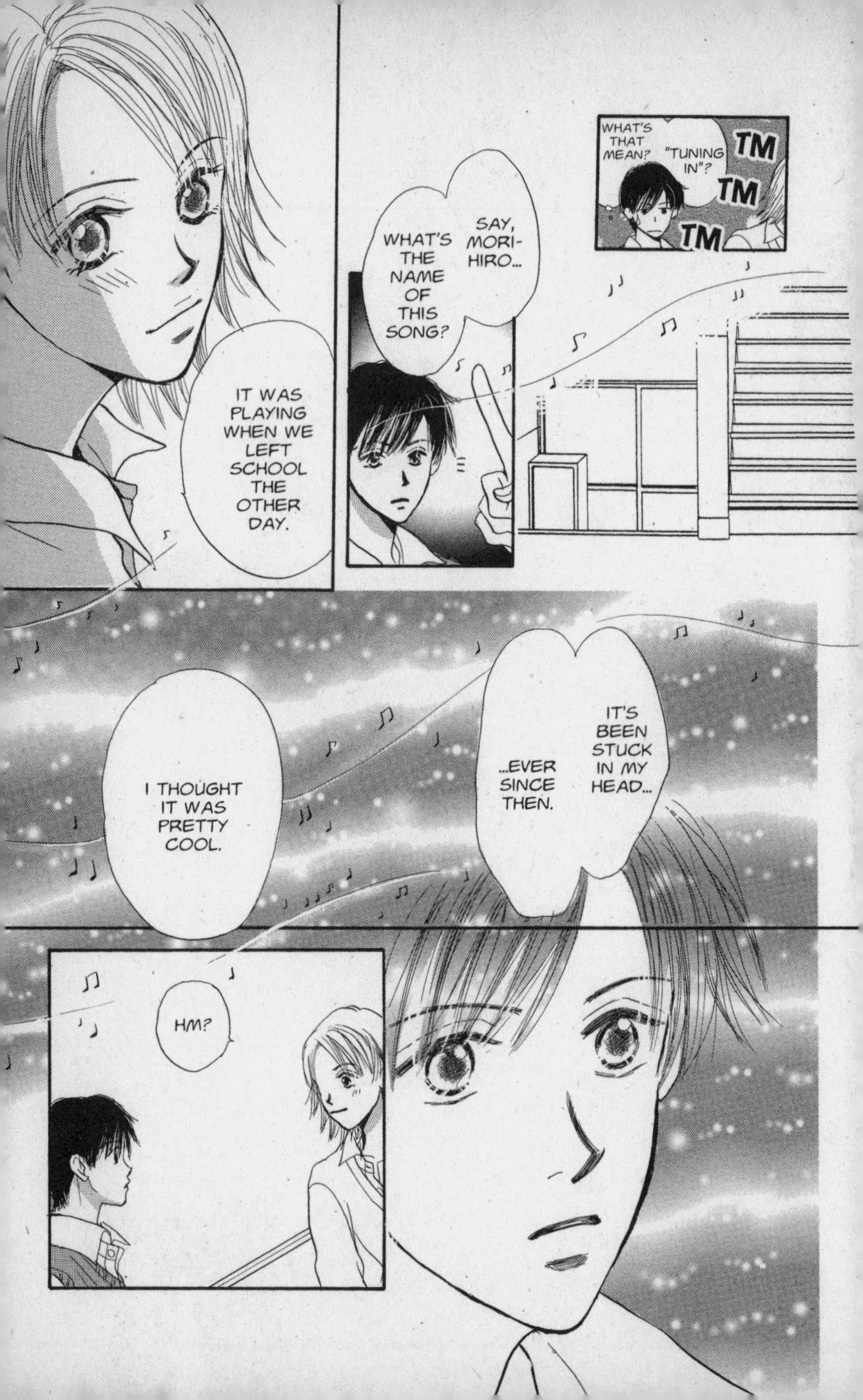
"TUNING IN"?
WHAT'S THAT MEAN?
TM
TM
TM
SAY, MORIHIRO...
WHAT'S THE NAME OF THIS SONG?
IT WAS PLAYING WHEN WE LEFT SCHOOL THE OTHER DAY.
IT'S BEEN STUCK IN MY HEAD...
...EVER SINCE THEN.
I THOUGHT IT WAS PRETTY COOL.
HM?

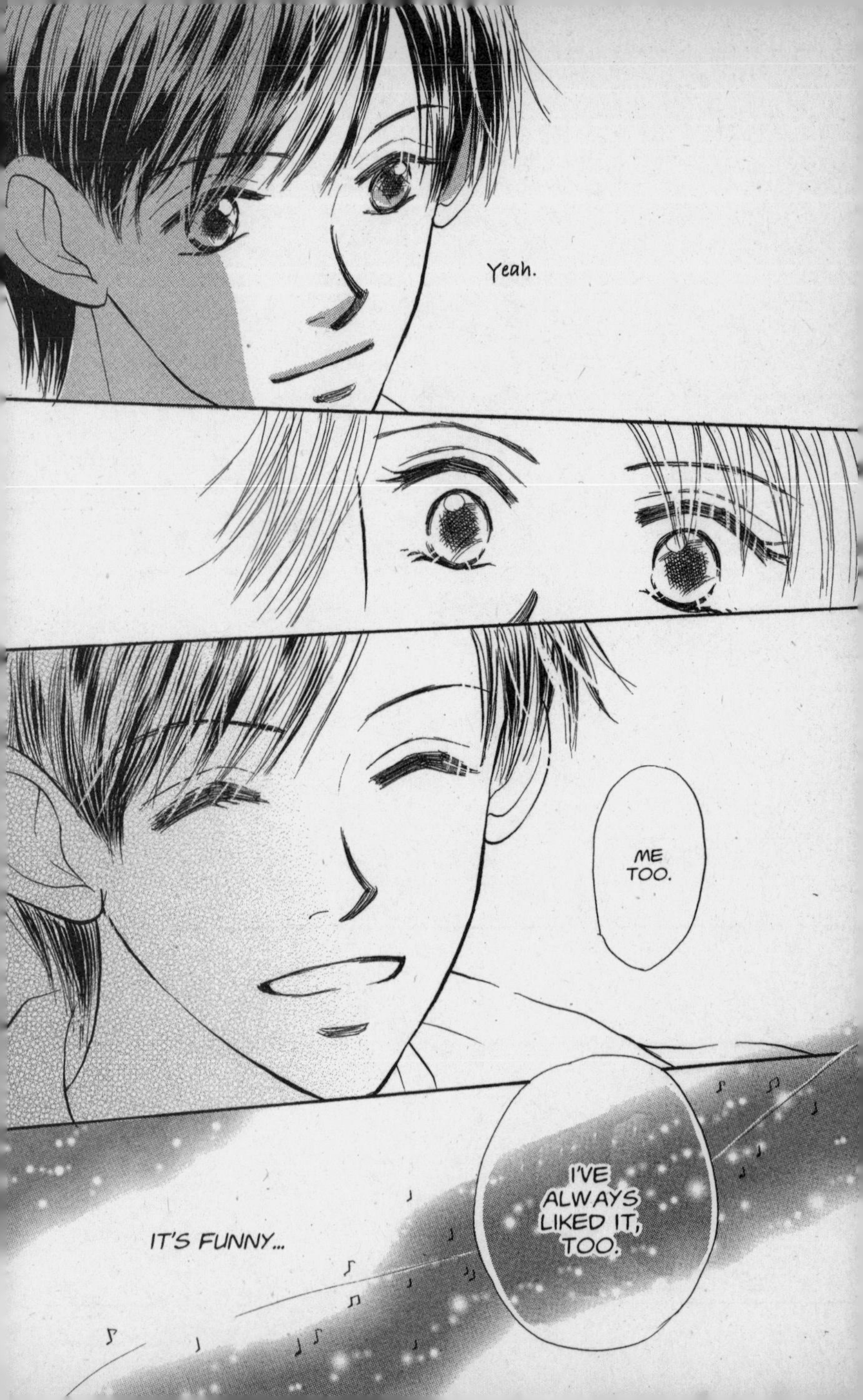
Yeah.
ME TOO.
I'VE ALWAYS LIKED IT, TOO.
IT'S FUNNY...

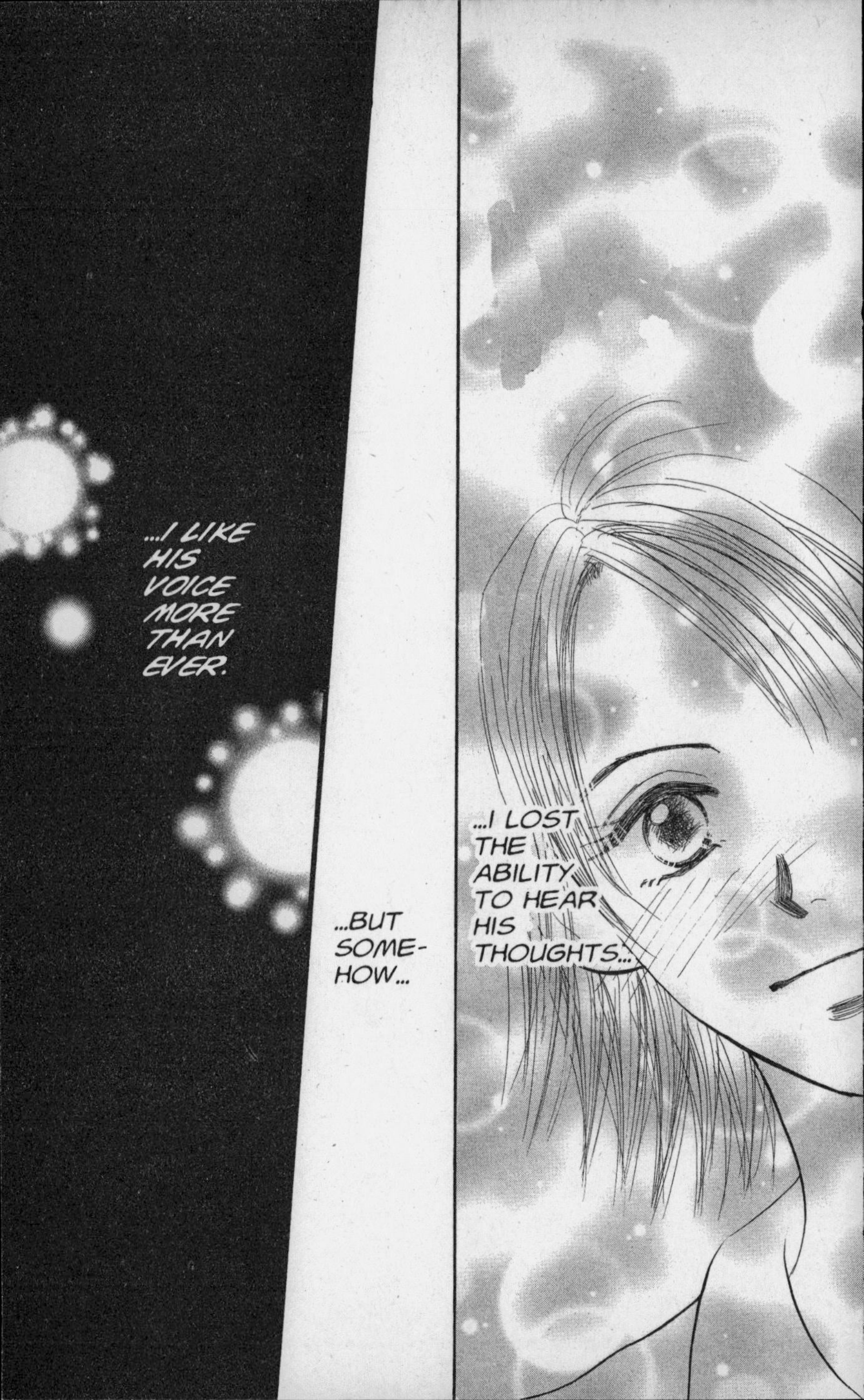
...I LOST THE ABILITY TO HEAR HIS THOUGHTS...
...BUT SOME-HOW...
...I LIKE HIS VOICE MORE THAN EVER.

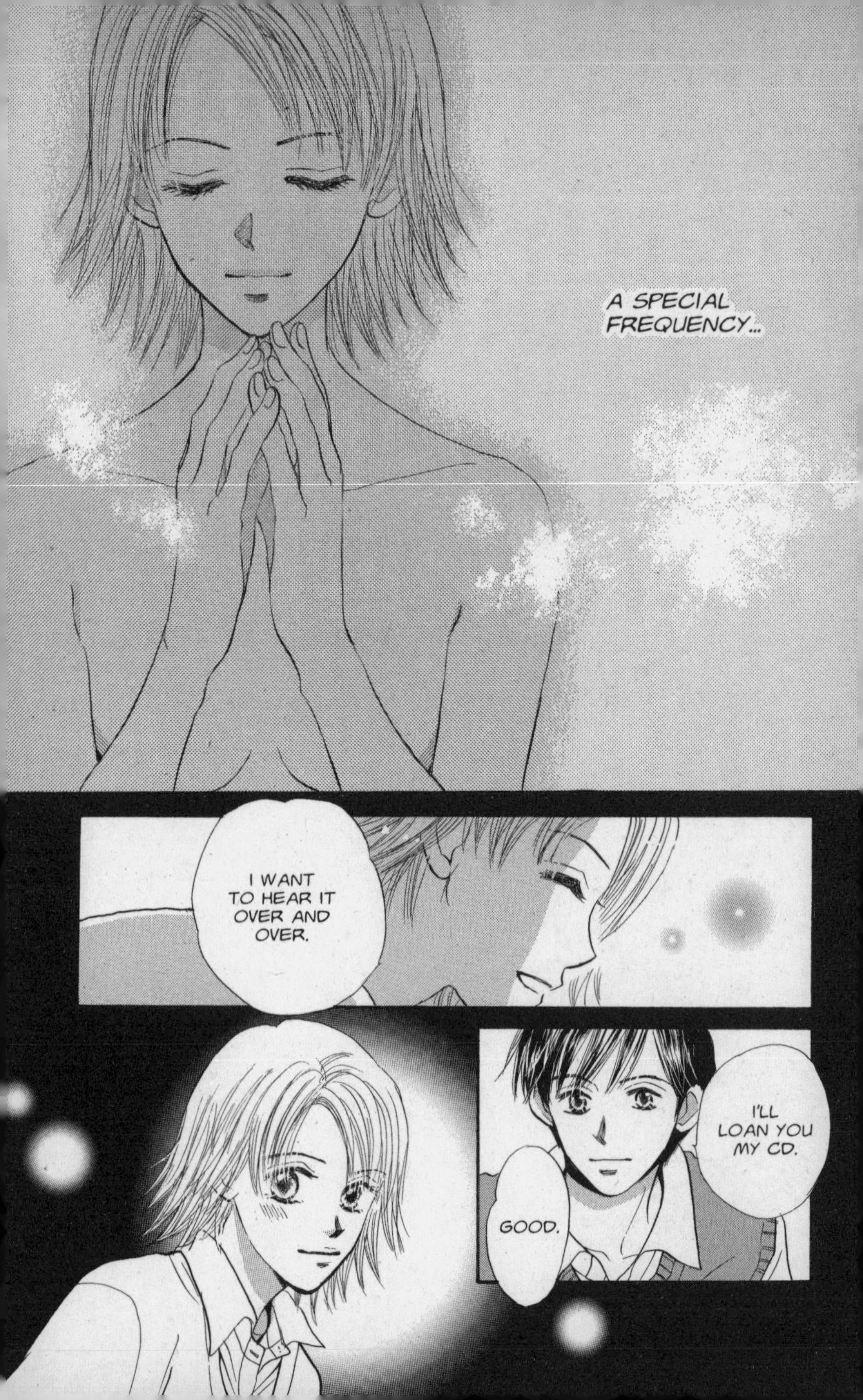
A SPECIAL FREQUENCY...
I WANT TO HEAR IT OVER AND OVER.
I'LL LOAN YOU MY CD.
GOOD.

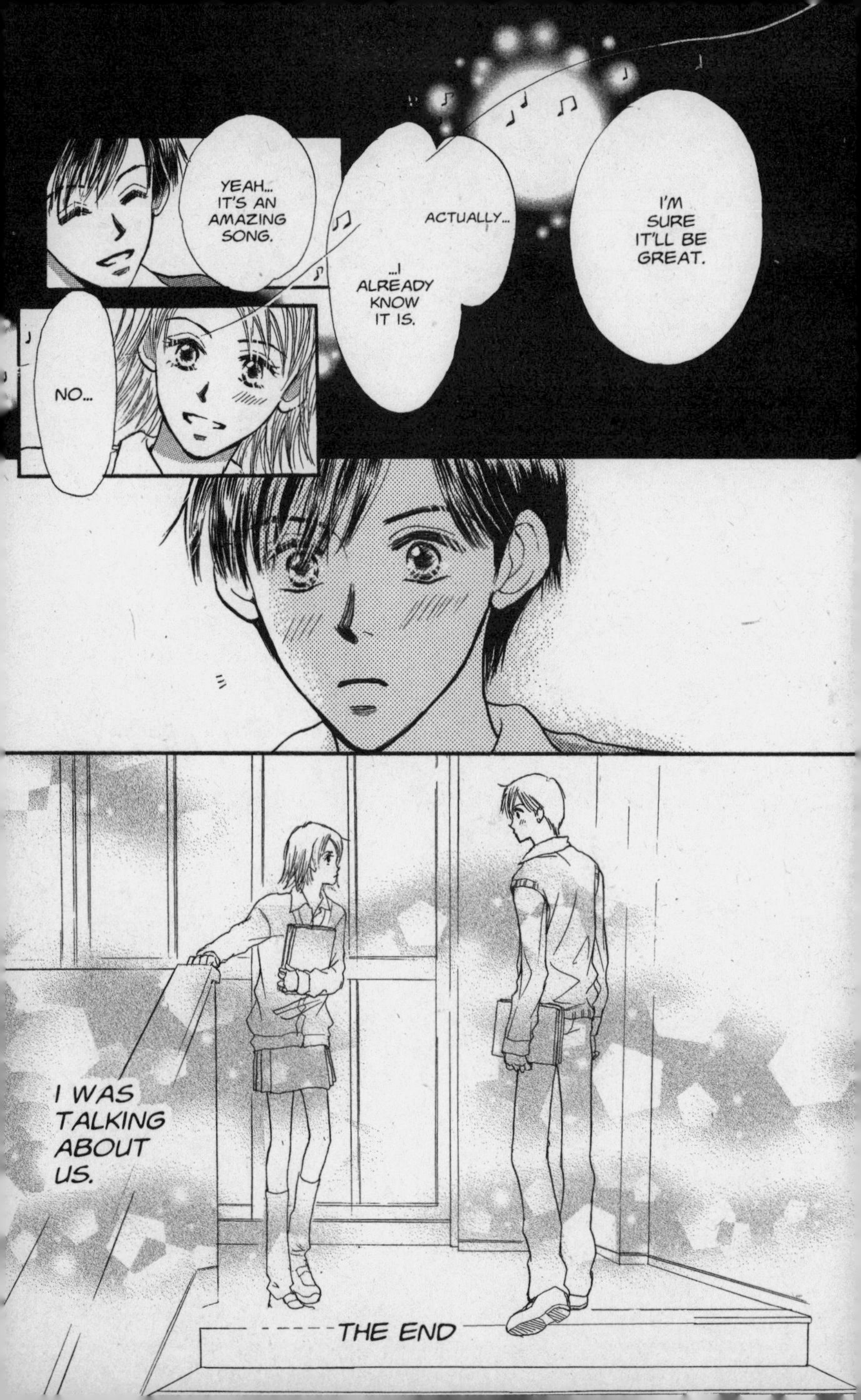
I'M SURE IT'LL BE GREAT.
ACTUALLY...
...I ALREADY KNOW IT IS.
YEAH... IT'S AN AMAZING SONG.
NO...
I WAS TALKING ABOUT US.
THE END

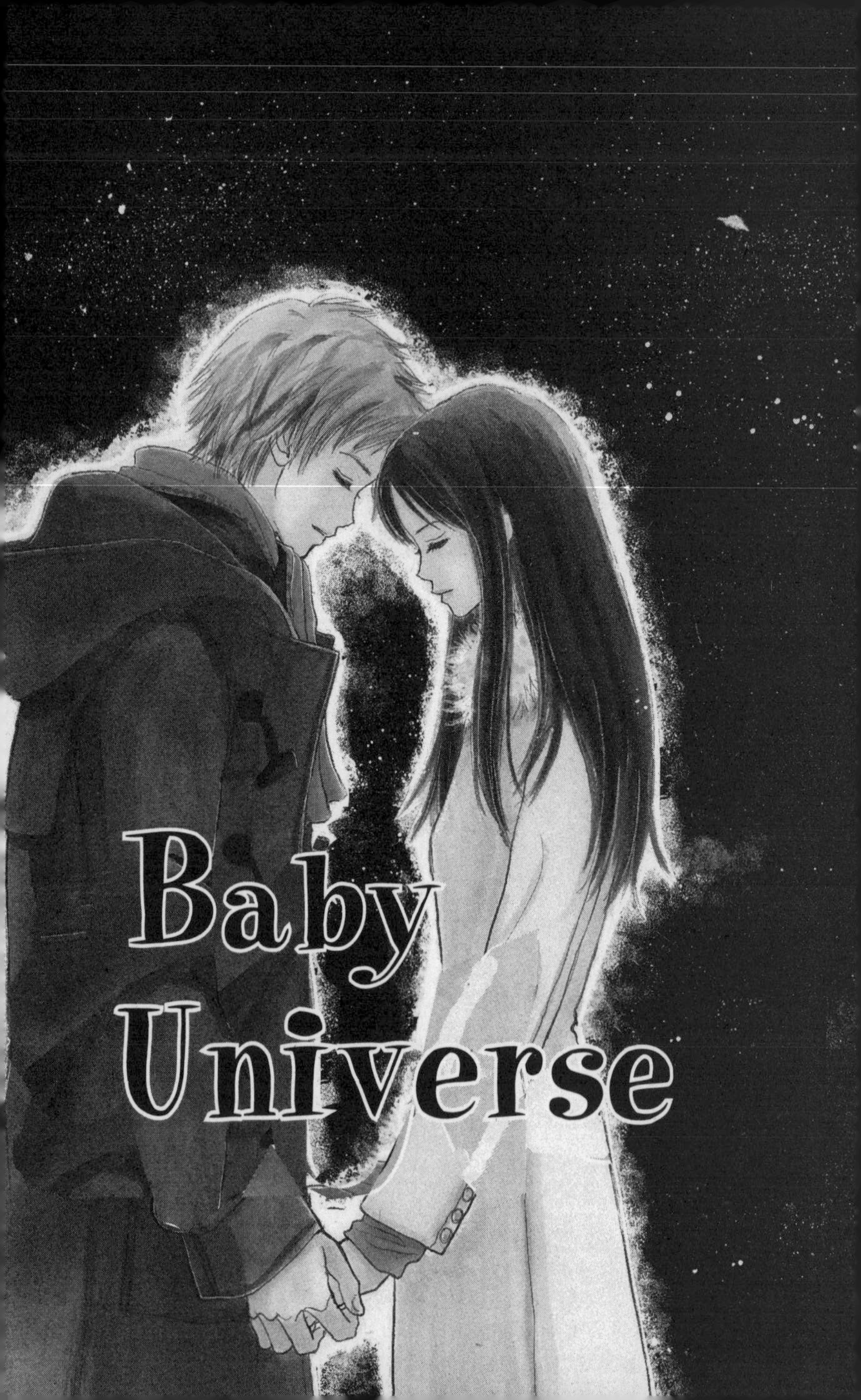
Baby
Universe

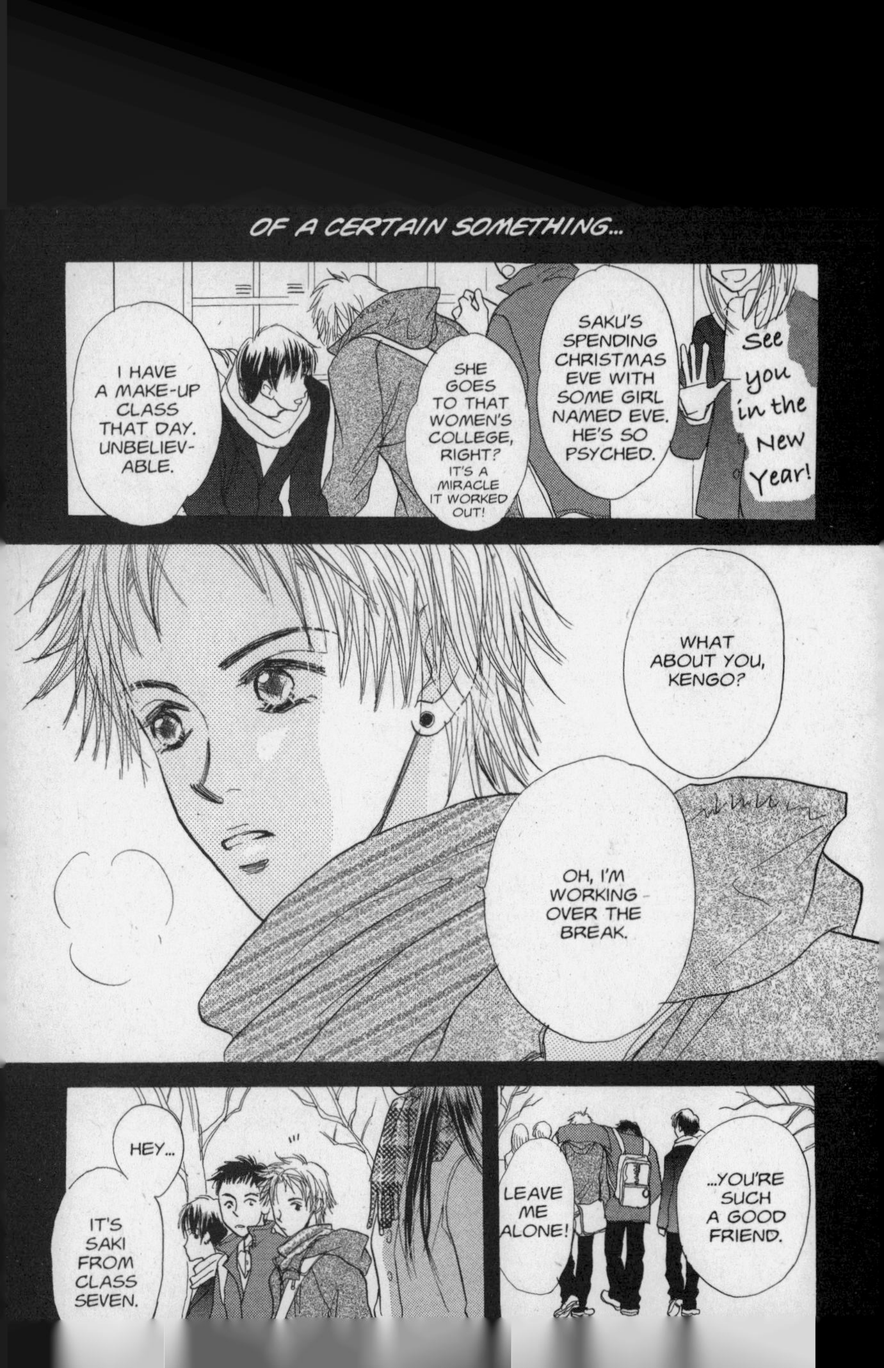
OF A CERTAIN SOMETHING...
See you in the New Year!
SAKU'S SPENDING CHRISTMAS EVE WITH SOME GIRL NAMED EVE. HE'S SO PSYCHED.
SHE GOES TO THAT WOMEN'S COLLEGE, RIGHT? IT'S A MIRACLE IT WORKED OUT!
I HAVE A MAKE-UP CLASS THAT DAY. UNBELIEV-ABLE.
WHAT ABOUT YOU, KENGO?
OH, I'M WORKING OVER THE BREAK.
...YOU'RE SUCH A GOOD FRIEND.
LEAVE ME ALONE!
HEY...
IT'S SAKI FROM CLASS SEVEN.

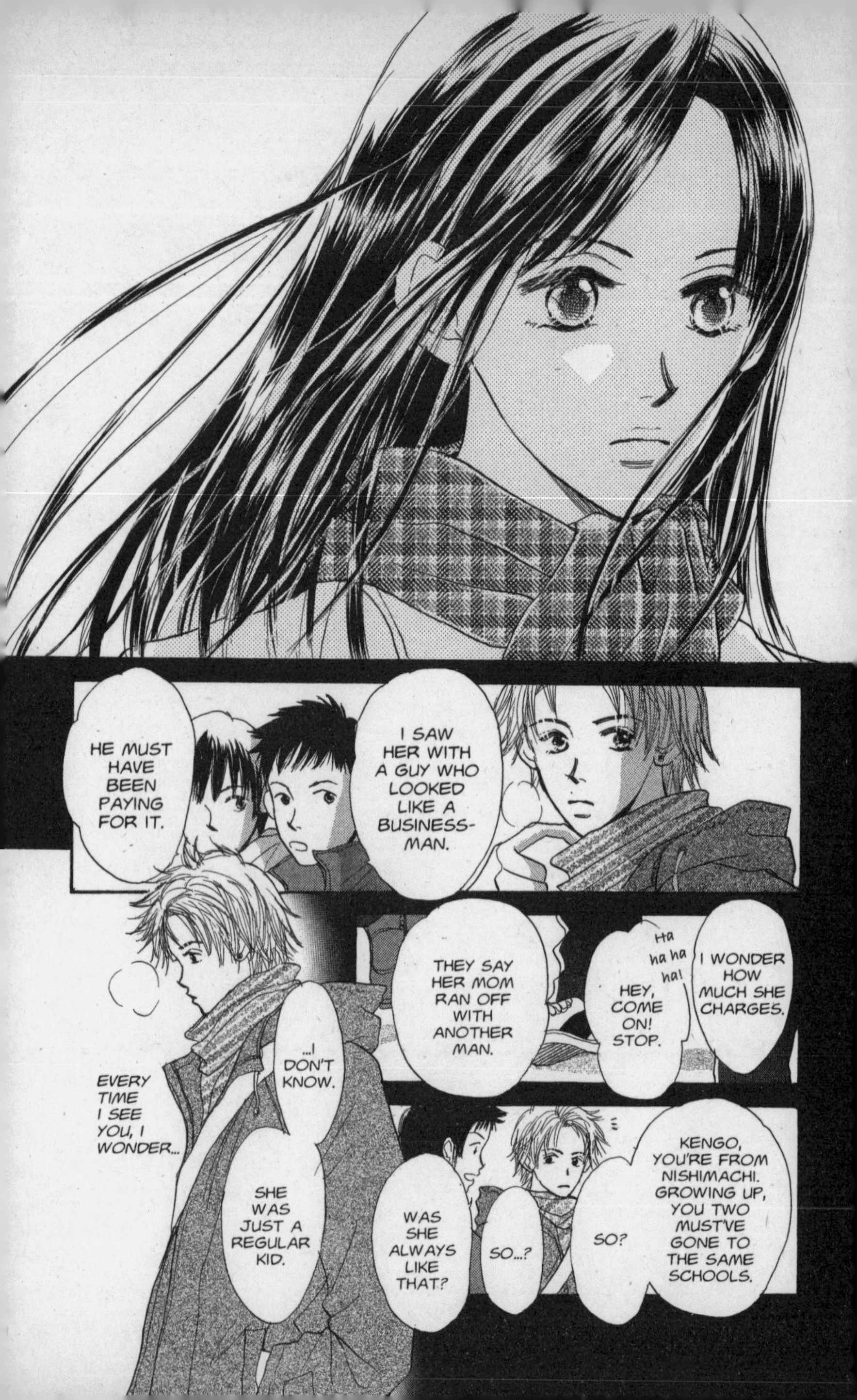
I SAW HER WITH A GUY WHO LOOKED LIKE A BUSINESS-MAN.
HE MUST HAVE BEEN PAYING FOR IT.
I WONDER HOW MUCH SHE CHARGES.
Ha ha ha ha!
HEY, COME ON! STOP.
THEY SAY HER MOM RAN OFF WITH ANOTHER MAN.
KENGO, YOU'RE FROM NISHIMACHI. GROWING UP, YOU TWO MUST'VE GONE TO THE SAME SCHOOLS.
SO?
SO...?
WAS SHE ALWAYS LIKE THAT?
...I DON'T KNOW.
SHE WAS JUST A REGULAR KID.
EVERY TIME I SEE YOU, I WONDER...

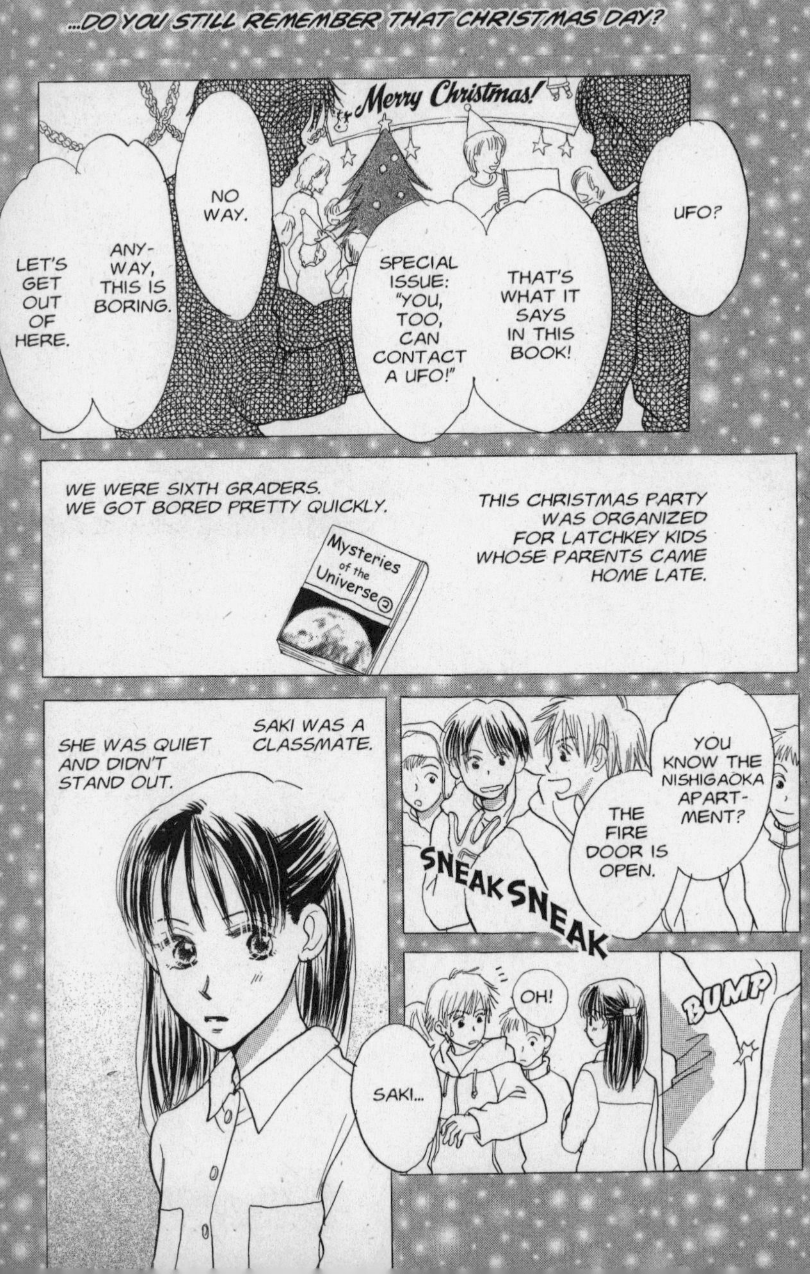
...DO YOU STILL REMEMBER THAT CHRISTMAS DAY?
Merry Christmas!
UFO?
THAT'S WHAT IT SAYS IN THIS BOOK!
SPECIAL ISSUE: "YOU, TOO, CAN CONTACT A UFO!"
NO WAY.
ANY-WAY, THIS IS BORING.
LET'S GET OUT OF HERE.
THIS CHRISTMAS PARTY WAS ORGANIZED FOR LATCHKEY KIDS WHOSE PARENTS CAME HOME LATE.
WE WERE SIXTH GRADERS. WE GOT BORED PRETTY QUICKLY.
Mysteries of the Universe
YOU KNOW THE NISHIGAOKA APART-MENT?
THE FIRE DOOR IS OPEN.
SNEAK SNEAK SNEAK
BUMP
OH!
SAKI...
SAKI WAS A CLASSMATE.
SHE WAS QUIET AND DIDN'T STAND OUT.

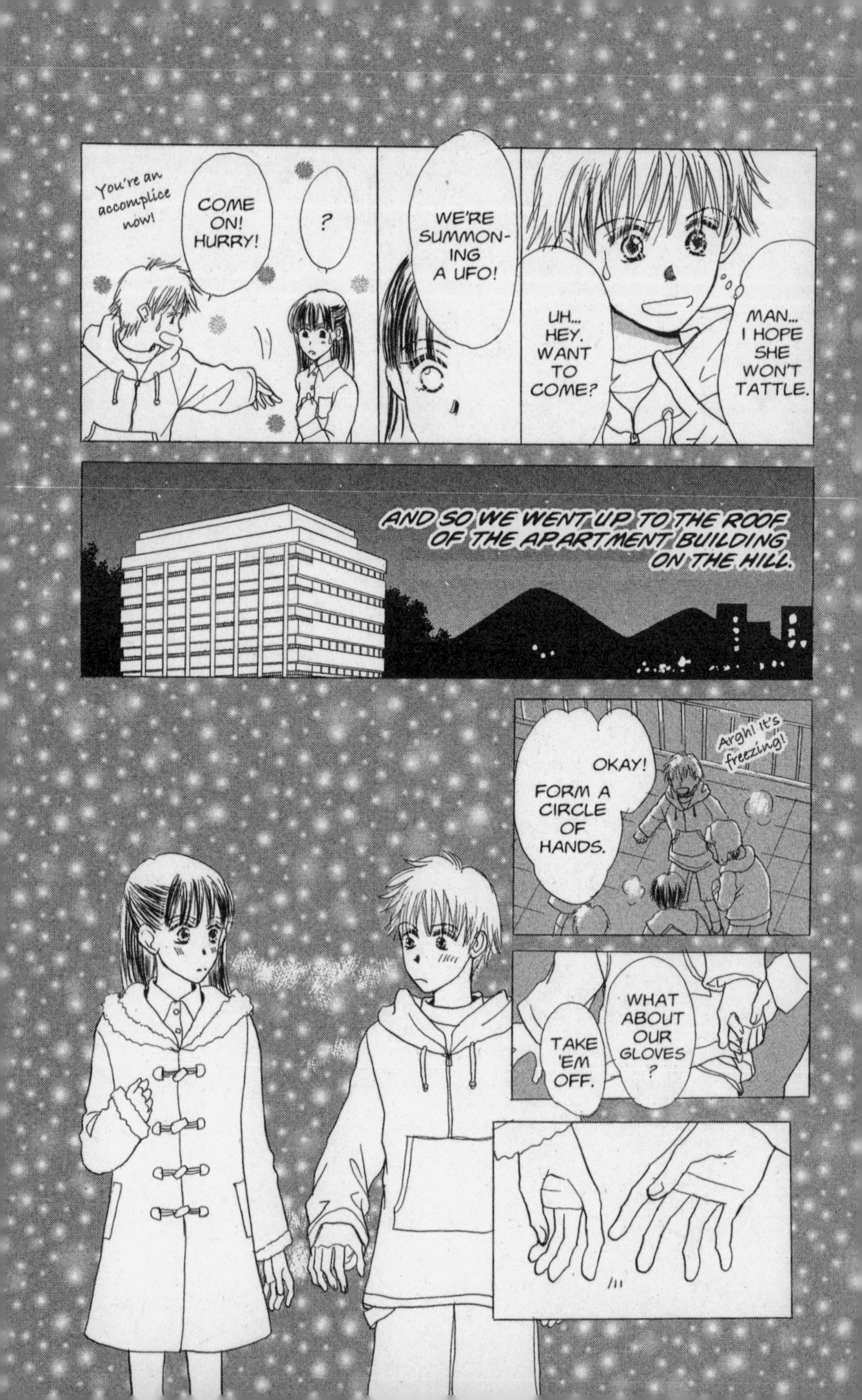
MAN... I HOPE SHE WON'T TATTLE.
UH... HEY. WANT TO COME?
WE'RE SUMMON-ING A UFO!
?
COME ON! HURRY!
You're an accomplice now!
AND SO WE WENT UP TO THE ROOF OF THE APARTMENT BUILDING ON THE HILL.
Argh! It's freezing!
OKAY! FORM A CIRCLE OF HANDS.
WHAT ABOUT OUR GLOVES?
TAKE 'EM OFF.

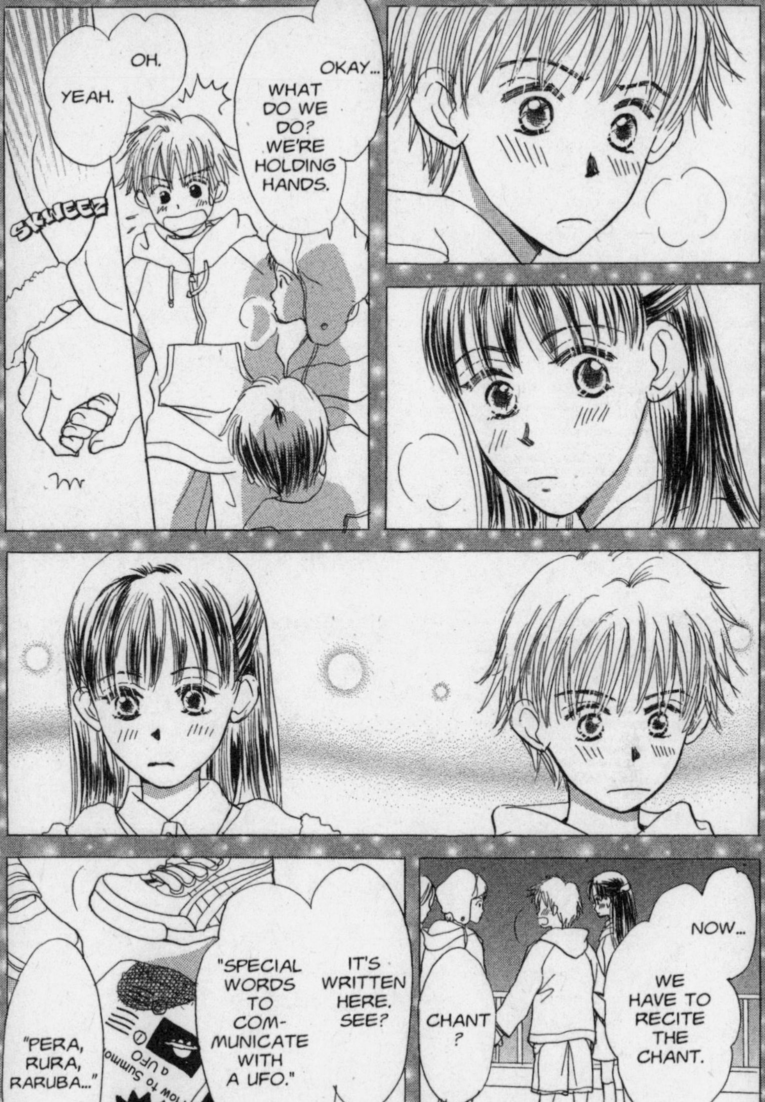
OKAY... WHAT DO WE DO? WE'RE HOLDING HANDS.
OH. YEAH.
SKWEEZ
NOW... WE HAVE TO RECITE THE CHANT.
CHANT?
IT'S WRITTEN HERE. SEE?
"SPECIAL WORDS TO COM-MUNICATE WITH A UFO."
"PERA, RURA, RARUBA..."

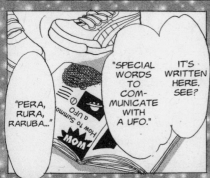

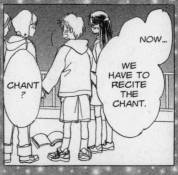

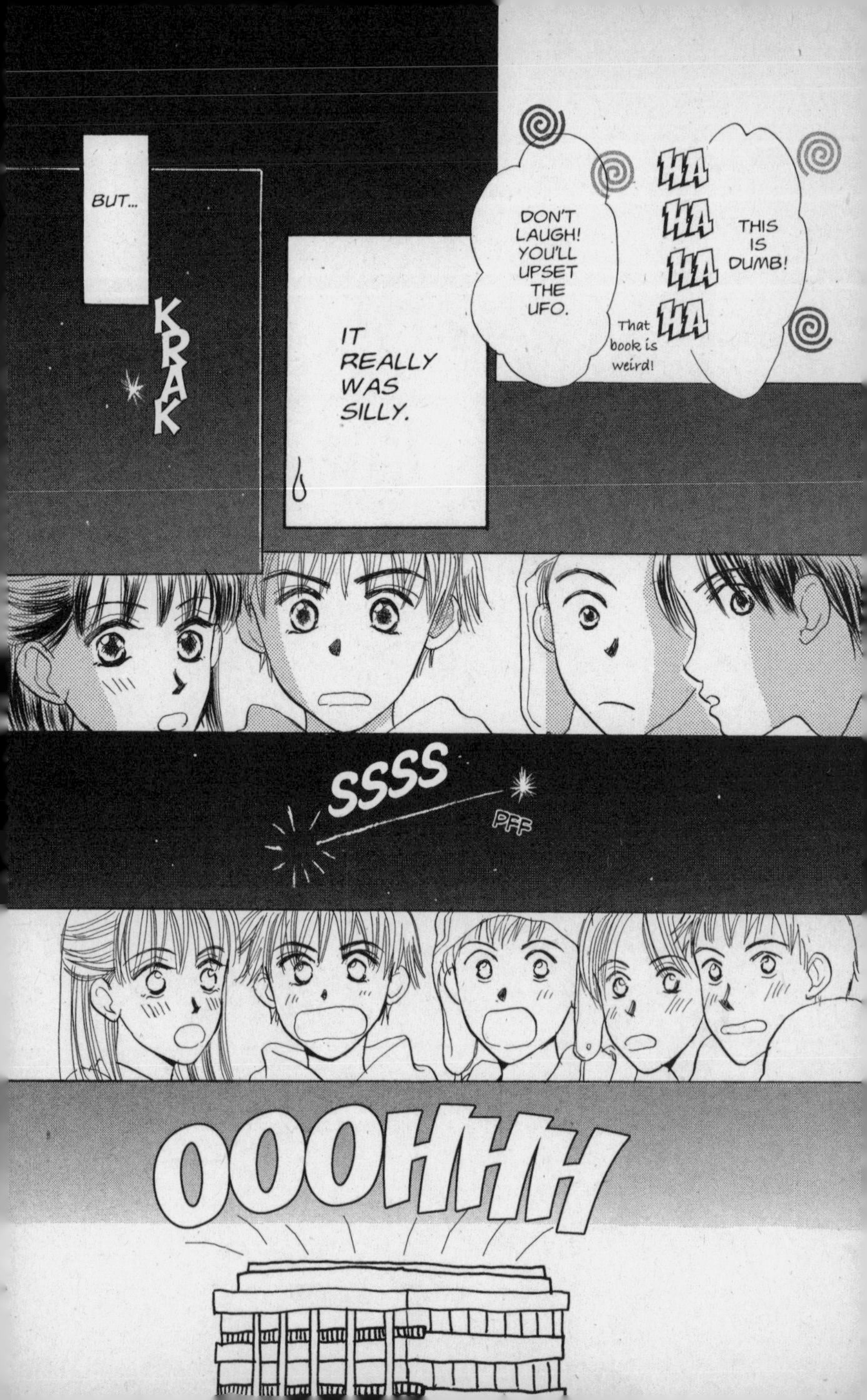
THIS IS DUMB!
HA HA HA HA
That book is weird!
DON'T LAUGH! YOU'LL UPSET THE UFO.
IT REALLY WAS SILLY.
BUT...
KRAK
SSSS
PFF
OOOHHH

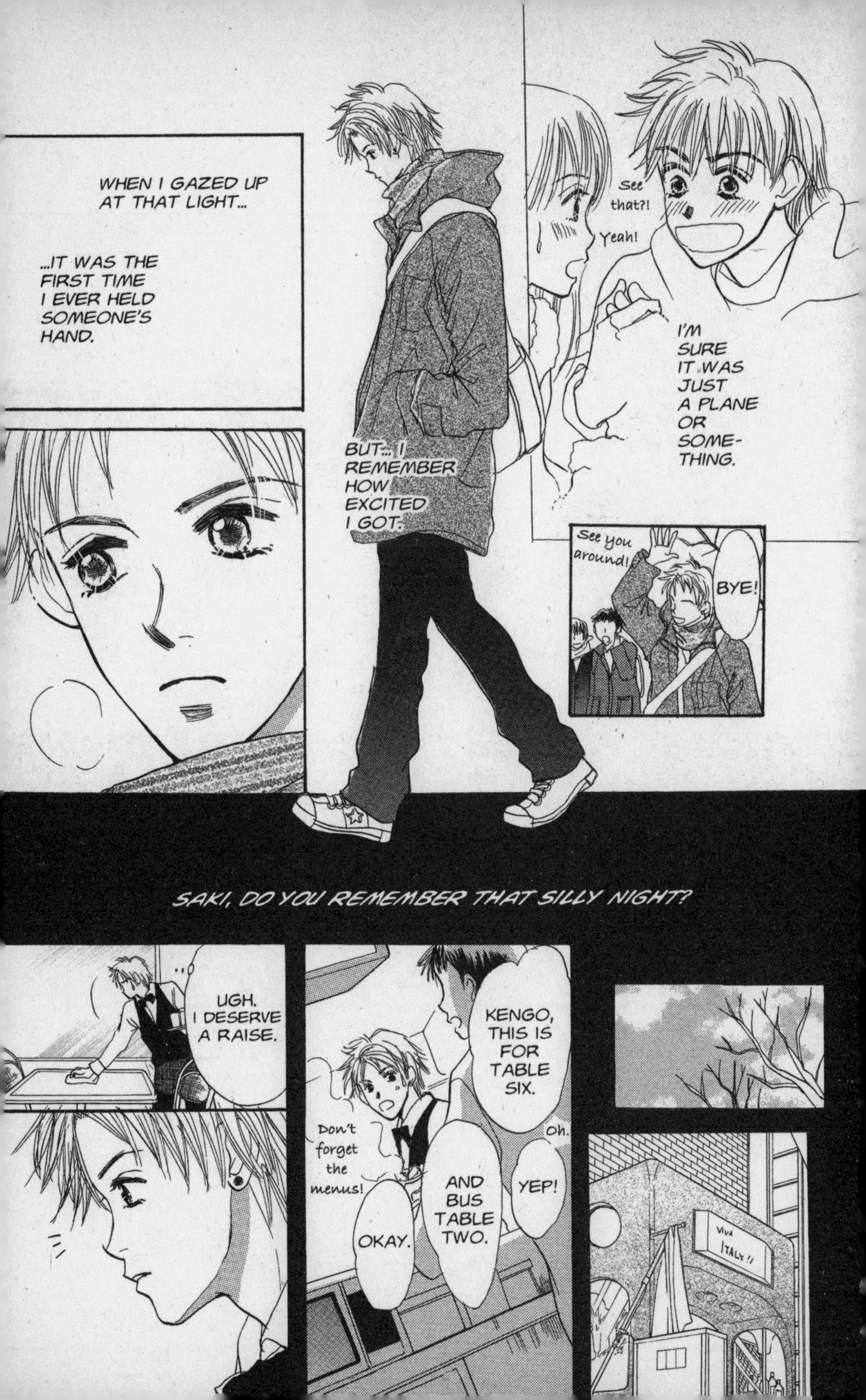
See that?!
Yeah!
I'M SURE IT WAS JUST A PLANE OR SOMETHING.
See you around!
BYE!
BUT... I REMEMBER HOW EXCITED I GOT.
WHEN I GAZED UP AT THAT LIGHT...
...IT WAS THE FIRST TIME I EVER HELD SOMEONE'S HAND.
SAKI, DO YOU REMEMBER THAT SILLY NIGHT?
VIVA ITALY!!
KENGO, THIS IS FOR TABLE SIX.
Oh.
YEP!
AND BUS TABLE TWO.
Don't forget the menus!
OKAY.
...
UGH. I DESERVE A RAISE.

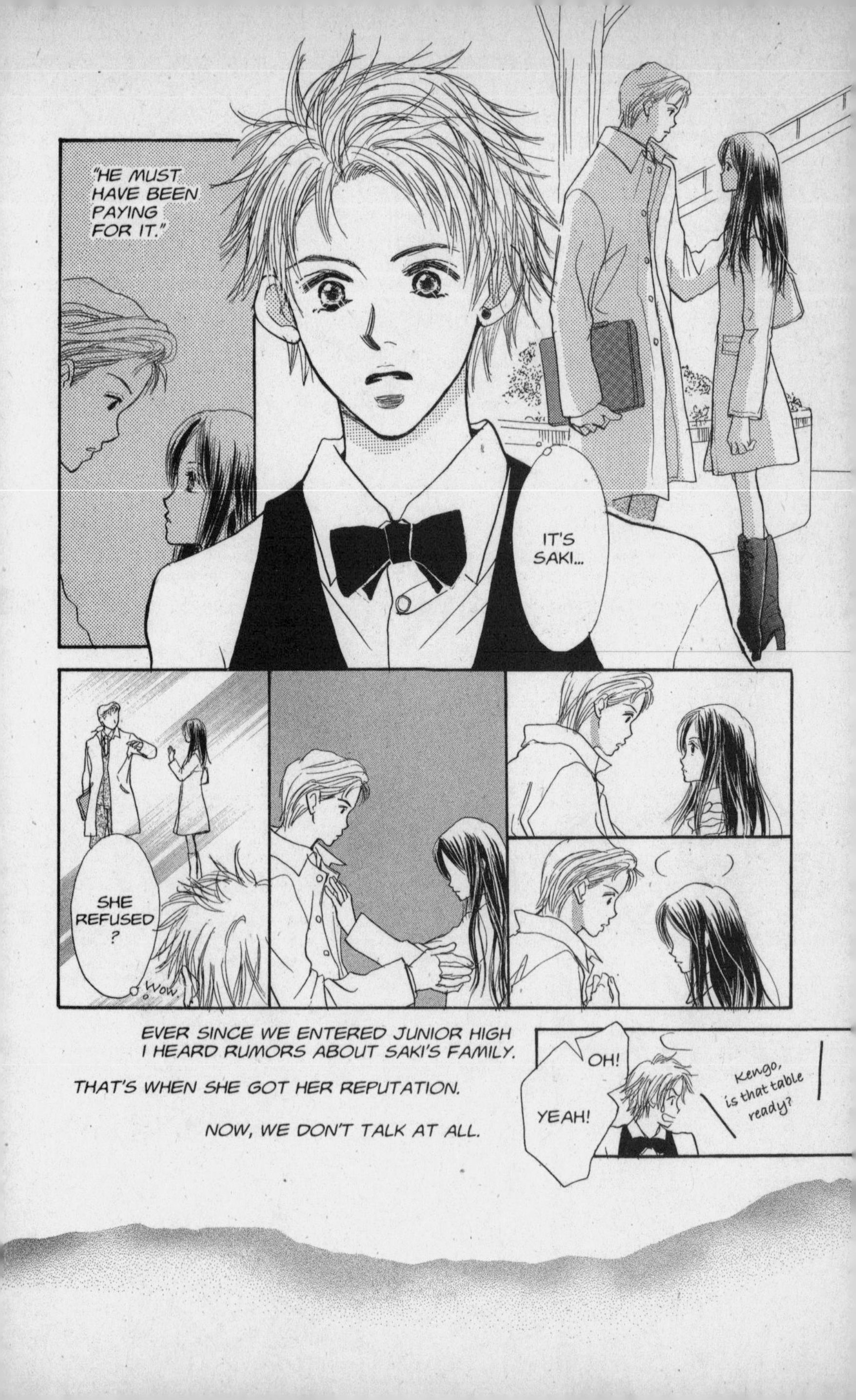
IT'S SAKI...
"HE MUST HAVE BEEN PAYING FOR IT."
SHE REFUSED?
Wow.
Kengo, is that table ready?
OH!
YEAH!
EVER SINCE WE ENTERED JUNIOR HIGH I HEARD RUMORS ABOUT SAKI'S FAMILY.
THAT'S WHEN SHE GOT HER REPUTATION.
NOW, WE DON'T TALK AT ALL.

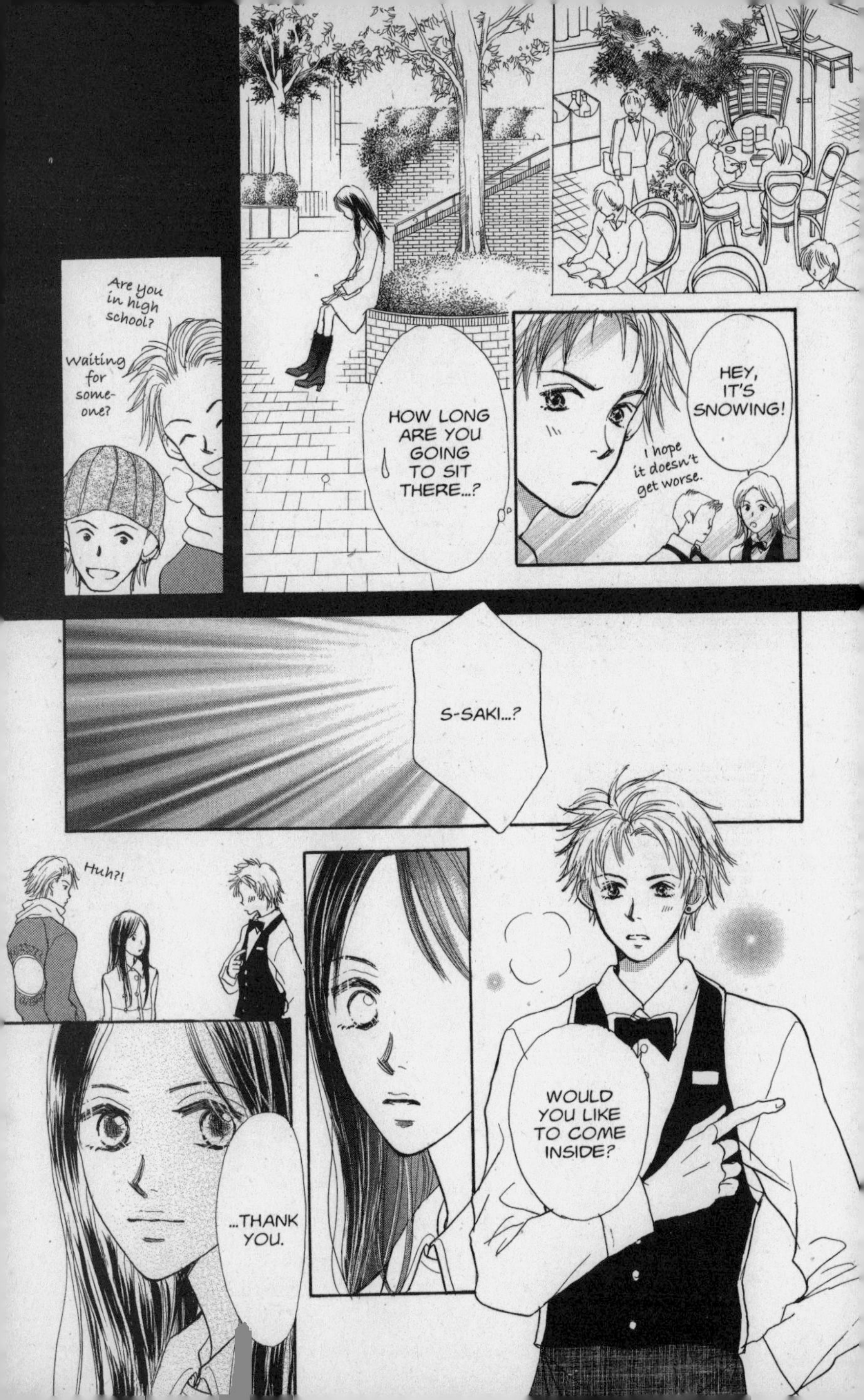
HEY, IT'S SNOWING!
I hope it doesn't get worse.
HOW LONG ARE YOU GOING TO SIT THERE...?
Are you in high school?
Waiting for some-one?
S-SAKI...?
WOULD YOU LIKE TO COME INSIDE?
Huh?!
...THANK YOU.

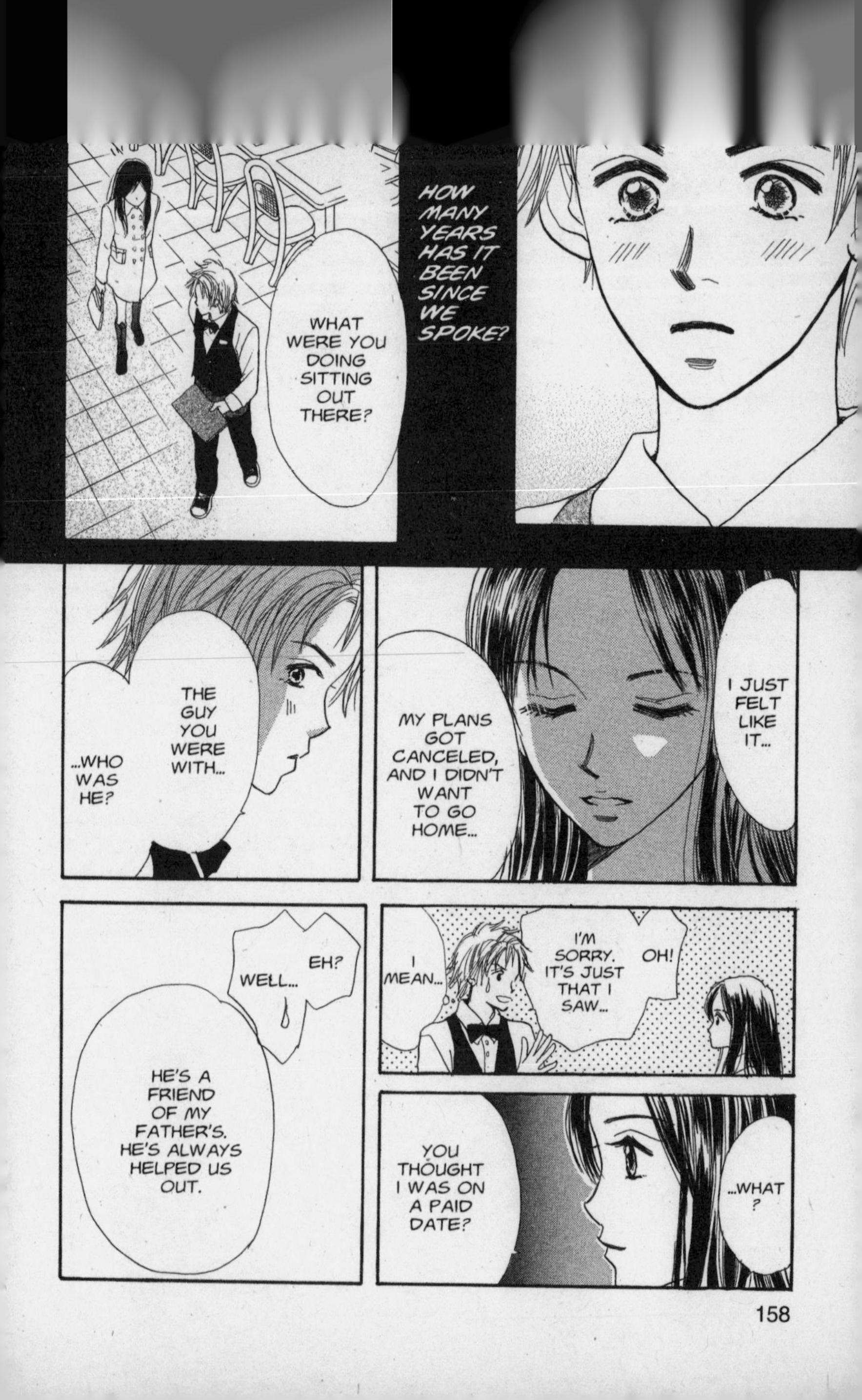
HOW MANY YEARS HAS IT BEEN SINCE WE SPOKE?
WHAT WERE YOU DOING SITTING OUT THERE?
I JUST FELT LIKE IT...
MY PLANS GOT CANCELED, AND I DIDN'T WANT TO GO HOME...
THE GUY YOU WERE WITH...
...WHO WAS HE?
OH!
I'M SORRY. IT'S JUST THAT I SAW...
I MEAN...
...WHAT?
YOU THOUGHT I WAS ON A PAID DATE?
EH? WELL...
HE'S A FRIEND OF MY FATHER'S. HE'S ALWAYS HELPED US OUT.

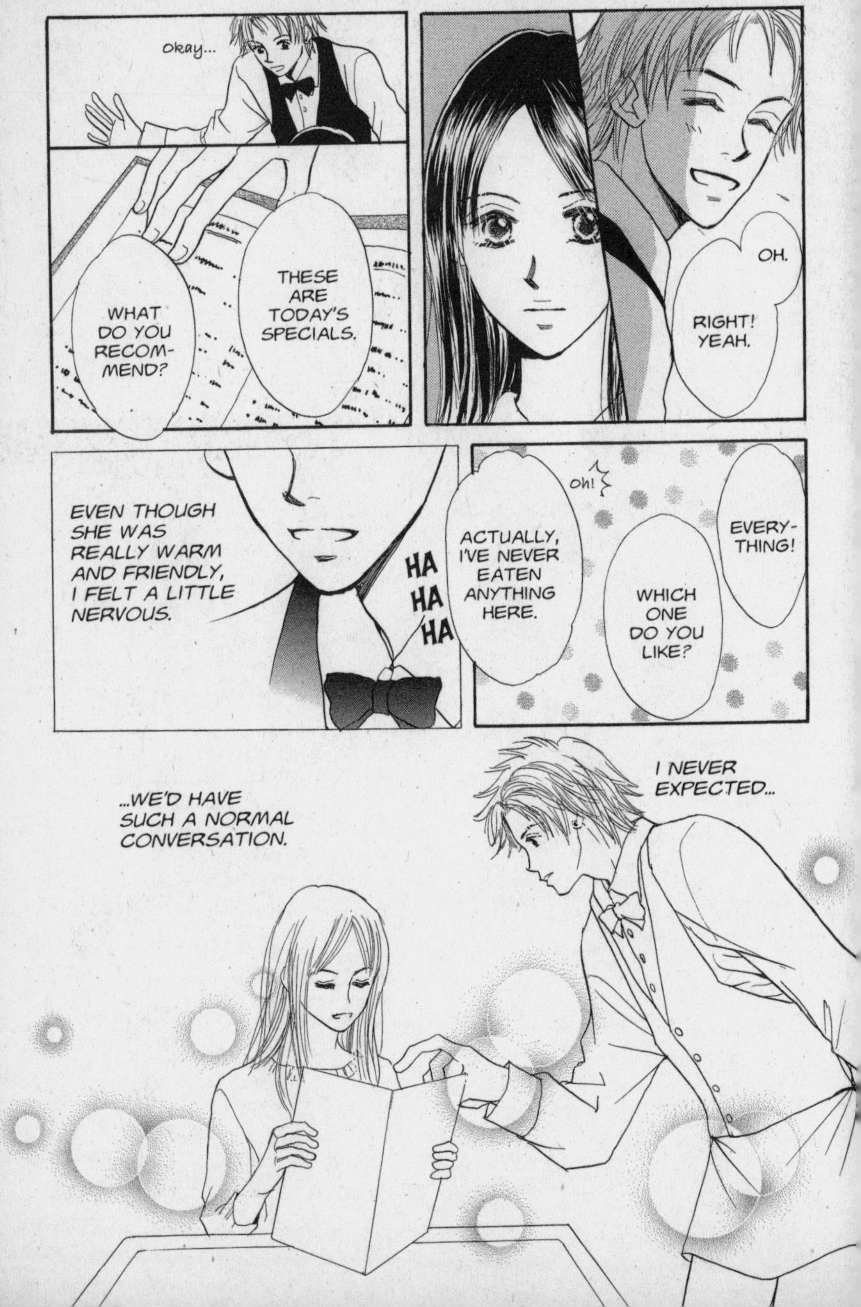
OH.
RIGHT! YEAH.
okay...
THESE ARE TODAY'S SPECIALS.
WHAT DO YOU RECOMMEND?
EVERYTHING!
oh!
WHICH ONE DO YOU LIKE?
ACTUALLY, I'VE NEVER EATEN ANYTHING HERE.
HA HA HA
EVEN THOUGH SHE WAS REALLY WARM AND FRIENDLY, I FELT A LITTLE NERVOUS.
I NEVER EXPECTED...
...WE'D HAVE SUCH A NORMAL CONVERSATION.

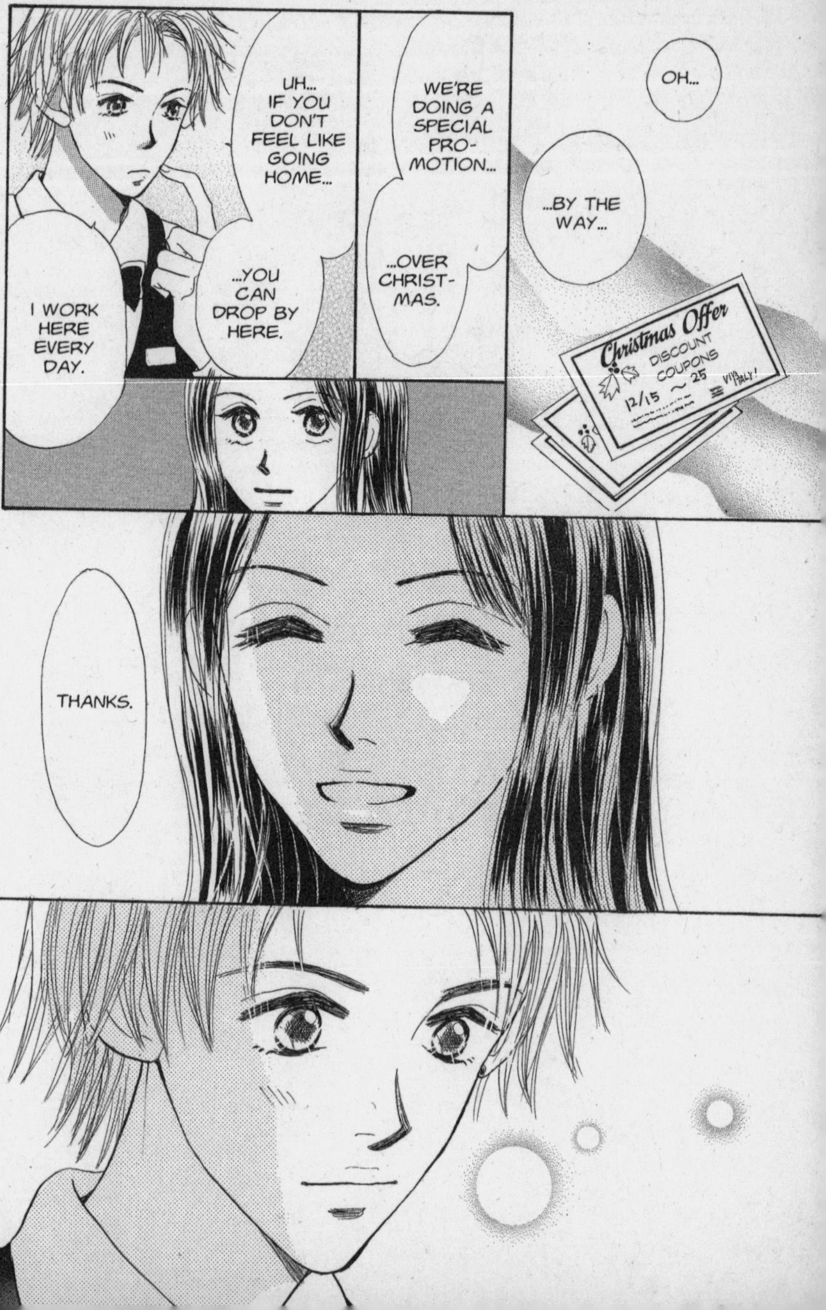
OH...
...BY THE WAY...
Christmas Offer
DISCOUNT COUPONS
12/15 ~ 25
VIVA ITALY!
WE'RE DOING A SPECIAL PRO-MOTION...
...OVER CHRIST-MAS.
UH... IF YOU DON'T FEEL LIKE GOING HOME...
...YOU CAN DROP BY HERE.
I WORK HERE EVERY DAY.
THANKS.

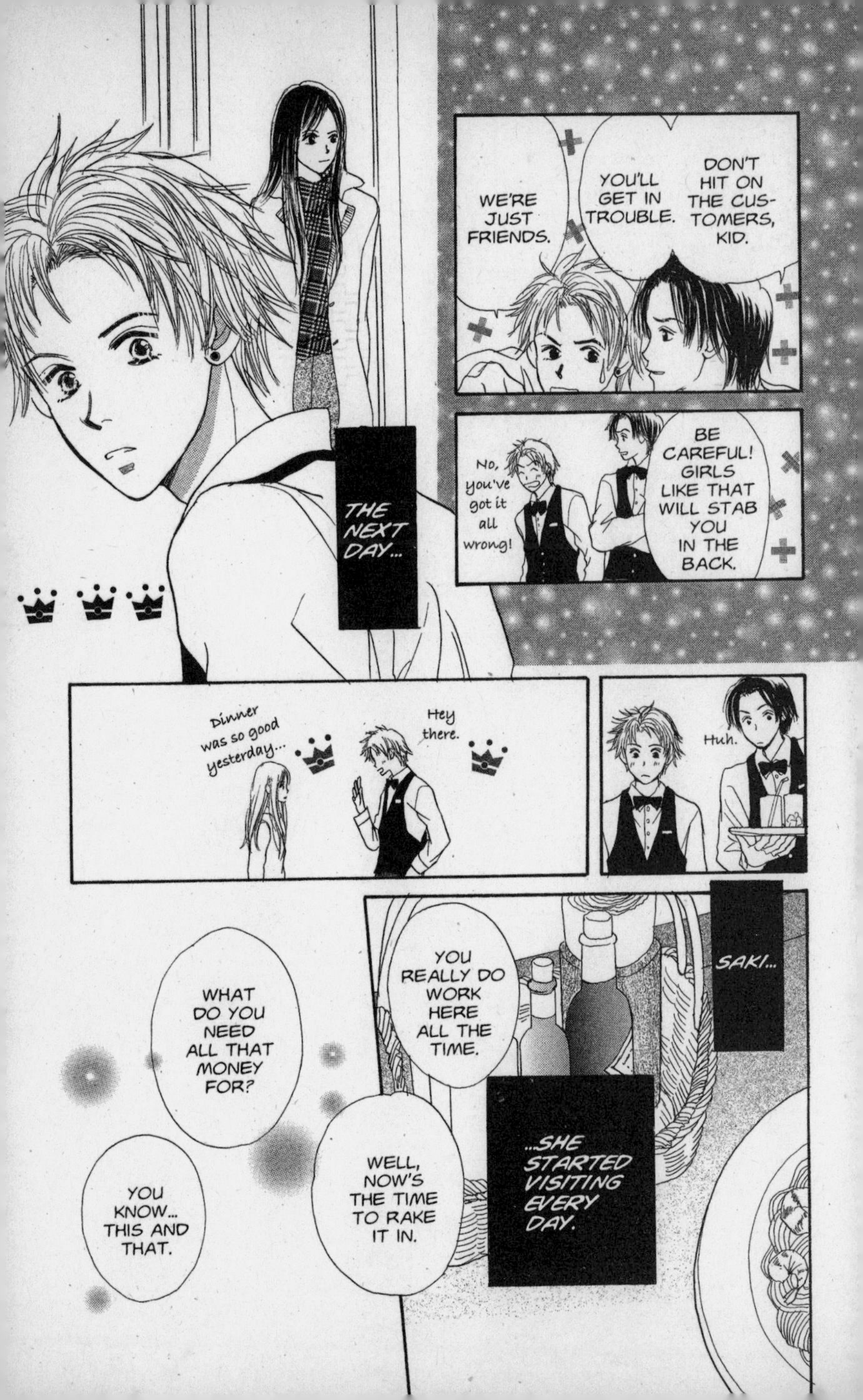
DON'T HIT ON THE CUSTOMERS, KID.
YOU'LL GET IN TROUBLE.
WE'RE JUST FRIENDS.
BE CAREFUL! GIRLS LIKE THAT WILL STAB YOU IN THE BACK.
No, you've got it all wrong!
THE NEXT DAY...
Huh.
Hey there.
Dinner was so good yesterday...
SAKI...
YOU REALLY DO WORK HERE ALL THE TIME.
...SHE STARTED VISITING EVERY DAY.
WHAT DO YOU NEED ALL THAT MONEY FOR?
WELL, NOW'S THE TIME TO RAKE IT IN.
YOU KNOW... THIS AND THAT.

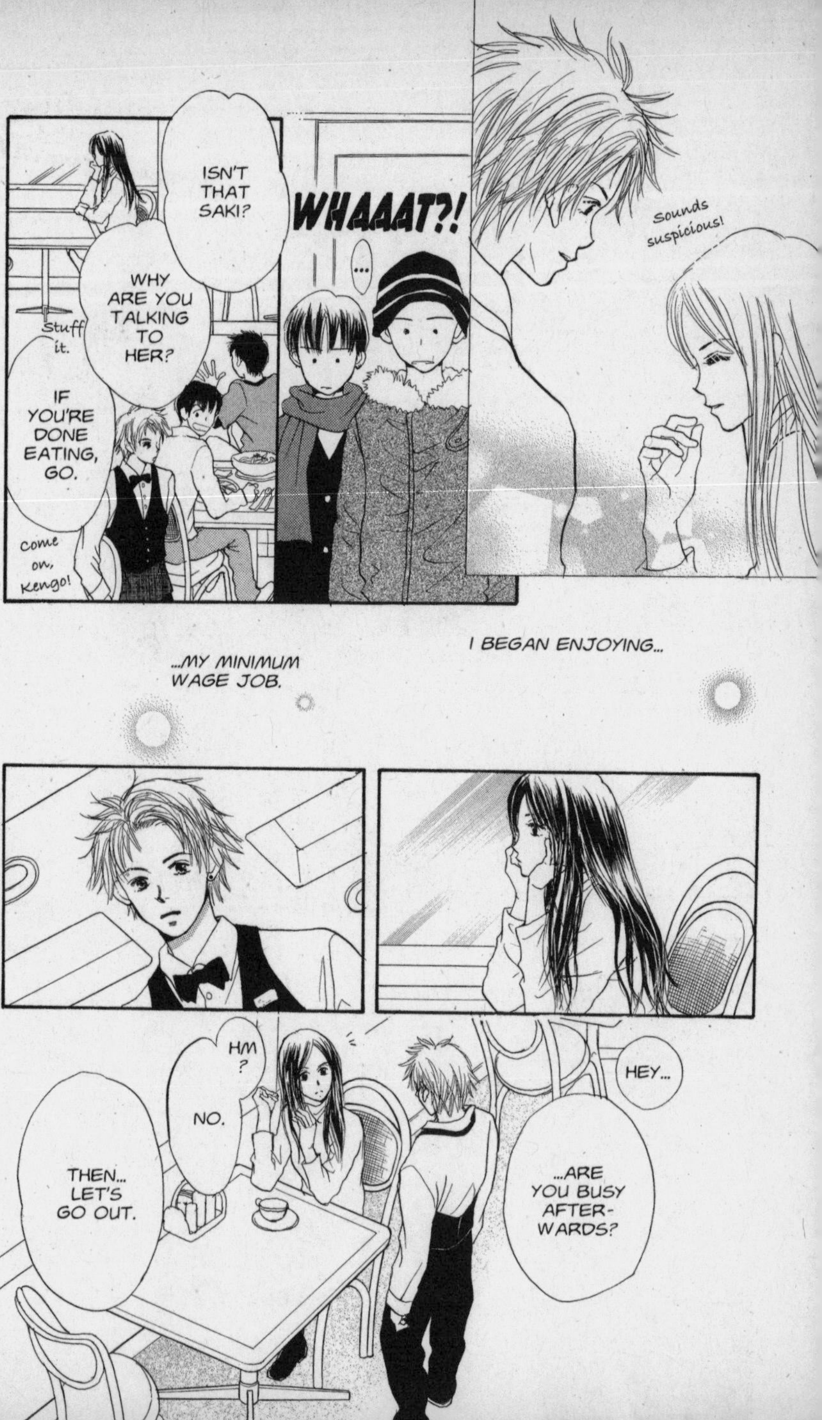
Sounds suspicious!
WHAAAT?!
...
ISN'T THAT SAKI?
WHY ARE YOU TALKING TO HER?
Stuff it.
IF YOU'RE DONE EATING, GO.
Come on, Kengo!
I BEGAN ENJOYING...
...MY MINIMUM WAGE JOB.
HEY...
...ARE YOU BUSY AFTERWARDS?
HM?
NO.
THEN... LET'S GO OUT.

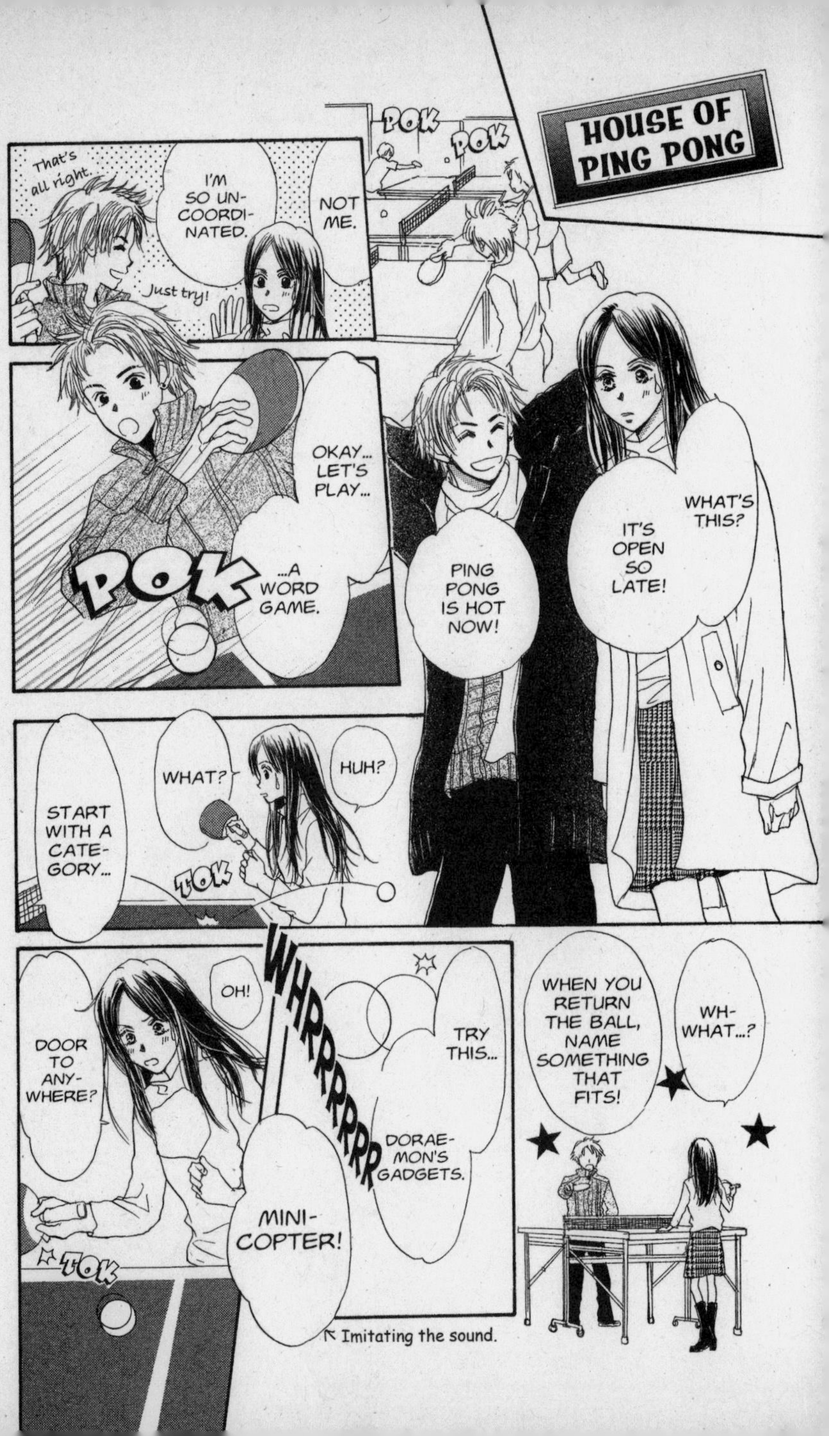

HOUSE OF PING PONG
POK
POK
WHAT'S THIS?
IT'S OPEN SO LATE!
PING PONG IS HOT NOW!
NOT ME.
I'M SO UN-COORDI-NATED.
That's all right.
Just try!
OKAY... LET'S PLAY...
...A WORD GAME.
POK
HUH?
WHAT?
START WITH A CATE-GORY...
TOK
WH-WHAT...?
WHEN YOU RETURN THE BALL, NAME SOMETHING THAT FITS!
TRY THIS...
DORAE-MON'S GADGETS.
WHRRRRRRR
MINI-COPTER!
↖ Imitating the sound.
OH!
DOOR TO ANY-WHERE?
TOK

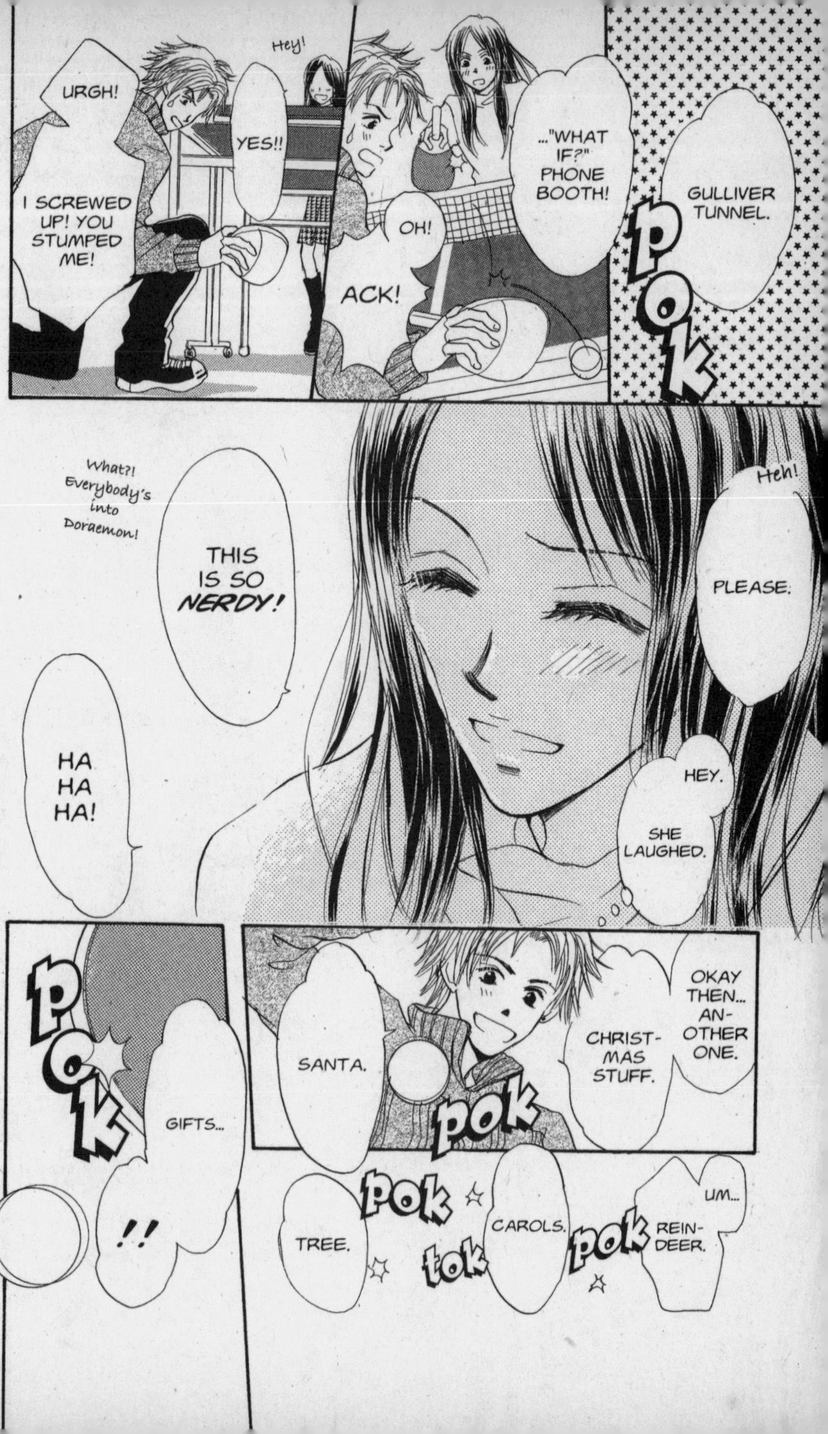
GULLIVER TUNNEL.
POK
..."WHAT IF?" PHONE BOOTH!
OH!
ACK!
Hey!
YES!!
URGH!
I SCREWED UP! YOU STUMPED ME!
Heh!
PLEASE.
HEY.
SHE LAUGHED.
THIS IS SO *NERDY!*
What?! Everybody's into Doraemon!
HA HA HA!
OKAY THEN... AN-OTHER ONE.
CHRIST-MAS STUFF.
SANTA.
pok
UM... REIN-DEER.
pok
CAROLS.
tok
pok
TREE.
pok
GIFTS...
!!

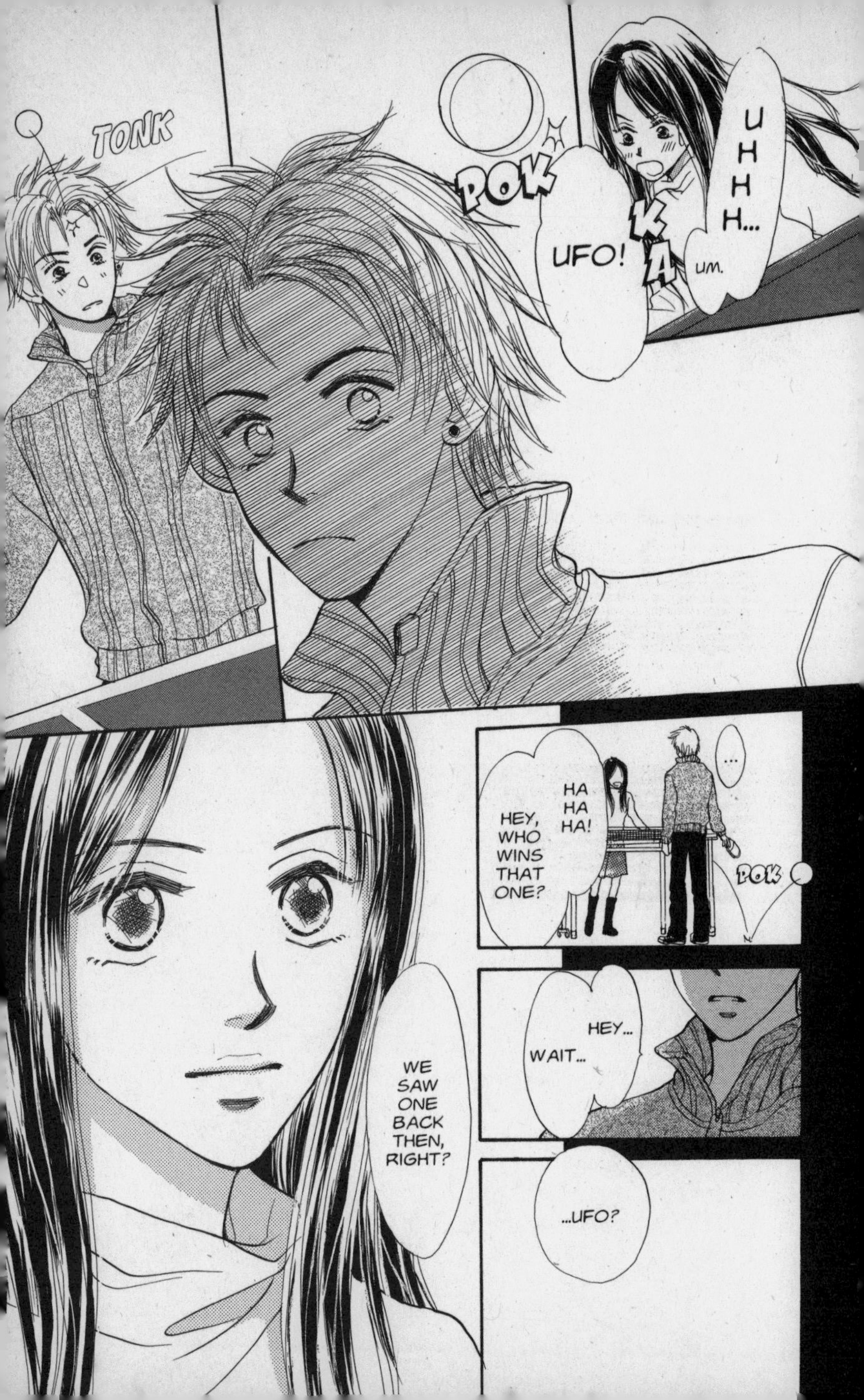
UHHH...
um.
UFO!
POK
KA
TONK
...
HA HA HA!
HEY, WHO WINS THAT ONE?
POK
HEY...
WAIT...
...UFO?
WE SAW ONE BACK THEN, RIGHT?

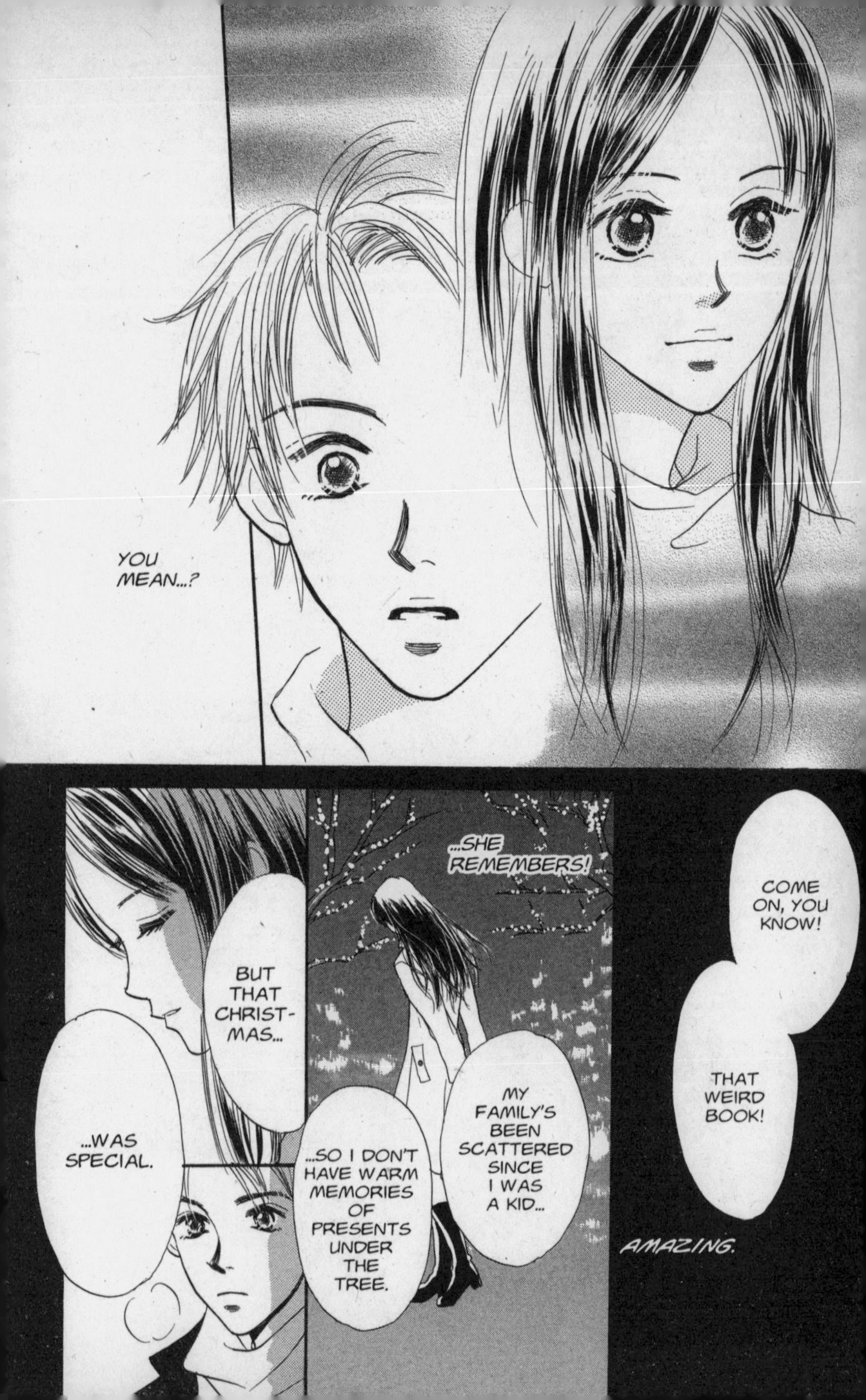
YOU MEAN...?
COME ON, YOU KNOW!
THAT WEIRD BOOK!
AMAZING.
...SHE REMEMBERS!
MY FAMILY'S BEEN SCATTERED SINCE I WAS A KID...
...SO I DON'T HAVE WARM MEMORIES OF PRESENTS UNDER THE TREE.
BUT THAT CHRISTMAS...
...WAS SPECIAL.

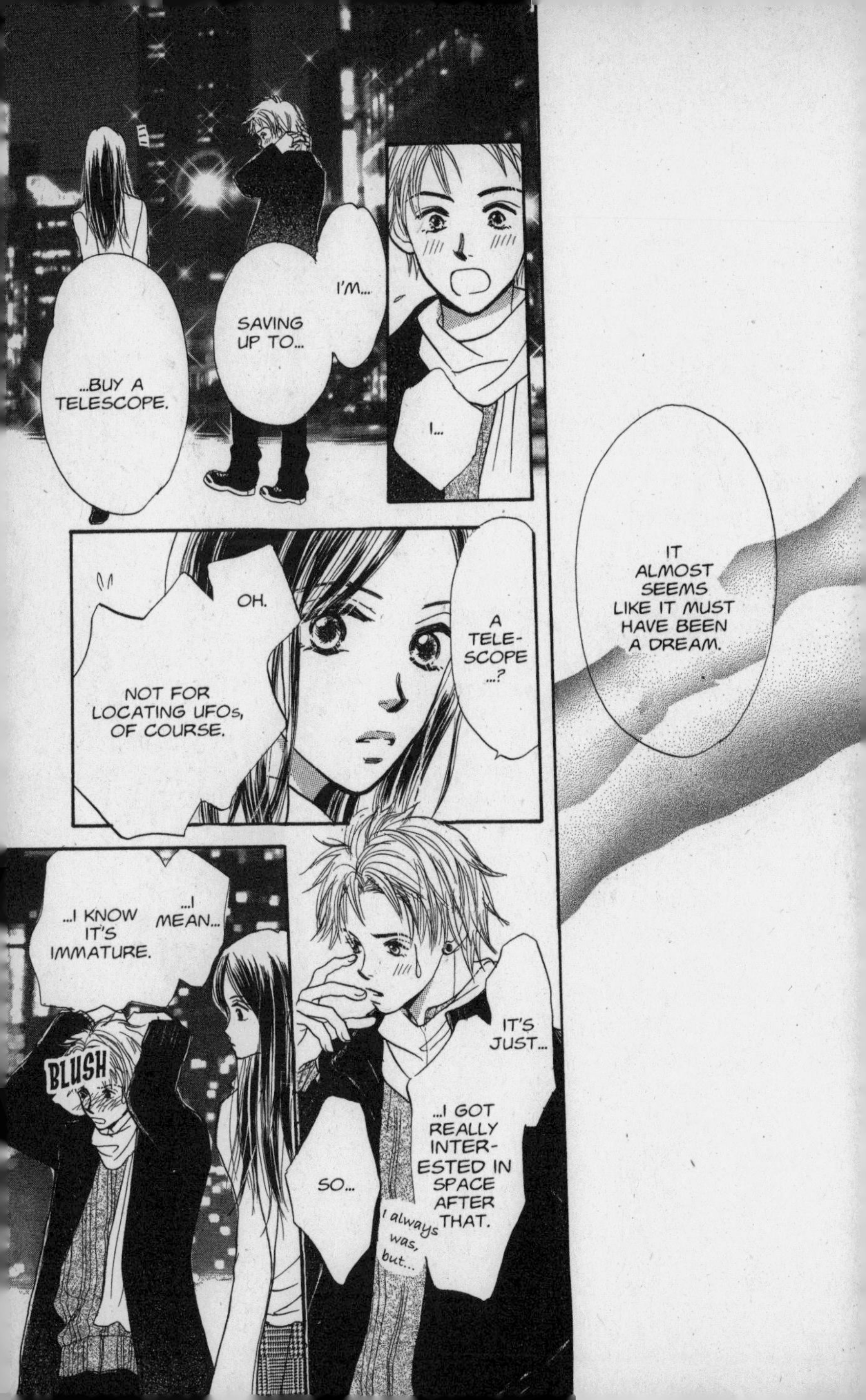
IT ALMOST SEEMS LIKE IT MUST HAVE BEEN A DREAM.
I...
I'M...
SAVING UP TO...
...BUY A TELESCOPE.
A TELE-SCOPE ...?
OH.
NOT FOR LOCATING UFOs, OF COURSE.
IT'S JUST...
...I GOT REALLY INTER-ESTED IN SPACE AFTER THAT.
I always was, but...
SO...
...I MEAN...
...I KNOW IT'S IMMATURE.
BLUSH

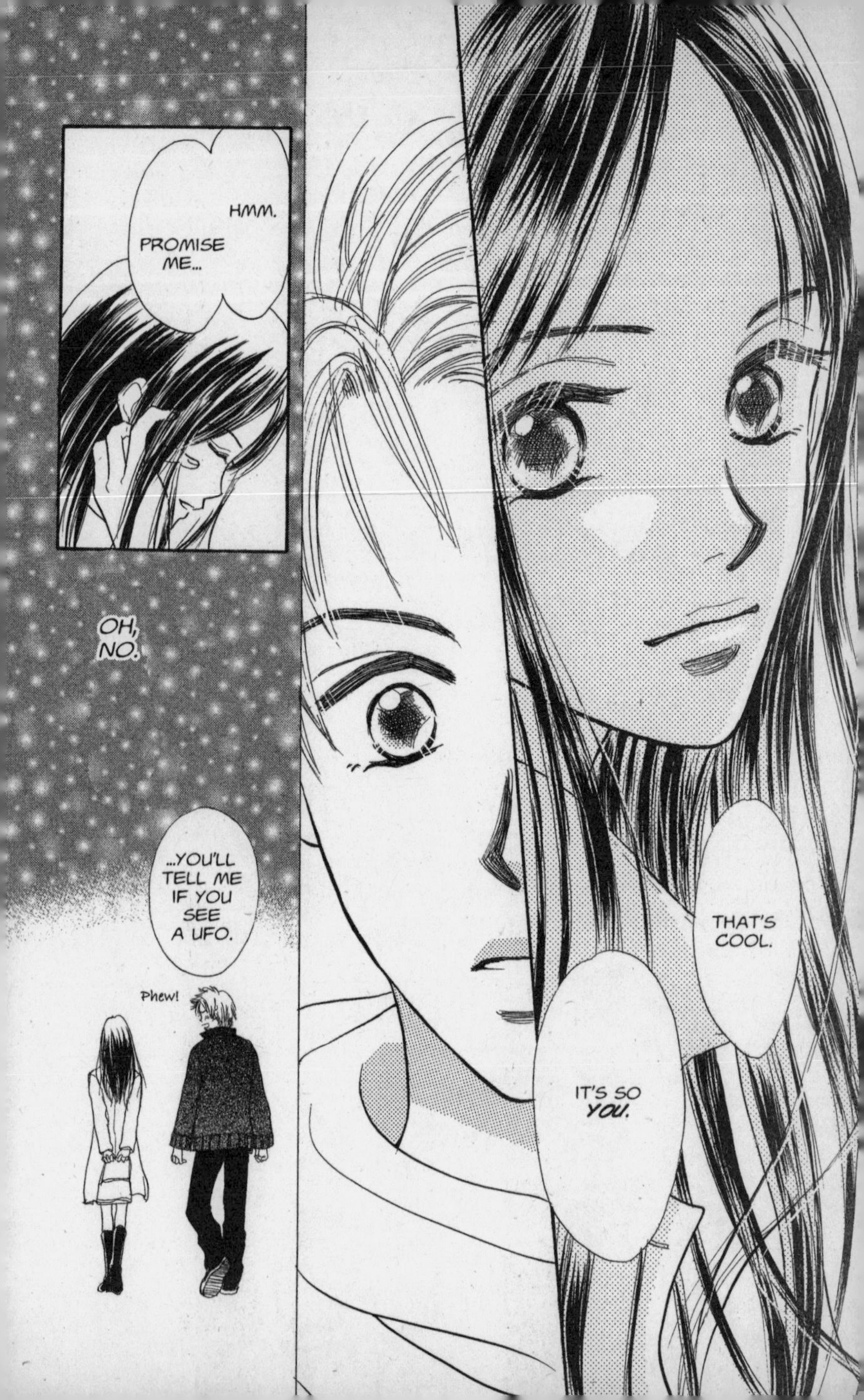
THAT'S COOL.
IT'S SO YOU.
HMM.
PROMISE ME...
OH, NO.
...YOU'LL TELL ME IF YOU SEE A UFO.
Phew!

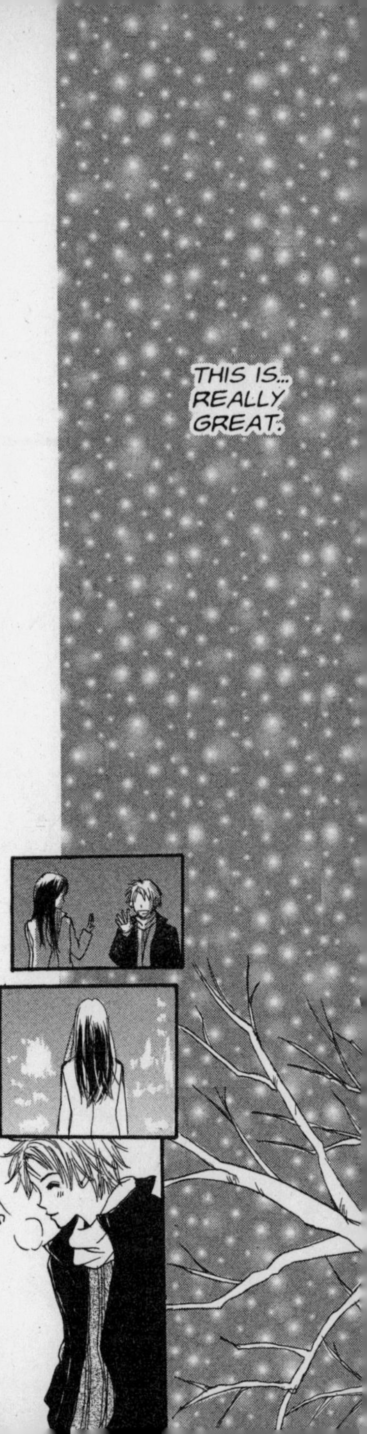
THIS IS... REALLY GREAT.

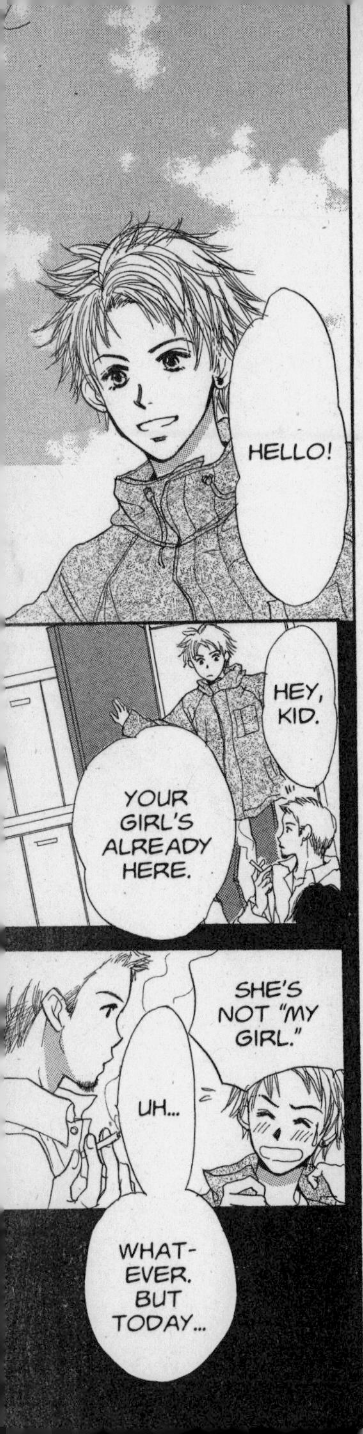
HELLO!
HEY, KID.
YOUR GIRL'S ALREADY HERE.
SHE'S NOT "MY GIRL."
UH...
WHAT-EVER. BUT TODAY...

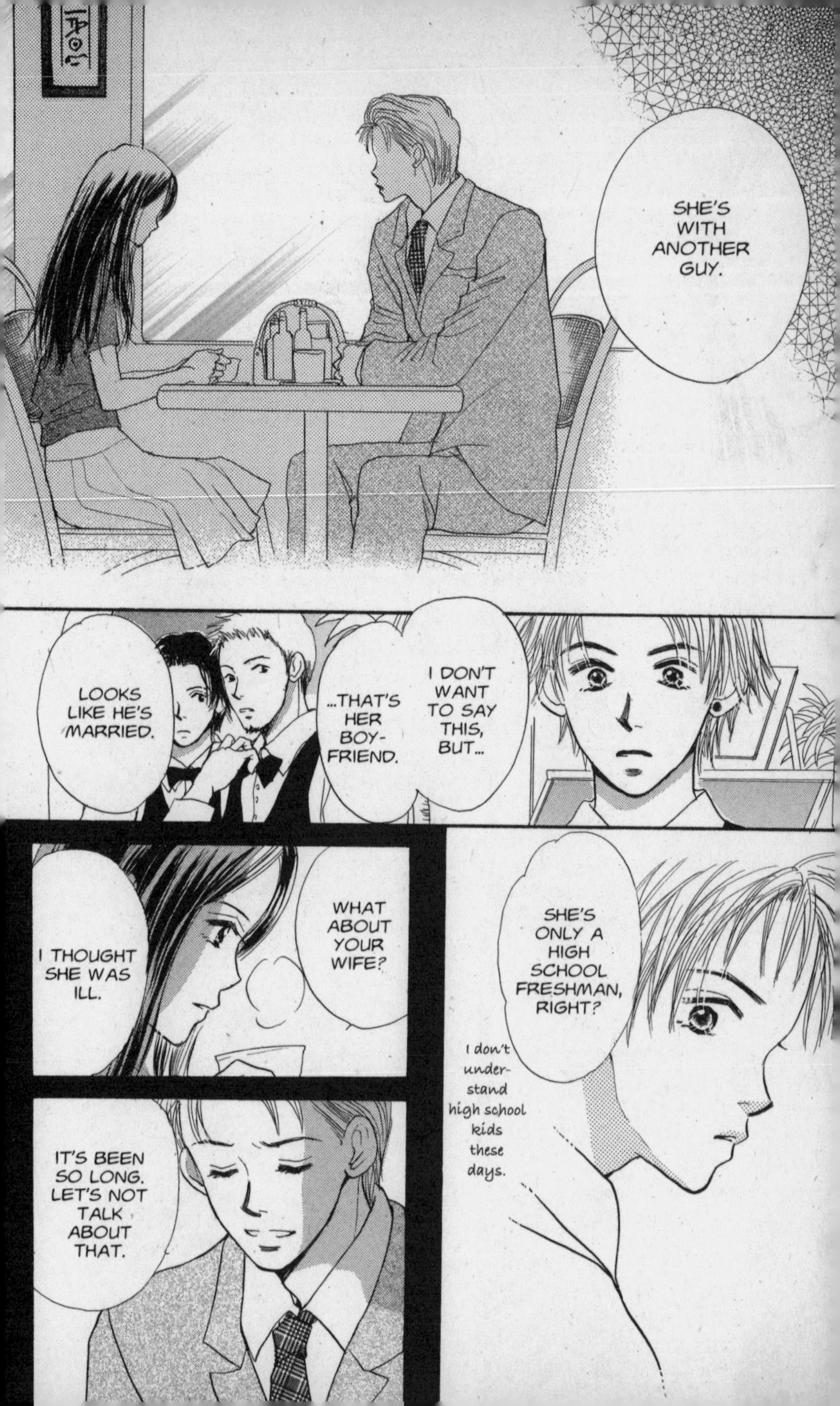
SHE'S WITH ANOTHER GUY.
I DON'T WANT TO SAY THIS, BUT...
...THAT'S HER BOYFRIEND.
LOOKS LIKE HE'S MARRIED.
SHE'S ONLY A HIGH SCHOOL FRESHMAN, RIGHT?
I don't understand high school kids these days.
WHAT ABOUT YOUR WIFE?
I THOUGHT SHE WAS ILL.
IT'S BEEN SO LONG. LET'S NOT TALK ABOUT THAT.

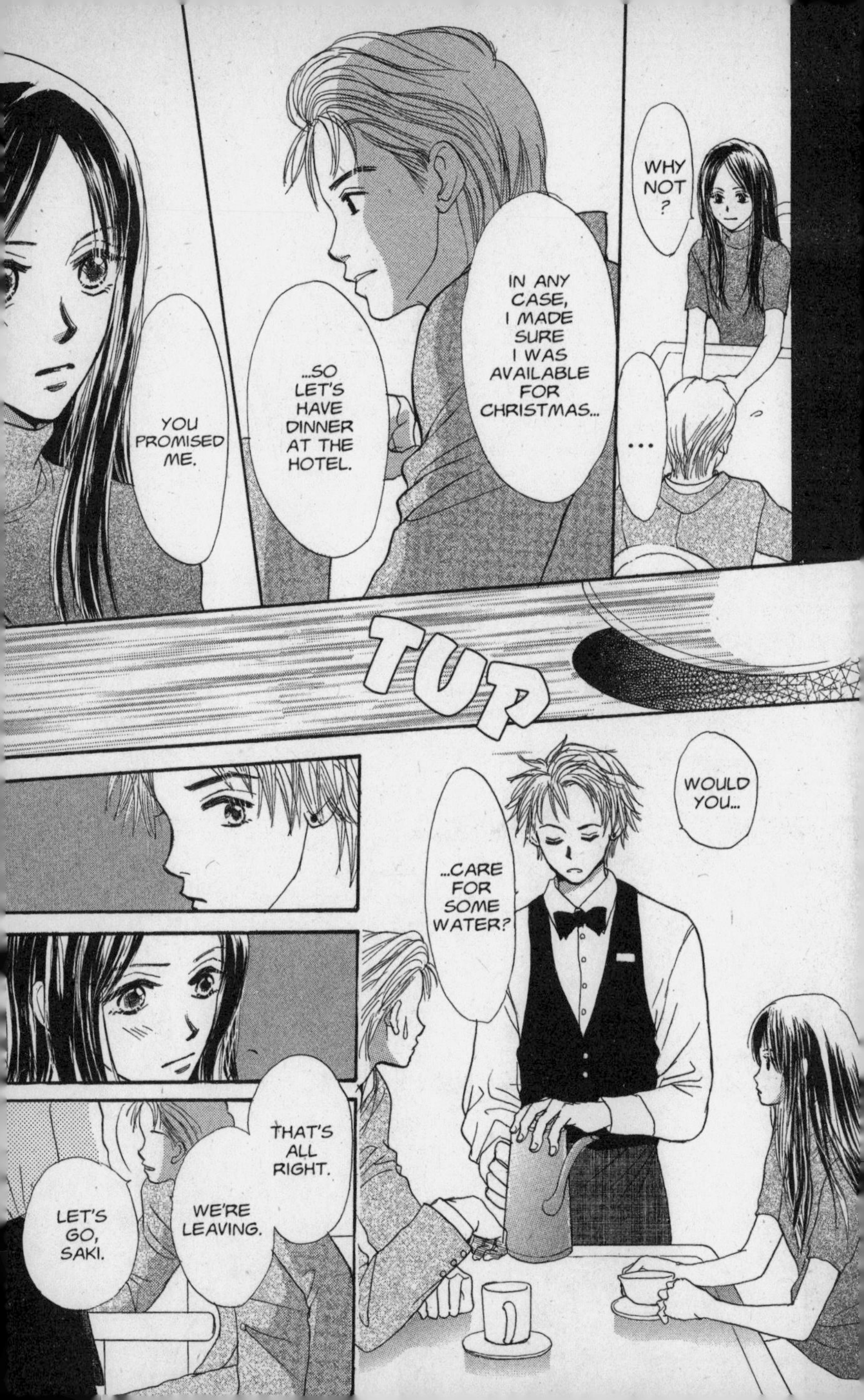
WHY NOT ?
...
IN ANY CASE, I MADE SURE I WAS AVAILABLE FOR CHRISTMAS...
...SO LET'S HAVE DINNER AT THE HOTEL.
YOU PROMISED ME.
TUP
WOULD YOU...
...CARE FOR SOME WATER?
THAT'S ALL RIGHT.
WE'RE LEAVING.
LET'S GO, SAKI.

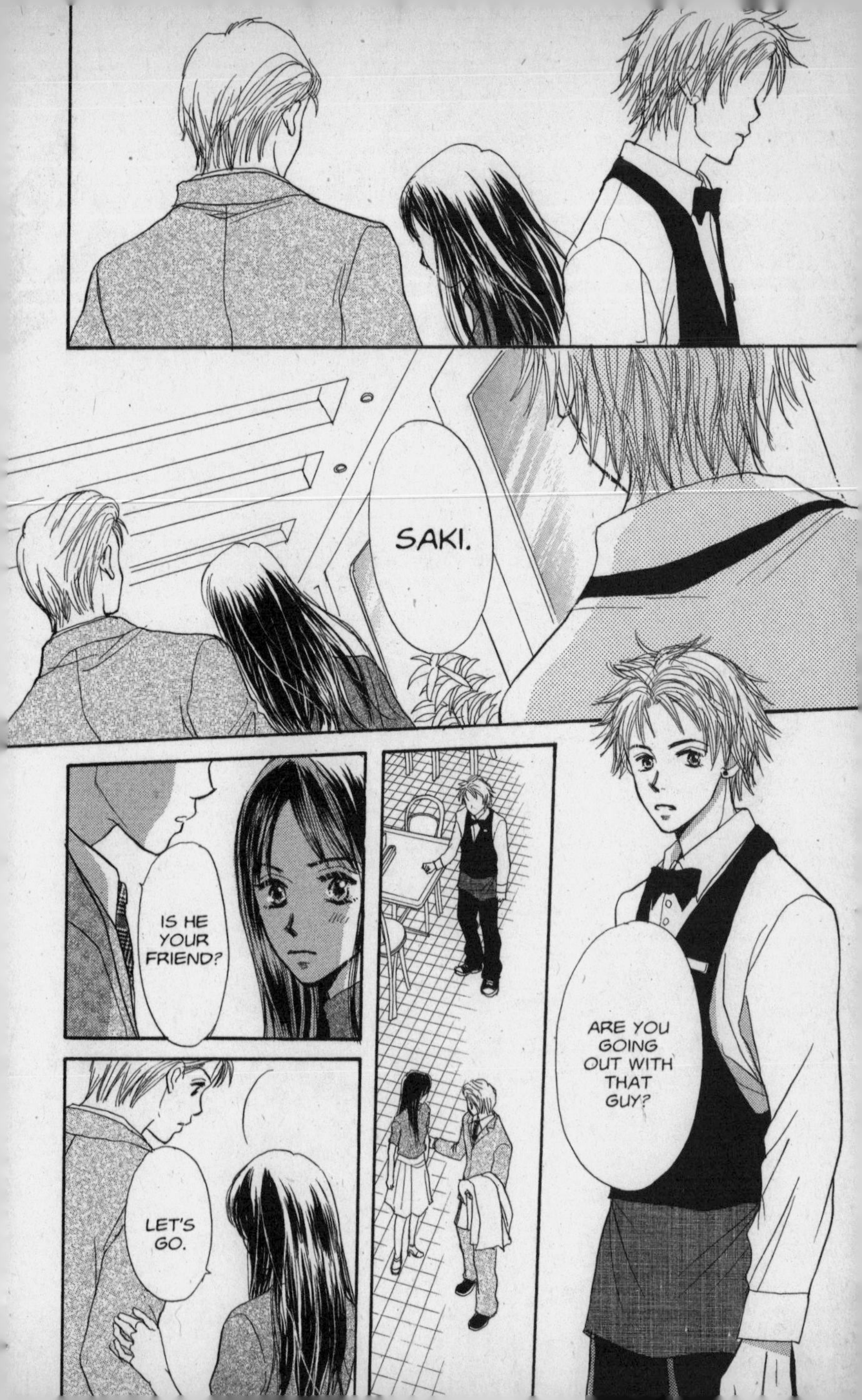
SAKI.
ARE YOU GOING OUT WITH THAT GUY?
IS HE YOUR FRIEND?
LET'S GO.

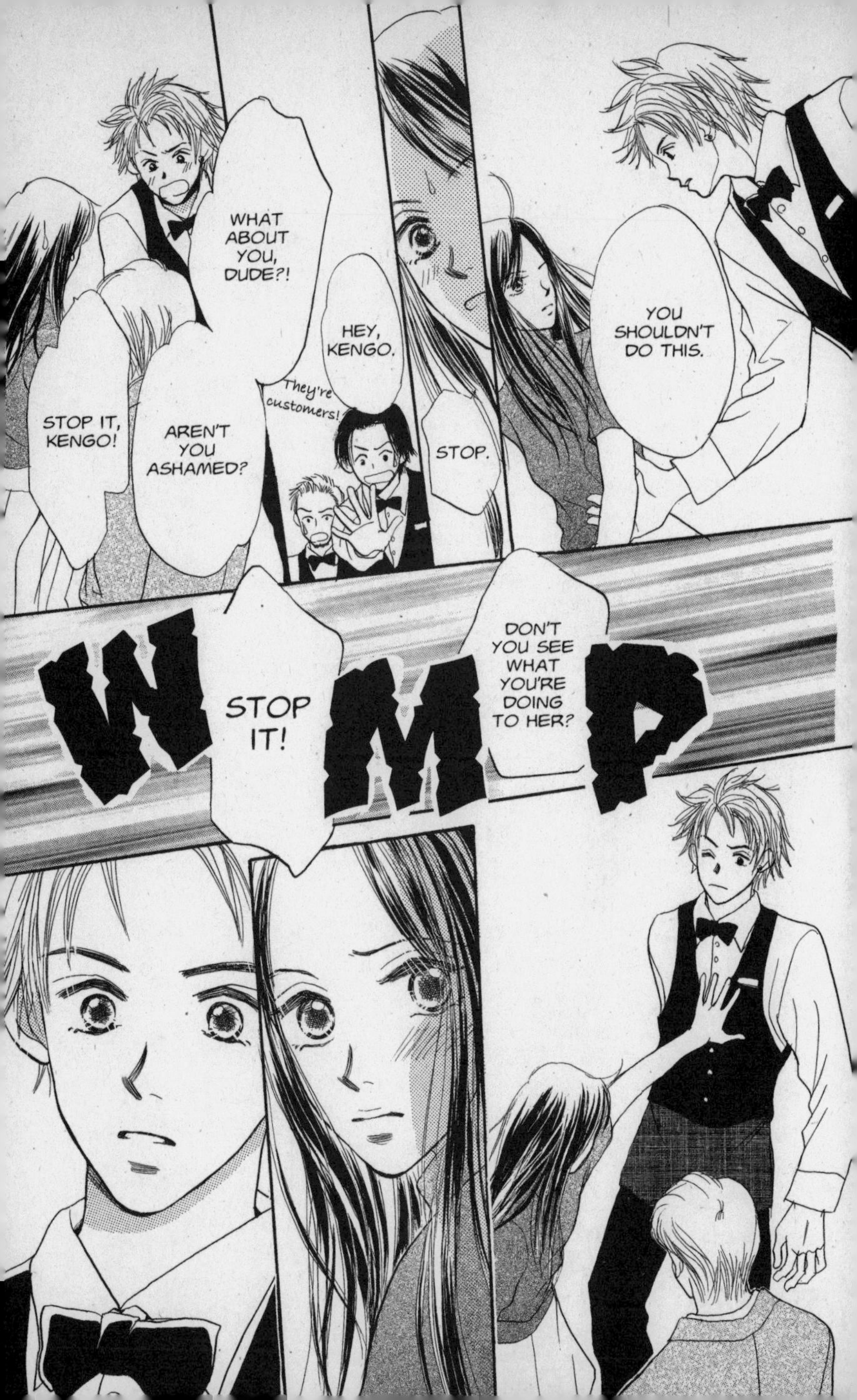
YOU SHOULDN'T DO THIS.
STOP.
HEY, KENGO.
They're customers!
WHAT ABOUT YOU, DUDE?!
AREN'T YOU ASHAMED?
STOP IT, KENGO!
DON'T YOU SEE WHAT YOU'RE DOING TO HER?
STOP IT!
WMP

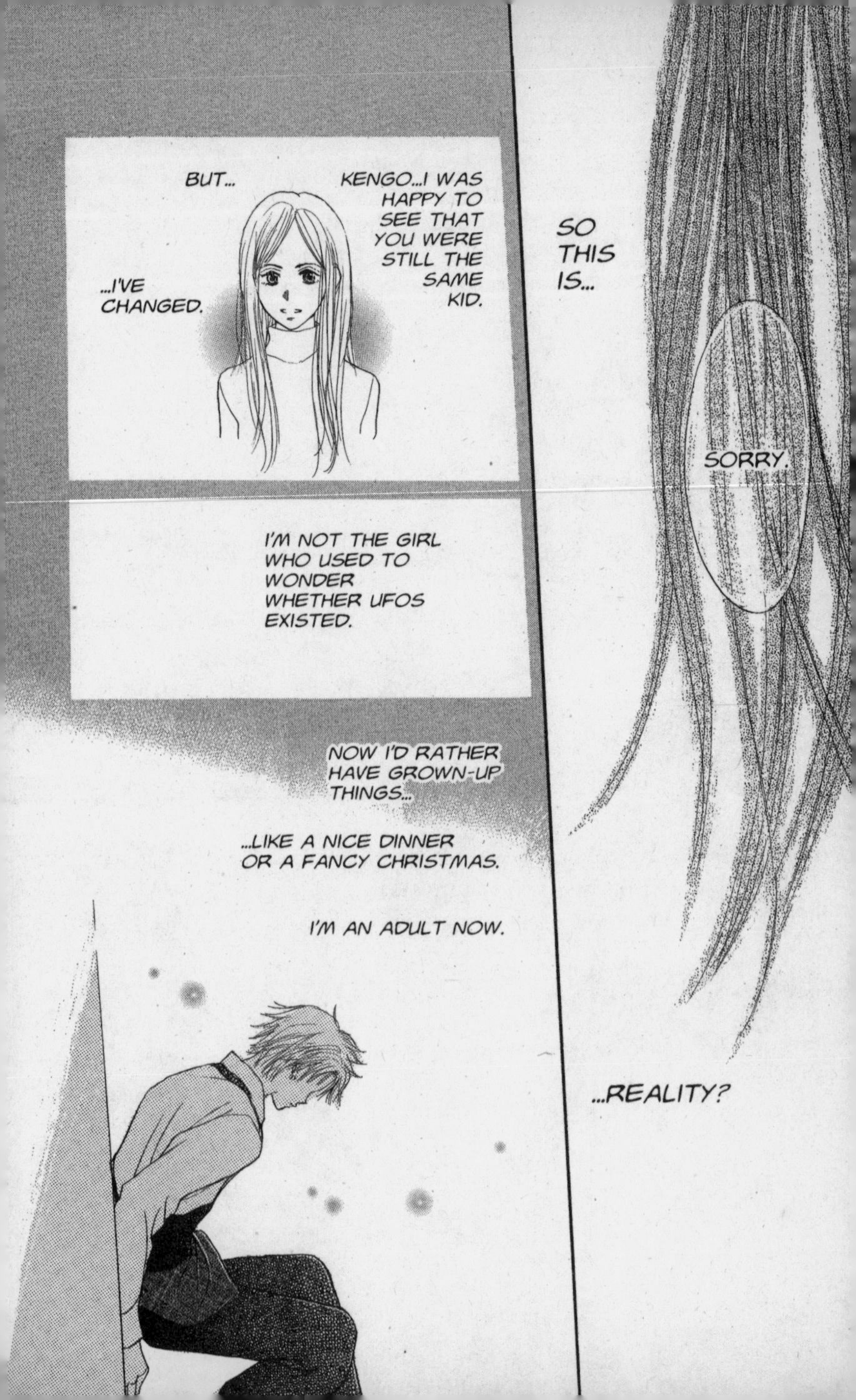
SO THIS IS...
SORRY.
...REALITY?
KENGO...I WAS HAPPY TO SEE THAT YOU WERE STILL THE SAME KID.
BUT...
...I'VE CHANGED.
I'M NOT THE GIRL WHO USED TO WONDER WHETHER UFOS EXISTED.
NOW I'D RATHER HAVE GROWN-UP THINGS...
...LIKE A NICE DINNER OR A FANCY CHRISTMAS.
I'M AN ADULT NOW.

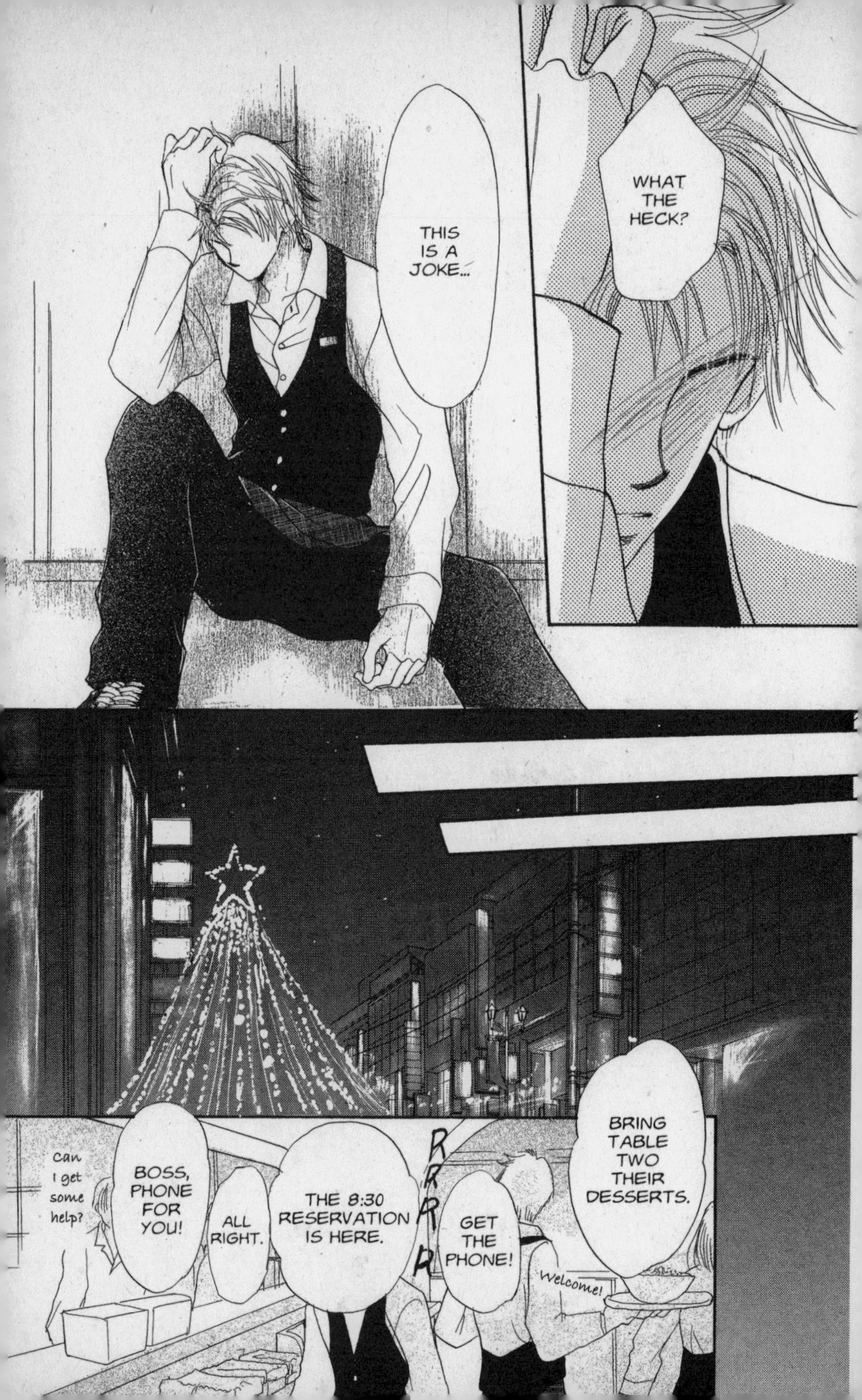
WHAT THE HECK?
THIS IS A JOKE...
BRING TABLE TWO THEIR DESSERTS.
Welcome!
GET THE PHONE!
RRRR
THE 8:30 RESERVATION IS HERE.
ALL RIGHT.
BOSS, PHONE FOR YOU!
Can I get some help?

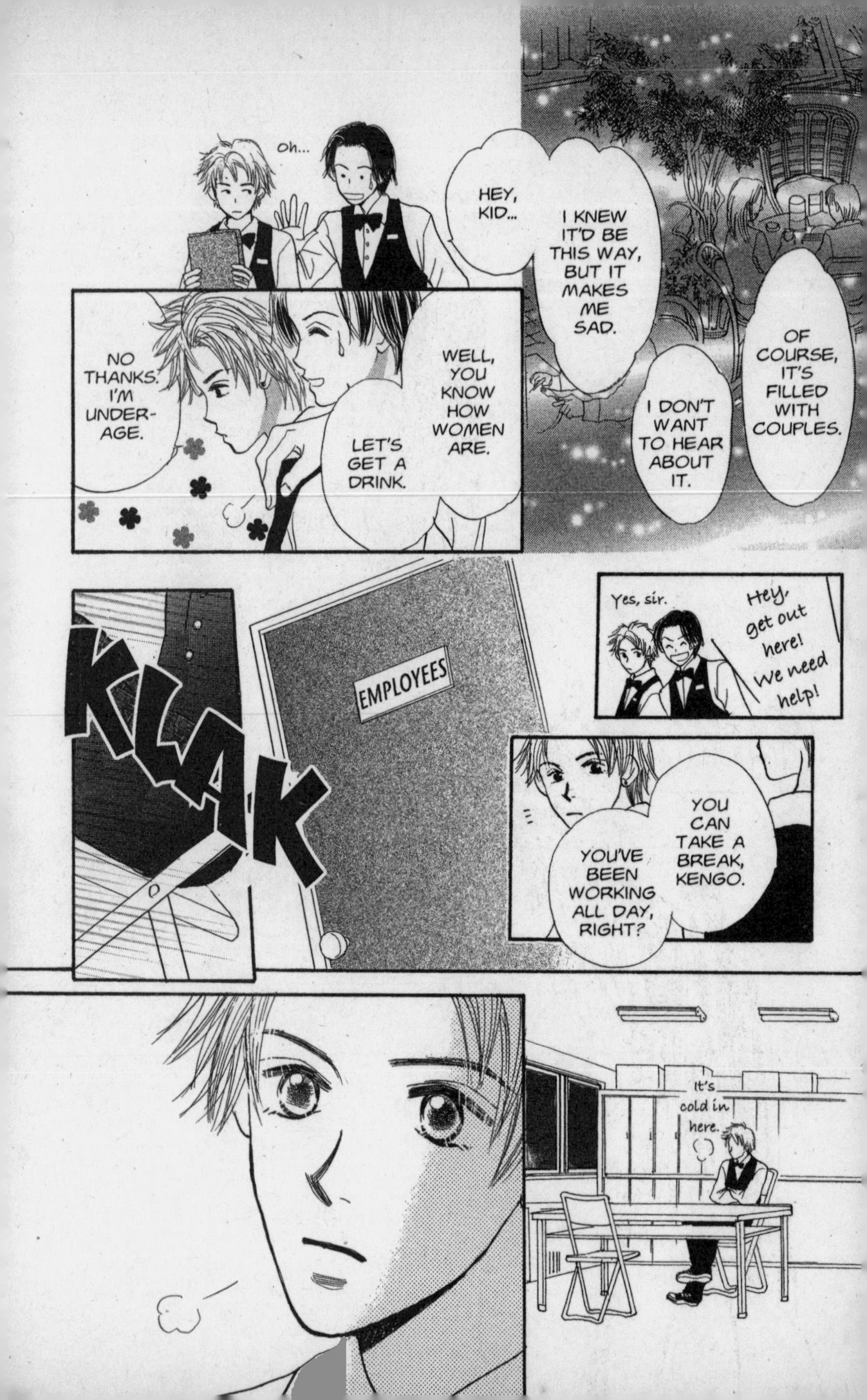
OF COURSE, IT'S FILLED WITH COUPLES.
I DON'T WANT TO HEAR ABOUT IT.
I KNEW IT'D BE THIS WAY, BUT IT MAKES ME SAD.
HEY, KID...
oh...
WELL, YOU KNOW HOW WOMEN ARE.
LET'S GET A DRINK.
NO THANKS. I'M UNDER-AGE.
Hey, get out here! We need help!
Yes, sir.
YOU CAN TAKE A BREAK, KENGO.
YOU'VE BEEN WORKING ALL DAY, RIGHT?
KLAK
EMPLOYEES
It's cold in here.

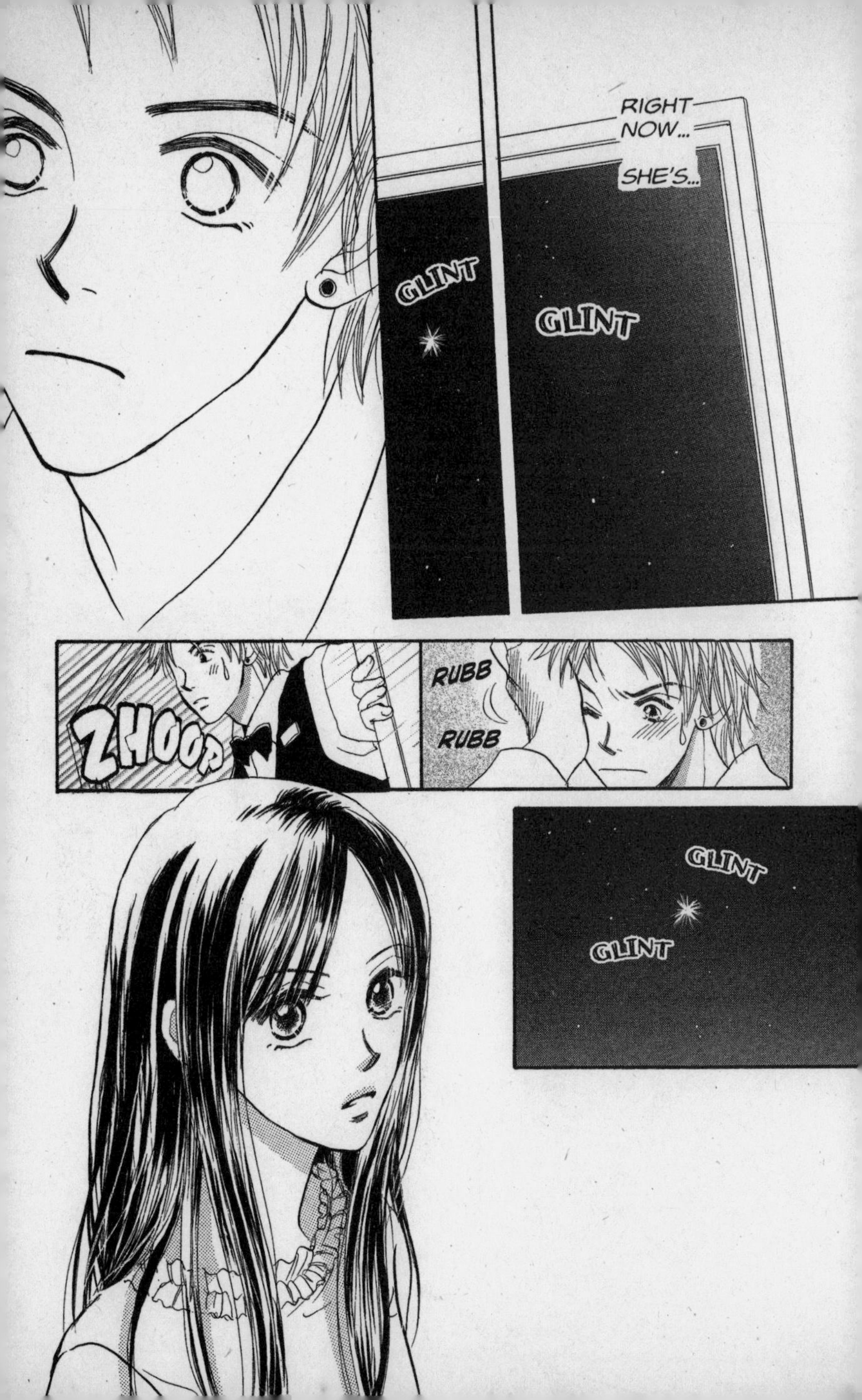
RIGHT NOW...
SHE'S...
GLINT
GLINT
RUBB
RUBB
ZHOOP
GLINT
GLINT

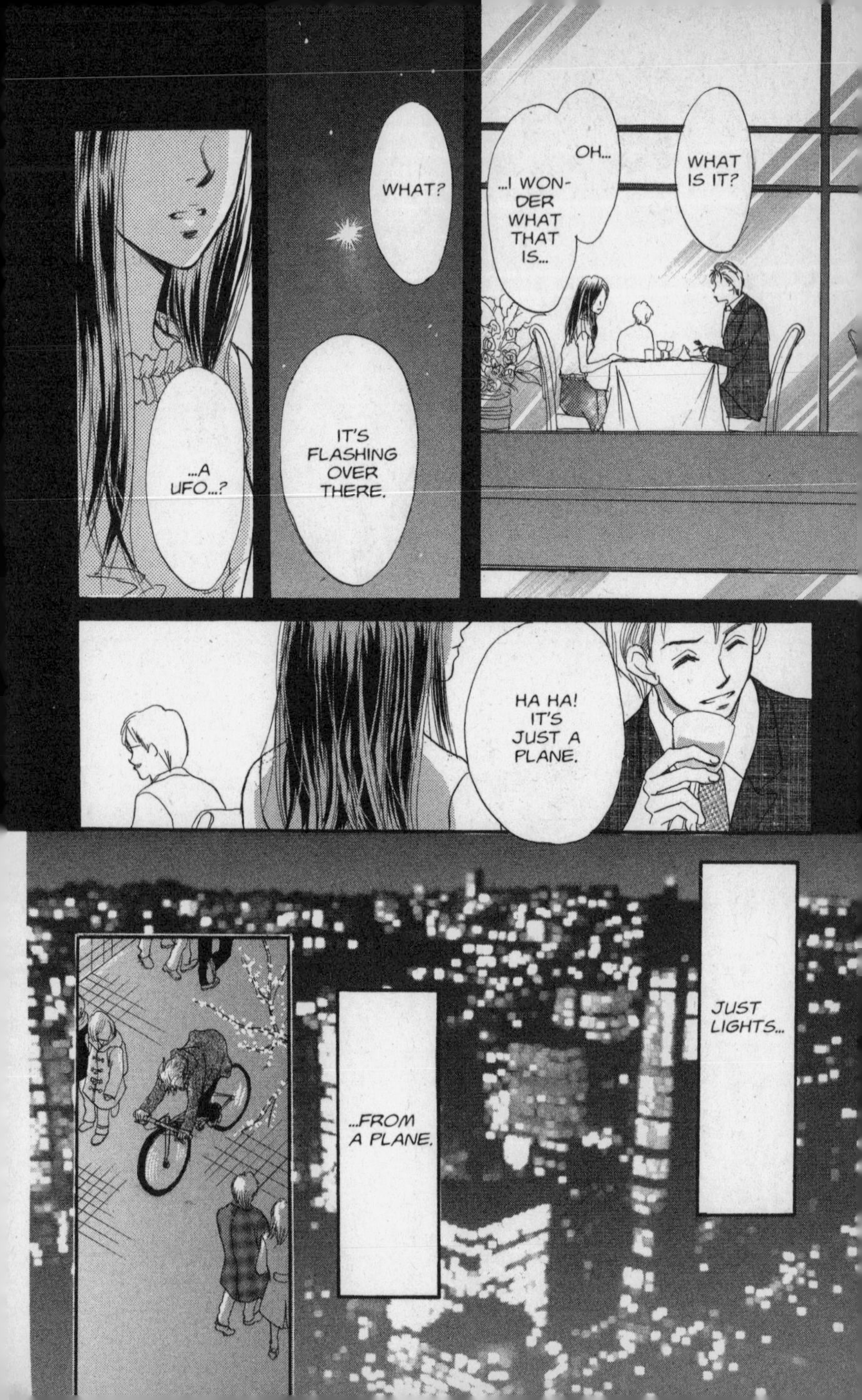
WHAT IS IT?
OH... ...I WON-DER WHAT THAT IS...
WHAT?
IT'S FLASHING OVER THERE.
...A UFO...?
HA HA! IT'S JUST A PLANE.
JUST LIGHTS...
...FROM A PLANE.

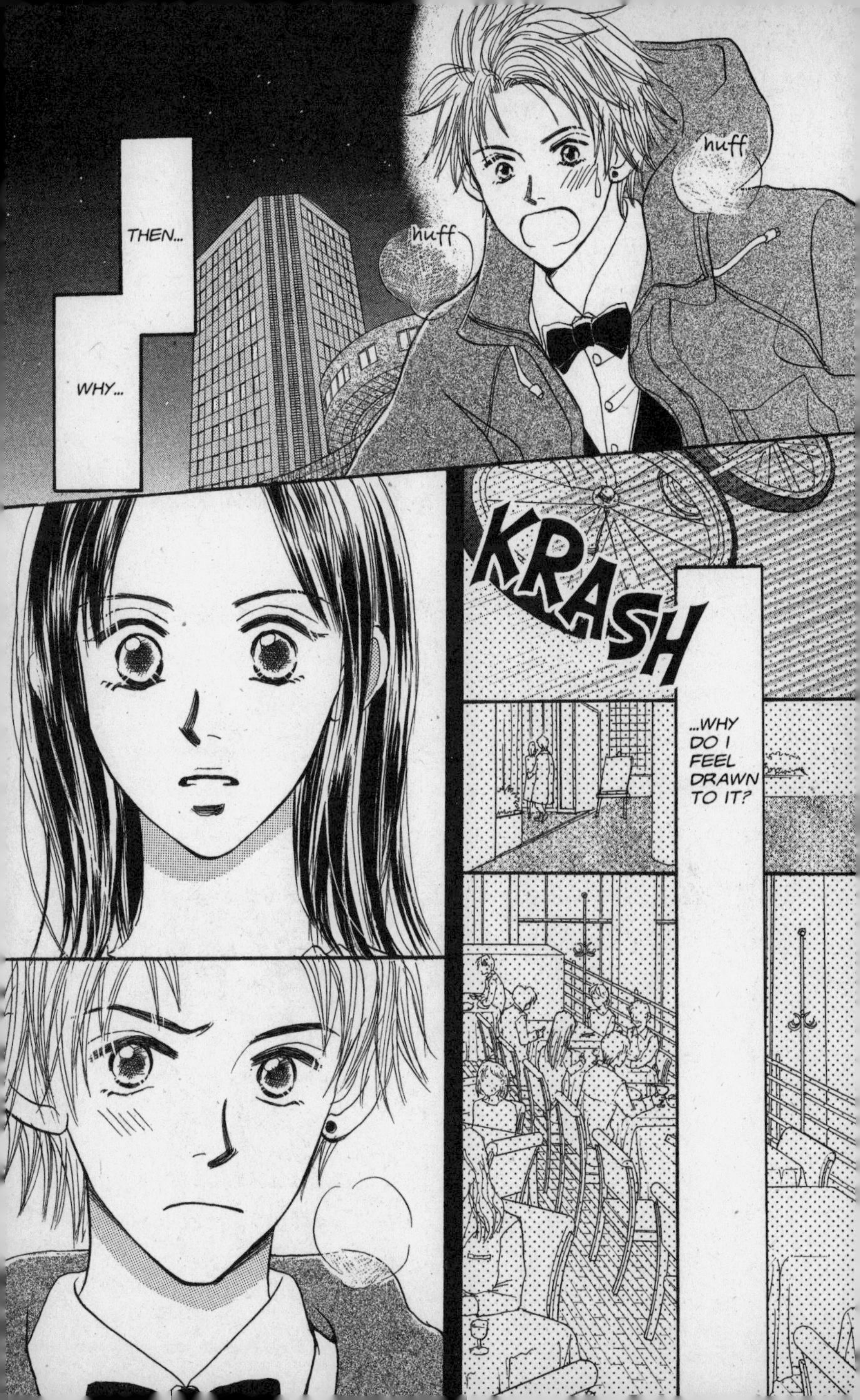
huff
huff
THEN...
WHY...
KRASH
...WHY DO I FEEL DRAWN TO IT?

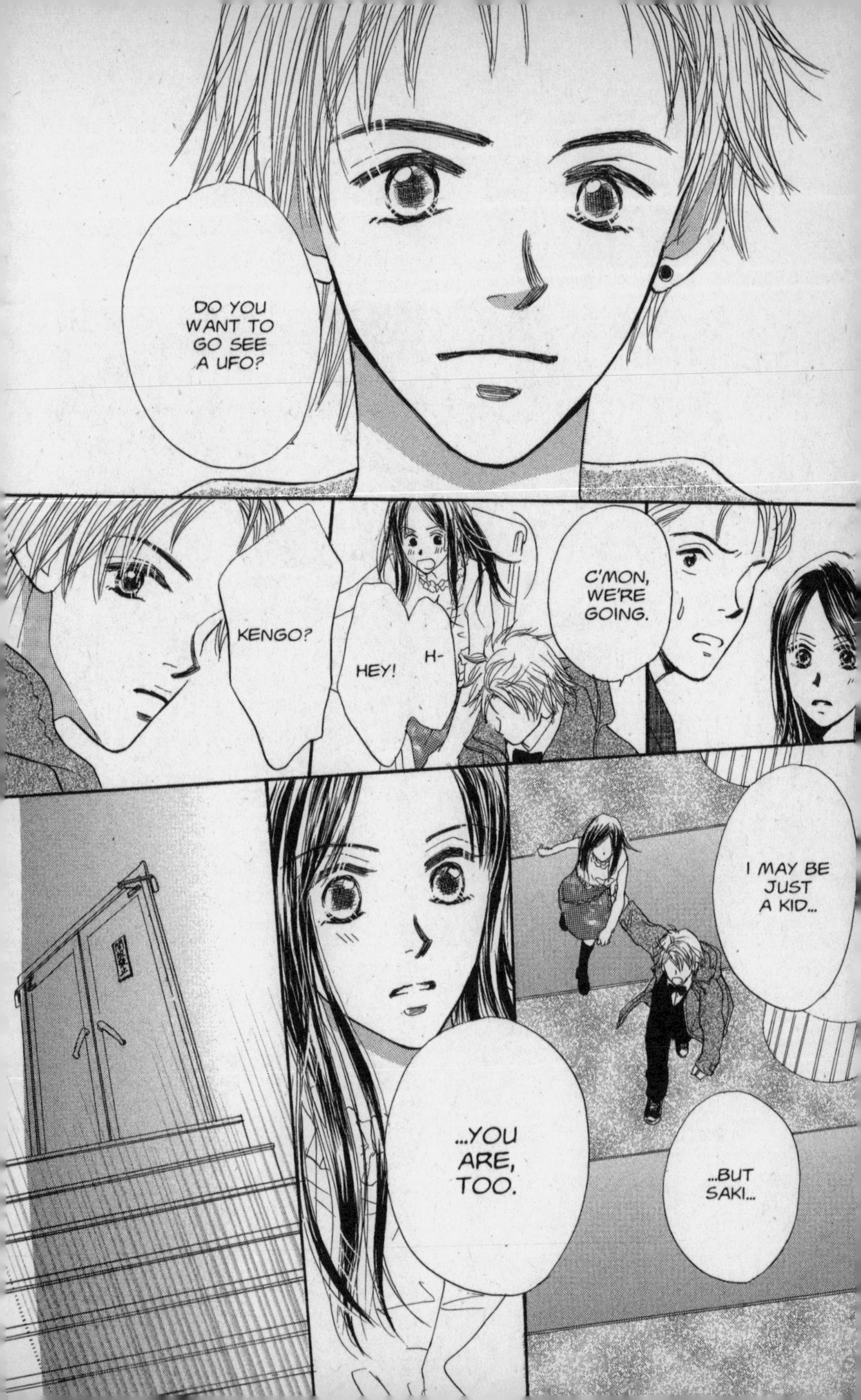
DO YOU WANT TO GO SEE A UFO?
C'MON, WE'RE GOING.
H- HEY!
KENGO?
I MAY BE JUST A KID...
...BUT SAKI...
...YOU ARE, TOO.

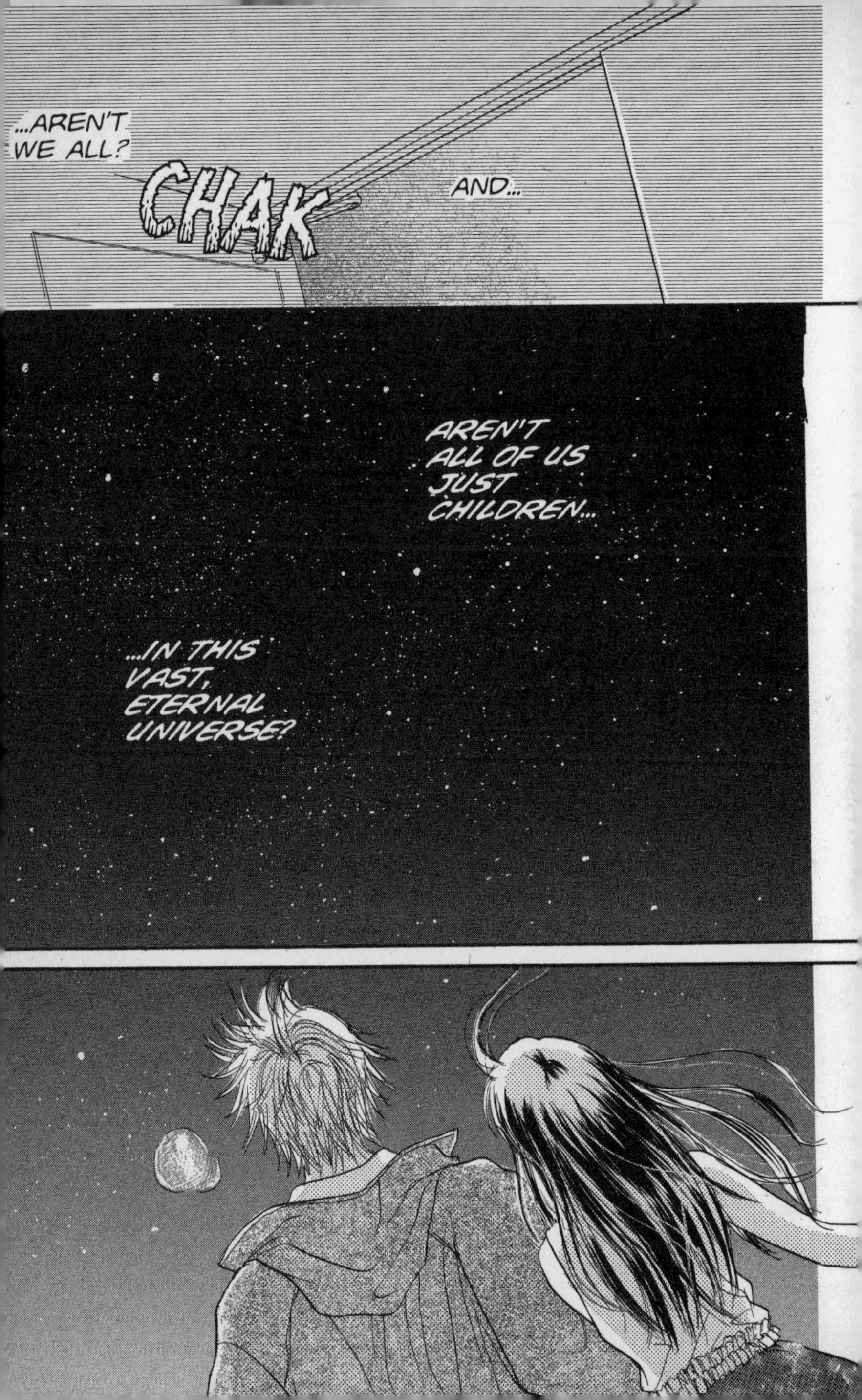
AND...
CHAK
...AREN'T WE ALL?
AREN'T ALL OF US JUST CHILDREN...
...IN THIS VAST, ETERNAL UNIVERSE?

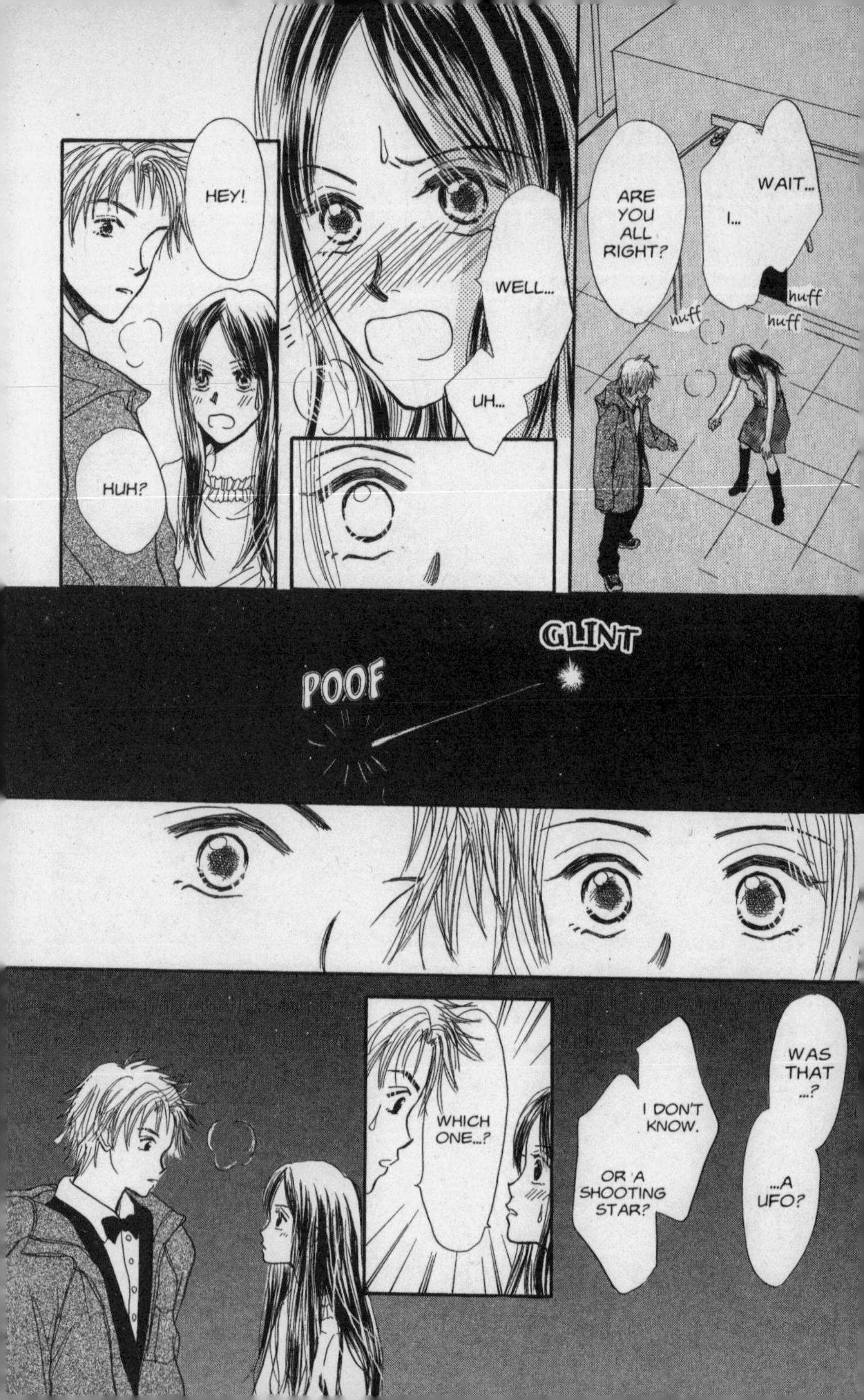
WAIT... I...
ARE YOU ALL RIGHT?
huff
huff
huff
WELL...
UH...
HEY!
HUH?
GLINT
POOF
WAS THAT ...?
...A UFO?
I DON'T KNOW.
OR A SHOOTING STAR?
WHICH ONE...?

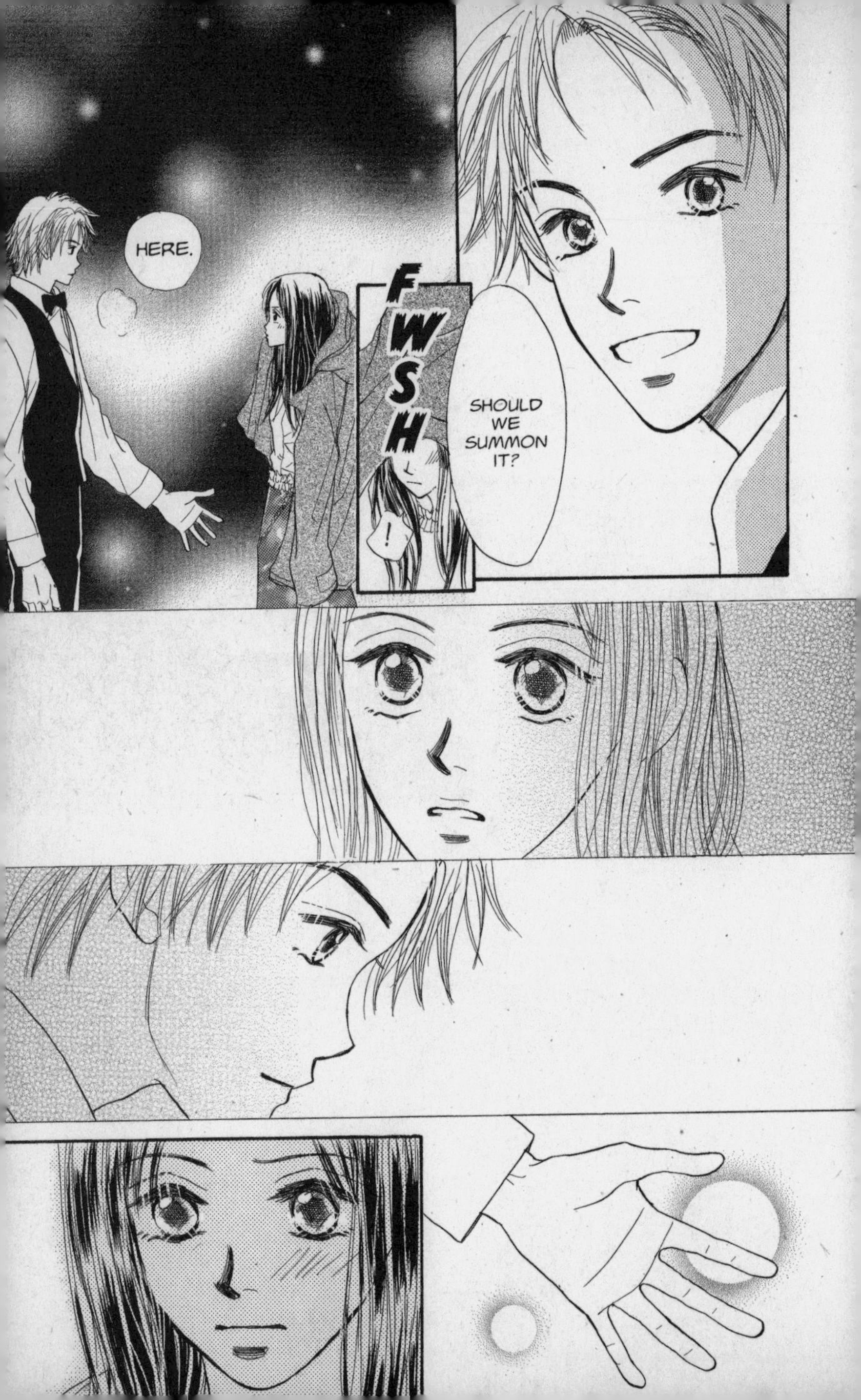
SHOULD WE SUMMON IT?
FWSH
!
HERE.

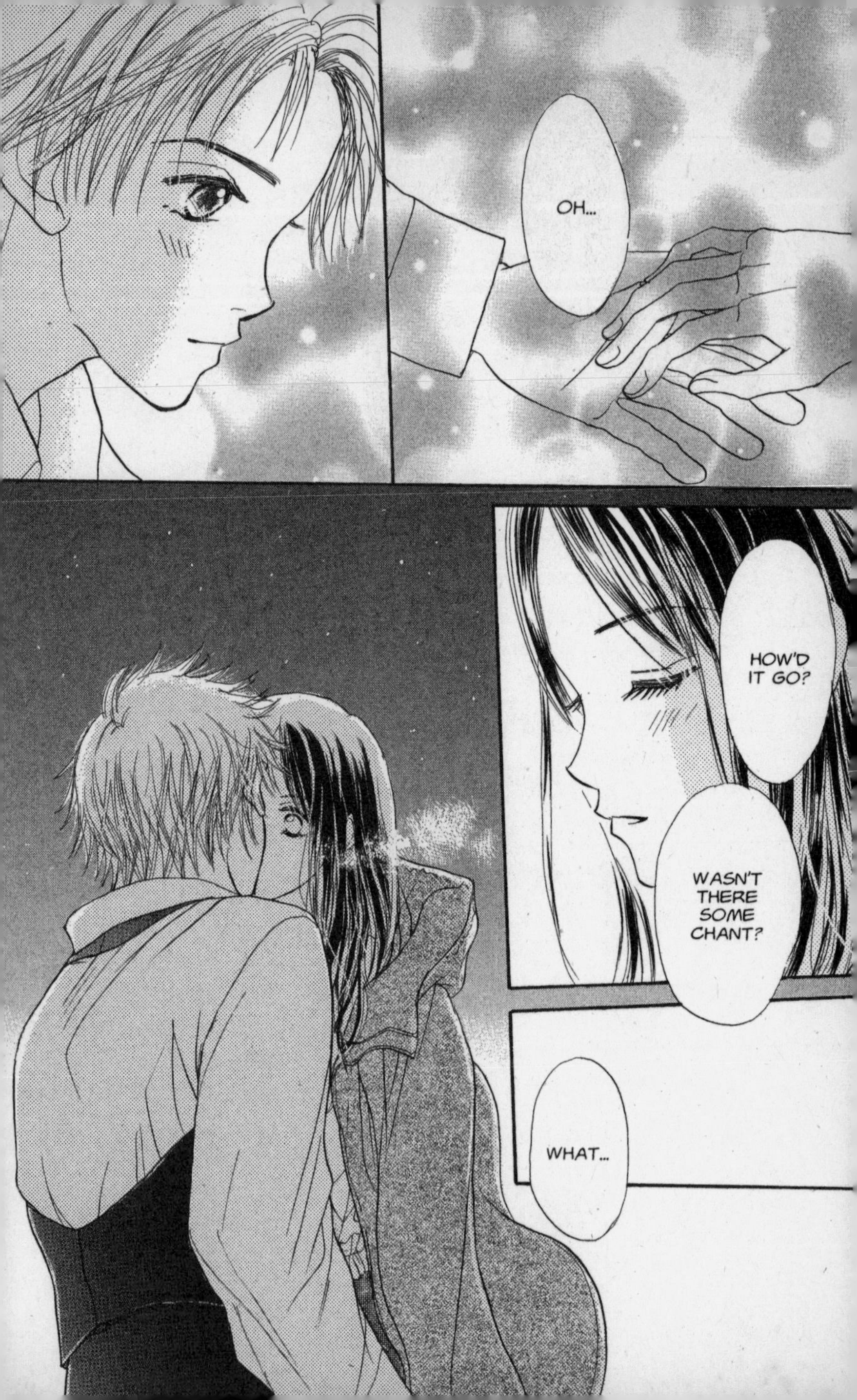
OH...
HOW'D IT GO?
WASN'T THERE SOME CHANT?
WHAT...

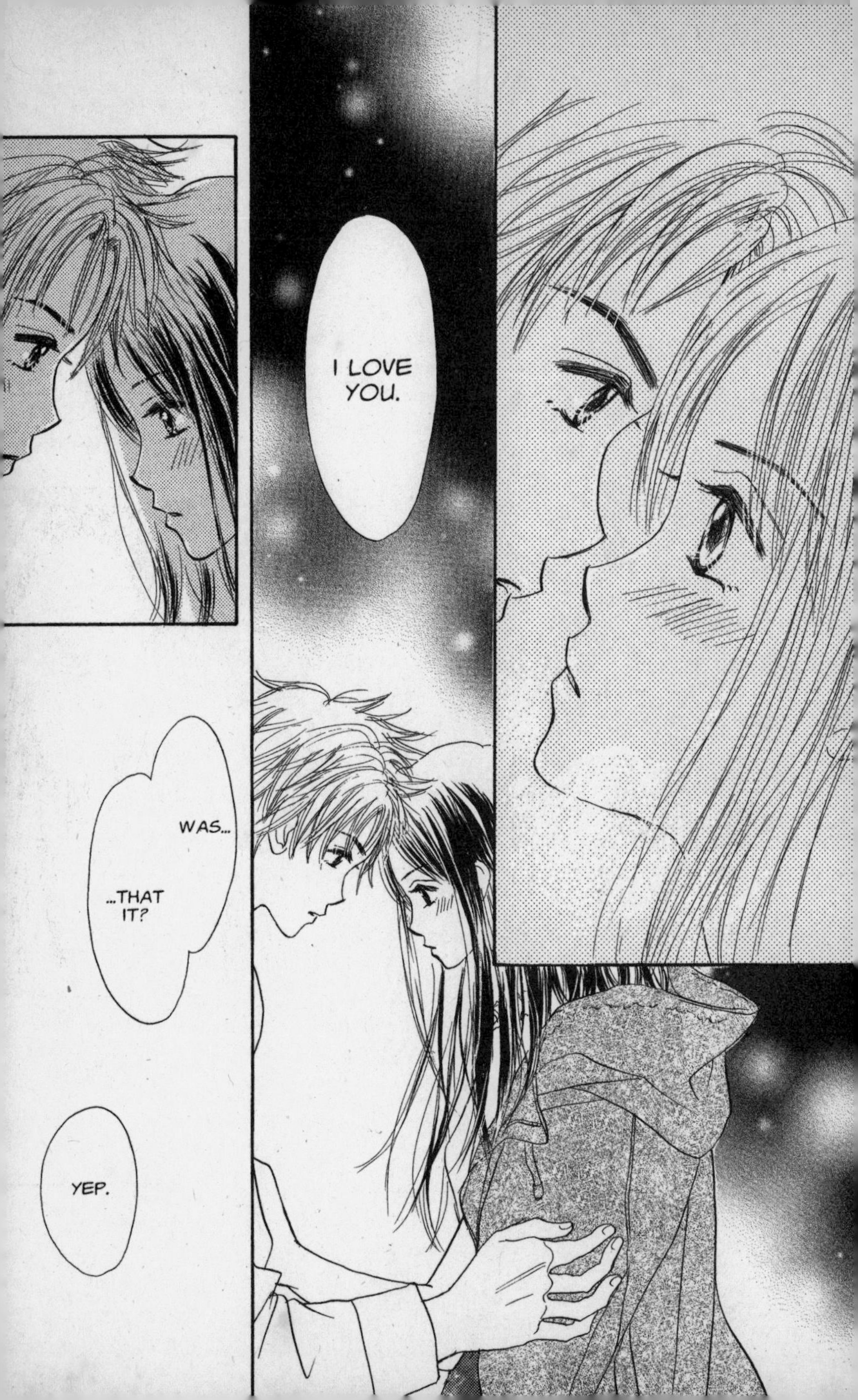
I LOVE YOU.
WAS...
...THAT IT?
YEP.

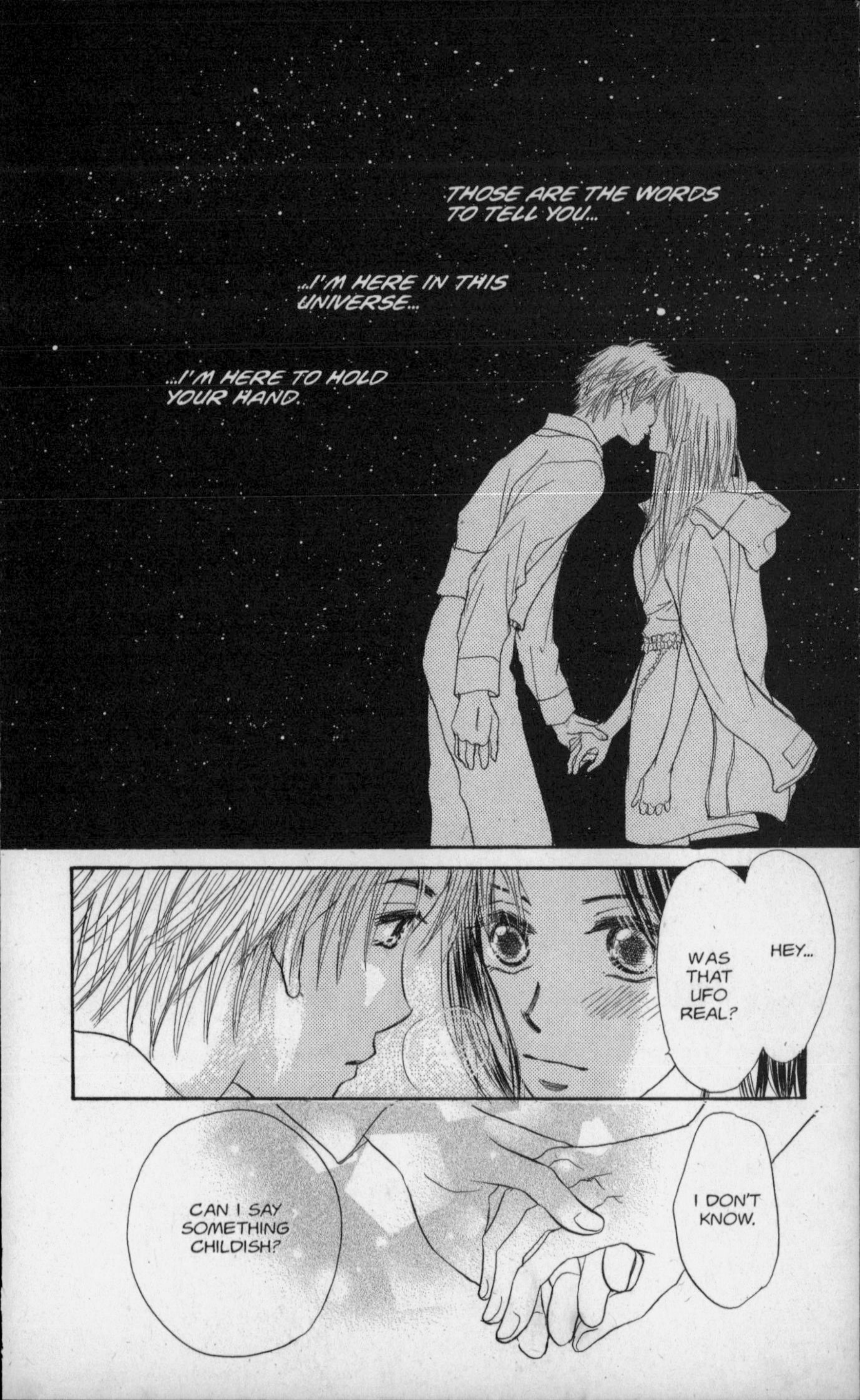
THOSE ARE THE WORDS TO TELL YOU...
...I'M HERE IN THIS UNIVERSE...
...I'M HERE TO HOLD YOUR HAND.
HEY...
WAS THAT UFO REAL?
I DON'T KNOW.
CAN I SAY SOMETHING CHILDISH?

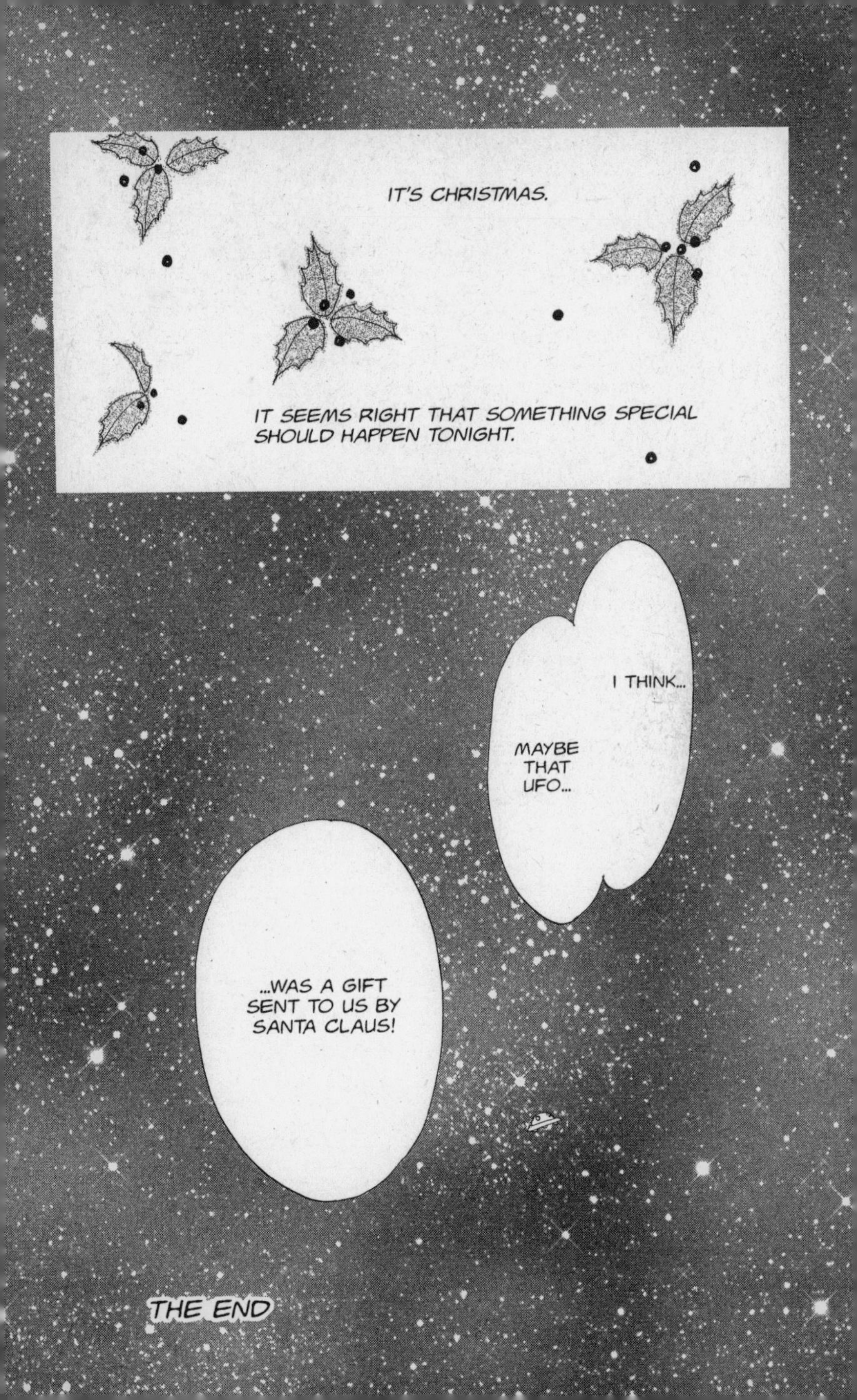
IT'S CHRISTMAS.
IT SEEMS RIGHT THAT SOMETHING SPECIAL SHOULD HAPPEN TONIGHT.
I THINK...
MAYBE THAT UFO...
...WAS A GIFT SENT TO US BY SANTA CLAUS!
THE END

"Frequency":
I borrowed my friend's name (without her
permission) for Kaori, the girl in this story.
My friend isn't hot-tempered like this Kaori, though.
The premise is a bit supernatural.
This is just an aside, but sometimes I look around
and wonder if there's someone who can hear
my thoughts. (Not that I have anything to hide...)

"Baby Universe":
This is actually my first story with a male protagonist.
(In fact, I really like stories where the main character
is a guy...I'd just never written one before.) I'd wanted
to tell a story like this for quite a while, so I'm glad it
finally materialized. I read a magazine feature on UFOs
when I was a kid, so my friends and I tried sending
signals them. Of course, they never came...

Afterword

Thanks so much for your readership.
I think I was going through a rough time
in my personal life while working on
these stories.
I wish I could be stronger.
I'll stay dedicated to my work, though,
so we'll meet again in the near future!

March 2002

Shouko Akira

Times Two

Shôjo Edition

This graphic novel contains material that was originally published in English in Animerica Extra Vol. 7, No. 7 through Vol. 7, No. 12

Story & Art by Shouko Akira

English Adaptation/Gerard Jones
Translation/Yuji Oniki
Touch-up Art & Lettering/Cato
Design/Andrea Rice
Editor/Frances E. Wall

Managing Editor/Annette Roman
Director of Production/Noboru Watanabe
Editorial Director/Alvin Lu
Sr. Director of Acquisitions/Rika Inouye
Vice President of Sales & Marketing/Liza Coppola
Executive Vice President/Hyoe Narita
Publisher/Seiji Horibuchi

Printed in the U.S.A.

Published by VIZ, LLC
P.O. Box 77010
San Francisco, CA 94107

10 9 8 7 6 5 4 3 2 1
First printing, February 2005

www.viz.com

RATED T FOR TEEN

PARENTAL ADVISORY
TIMES TWO is rated T for Teen and is recommended for ages 13 and up. It contains mild language, suggestive themes, and mild sexual humor.

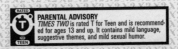

store.viz.com